INDIA
An Investor's Guide to the Next
Economic Superpower

INDIA
An Investor's Guide to the Next
Economic Superpower

Aaron Chaze

WILEY

John Wiley & Sons (Asia) Pte., Ltd

Other Wiley Editorial Offices
John Wiley & Sons, Inc., 111 River Street, Hoboken, NJ 07030, USA
John Wiley & Sons Ltd, The Atrium, Southern Gate, Chichester PO19 BSQ, England
John Wiley & Sons (Canada) Ltd, 5353 Dundas Street West, Suite 400, Toronto, Ontario, Canada
John Wiley & Sons Australia Ltd, M9B 6HB, 42 McDougall Street, Milton, Queensland 4046, Australia
Wiley-VCH, Bosch Strasse 12, D- 69469 Weinheim, Germany

Library of Congress Cataloging-in-Publication Data:
ISBN-13: 978-0-470-82194-7
ISBN-10: 0-470-82194-9

Typeset in 11/13 point, Garamond by ChungKing Data Systems
Printed in Singapore by Saik Wah Press Pte Ltd
10 9 8 7 6 5 4 3 2

CONTENTS

For Sanaya and Sanath

ACKNOWLEDGEMENTS

The book is a culmination of years of observation and study in India of the investment opportunities. Several factors and people have contributed to my thinking on the Indian investment scene and the potential it holds for all Indian and global investors and, as a result, have been indirect contributors to this book.

Its one thing to conceptualize a book and another thing to get it done in a very short time frame, with all the attendant pressures of work and family commitments, and this could not have been achieved through my efforts alone. This book therefore is also a testimony to the strong and unquestioning support of my family, especially from Ferzana, my wife, who though very accomplished in her own right has made numerous sacrifices over the years that I may be able to pursue my dreams. I have learnt from her example that it is important to do what is right and not what is convenient. My gratitude to her knows no bounds, as it does to my father Thomas Chaze who introduced me to the world of equities. My sister Orlova Chaze too has been an outstanding source of support and encouragement.

It is also a testimony to the support I enjoyed from my closest friends at a time when I really needed them. Raju Vasantraj, over the years has been a guiding light; pushing me into believing that I can excel, and Shishir Asthana, who no matter what the pressure on his time was always around. Urmik Chhaya, an expert on the Indian building materials, power and capital goods sectors endeavored to read the relevant sections of the book and gave me very useful feedback. Deepak Tanwar and Anurag Khetarpal unhesitatingly shared the fruits of their research with me. Sunder Subramaniam helped considerably with the corporate databases.

I have benefited from the guidance and wisdom of several individuals both when I lived and worked in India and subsequently in Canada. My mentor and coach in the equities business was Rajashekar Iyer, who is widely regarded as one of the original practitioners of the art of value investing in India. I have also benefited from observing the investment thought processes of other gifted practitioners, notably Deepak Agrawal of Impetus Advisors and Ketan Sheth of Way2Wealth Securities. I am also deeply grateful to the friendship and counsel of Jawahir Mulraj, one of India's longest running financial columnists, to Keya Sarkar, and to Manas Chakravarty, a self-anointed "super skeptic", whose sometimes caustic musings in newspaper columns have become staple for innumerable readers over the years.

I also wonder at the remarkable sequence of events that brought me and kept me in touch with Ernest McCrary, editor and publisher, special projects with *Institutional Investor* magazine, now a very dear friend, and Tom Leander, Editor in Chief, *CFO Asia,* who was instrumental in helping take this book forward, as was Steve Schwartz of Walek & Associates.

In Canada I have had the good fortune to benefit from the wise counsel and support and encouragement of a cross-section of very distinguished and accomplished individuals. Dr Jagdeep Bachher, my "mentor" in Canada, has been and hopefully will continue to be a source of encouragement and ideas. Nitin Amersey, who was and remains instrumental in backing my efforts at launching *The Midas Touch,* a magazine on global and Indian investments, and who continues to work closely with me on several projects. And Rajendra K Kothari, Partner, PricewaterhouseCoopers, whose insightfulness, guidance and forthrightness I have been fortunate to have.

Needless to say I am extremely lucky to have stumbled onto Nick Wallwork, publisher, John Wiley Asia, with whom I've had many an enjoyable conversation discussing and debating this book at various stages, and to two very patient editors: Janis Soo; Wiley Asia's managing editor, and Micheal Hanrahan, this book's exceedingly competent copy editor.

Aaron Chaze
Toronto, Canada
June 2006

INTRODUCTION

Millions of Indian investors have already capitalized on the superb investment opportunities created by the strength, resilience and growth of the Indian economy over the last few decades. I feel strongly that the story of the wealth-creating opportunity that is India should now be shared with investors in the rest of world.

This book seeks to uncover the investment opportunity in India for a global investing audience. India is the new investment frontier, the place where the next "gold rush" will happen and is already happening to some extent. Misconceptions and myths about the true nature of the Indian investment opportunity are considerable. That became alarmingly apparent to me after I moved to North America. I decided to do something about the myths, the gaps in knowledge and plain ignorance that much of the world has had about India for so long. The rise of China has been a blessing for India since investors across the world, having seen the Chinese miracle unfold, now increasingly accept India as the next and probably last miracle mega-economy. However, they lack the knowledge on how to benefit from India's rising status as the next economic superpower. Hence the need for an investors guide to this market.

It is my hope that the book is actionable for both existing and future investors. The book will have served its purpose if it successfully unveils the depth and quality of the investment opportunity in India and whets the reader's appetite to begin a rewarding journey into a market that is even more fascinating and multi-faceted than the country where the underlying assets are located.

The book is divided into three sections. The first section showcases contemporary India and takes the reader through the economic, financial, political, intellectual and social developments that blended to create this superb investment canvas.

The second section is a guide to creating wealth from this investment canvas. It brings out the various investment themes, companies and industries at the forefront of India's new economic expansion, and provides clear pointers to the key drivers and catalysts of growth. It details India's corporate history, and paints a picture of what was, what has changed, and what that means for an investor looking at India afresh or for the first time.

The third section discusses the threat and opportunity facing India as it confronts its growing energy deficiency. It presents key lessons for India from the growth path blazed by China, and provides a perspective on the India–China economic rivalry.

For all its fantastic potential, India still has many problems to address. The key one is ensuring that the benefits of the new economic growth quickly reach all segments of society especially those that need it the most. The devastating reversal suffered by the NDA government in the 2004 elections was a warning to the political class that the benefits of growth are to be felt and not just seen by the vast majority of the population.

Serious investors will have to do more study tailored to their specific circumstances, objectives and risk tolerance, but I hope that reading this book will be the beginning of a profitable journey into the world of investing in India.

THE INVESTMENT CANVAS

WHAT IS DRIVING THE SURGE OF OPPORTUNITY IN INDIA AND THE OPPORTUNITY FOR INVESTORS?

To say today that India is bursting with investment opportunities and the potential to create wealth over the long term would be an understatement. Wherever one looks in India, whether in the big cities or small towns, there seems to be an economic atmosphere charged with enthusiasm, with businesses and consumers expressing new-found confidence in the sustainability of the country's economic growth. Roads are feverishly being built, grand expressways are sprouting up linking India's major cities, airports are being expanded and modernized, and gigantic cities of concrete, steel and glass are emerging within and in the vicinity of the metropolises as India's youthful, newly rich middle classes search for the perfect urban existence.

DOMESTIC ENTHUSIASM EQUALS INVESTMENT OPPORTUNITY

India is a young country, with the median age of the population being 24.6 years, and one-third of the population is below the age of

14. This youthful population – increasingly educated, entrepreneurial, and with rising disposable incomes – is the fulcrum of the opportunity in India, driving demand for everything from cars, brand-name clothing, cell phones and consumer electronics to real estate and a host of other goods and services, including insurance, health care and travel. Sectors that were once tightly controlled by the government are racing away at incredible growth rates after being thrown open to domestic and foreign private investment and with the injection of competition. The fastest growth rate is coming from sectors that did not even exist or barely registered a presence a decade and a half ago, such as software services, information technology–enabled services, automobile components, pharmaceuticals, biotechnology, refined petroleum products and mobile telephony. And new opportunities are springing up almost constantly in older and more established sectors, such as in commodity-linked industries like steel and cement, automobiles, petrochemicals, oil and gas, and insurance and banking, due to restructuring and repositioning coupled with an explosion in domestic demand, an infusion of competition and the growing emphasis on exports.

The long run average GDP growth from the mid-1990s has now stepped up to 6.5%, from an average of 5% a decade and a half ago and less than 3% over two decades ago. Annual average growth for the next few years is expected to be 7% to 7.5%. This rate of growth is one of the fastest in the world, and the efforts underway to introduce the necessary structural changes that can raise growth rates further will turn India into a global economic power, throwing up huge investment opportunities along the way. The opportunity unfolding in India is a function of the reforms enacted from the early 1990s as well as a result of India's increasing competitiveness and confidence.

Almost every critical sector of the economy is seeing new investment flowing in, both domestic and foreign. Bidders are being invited for the expansion and management of airports and sea ports and contracts have been awarded for the first time ever for the expansion, modernization and management by a private company of the Mumbai and New Delhi airports. The government's policy to open oil and gas exploration and production to private domestic and foreign companies since the year 2000 has been fabulously successful, with some of the largest gas deposits in the world being found in India since then. Just three gas finds between 2002 and 2005 have produced estimated gas reserves of over 40 trillion cubic feet. Now, riding on early successes in getting big-ticket automobile, oil and gas, telecom, roads and infrastructure-related investments, Indian state governments are competing with each other in trying to bring in larger domestic and foreign investments to their states faster. News that a government-sponsored delegation from some Indian state or another is on a global road-show selling their investment potential to investors and corporations and demonstrating how their policies are most friendly to foreign investors barely raises an eyebrow.

More cars are being built in India than ever before, with 1.2 million being produced in 2005, making it the fourth-largest car market in Asia. India today is the second-largest producer of motorcycles and mopeds in the world at 6.5 million a year. More important are the projected growth rates than the current level of sales of cars and motorcycles and other products. Both car and motorcycle sales are estimated to grow at 20% compounded for the next few years. Goldman Sachs estimates that by 2020 one in six cars produced in the world will be bought by an Indian. More than 30 million new cellular subscribers are being added annually, exceeding growth rates even in China. Korean electronic giants LG and Samsung, auto manufacturer Hyundai and Japanese automobile manufacturers Suzuki and Toyota are among a growing list of multinationals already successfully riding the consumer boom, and it is very likely that their long-term growth is intricately tied to the growth of India, which explains why they are more focused on India than ever before. Suzuki, for example, derives nearly one-quarter of its annual sales volume and net income from its Indian operations.

Things were not always this exciting, and the thought of India as a rising economic superpower for a long time seemed like a contradiction in terms. But that was before the country faced near economic collapse that in turn triggered an epochal response from the government of the time. More importantly, Indian industry rose superbly to the challenge, transforming themselves from managing trivial domestic fiefs under the government's protectionist policies to potentially building empires in a competitive global environment. The opportunity wrought by this change in corporate thinking and economic policy and practice is now intriguing corporations, fund managers and investors worldwide, and will continue to occupy them for decades to come.

The Indian economy: a perspective

In the decades preceding the Indian economic crisis of 1991, barring a few, businesses and investors in the developed world consistently ignored the investment potential in post-independence India, eventually relegating it to an afterthought, a hopeless case, dismissing it as a land of soothsayers and snake charmers run by avaricious politicians and vacillating bureaucrats. The fact that the opportunity in India was indeed controlled by politicians, bureaucrats and vested interests bred out of a controlled economy did nothing to ease the negative perception. The frightening experience that Western multinational companies had at the hands of a left-leaning government in the late 1970s – where many, including Coca-Cola, were kicked out of the country without compensation, and others were forced to divest in favor of minority shareholders – and the long gestation periods that Japanese companies faced more than a decade later further worsened the perception that India had few, if any, wealth-creating opportunities. Indians compounded their own investment isolation and shunned competing on the global stage by shutting out any thoughts of attracting foreign investments and discouraged domestic private investment, thus gradually turning into a closed, inward-looking economy. The overriding economic theme was import substitution rather than the export-oriented growth strategy of the East Asian economies or even China.

For well over two decades, beginning in the 1980s and right through the 1990s, China and other East Asian economies took center stage as far as the attention of global investors and companies was concerned, further relegating India into investment obscurity. China's experiment with capitalism, the tremendous success it enjoyed in attracting foreign investment by creating the right environment, and more importantly, the fact that it could significantly raise the standard of living of its citizens laid bare India's flawed approach of selectively allowing foreign investments. India's approach to attracting foreign capital was not only very arbitrary and selective but also subjected those few that bothered to venture in to layers of myriad regulations, controls and trying delays.

By the start of the 1990s, just as China was beginning to hit its stride as a great place for investors to be involved in, India was in the throes of economic agony as years of isolation, stifling government control over economic activity and fiscal mismanagement finally caught up. By the middle of 1991, the Indian government came to the brink of default on its foreign currency loans, and its foreign exchange reserves position was such that India had about enough dollars to cover just two weeks' worth of imports. This situation was the result of the half-hearted attempts made by the Rajiv Gandhi government in the mid-1980s to selectively open the economy to foreign trade and relax import restrictions, which did not have the intended consequence of stimulating investment and eventually pushed the balance of payments out of gear. Export growth had turned negative and for the first time Indian industrial production recorded negative growth. GDP growth for the fiscal year 1991–92 was a shade below 1%. Historically India had never seen negative GDP growth, and that was the first time the country came so close to that ignominious situation. And the situation was compounded by the oil shock effected by the first Gulf war and the drying up of remittances from Indian workers in that region, which until that point provided a substantial amount of the invisibles that supported India's current account balance.

From mandarins to the market

The situation that India found itself in by the middle of 1991 was untenable. The government was bankrupt and near default on foreign currency loans. What was worse was that with foreign exchange reserves dwindling to $1 billion – just enough to fund two weeks' worth of imports – foreign lenders had virtually shut the door on India and the sovereign foreign currency rating was pegged at junk status. The Indian banking system was in a pitiable shape, with most banks being hit by astronomical levels of non-performing assets and many were in crying need for recapitalization. Economic growth had picked up in the mid-1980s to 5% (the average during the 1980s) as a result of the Rajiv Gandhi government's attempt to jump-start faster growth. But since the measures taken to liberalize trade and investment were half-hearted and did not result in investment-led growth the economic growth that happened came at a heavy price, with unsustainable government borrowing overseas and high fiscal deficits locally. The short-term external debt as a percentage of foreign exchange reserves was 146%. By 1990–91 the current account deficit reached 3.1% and inflation was running at 12%. Things had begun to boil over when the government had to pledge gold held by the Reserve Bank of India – the country's central bank – with lenders abroad in order to raise short-term loans and tide over the financial crisis.

The subsequent political storm that it caused and the recognition of the severity of the fiscal situation finally forced the politicians and bureaucrats to release their iron grip on the economy. The crisis achieved something unbelievable and unthinkable until then; it induced the change from uncompromising centralized control to a market-driven system with regulatory oversight enforced independent of the state in several key sectors of the economy. This was a significant response from the government of the day, engineered by an economic team of rare resolve, led by an economist and former governor of the Reserve Bank of India and current Prime Minister, Dr Manmohan Singh. His appointment at that time of adversity was a masterstroke by India's visionary Prime Minister, P V Narasimha Rao, who avoided appointing a politician and instead chose a brilliant bureaucrat with plenty of both international experience and acceptability to what was then the least-coveted job in the country.

The severity of the economic straightjacket that India was in and the backdrop of policies that brought it about are very important for anyone investing in India to understand. It led to a very powerful series of reforms that catalyzed growth. The reform process built on the large, diversified but inefficient industrial base that decades of protectionism had created and on the huge pool of technical manpower that the emphasis on higher education provided. These factors had very important, positive consequences of unleashing growth and raising the standard of living. Huge entrepreneurial opportunities have emerged as a result. But for that economic crisis and the country's response to it, especially the recognition of the faulty policies and systems that led to it, India would not be filled with the kind of wealth-creating opportunity that is available today for investors both within and outside its borders. The history of misdirected economic policies in India and the near disaster that eventually visited the country as a result is one solid reassurance investors have that the reform process cannot and will not be rolled back.

In the decades after independence, India followed a broad economic policy based largely on Fabian socialism and what is now derisively known as "Nehruvian socialism", named after India's first prime minister, Jawaharlal Nehru. He wanted to pursue Soviet-style heavy industrialization and central planning minus the collectivization and loss of individuality. His thinking was that the state should bear the responsibility of putting up the gigantic investments required to turn India into an industrial power, while private sector "for profit" businesses should play a minor but supporting role. Subsequent political dispensations increasingly interpreted this quasi-socialist philosophy to mean control of assets and resources by the state as an end in itself, and this gradually led to a government stranglehold over economic decision-making, government monopoly over vital physical and financial resources, inefficient allocation and wastage of national assets. It was understood that the government controlled most assets and decided on the priority of their use, thus the private sector was forced to function as little more than an extension of the state with no freedom over labor, capital or raw material use, and in the case of many industries, there were state-mandated market-ing and distribution restrictions. Companies could not close down if they were losing money, and the state usually provided some form of subsidy to keep such companies afloat in order to avoid retrench-ment of labor.

India began to use Soviet-style five-year plans to further its develop-ment agenda, and the approach was outlined by the Industrial Policy Resolution adopted by the Indian cabinet in 1951. Legislation such as the *Foreign Exchange Regulation Act* (FERA) and the *Monopolies and Restrictive Trade Practices Act* (MRTPA) were introduced, which for all practical purposes shut the door on most foreign investment while limiting growth opportunities for Indian companies. Foreign investments were permitted in only a handful of industries deemed critical to the national interest, that too with a 40% ceiling on equity holding. The private sector that was to play a smaller, supportive but independent role under Nehru's economic policies began to come under increasing state control to the point where every level of ac-tivity, including capacity expansion, had to have the government's explicit stamp of approval. As this economic dispensation evolved it led to the creation of a compulsory licensing system known as the "license raj", without which no private industry could commence or expand. Thanks to licensing, the state now essentially decided who got to do what and to what extent. This unquestioned power cre-ated a class of capitalists that were dependent on the government for their survival and growth, and in turn greased the state machinery to keep out competition and ensure the flow of industrial licenses irrespective of which industry it allowed them to get into and how it correlated with their existing businesses. By the early 1980s the situ-ation was such that government departments routinely rejected 50% to 60 % of applications for licenses, mostly on the premise that there was adequate existing capacity. This thinking was partly motivated by the fact that companies did not want to give up their monopolis-tic control of their markets. Existing companies also discovered the strategy of applying for such licenses to thwart potential competitors from obtaining licenses.

There was a tendency on the part of the government to restrict suc-cessful firms from growing by controlling the expansion of existing capacities, perhaps out of the irrational socialist fear of large private enterprise. This trend, seen in tandem with the fact that by the 1990s nearly 800 product segments were reserved for small-scale indus-tries, showed that the Indian establishment's economic thinking was the antithesis of sensible growth-oriented policies where the thrust should have been on economies of scale and on growth momentum.

Instead, the Indian government through a mix of regulation and fiscal incentives sought to restrict industries and product segments that private enterprise could get into, and once there they were to remain small. The tragedy was that many of the products reserved either for the public sector or for the small-scale industry had high investment and export potential which were not allowed to develop.

By the time Nehruvian socialism ran its course, India had a government that comprised most of the economy, controlling almost everything from the large-and medium-sized banks – which were nationalized in the 1970s – to manufacturing cars, watches, cement, steel and textiles, besides operating refineries, supplying electricity to rural and urban consumers, running telephone exchanges, gas stations and airlines, exporting minerals, and selling general and life insurance, among other things. Thanks to the constituencies that developed after years of state largess being splurged on a populist agenda and an inefficiently run economy the government was heavily in debt, with external debt that was close to the size of the total annual GDP, annual fiscal deficits as high as 8.5%, huge revenue deficits, unhealthy public sector corporations increasingly supported out of the government's annual budget, a debilitated banking system and an uncompetitive, monopolistic private sector.

The government, realizing early on in the game that its own revenues were limited despite high taxation and that deficit financing could only go so far, had begun to dip into public bank deposits through various means. The first means was through the preemption of funds, where a high cash reserve ratio was imposed, on top of which lay a statutory reserve ratio, absorbing over 40% of deposits. Banks were also expected to lend a significant portion of their liabilities to the priority sector, including agriculture, and were expected to buy government bonds at below market rates. Thus, net of these social objectives and the government's frequent bond placement programs the availability of funds to the private sector was both limited and expensive. Further compounding the problem was the balance that the government tried to achieve by controlling deposit and lending rates, by setting ceilings for deposit rates and floors for lending rates. Public sector bank managements were forced to look at the social aspects of their business and meet predetermined lending parameters rather than worry about credit quality and lending risks.

As can be imagined the economy was a nightmare where no foreign investors would dare want to enter, and were probably deterred by the regulations and bureaucracy even if they wanted to. Decades of restrictive economic policies, designed to control rather than nurture, saw a per capita GDP of just $1,100 (on a purchasing power parity or PPP basis, which conceptually states that a basket of goods in one country should cost the same in another country if the currencies are exchanged at that rate) by 1990–91. Adult literacy was just 52%, and there were high infant mortality rates and an average life expectancy of just 57 years. Infrastructure was poor, the road network was vast but of poor quality, and the country was crisscrossed with two-lane highways. Ports had such low capacity and high turnaround times that the major ports servicing India were Colombo in Sri Lanka, and Singapore. At the time of independence in 1947 India had a 2.4% share of world trade, which had collapsed to 0.5% by 1991. According to the World Bank, agriculture still comprised 31% of the economy as compared to a 27% share of industry. According to a UNICEF report only 14% of rural India had access to sanitation facilities at that time.

A class of economic elite was being created with state connivance, and the resulting concentration of wealth pushed a majority of the population below the poverty line. The poverty ratio in 1991 was 40%. The poor increasingly became dependent on ever-rising subsidies from the government and simultaneously a large middle class emerged without any purchasing power. This was the state of an economy after following policies for decades that were designed to build a new industrialized India, where servicing the government's debt alone took up almost all its revenues and the government was actually borrowing to pay salaries to public servants and subsidize the economy. The biggest casualty of poor allocation of resources was the absence of physical infrastructure that was so badly needed to push growth. It took the Indian economic and political establishment a long time, at least until the crisis struck, to realize there cannot be growth without physical infrastructure.

The combination of external and internal economic reforms that the government started pushing through after coming to the brink of disaster in 1991 brought in three elements that India was never previously allowed to have: competition, entrepreneurship and the beginnings of world-class infrastructure. The government reducing its role in the economy quite dramatically since the mid-1990s also meant that – with state control of economic activity ending – resource allocation was being taken over by market forces, as a result of which pricing and availability across economic sectors are now competitive rather than monopolistic.

Reforms; making the right call

To give an example of the kind of resource allocation a tightly controlled state economy is able to achieve versus the miracle a market economy is able to produce, one only has to look at the Indian telecommunications sector. Telecommunications was a state monopoly until the mid-1990s. In nearly 50 years after independence in 1947, the department of telecom, through various agencies controlled by it, managed to install six million fixed telephone lines across the country, and no mobile connections, effectively yielding a telephone density of just six per thousand people.

After the fiscal crisis, when the government began to relax its grip on resource allocation, the telecom industry was among the first to be decontrolled and offered up to the private sector for investment. Within a decade from when it was decontrolled, the Indian and foreign telecom companies that came in added nearly 120 million fixed and mobile telephone connections across the country, including 30 million in 2005, doubling the telephone density in this period.

The entire government-owned infrastructure was very quickly eclipsed and several times its investment was made in just a few years, largely by the private sector. As this book is being written the privately owned companies that invested – now including regional giants such as SingTel (Singapore) and Hutchinson Whampoa (Hong Kong), and domestic giants Reliance Infocomm, Bharti Televentures and others – are adding as many as two and a half million new subscribers a month to their services.

The difference can be felt not only in terms of the size attained by the industry and its growth rates but also its quality. India has leapfrogged the "copper" age in telecom and has landed in the digital age with a state-of-the-art fiber optic backbone now laid across the country, with the stage being set for the introduction of 3G telecom networks. Telecom carriers are looking at data and cross-border traffic and not just domestic voice traffic as the real growth opportunity in the Indian telecom space, where currently less than 10% of revenue comes from data transmission. Equally important is that the cost of telephony has reduced tremendously, making it an affordable option for even the common man besides making the business of offering IT-enabled services increasingly viable.

WHAT IS DRIVING THE SURGE OF OPPORTUNITY IN INDIA AND
THE OPPORTUNITY FOR INVESTORS?

13

TRADE, FINANCIAL AND CAPITAL MARKET REFORM AND THE CREATION OF THE OPPORTUNITY

Since the main cause of the 1991 crisis was linked to India's external trade and capital flows and was triggered by the rickety nature of its balance of payments system most of the early blast of reform was centered there, and it was only when the positive effect of that was felt were reforms quickly and logically moved to other sectors. The first and long overdue step was to take the Indian rupee off the fixed exchange rate mechanism, where it was pegged to a basket of major global currencies and where its value remained largely discretionary. The rupee was effectively and substantially devalued after it was un-pegged, but it brought about harmonization of external trade and a tremendous stability in the exchange rate. Though the rupee slid sig-nificantly against global currencies in the years after reform the slide was measured and expected. The earlier pre-crisis exchange rate was artificially kept high and was naturally a huge export disincen-tive. In the crisis year, and even preceding it, export growth ranged between being marginally negative and being marginally positive. Today exports from India are growing at a compounded rate of 25% per annum and are expected to hit $150 billion by 2008, comprising largely of goods and services from sectors that did not even exist in India's pre-reform economy. Exports as a percentage of GDP have increased from 6.6% in 1989–90 to over 10%. There is also evidence that India is integrating with the world economy, with the external sector now comprising nearly 30% of the economy.

As India's foreign exchange reserves continue to increase at a rapid pace (now enough to cover well over two years' worth of gross imports), the focus of the central bank is on whether to go in for full convertibility of the rupee. Currently the rupee is fully convertible on the trade account and partly convertible on the capital account. The likelihood is that irrespective of the viability of regional trade blocks on the Indian sub-continent, the Indian rupee could well become a regional currency of choice if freely convertible. Full convertibility of the rupee is being discussed by an expert committee constituted by the central bank. Some pundits have opined that if the rupee is freely convertible it could become a major global currency.

A truly significant step taken during the early reform process was in slashing import tariffs. It was long known in globally competi-tive economies and only just being understood in India that there is a close correlation between allowing imports and pushing exports. This one step of increasing liberalization in imports in tandem with relaxing foreign equity ceilings in various industries has been a critical contributor to India's competitiveness. The peak level of customs duties in 1991 was 300%. The reduction in tariffs was gradual but sustained, and at present the peak customs tariff is around 20%, with numerous products attracting nil tariffs or tariffs in single digits, including items such as cell phones that once would have attracted peak duties, and computer equipment that at one point in the 1980s was actually banned from imports. Both telecom and IT are key economic drivers today.

The impact of the reduction in tariffs, especially early on in the reform process, was a bit of a *fait accompli* for Indian corporations that knew they had to restructure or die in a post-protectionist India. As part of the external sector reforms the government began to dismantle foreign equity ownership restrictions in several sectors, even those considered to be sensitive. The number of sectors where foreign equity ownership of up to 51% was automatically granted was increased dramatically. Today the government's and Indian industry's comfort levels with foreign ownership is so great that 100% foreign equity ownership is now allowed in several sectors, including some segments of real estate, and automatic approvals for ownership up to 74% have increased dramatically, including in insurance and telecom, sectors that were once considered very sensitive to the national interest and were completely inaccessible to foreign investors.

The first foreign portfolio investor was allowed to enter the capital markets in 1993, a couple of years after the economic reforms began. The first step was to allow foreign brokers to set up shop, since the thinking was that if the brokers came in they would bring their institutional investor clients along, and also for the institutional investor dealing with a familiar-name broker made a big difference initially. But from the very beginning the government and the Securities and Exchange Board of India (SEBI – the capital market regulator) were adamant about not allowing short-term money to enter the country. As a result, SEBI decided that only those institutional investors that were established in their country of domicile and were supervised by market regulators in their own countries could enter freely as foreign institutional investors (FIIs). At first, the inflow of portfolio funds was only a trickle and hit only a few hundred million dollars per annum for several years. But seeing India's commitment to reform and the dramatic change in the Indian economic environment and the improvement in the quality and depth of Indian companies, foreign portfolio flows have now begun to exceed $1.0 billion to $1.5 billion per month.

Reforming the financial sector: greasing the path to progress

While the external trade, capital and foreign exchange situation was being drastically changed and the external sector was being stabilized, the next burst of reform came to the financial sector, especially the government-run banking system. A large number of weaker banks were recapitalized or merged with larger public sector banks and loan loss write-offs were facilitated. The Indian private sector was allowed to come forward and establish what have come to be known as the new generation banks, which are high on technology and growth and have shaken up the entire banking sector with their presence. Reforms were also simultaneously extended to the capital markets and to internal trade and industry.

With the reforms in the banking sector, state-directed credit and ad hoc credit and social responsibility norms were no longer a factor that corporations had to look out for. Preemption of funds from banks by the government reduced considerably. As a result, not only did the cost of credit come down, but the availability increased as banks focused on credit quality, corporations enhanced their credit appeal and the money markets deepened considerably, with instruments such as commercial papers, inter-corporate deposits and certificates of deposits being very actively sought after. Corporations would now have to bring in some amount of sophistication in raising resources from banks and take advantage of relaxations in raising capital where they could now access external lenders and the capital markets on their own strength.

The equity market as a source of capital has always been integral to the Indian economy, not only during the days of India's disastrous experiment with socialism but even earlier during the days of British rule. A little-known fact is that India is home to the oldest stock exchange in Asia. The Bombay Stock Exchange, which was the first of 18 stock exchanges in the country, was established as a merchant association in 1875. Apocryphal stories abound that even before the establishment of the stock exchange, merchants would gather to trade stocks under a banyan tree. Most of India's large smokestack industries, banks and even several new-generation industries owned by the private sector were products of India's controlled equity markets that, for a long time, existed as providers of venture finance for start-up companies rather than a quality-conscious arbiter of value. During the 1990s the reliance on the capital markets increased dramatically, which at the same time improved qualitatively, especially since the capital markets went through their own process of reformation.

The government facilitated the process of improving the quality and depth of the equity market by repealing the *Capital Issues Control Act, 1947* and abolishing the office of Controller of Capital Issues (CCI). Setting the price for initial public offerings (IPOs) was the CCI's responsibility during the years of centralized planning and control; this function was handed back to the market. As a result, equity issues were better priced and brought more money into the market, which led to a major equity boom in the mid-1990s and triggered the subsequent de-leveraging of Indian corporations (the average debt equity ratio in 1991 for a large Indian company was 1.64:1 as against below 1:1 now). This development – along with the creation of the National Stock Exchange, an electronic order-driven market linked by satellite across 240 towns and cities of India – led to a sea change in the size and quality of companies that could now access the market. Simultaneously, the Securities and Exchange Board of India began to introduce regulations that further streamlined the issue of and the trading in securities and provided very strict oversight of the market. These changes had far-reaching effects, as foreign investors could now come in knowing they were dealing with first-world systems and within a regulatory framework no different than those being exercised in major global economies. In addition, transparency and fault-free settlement systems also enabled the introduction of index and stock options and futures. India is probably one of the few countries in the world where stock futures have been a huge success. Stock options and futures on some 119 large cap stocks and options and futures on key indices trade volumes of around $10 billion a day. The cash market trades roughly $3.5 billion per day.

Change management and the genesis of competitiveness

As the reform of the external sector was underway the government began to turn its attention to reform of Indian industry. The excessive regulation – where companies had to seek the government's permission on issues such as what it could produce, how it could be financed, where products could be produced and to whom it could sell – that had served to stifle enterprise was ended for good. With the abolition of restrictive laws such as the *Foreign Exchange Regulation Act* (FERA) and the *Monopolies and Restrictive Trade Practices Act* (MRTPA) that controlled external and internal competition respectively, competition was introduced in consumer sectors and foreign investors were wooed with clearer policies that protected their investments and allowed them larger stakes in a wide variety of industries. One leg of this policy that sought to seed an environment of competitiveness was creating a more even playing field between Indian and foreign companies and giving foreign investors more control over the companies they invest in. The other leg was the reduction in import tariffs that brought in immediate competition and forced Indian companies to be competitive.

In addition to direct foreign competition the internal reforms process also brought a commitment to reduce tariff barriers still further, but the manner in which Indian companies have restructured themselves – by reducing operating costs, building in capital and resource efficiencies, increasing the scale of operations and turning to value addition – has made tariff protection a redundant concept. But creditably, despite entrenched incumbents several foreign companies are doing well in breaking into the Indian market. Korean companies in particular are doing exceedingly well in India by playing the game that Indian consumers understand; offering products at a price point they cannot refuse and identifying with popular culture and localized themes.

The culmination of these factors and a tremendous sense of stability have led to a transformation of the Indian economy from inward-looking, self-contained and managed by political diktat to outward-looking, competitive and managed by global economic reality. Once high tariff barriers protected Indian companies from what the government thought would be a damaging onslaught of imported goods, but a decade and a half of reforms has seen most of Indian industry restructured, leaner and now raring for cross-border competition, taking imports in their stride. Besides, thanks to rising purchasing power and the growing clout of the middle class, the consumer market itself has expanded. The changes that have been effected from within, such as cost consciousness, ensure corporate India's competitiveness, but this also builds on decades of resourcefulness that emerged as companies negotiated labyrinthine regulations and controls.

Corporate managements: India's leading edge

Indian managements are learning how to be nimble and seem to be aware of global opportunities in their sectors. They have all understood the need and advantage of size and large-scale global operations and are developing a taste for aggression. A few years ago it would have been unthinkable that ONGC Ltd, India's largest oil and gas exploration and production company, would have bid for and come close to snapping up Petrokazakh, a Toronto Stock Exchange-listed company with huge gas interests in Central Asia. The largest and most valuable steel group in the world belongs to the LNM group controlled by Laxmi Mittal, an Indian steel trader turned global tycoon. Three of the largest IT companies in Asia are Indian, and India is also home to the world's second-largest market for motorcycles and mopeds, producing 6.5 million vehicles a year and growing at 25% per annum, the rate at which it is expected to compound for the next few years. Bharat Forge, the world's second-largest manufacturer of castings and forgings, is located in India, as is one of the largest manufacturers of fasteners and radiator caps. At 33 million tons per annum, the world's third-largest oil refinery is in Jamnagar, India, and so is Asia's largest inorganic chemicals complex, the world's third-largest manufacturer of optical media, the world's largest manufacturer of denim fabric and the world's largest manufacturer of flexible packaging. These are some of the notable achievements of corporate India and are a testimony to the ability of Indian managements and the quality of the opportunity available in India. Tata Steel, the world's lowest cost producer of steel, is located in eastern India. And India is also home to the world's fastest growing insurance sector and automobiles sector. Many companies in sectors such as steel, auto components, pharmaceuticals, engineering design, IT and apparel manufacturing have either bought or are now scouting for acquisitions globally. In the first few months of 2005 Indian automobile component and pharmaceutical companies have invested several hundred million dollars buying companies in Europe and North America, as they seek global markets for their products. Even as this book is being written Dr Reddy's Laboratories made a successful €550 million bid for Betapharm Arzeniemittel, Germany's fourth-largest generic drug maker.

After a decade of rapid domestic growth and with Indian companies flexing their muscles overseas, the realization is dawning among investors globally that they have been ignoring the potential in India at their own peril. Institutional investors have piled into India first, as is always the case with economies witnessing a major transformation, with investors in hard assets only just beginning to follow through. The Indian capital market was opened to foreign investments in 1993; since then nearly $42.5 billion has come in as portfolio investments (as of end January 2006), most of it in recent years. At the time the reforms began, India attracted $100 million in foreign direct investment (FDI) a year; by the year 2000 the level of FDI had reached $2 billion a year, while in 2005 it hit $6 billion. The expectation is that FDI inflows will skyrocket over the next few years.

Framework for the continuation of reforms

Sustainability of the reform-ignited growth is now a cornerstone of the government's economic policy. And the objective of this policy now has seamlessly transcended political ideology. The change of the ruling political coalition from center-right to center-left in mid-2004 has brought in new rhetoric and a new emphasis, but essentially the economic policy is to remain married to reform, given its major accomplishments. The thrust of the economic policy now is to sustain the shift away from an agrarian and rural-centric economy, where self-sufficiency was the key, and move towards a dynamic, industrial, service and export-oriented economy, where staying globally competitive is the key. In the next generation of the reform process, which in part is already underway, it is the internal trade and domestic industrial issues – such as internal tariffs that hamper the free flow of goods between states and the mobility of labor – that are being addressed, along with the much delayed creation of physical infrastructure. While the reforms have been very good for the economy and the external sector in general, the government's financial health, though substantially better, still suffers from some structural problems. India is already on the ascendancy – there is no question about that. The pace is good, though it could be better, and there are important macro issues that need to be addressed. The tax to GDP ratio needs to improve substantially from the current level of 10% (in China it is 20% according to the Chinese goverment's State Administration of Tax department). The savings to GDP stands at 29.1% and the investment to GDP ratio stands at 30.1% (see figure 1.1). Though these figures have improved over the last few years, they need to improve further in order to step up the growth rate and raise the standard of living. The East Asian economies and China have far higher savings and investment rates, and this is something that is left for India to achieve, though the ratios have been improving considerably and very evidently over the last six or seven years.

Figure 1.1: Trend in domestic savings and investment rate as a percentage of GDP

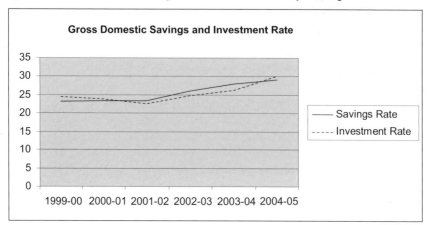

Source: Ministry of Finance

The new economic face of India

The recent economic surveys from the Indian government, as well as the budget documents, clearly signal the new government's focus on neglected areas of the political economy, education, health care and rural infrastructure. Significant investments have been earmarked and will now begin to address the inequity in the system and permit a more equitable distribution of wealth in India.

The quality of the economic growth numbers is beginning to reflect the opportunity that has been unleashed in India. In the past, India never managed to maintain two consecutive years of high GDP growth (7%+). Inevitably a year with high GDP growth would be followed by a disappointing GDP growth rate. There was a comical concept that all Indian economy watchers adhered to, called the "Hindu rate of growth", where an average annual growth rate of 3% to 3.5% was considered to be the norm and exceeding that band on a sustained basis was impossible. A great year – one in which the monsoon was very good – would see a rate of growth in excess of 5% or 6%, since a good monsoon greatly improved rural India's purchasing power and led to a temporary liquidity-driven consumer boom that would typically dry up once the latent demand was absorbed.

Today, thanks to the impact of deep economic reforms throughout the 1990s, the economic growth rate band in India has doubled to 6% to 6.5%, and the impact of exceptionally strong monsoons such as the one in 2003 would now simply push the GDP growth rate to 8% or 9%. But more interesting is the impact in the years when the monsoon fails. In earlier years a monsoon failure would mean growth of just 2% to 3%, or sometimes less. For decades the phenomenon that domestic corporate and individual investors in Indian stocks and the economy – and later global fund managers – worried about most was the monsoon's unpredictability and the impact its failure would have on the economy and on the spending power of a vast segment of the economy. The year 2004 was a telling example of the type of fundamental transformation that the Indian economy has undergone and continues to undergo. In 2004, when the monsoon failed miserably, GDP growth still stayed at 6.5%, driven by growth in the services sector and sustained growth in industrial production and in exports. The robustness of domestic demand that has been emphasized all along is now evident and assertive.

India is now a non-traditional economy that has de-linked itself from its agricultural roots. On the face of it, that seems to be a strange comment to make when according to the Reserve Bank of India 57% of the workforce is still engaged in agricultural activities in some form or another, while agriculture contributes just 23% of the GDP, a sharp decline from the pre-reform days. Despite the dependence of a large percentage of the population on agriculture for their livelihood, the change is that India is turning from being dependent on its agricultural sector for growth to a rapidly developing industrial economy, where the direction and pace of growth is no longer dependent on the vagaries of the monsoon but on its ability to break through to the global marketplace for goods and services and satisfy the huge emerging domestic appetite. Today it does not seem improbable that India can sustain multiple years of high growth rates irrespective of what happens with the monsoon. Significant purchasing power has emerged from the service sector, which comprises 52% of the Indian economy, driven by the millions of new high-wage jobs created by software services, IT-enabled services, banking, insurance, capital markets, telecommunications, hospitality, travel, global technology research and development initiatives, and lots of other service industries.

India has a level of economic maturity not consistent with its status as a developing economy. The unusual part of India's rapid ascent to be the world's fourth-largest economy – with annual GDP of $3.36 trillion in PPP terms (in US dollar terms it is ranked tenth with a GDP of $691 billion) – is the role being played not by manufacturing but by the services sector in pushing growth rates. Most of Asia's rapidly growing economies, including China, have ascended based on their manufacturing muscle and their success in the external sector. India is rising on the strength of its service industry that, thanks to increasing purchasing power, is taking manufacturing up along with it and is still largely driven by the expansion of the domestic economy. India is beginning to stand out qualitatively thanks to the potential of its huge domestic market. As Stephen Roach – managing director and chief economist, Morgan Stanley – once argued, India stands apart from other Asian economies thanks to it not being unduly dependent on the external sector and for its IT- and services-led growth.

The new middle class: hedonistic, hungry and in a hurry

The difference between what the domestic and foreign companies that came in the 1980s and early 1990s experienced and those that are actively marketing to the Indian middle class today is that back then the middle class in India was just a large hypothetical number. Companies made investments in the 1990s with an eye on the impact of reforms and their belief that India has a huge 300-million-strong untapped middle class (a number that has never been verified) that was just waiting to lap up whatever was on offer. This led to domestic companies doubling and tripling manufacturing facilities, and foreign competition entering the Indian market for the same reason, investing hundreds of millions of dollars. But the middle class and most certainly their much-touted purchasing power turned out to be a mirage. Indian companies – especially in consumer industries, housing, materials and automobiles – were all left with underutilized capacities, leveraged balance sheets, increased competition and a market that did not really exist. But the middle class that proved to be so elusive to so many companies back then is finally beginning to emerge as a market with growing purchasing power and the inclination to use it. Members of this class are still reticent about the volume of purchases they make and are still considered – by Western standards – conservative in their choices of financing, but the signs are unmistakable that the consumer businesses in India are now looking at many years of high growth. The next step would be the opportunity provided by consumers upgrading to luxury products, the way it is happening in China right now.

The emerging of the consumer and real estate boom is one of the new and great opportunities in India, triggered by an increasingly powerful and assertive middle class. Increasing consumer sophistication, rising income levels, increasingly smaller families, the end of traditional joint family systems and falling mortgage costs are factors driving a real estate boom in India. The boom is also powered by the demand for and the availability of high-quality construction by reputable Indian brands. In the post-reform years there has been a qualitative improvement in the standard of living for the middle class. The income level of an average Indian middle class family has gone up substantially and is symptomatic of an evolving economy. In the 1980s, average mortgage payments would comprise over one-third of a typical middle class family's income; now that figure is down to less than one-sixth. Affordable housing is a cornerstone of the consumer revolution in India and the catalyst for a substantial portion of the consumption growth in the rest of the economy. The Western image of a typical Indian consumer would be of one that eschews consumerism. But that could not be further from the truth. Most Indians, despite their cultivated image of detachment from materialism, are in reality among the most hedonistic people that could be found anywhere. And materialism has always been evident and encouraged in Indian culture. Now combined with availability and purchasing power there is an unbelievable growth in consumer industries and in retailing.

Growth of organized retailing has already taken a momentum of its own in India. The convergence of retailing, entertainment and tourism has led to an unprecedented demand for modern retailing space. By the end of 2007 it has been estimated that there will be 358 malls in operation across the country, with 87.8 million square feet, according to a study done by *Images* magazine. An interesting concept taking root is the hotel-malls, where up-market hotels are also creating a high-end shopping experience. Organized retailing (versus the traditional Indian fare of stand-alone retail or department stores) has to be one of the most exciting growth industries in India today, with branded stores and malls thus far covering a miniscule 2% of the total market. Changing lifestyles, rising incomes, exposure to global trends, increasing mobility and the rapid growth of suburban life are creating the perfect environment for an explosive growth in retailing. With the government now thinking along the lines of allowing foreign direct investment in retailing, at some point there is bound to be a significant increase in investments and an uncovering of opportunity. The fact that there has been a quantum jump in lifestyles and the availability of higher value products in India – straddling clothing, consumer electronics, food retailing, restaurants and home products – underscores the rising sophistication of the Indian retailing market. The change in manner in which Indians increasingly seek to indulge in their newfound lifestyles is driving the opportunity for a host of companies in apparels, fashion accessories, hospitality and lifestyle products.

As Indians begin to prosper, more and more of them also seem to get bitten by the travel bug. This is a common trend, and economies across the world have seen it over the years as economic prosperity took root. Ever-increasing hordes of Japanese, Koreans, Taiwanese and Chinese have become enthusiastic tourists. This is symptomatic of rising income levels and economic clout. Now countries, especially in India's vicinity, are playing host to tens of thousands of new travelers from India. The domestic Indian hospitality sector has also geared up for the boom in domestic travel, with hotel rooms being created across various budget categories at great speed.

Even airlines in India – both the state-owned Air India and Indian Airlines, and private airlines such as Jet Airways – have decided to expand like never before, and new airlines are being started by various industrial groups. The state-owned airlines combined have placed the largest order ever with Boeing and Airbus in 2005 for purchases of dozens of new-generation aircraft. India ordered more new aircraft in 2005 than any other country. At the 2005 Paris air show, four private Indian airlines ordered a total of 150 aircraft of varying sizes worth over $16 billion, which was an unprecedented development. Successful domestic airlines like Jet Airways are looking to fly to destinations overseas, including the United States, and more importantly are looking to list on NASDAQ or the New York Stock Exchange giving global investors one more opportunity to gain exposure to a rapidly growing sector. The *Aviation Daily* news magazine quoted Dinesh Keskar, president of Boeing Aircraft Trading, in early 2005 as saying that Boeing expected to sell 492 aircraft to India between 2005 and 2024.

But the opportunity is not just defined by India's innate hedonism and the consumer mantra that seems to have taken hold of the country. It is also defined by the scientific skills honed in universities and technical institutes across the country and sharpened in top Indian and global corporations. For example, it is acknowledged in pharmaceutical companies across the globe that India has very strong skills in molecular chemistry and has the home-grown entrepreneurial ability needed to capitalize on this skill. This has been amply demonstrated by the fact that there are a growing number of Indian companies active in new drug discovery programs, either on their own or in conjunction with global pharmaceutical majors. India's strength is being recognized in bulk drugs, especially in the generic space where its companies compare very favorably with those in other countries with strong generic drug companies, such as Israel, Brazil and Canada. The largest number of US Federal Drug Administration (US FDA) approved pharmaceutical plants outside the United States is located in India. A large number of global pharmaceutical companies are increasingly setting up research centers in India, and the country could also become a leader in clinical trials prior to global drug launches, some of which are already underway. The quality of its manpower is a defining element of the sustainable opportunity in India.

But the key question that will define the investment opportunity in India is whether or not Indian economic growth can accelerate from the 6% to 8% annual growth band that it is in currently to the 10% to 12% band that it needs to be in if it is to count itself amongst the economically powerful group in the world within the next decade or two. Rodrigo De Rato, managing director of the International Monetary Fund (IMF), said that if India can simply raise growth rates to 8% from 6%, the country will double average incomes in 11 rather than 16 years, dramatically improving the standard of living in the country. And the structural changes needed for that to happen are being put into motion, the impact of which will be felt in the years ahead. The next stage of this continuum will be the broadening and deepening of the Indian capital markets, the creation of new markets and instruments such as real estate investment trusts (REITs) that will help investors participate in the massive boom in the real estate sector, and also more importantly the flow of Indian companies to Western capital markets as both their maturity and acceptability grows, throwing up further opportunities for global investors. Already smaller countries and economies such as Taiwan and Israel have more American Depository Receipts (ADRs; issued by foreign companies to equity investors in the United States) trading on the NASDAQ and the New York Stock Exchange than India, which has 12 ADRs trading in the United States and a few dozen Global Depository Receipts (GDRs) in the London and Luxembourg stock exchanges. This will change in the near future, considering that the option of listing ADRs has been given to Indian companies by the government only a few years ago.

The appetite for investing in Indian securities is strongest in the foreign currency convertible bond market (FCCBs). Strong global institutional demand has reduced the yield to maturity (YTM) on Indian paper substantially. According to investment bank Jefferies & Co Inc, the $100 million FCCB by Tata Motors in February 2006 produced a negative yield of 15 basis points, which is uncommon for companies from the Asia Pacific. The YTM of an FCCB is the premium payable in case the option to convert to equity is not exercised and reflects the relative attractiveness of the issuer.

Can Indian manufacturing rise to the challenge?

Success in India is defined by the success of the service sector, but if India is to claim its place among the truly great economies of the world the manufacturing sector has to take up the growth momentum. And fortunately there are clear signs that this is happening. This shift to growth of the manufacturing industry is being captured in a variety of sectors, but most notably in automobiles and auto components. According to the global association of automobile companies, India has the fastest growing automobile industry in the world, with growth rates twice that of China. India is also rapidly becoming the global hub for auto component manufacturing. The list of global automobile names that are outsourcing from India is impressive, and auto component exports are expected to grow by 33% annually for the next few years. The automobile trade associations as well as global consulting firms estimate that between $3 billion and $5 billion of auto investments are headed towards India in the next few years that will further bolster its manufacturing capability. While this may seem small compared to the fact that the Chinese auto sector received $13 billion in 2004 alone, it would be wise to remember that before the year 2000, India hardly made a ripple in the global auto scene.

The realization is dawning on the powers that be that relying on services alone to fuel growth is impossible. The reason is that for an economy to grow large and provide the necessary jobs, manufacturing – which is a voluminous activity – has to grow. Due to neglect, India was poor in physical infrastructure but rich in high-caliber manpower, which is why it was able to capture the wave of globalization in the services sector but not the one in manufacturing, which went China's way. But that lacuna is now being addressed and will contribute significantly as the Indian economy now braces for faster growth. India's move to allow manufacturing foreign direct investment and to build the infrastructure they need will rapidly increase the pace of growth. The private sector and noted Indian academics have been pressing the government for years to recognize the correlation between investment in infrastructure and labor flexibility and economic growth, and to address the infrastructure shortages and labor issues and other rigidities in the economy. The fact that India has already made such great strides in exports despite severe handicaps shows its tremendous prowess and hints to its true potential. The IMF pointed out that India will need 110 million new jobs by 2015, and even under the most optimistic scenario the IT sector will not provide more than two million jobs, which is less than 1% of the workforce, so the real employment will have to come from manufacturing and labor-intensive industries.

Indian companies have been able to create, however slowly, a reliable and growing market for the "Made in India" label, beginning with services, thanks to its software and IT-enabled services companies, and now in manufacturing, thanks to its automobile components and pharmaceutical companies. In addition, Indian companies have been looking globally for their benchmarks, and in many cases are exceeding them.

While Indian companies have realized the importance of thinking global and now have the expertise, resources and aggression needed to deliver solid growth and returns, the question remains: how well prepared is the Indian marketplace to deliver returns to those that venture in now? The lessons that early investors such as the big Japanese companies learnt in the 1980s and 1990s are relevant even today.

The Japanese experience in India

The Japanese were the first major investor group in India, investing heavily in automobiles, auto components and some industrial sectors. Many Japanese companies did poorly, and several fled. But those that hung around and continuously kept up the flow of investments have been rewarded. Suzuki in passenger cars, Honda in motor cycles, Mazda in engines, Showa in shock absorbers; all have created significant value for themselves and their consumers and stakeholders. Suzuki's joint venture in India, Maruti Udyog Ltd, was the first major foreign investment in India in 1982, and after nearly 20 years in India this was one of the crown jewels that was partly offloaded by the Indian government in 2003 as part of its drive to disengage from non-strategic businesses. The 20% stake that the government retained is worth $700 million to $800 million at current stock value. This stake will be offloaded sooner or later. Suzuki's subsidiary alone produces nearly half a million cars annually in India, which is half of India's total car production, and its Indian operations contribute one-quarter of its global volume and profit. Honda Motors is the largest producer of motorcycles in the world thanks to its Indian joint venture Hero Honda Ltd, and is one of the biggest exporters from the country as well. Besides the automobile industry, Japanese companies initially were active in power generation, agriculture and irrigation.

Though the Japanese were the first to enter India, few of the early entrants, except for Suzuki and Honda, hung around. Now that is changing, with Japanese companies beginning to see value in India again. Companies such as Toyota, Mitsubishi Chemicals and consumer electronics firms Toshiba and Sansui are beginning to bet on India, and in a fairly significant way. The interesting point is that India has moved forward so slowly in Japanese minds that 23 years after the first major investment by Suzuki Motors and despite the significant Japanese successes in India, smaller- and medium-sized Japanese companies are only just beginning to look interested. Some notable successes have also been seen among smaller Japanese companies such as Igarashi Motors, ASB Nissei and Koyo Steering. It was this interest from smaller companies that defined Japan's commercial interest in China (at least a couple of thousand Japanese firms are active in China) and will do so in India too. Japanese companies are looking to de-risk their exposure in China, especially with the rise in anti-Japanese sentiment and the potential of an erosion in Chinese manufacturing competitiveness as and when the yuan is allowed to rise, which over time could become an influential factor pushing capital flows India's way.

Whatever the compulsions that drive future investment trends, the Japanese experience in India shows that the greatest reward to investors comes to those who recognize two infallibles. First, no matter what the nature of investment few opportunities in India unfold in a hurry. And second, it is a highly price-sensitive market such that most in the West have never encountered, and that to most consumers a low price point, especially at the entry level, scores over value addition. The greatest pitfall of investing in India is having king-sized expectations. Transplanting growth and returns expectations from other markets, even similar emerging ones, can lead to wrong decisions. The best returns from India have come to those that have decided to hang in there for the long haul. A plethora of experiences has been captured by Japanese investors who were the first to venture in, and these serve as valuable guideposts to expectations, even in a post-liberalized, high-growth era in India.

A large portion of the changes being seen in global investors' attitudes towards India have been prompted by the change within India, its economic structures, the political maturity that it has consistently displayed and more importantly the quality of Indian managements and the global ambition of its corporations. The outcome is that India is now an open, market-driven economy with transparent systems, and with one of the better foreign investment policies found anywhere in the world and even more so among emerging markets.

There has always been an implicit recognition of India through its greatest export yet; its highly trained manpower that is seen at work in global corporations. That implicit recognition is leading to the understanding that the country has a burgeoning mass of educated people with rising income levels and unmet expectations, a valuable mix that simply cannot be ignored any longer. The combination of political stability, economic policy credibility and a well-developed human resource base places India at a tremendous advantage today.

2

THE INTELLECTUAL STRUCTURE AND FRAMEWORK OF THE INDIAN ECONOMY: A HISTORICAL AND CONTEMPORARY PERSPECTIVE

India is often called a country of paradoxes, the greatest paradox of which is the skewed development of its manpower. India produces 200,000 engineers and 50,000 to 60,000 MBAs a year, and thousands of doctors from its 250 medical schools. Its 177 universities and thousands of colleges have four million students enrolled at any time. The seven Indian Institutes of Technology (IIT) and six Indian Institutes of Management (IIM) are now global brands whose graduates, needing no introduction, usually walk into the best global corporations and into plum jobs. There are 50,000 physicians of Indian origin in the United States alone, three-quarters of whom graduated from Indian medical schools.

On the other hand, India suffers from the travesty of having probably the largest number of illiterates and semi-literates anywhere in the world. Rather than being a function of having too many poor people, this is a function of poorly directed, poorly funded and poorly executed state education policies. This is an inexplicable paradox since the storied institutions of higher learning – whether universities, medical schools, regional engineering colleges, IITs and IIMs

– are after all products of a very conscious state policy to create a large pool of technical manpower. These institutions have benefited from consistent investments and budgetary supports from both the central and individual state governments. Financial and infrastructural support to science and technology education and research has been a priority that is even reflected in the government's five-year development plans. Even a relatively new subject like nanotechnology has begun to receive significant funding from the government by way of grants to prestigious engineering colleges and private and public research laboratories, an effort coordinated by the ministry of science and technology.

India has benefited from nurturing the higher educational aspirations of its people but has unfortunately failed in its attempt to provide the most basic education framework to a vast segment of the population. The classic difference between India and China is this: India has invested heavily in higher and technical education, producing a huge segment of an English-educated and trained workforce capable of competing with the best in the world and who are at the forefront of its economic growth. China, on the other hand, has invested heavily in high-quality primary education for all the people, who have become the cornerstone of its success in manufacturing. Economists have hypothesized after studying industrial economies that in tandem with physical and financial infrastructure it is the availability of a workforce equipped with a minimum level of education and skills (often obtained with a basic high school education) that leads to the creation of a successful industrial economy.

India has come to that realization rather belatedly. The policy direction coming from the government is now to match the investments it has made in higher education and in scientific and technical research with increased spending on primary schooling, especially rural education. The established quality of Indian higher education and the increasing availability of primary education should also be seen in the context of demographics and the opportunities it throws up. There is a concept being applied to the emerging story in India called the "demographic dividend"; the fact that India is the only major economy in the world where a significant portion of the population is entering or is still to enter the workforce over the next 10 to 15 years. Today, 54% of the Indian population is below the age of 25. All the other major economies, including China, are looking at the prospects of dealing with an ageing population. This demographic fact and its improving quality have to be seen in the context of the investments being made or considered in physical infrastructure and in manufacturing capability. It portends explosive economic growth, driven by rising purchasing power. Real sustainable growth in the economy will come when the volume of better paying jobs increases and enables the shift of employment demand from agriculture (that currently employs 57% of the workforce) to industry.

The ignored factor in all the talk of Indian talent and quality manpower is the demonstrated ability to innovate and the long history of entrepreneurship and industry in the country. According to author and journalist Paul D'Amato, at the end of the seventeenth century, India and China were two of the most prosperous nations on earth. He pointed out that by 1750, 24.5% of the world's manufacturing output came from India. By 1900, thanks to over a century of colonial exploitation, India's share of world manufacturing had dropped to 1.7%. Investment opportunities will now arise as Indian entrepreneurs – coupled with access to greater capital pools and the cross-border flow of manpower and technology – seek to rebuild its eminent place among the great economies of the world. This natural talent for entrepreneurship was suppressed during India's experiment with Fabian socialism. And the big opportunity today lies in the manufacturing sector where a large number of both listed and privately held Indian companies are clustered.

The opportunity to buy large stakes in relatively young or new companies has not gone unnoticed by global private equity players. A number of ivy-league private and venture fund management companies representing some of the wealthiest individuals globally – such as the Carlyle Group, Blackstone Plc, Warburg Pincus and Walden Nikko – are already making their presence felt. A San Francisco-based private equity firm, Thomas Weisel Partners Group has created the first known United States-based fund of funds for venture capital and private equity going into India, with a $300 million corpus. Global corporations too are investing in Indian companies that are developing new technologies. Intel Corp announced that it will invest $250 million in Indian companies developing cutting-edge technologies. According to ICICI Venture Funds Management, India's largest domestic venture funding company, the pool of venture funding in India could rise to $8 billion annually in a couple of years, from $2 billion in 2005. Several large global venture funds are establishing India-specific funds or earmarking a large component for India from new Asia-specific funds. And given the quality of companies that are sloshing around, the returns are turning out to be phenomenal. Take Warburg Pincus for example; they bought a large stake in Bharti Televentures, one of the fastest growing telecom companies in India, for $300 million and sold just a portion of it for $560 million in 2005. (Warburg incidentally has over $1 billion invested in private Indian companies. ICICI Venture Fund too has over $1 billion invested, and according to the company they have funded 250 companies since 1988 and earned an average return of 39%.)

Along with entrepreneurial talent the key differentiator in the quality of the opportunity in India over other emerging economies is the embedded history of risk-taking and development of localized and sometimes rudimentary but institutionalized mechanisms of mitigating that risk. India has the oldest stock exchange and some of the oldest and largest commodity derivative exchanges in Asia, and even globally (though it is generally accepted that some form of rice futures were traded in Yodoya, Japan, in the mid-seventeenth century). Commodity derivatives trading in India commenced in 1875 with the opening of the cotton exchange in Bombay. The oilseeds exchange opened for trading in forward contracts in 1900, also in Bombay, and was followed in 1912 with the opening of a derivative market for raw jute and jute products in Calcutta. Forward trading in wheat commenced in 1913 and in bullion in 1920. These exchanges have historically traded forward and futures contracts, as well as option contracts, at roughly the same time that these products were being popularized by better-known markets such as the Chicago Board of Trade from the late nineteenth century.

India has thought through its own path to economic growth with a model that emphasized developing high-quality manpower and building a very strong service economy; the success of which is beginning to provide the momentum and confidence to expand its manufacturing base. This is the reverse of what has happened in the rest of the developing world, and is worth emulating. However, it has often been said that India's curse has been its bureaucrats and the legions of socialist-minded economists that the country has been wont to produce, who have had undue influence on the economic route that India took. Jairam Ramesh, the secretary of economic affairs of the Congress party (which heads the current coalition government), once said tongue-in-cheek that the rate of growth of an economy is inversely proportionate to the number of economists in the country! Going by the strange and sometimes inexplicable economic policies followed over several decades, one would accept that perspective without any reservation.

But India's trained manpower – its legions of engineers, biochemists, computer scientists and science and technology PhDs – is the clear edge that the country possesses today, now that the government has decided to unshackle the economy and commit it towards a truly free market. Although India was slow and very late in modernizing and expanding industry and infrastructure, it has been buoyed by its intellectual capital and their success in the global knowledge economy. India's success in information technology is well known, but there are other interesting examples of its prowess. According to a study done by Ernst & Young, the government, through its agency the Council for Scientific and Industrial Research (CSIR), has funded and runs 40 biotech laboratories with 80 field stations employing thousands of people over the last several decades. Indian biotechnology companies are now beginning to be recognized for the development and manufacture of genomic drugs. According to the Indian ministry of commerce, there are 170 biotechnology companies in India, many of which are beginning to collaborate with global companies in gene sequencing and delivering of genomic research.

The other way in which the fusion of capital and talent is taking place is in the outsourcing of scientific research. Around 100 global corporations have made a beeline for India to set up their research facilities and manufacturing hubs. This is a significant tribute to Indian scientific ability. Ever in the search for increased efficiency at a lower cost, global corporations are thus drawn to India by its talent pool and by its high-quality intellectual infrastructure. The world's biggest corporations and technology giants, such as GE, Microsoft, IBM, Texas Instruments and Intel, have begun to make significant investments. Corporations such as Bell Labs, Du Pont, Daimler Chrysler, Caterpillar, Cummins and GM have established R&D centers. The R&D center of GE in Bangalore is the largest outside of the United States, employing 1,600 researchers. And Intel has located its only R&D center outside of the United States in India, employing 1,800 people, and it has committed to investing $1 billion in its development effort in India over a five-year period. AMD has committed to spend $900 million in setting up India's first hi-tech computer chip manufacturing plant. Several global pharmaceutical companies, such as Eli Lily and Monsanto, are also beginning to locate R&D centers in India. Bayer AG, the German chemical giant, has identified India as a global manufacturing hub and R&D center. A coup of sorts occurred when the San Jose, California-based Cisco Systems announced in late October 2005 that it would invest $1.1 billion into R&D and manufacturing in India. This is to be its largest investment outside of the United States. The company's business is growing at 50% compounded for the last few years in India, and they expect to continue to grow at a minimum of 30% in the next few years. Cisco will look at manufacturing of telecommunications equipment too, first for the Indian market and then to source products for global distribution; this is the route that many multinationals are looking at. Impressed with the culture of innovation and the educational environment,

Cisco will also add to the private equity pool heading into India with a $100 million contribution for Indian start-ups.

But the emergence of India on the strength of its scientific talent is no accident, nor will it diminish with time. Scientific research and thought has been an ancient tradition in India that continues to live on. Before the enlightenment of the Renaissance altered European perspectives and attitudes towards science, India was considered to be a thought leader in science and mathematics, besides being an economic power. Indian scientific discoveries – especially related to mathematics, physics and astronomy – were much sought after in the West, and Indian ideas were carried across through trade links and often by Arab travelers and scholars. It is the Hindu numbering system involving 10 numerals and the development of the place value system that is the standard today. The mathematician, Aryabhata, wrote a book on mathematics and astronomy in AD 499 and is considered to be the inventor of modern algebra. Before being introduced to the Hindu numbering system, much of the European world used the abacus and Roman numerals. The old system limited their ability to delve deep into mathematics. It was the use of zero as a numeral by an unknown Indian mathematician in 2 BC that revolutionized the world of mathematics, and everything else too. The decimal system was invented in India and recorded to be in use from 1300 BC.

Chemistry was practiced in India and was well developed well over 2,000 years ago, as was the practice of metallurgy. Indian chemistry skills were well utilized in understanding the use and manufacture of dyes for textiles, manufacture of paints and cement and in the development of medicines. The West eventually caught up with Indian science during the European Renaissance. India always had brilliant theorists, who for various reasons did not pursue experimentation to augment their scientific observations, and their work – though brilliant and intuitive – was difficult to actualize. Scientific leadership eventually moved to the West, with their emphasis on experimentation and the development of the tools to convert observations to experimentation and experimentation to practical application.

Today there is a reverse flow once again. During and after the process of colonization the emphasis that India put on the Western system of education has led to the cross-fertilization of the long and venerable tradition of Indian scientific enquiry and the emphasis on learning with Western rigor, practicality and orientation towards results. This is very evident in the pharmaceutical sector where numerous Indian companies have evolved with very strong product and process development skills, with strong commercial applications.

Now, there is little doubt that the scientific and technological man-power and research and development institutions in India are far superior than ever before and can match the skills available among the top global institutions. India has 1,500 research laboratories op-erating, and according to the Indian commerce ministry, in 2002–03 Indian companies and laboratories filed 1,700 patents with the US patents and trademarks office and 15,000 patents were filed domesti-cally.

Funding of scientific efforts post-independence has always been an issue with Indian scientific organizations, but even on meager gov-ernment funding a lot has been achieved. Today with the increased participation of the corporate sector and the remodeling of the na-ture of scientific enquiry, Indian institutions – especially the premier ones – are becoming incubators of ideas, processes and products. For example, a group of technologists and scientists from Banga-lore's premier Indian Institute of Science, often referred to as India's knowledge hub, conceptualized, designed and built the world's first hand-held computer called the "simputer", designed for rural users in India. As a part of its concept and design the cost of the unit was kept below $200, and it has proven to be commercially viable and is being tested prior to introduction in various parts of the third world, with far more applications than was first envisaged. In 1998 India tested nuclear weapons, an act that led to sanctions against it by the United States, which denied it crucial supercomputing technol-ogy. India's response was to quickly assemble a team from various government research laboratories and public sector corporations that went on to create an indigenous supercomputer christened "Param". Only two other countries – the United States and Japan – have indig-enous supercomputing technology.

The role of the Indian public sector too has been paradoxical but largely beneficial in developing India's intellectual capital. While the public sector controlled a lion's share of resources, and though by the time economic reforms were introduced many of them could not even produce a positive return on capital employed, their contri-bution to developing India's scientific and technical manpower has been phenomenal. Most of today's Indian scientists and technologists being sought after by the Indian private sector and foreign compa-nies were incubated in public-sector corporations and in govern-ment-run laboratories. India is one of only a handful of nations with a permanent research station in Antarctica, is one of just six countries that has a successful space program and satellite launch capability, and is one among just a few countries with the capability to design and manufacture a car completely indigenously.

The government aided and sponsored scientific and technical institutes and laboratories have developed world-class research in diverse and complex areas such as agriculture, defense technology, biotechnology, communications, avionics, pharmaceuticals, tropical diseases, environment, mining, nuclear power, oceanography, supercomputing, telecommunications and space research. These were all segments that were once exclusively handled by the public sector and are now seeing a lot of participation from the private sector, even in once-closed sectors such as defense.

India's progress in fundamental science and technology makes it stand out among developing nations and put it in a league of its own in terms of available intellectual capital. India produces close to 6,000 PhDs in science and technology every year – only China and Japan produce a higher number. But that was not always the case; in 1991 India produced around 5,000 science and technology PhDs, which was more than in China, Japan and South Korea combined. India's annual output of PhDs has risen by only 15% in the one and a half decades since, while China and Japan have increased between 150% and 200% and only then have they caught up with India.

The cross-fertilization of intellectual capital with the real world has happened in the best global traditions. Institutions such as Stanford University and laboratories run by major United States corporations helped fuel innovation and growth in Silicon Valley. Bangalore, the hub of India's IT industry which is often compared to Silicon Valley, has benefited from an identical model, where high-quality engineering institutions and the presence of several large public-sector laboratories in industries from aerospace, computing and heavy engineering provided the human and intellectual infrastructure needed by the rapidly growing and futuristic information technology campuses in the city. In fact, the four southern states – Tamil Nadu, Andhra Pradesh, Karnataka (where Bangalore is located) and Kerala – and the western state of Maharashtra produce over two-thirds of the total engineering graduates in the country, emerging from hundreds of engineering colleges (half the total number of engineering colleges in India are estimated to be in these states). These same five states also contain nearly half of the medical schools in India and supply most of the physicians of Indian origin in the United States.

Pre-reform, India's surplus of talent in its scientific and technical pool did not find adequate opportunity. The emphasis on developing human capital was independent of economic policies being followed, so while the opportunity to earn a masters or a doctorate was certain, the opportunity of utilizing it was by no means certain. Thanks to a restricted economy where employment prospects were not always bright and compensation not particularly great, there was a mass migration called "the brain drain" away from India to largely to the United States and also to South East Asia. According to Indian government statistics nearly one-third of Microsoft and IBM today are staffed with Indians, and they form a large portion of the pool of talent at NASA and various other top corporations. But now the talent pool is beginning to find increasing avenues of deployment at home, as new employment opportunities are constantly springing up in dozens of industries. From a negligible amount a few decades ago, Indian corporations now contribute to around one-third of the total research and development spend in the country, and most have committed to increasing this several fold. According to the OECD, India's R&D spend today puts it amongst the top 10 spenders globally.

There is a recognition both within and outside of the government that if this is to be India's century then the huge and growing pool of entrepreneurs and skilled workers needs to be given every incentive to be productive. India's edge, clearly, is its human resource base or its intellectual infrastructure that has the capability to shape world-class talent and has already notched up notable achievements. This development is unique in the world of emerging economies. The tremendous success of Indian software and systems integration firms and in select manufacturing and process industries after the opening up of the economy in 1991 attests to the validity of the model where successful human capital formation accompanied by market-friendly economic policies can propel developing countries into higher value-added activity. Jawaharlal Nehru summed up the potential for India, saying, "India, constituted as she is, cannot play a secondary part in the world. She will either count for a great deal or not count at all." It seems India, powered by the intellect of its people, has chosen the former.

3

CHANGE CATALYSTS: COST OF CAPITAL, CORPORATE GOVERNANCE AND THE EMERGENCE OF VALUE

There were always a number of companies in India that paid very careful attention to enhancing shareholder value, and appreciated the importance of earning more than their cost of capital. They were more the exception though, and until recently the vast majority of companies never did either. The gradual but growing recognition among Indian corporations that all capital, and especially equity capital, does carry a very heavy cost even if that cost is not accounted for in the financial statements has gone a long way to boost the quality of the investment opportunity in India.

Traditionally, Indian companies were especially inclined to treat equity capital as "free money" and did not pay attention to the implicit cost that using it entailed because capital in any other form obviously carried an explicit pre- or post-tax charge to the income statement. It was common for companies to access the equity market – even for greenfield projects as well as for routine expansion projects – until the mid-1990s. This flawed thinking was also widely prevalent within the financial community. Due to the fact that India was a closed economy where outside influences were not easily digested, the change in understanding investor expectations in the financial world outside – brought about by the modern portfolio theory (MPT) and the capital asset pricing model (CAPM) – to a large extent bypassed the Indian capital market.

Among others, the common manifestation of this ignorance over the true cost of capital and how it relates investor expectations to corporate behavior is that companies would tend to enter businesses that were not necessarily economically remunerative, funded through an unhealthy mix of equity raised from state-owned mutual funds and financial institutions and the IPO market – where new-issue pricing was controlled by a government department – and through large dollops of debt. Companies would also tend to retain a large portion of their earnings, building up assets, investing in securities of other companies or depositing cash with companies controlled by the promoter group, simply because there was no incentive to reduce assets by returning cash to shareholders or maintaining a more efficient working capital flow and thereby improving the return on capital employed (RoCE).

There was always a clear demarcation between those companies that understood the economic concepts linked to shareholder value and those that did not. There were companies that produced extremely high returns on capital employed, high rates of incremental return on capital, threw up mountains of cash, squeezed every penny out of working capital and carried as little investment in assets as possible. These companies traded at a significant premium to the market, but the reason for that was not easily understood by the investing establishment at large and even less so by the average company managements. Besides, most Indian companies looked askance at economic profits and only worried about accounting profits since the markets used variations of price earnings multiples and other relative and accounting-profit-based valuation methods as the preferred pricing methodology. Most corporations were not concerned whether their businesses were generating an adequate return on net worth (RoNW), RoCE or incremental RoCE, or whether they were earning more than their cost of capital. Companies had no incentive to be efficient with their capital allocation decisions, nor did they need to be concerned with processes that enhanced shareholder value because other than an astute few, the market in general did not fully digest these concepts.

But there were other reasons for this thinking. First, because of industrial licensing policy the government decided who could enter new lines of business and whether they could expand, and those that did usually also managed to get more than adequate debt funding from state-owned institutions, sometimes to the extent of two-thirds of their capital employed. Second, the bulk of Indian corporate equity was held by promoting families, so there was no-one to really answer to. Third, through the Controller of Capital Issues, the government decided on how much they could raise to fund projects and the price at which equity could be raised, so if companies were tapping the IPO or new issues market they had to sell equity on the cheap anyway. Fourth, there was absolutely no global competition since the economy was closed, and limited domestic and international competition meant there was limited need for operational and capital efficiency. And last, there were no knowledgeable or powerful institutional or activist shareholders, and the laws surrounding the transfer of shares were so restrictive that few if any could challenge incumbent managements with "greenmail", as happened regularly in the United States in the 1980s and 1990s, where large blocks of stock were acquired by professional corporate raiders and the targeted managements were either forced to shape up or had to buy back this stock at a premium. These factors severely impacted the quality of available investments.

Despite valuation being an enigma in India and the disparity in the pricing of equity in the market, there were dynamic companies that stood out as investment-worthy, led by high-quality managements and that commanded significant market premiums. Companies such as Hindustan Lever (the Indian subsidiary of Unilever Plc), Asian Paints, Castrol India, MICO, MRF, Madras Cement, Bajaj Auto, a host of multinational companies – especially pharmaceutical companies such as GlaxoSmithkline, Pfizer, Hoechst and Bayer – and others such as Cummins India, Ingersoll Rand and Atlas Copco were traded at a premium to the Indian market. Indian pharmaceutical companies emerged as outstanding value creators only since the late 1990s (today the valuation appended to Indian pharmaceutical companies is significantly higher than that appended to the multinational pharmaceutical companies, and with very good reason). In essence, there were really two sets of companies: those multinationals that followed the best financial practices of their parent organization and the Indian companies spread out in different sectors that emulated those practices, and those companies that were clueless with managements that were perfectly happy to run corporations like their personal fiefdoms.

The irony of something so twisted as controlled pricing of new issues and a regulated industrial environment is that it actually helped some categories of committed equity investors to make money, and it helped the spread of the equity cult. Indian capital market professionals humorously referred to this government-controlled equity pricing environment as a capital market subsidy. But lax governance and ignorance over what equity investors really expected delayed the growth, expansion and maturing of the Indian capital markets, which was a steep price for a capital-starved economy to pay.

The eventual result of industrial licensing and the proclivity to raise money from ever-obliging financial institutions and an ever-yielding capital market was the creation of the conglomerate structure and the evolution of large diversified companies or diversified groups where companies within have close financial and management ties with each other. Interestingly, there were several cases of corporate groups having more than one company in the same line of business. It also became a convenient way for corporate groups to simply move funds from one company to another.

Despite the fact that there were 7,000 issues listed for trading on the Bombay stock exchange by the early 1990s, there were only about 50 to 100 companies that really understood investor expectations and the essence of cost of capital and so by their actions tried to enhance shareholder value. But the liquidity and the depth of all the companies that were publicly traded were very poor, even among the better-valued ones. In effect the Indian capital market was a large but shallow pond.

The growth of the capital market, its qualitative change and increase in trading depth came about only from the mid-1990s, brought on by sweeping changes in regulation, knowledge and attitude. As the government reversed its compulsory licensing policies and opened the economy to competition the canvas of the shortage economy disappeared, and the survival of companies – let alone growth – was by no means certain. Companies had to change and become more competitive, and recognize the need for capital efficiency. And adapting to change – including understanding shareholder value and the corporate practices that led to it – was a major development for the Indian capital markets. The change in laws that governed corporate takeovers and the events that led to the emergence of corporate raiders and "greenmailers" in the 1990s hastened this process.

A large number of Indian companies went through business process re-engineering in order to enhance their competitive strengths and eliminate value-depleting activities. It is now becoming widely accepted among corporations that once considered equity to be "free money", that it carries a cost that is usually steep. Along with business process re-engineering there also began a conversion from the conglomerate structure to leaner and often single-business enterprises. That change is still happening, and de-mergers are all the rage now in corporate India.

The coming of foreign investors saw the valuation premium for well-run companies increase dramatically. With the scrapping of the office of Controller of Capital Issues, the power to price issues was handed back to the market, and with valuations now becoming of paramount importance it prompted companies to adopt value-enhancing practices and attempt to close the valuation gap. This change has also begun to have a profound effect on the Indian IPO market. Where once all and sundry turned up to place equity to fund anything from start-ups to investing in group ventures, now only well-established companies have begun to appear, especially after the last IPO debacle of 1994–95 where dozens of start-ups and unheard – of companies suddenly appeared on the scene, taking advantage of strong market sentiment to raise capital and then disappear overnight – and that too only for well-thought-out projects closely related to the company's existing business or in businesses where the company or management has some strategic advantages.

THE EMERGENCE OF CORPORATE GOVERNANCE AND RECOGNITION OF THE VALUE GAP

Closely linked to efficient capital allocation and the ability of corporations to consistently earn a return in excess of their cost of capital was the corporate attitude towards their shareholders and how that has influenced value. Investors traditionally received the short end of the stick from corporations, and minority shareholder rights for the large part were laughable. Mark Mobius, Franklin Templeton's celebrated emerging markets fund manager, wrote about the pathetic experiences of shareholders in Russia, where corporations reserved the right to refuse to transfer shares if they felt threatened by new investors, or sometimes they simply sat on the shares for years without transferring them, thereby depriving the market of liquidity and keeping stock prices artificially higher. Malpractices of a similar nature used to be the norm in India, and early foreign investors no doubt suffered through it as Indian shareholders had done for decades. Mobius said that the critical criteria he used before entering any emerging market was to check whether or not there was a central share registry. In India, the creation of a central share depository as part of sweeping capital market reform solved the problem of delays in share transfers and the resultant improprieties entirely.

Let alone corporate governance, corporations were literally known to treat shareholders as little more than a footnote, whereby simple shareholder rights were difficult to enforce amongst the bulk of the companies (of course there were plenty of exceptions). The threat of company funds being siphoned out was a huge problem that minority and institutional investors faced in a majority of Indian companies. The tell-tale signs were always there: interest-free loans to group companies, complex cross-holdings where company funds were diverted to buy company stock or stock of group companies, over or under invoicing, distorted input/output ratios, and a host of others.

Investors were actually paying the price for an over-regulated economy, and there is some merit to the argument that managements had little choice but to devise alternate means to take money out of the companies since all the value they created was locked into the company by the laws of the time. There was a ceiling on how much salary and bonuses managements could pay themselves, and stock options were disallowed. Even dividends paid out by corporations were controlled by government diktat in the pre-reform era. It has been argued that the unreasonable restrictions on management compensation were undoubtedly the genesis of these malpractices. An excellent and scholarly treatment of corporate practices in India was published in an Oxford University study titled *Corporate Governance and the Indian Private Sector*, authored by Jairus Banaji and Gautam Mody. They summed up the situation in India well: "Corporate governance is at the heart of the drama of liberalization, because key issues are those of ownership and control as well as management integrity, accountability and transparency and the impact these features have on the growth of the economy and the vitality of the business sector. The subordination of boards to management, self dealing, manipulation of accounts and corruption in the allocation of finance have all contributed to the endemic lack of credibility Indian businesses have suffered from and a crucial part of the reform of the corporate sector is how soon and how consistently those legacies can be discarded and overcome. India is still a developing country and it can scarcely afford to live with the incubus of a corporate system that constrains growth because business families are unwilling to yield control and because the management of companies lacks credibility with investors."

The effort to change the Indian capital market and especially corporate practices was never taken seriously, until foreign investors began to look at India as an investment destination after the capital market was opened to them in 1993. Investment practitioners subsequently began to develop the ability to recognize, differentiate and quantify investment value and risk. The different approaches to corporate governance were also quantified and appended as differential multiples to companies. There is definitely a premium being paid for companies considered to be ethical and upholding strong corporate values. Linking value to the perception of a company besides its performance has played an important role in spreading the idea of better corporate governance.

Managements too took notice as some companies suddenly became very valuable. This is clearly observed within the software services industry, where the top-tier firms – especially Infosys Technologies, TCS and Wipro – record high multiples while other large firms do not command the same, even though there is equivalence in growth expectations. This value gap has begun to be recognized as the price of neglecting corporate governance.

But despite the recognition of the value-enhancing characteristics of observing a better standard of corporate governance, it has not been widely adopted even though more companies follow it than before. Even within the software industry not all companies follow the high standards set by Infosys Technologies and Wipro. But compared to the rest of Indian industry the software services industry is a different kettle of fish. Firstly, this sector is relatively new and was among the first to be created and run by technocrats and not traditional industry groups or family-run conglomerates. Many of the entrepreneurs came from Silicon Valley or were influenced by it and brought corporate best practices from that world to India. Secondly, these companies dealt almost entirely outside India and conformed to practices in countries that have higher governance standards, such as the United States. And thirdly, there was a need for these companies to attract cross-border talent, especially in countries where they operate, and this was possible only with a very good image.

A few Indian family-run conglomerate groups have initiated the move towards better corporate governance practices. Companies such as Birla 3M (joint venture with 3M Corp), Indian Shaving Products (Gillette) and Paper Products (Van Leer, Netherlands), among several others, realized that it was better to allow their MNC partners to control the company (separation of ownership and management) and benefit from the higher valuations rather than control the company and constantly battle the negative perceptions that surround most industrial groups in India. Other conglomerates and corporations have benefited from best practices like untangling cross-holdings (the OP Jindal and Aditya V Birla conglomerates), bringing in valuable brands once held by the promoters through private companies (Nirma Ltd and Navneet Publications Ltd), reducing the number of subsidiary companies (BSES Ltd; now known as Reliance Energy Ltd), avoiding share issues to promoter groups at preferential prices, compensating the company for fiscal mismanagement by the promoters (Jain Irrigation Ltd), and increasing compliance with consolidation of financial statements.

But these are still not representative enough, and more needs to be done. The factors that will drive greater adoption of corporate governance practices are the increasing number of Indian companies that are looking to list on overseas exchanges, the gradual but certain reduction in promoter or single-family control of Indian businesses and the demand from increasingly vocal institutional shareholders for more value-enhancing practices. However, on the litmus test of independent directors almost all Indian companies would still fail miserably. But truly independent directors is a tall order, and even companies in more developed economies with better corporate governance practices find it difficult to meet the intended objective behind this.

Even today, despite all the major transformation that has happened, almost 95% of the market cap is concentrated in fewer than 1,000 companies, of which about half are still not fully investment grade (though it is still a big jump from the early and mid-1990s). But it is due to the remarkable metamorphosis of the capital market that the investment worthiness of companies has been rising and that the type of companies that have been approaching the market for the past couple of years have been of the highest quality, both from the private and public sector, with long-established businesses and reputations. Even though some of these names are relatively new, they have a solid operating track record. Thus there is evidence that the Indian capital market is maturing. The companies that once chose to stay away from the public market are now confident enough of the systems and market practices and are beginning to come forward, thereby increasing the choice of better quality and investment-worthy names. And we will see subsequently just how much bigger the investment pie has become as a result of these value-enhancing changes, and how deep the opportunity now runs.

THE LANDSCAPE OF POLITICAL REFORM AND DIMINISHING RISK

When John Chambers, CEO of Cisco Systems, announced his company's plans to invest over $1 billion in India in October 2005, he said that it was "India's economic potential, educational infrastructure, culture of innovation and a supportive government" that prompted Cisco to increase investments in India. That anyone, let alone a high-profile CEO of one of the largest technology companies in the world, would cite India's government as supportive and that it could be part of a reason to invest would astound even those most convinced of the country's potential. But this is the reality in India today; the government that once existed solely to regulate and obfuscate is now an economic cheerleader focused on improving people's lives with deeds and not merely words or slogans. One of the more significant elements of political risk faced by investors that emanates from government policies has greatly diminished as a result.

The catalyst for change in the economy has been the shift in the political will of the nation. It is true that the momentum of reform had risen to unprecedented levels during the five years under the BJP-led coalition, the National Democratic Alliance (NDA), beginning in 1999, yet that coalition was defeated during the 2004 general elections. The reason for the defeat was not popular opposition to the reform process – as was put forward by the leftist parties and other victors of that election – but an expression of resentment that the benefit of the reforms was not spread around faster and the feeling of alienation, largely among the rural population since the success of the reforms was seen as a predominantly urban phenomenon.

It is evident that democratic rights are taken very seriously in India and politicians are made to pay dearly for their perceived failures. The direction of reforms and the speed with which they impact different segments of Indian society are now critical inputs in determining political destinies. This growing political and public momentum in favor of faster and sustained reform is the least understood of all the developments in India by global investors. Major misconceptions exist regarding the degree of political risk that India still poses to overseas investors, and how much of real continuity and stability there is in economic policy and direction.

Political risk can be defined from the practical standpoint of an investor's generic need for regulatory and policy stability and the assurance that the rules will not change *ex post facto*. This used to happen a lot in India; investors would enter based on certain rules only to see the rules or their interpretation change later. Now, there is a recognition in political and government circles that ad hoc policies aimed at short-term political interests do backfire in the long run. Each of the critical sectors in India that were opened to private investment are now subject to independent regulatory oversight distinct from the government. One by one various industries are being brought under the purview of independent regulators, including insurance, power and telecommunications. Legislative efforts are now underway (through the introduction of the Petroleum and Natural Gas Regulatory Board Bill) to bring the petroleum and natural gas sector under the purview of an independent regulator. A key power that will be given to this regulatory board once the Indian parliament passes the Bill will be the pricing of natural gas with respect to transportation charges and pipeline usage. An existing government department – the Directorate of Hydrocarbons – will also have regulatory oversight over oil and gas exploration and production activities, and will have oversight over pricing of natural gas in terms of production-sharing contracts. Developments like this obviously go a long way to reassuring investors that there cannot be any arbitrary change of rules and that no-one will be discriminated against, and that a statutory body exists to address significant issues, including pricing and any grievances that may arise.

The will to change the old pervasive mindset was tested a couple of years ago when demands were made in some political quarters that the preferential capital gains tax treatment for foreign investors be revoked. Most foreign institutional investors in India use either Mauritius or Singapore to route their investments into India, though they may not be domiciled there since India has a double tax avoidance treaty with both nations. The objection raised by some politicians was that this route had become a means to defraud the Indian exchequer. The government was forced to raise the possibility of revoking the tax status of some funds suspected of "abusing" the system, and a full-scale investigation by the market regulator and tax authorities loomed. This threatened the very structure of foreign portfolio investments in India. Eventually it became clear that the government had no intention to take any action that altered the rules *ex post facto*. But something like this could have blown into a serious crisis of confidence with foreign investors, and it nearly did. It was not lost on anyone that the problem was managed without any change in the ground rules, and this showed a more refined, mature and sensitive understanding of the expectations of foreign investors.

Fear factor: Overcoming Indian bureaucracy

A joke was that in the past if a foreign investor wanted information on investing in India he or she needed to make an application of enquiry to an appropriate authority in triplicate. That may have been said in jest, but the impression that foreign investors in general have about investing in India is one of endless red tape, endless requests for permissions and consequent delays. This has long hampered the flow of investments into India.

However, in contrast to this sentiment, the FDI Confidence Index (the annual survey conducted by consulting firm AT Kearney) showed that India has replaced the United States as the world's second most popular destination for foreign direct investment. The factors that contributed to this enhanced view of India as an investment destination include reduced interaction with the bureaucracy, setting up of an investment facilitation cell within the government, single-window clearances and substantial hikes in FDI caps for various industries. But old perceptions have not entirely died out, especially those relating to the nature of politics.

THE FRUITS OF COALITION POLITICS

The emergence of coalition politics from 1991 has led to the rise of regional political parties. As a result, regional development issues were pushed to the forefront. This has led to a slackening of political opposition to vital issues of reform since a large part of the opposition did come from regional parties. The reform process is now gathering momentum from within the individual states, and many of them (run by a range of political ideologies) are leading the effort to bring in foreign investment. When the NDA coalition came to power in 1999 there was a strong political consensus for accelerating the reform process both at the state and national levels. Now after the NDA has been voted out and with a communist-backed government in power the reform process is taking on a more human face, in the form of investment in rural literacy and building rural infrastructure in an effort to speed up the impact of economic growth to the rural masses.

The voting out of the BJP-led NDA government was initially seen as a setback since a reforming India that was beginning to throw up significant investment opportunities was closely identified by global investors with the BJP's economic policies. But no-one had foreseen the propitious events that would follow the creation of a new coalition led by the Congress party that had ruled for the greater part of post-independence India. Both the architect of India's early reforms initiative, former finance minister Dr Manmohan Singh, and its subsequent champion as finance minister under different governments, P Chidambaram, came together to form a formidable team as prime minister and finance minister respectively. A look at what they have set out to do in the first year and a half in office is a testament to the fact that India will look a lot different a few years from now.

This transition, and the fact that no matter which of the two major coalition blocks is in power there are strong and firm hands to guide the economy, has been very positive for India's image among global investors and is a remarkable development in itself. The evidence is that there is continuity of major policies, though with some differences in priorities. India now does appear to be a more mature and stable political economy where even a drastic change of government from right to left does not or cannot alter the essential reformist direction of the economy.

Indian states: The new engine of reform

- There has been a diffusion of real political power from the center to the states; the new political approach has been coined as "cooperative federalism". The seven or eight high-income states, which are also fast-growing ones commanding a large share of investment and savings, have long pushed for greater economic autonomy.
- The emergence of regional politics over national politics has brought about the means to better understand the needs of individual regions, and policy-making has been more effective.
- Individual state governments have been taking very progressive economic actions based on their assessment of what is best for them, including disinvesting from government-owned companies, closing down loss-making public sector companies, and privatizing services.
- Increased competition among states has spurred more reform, even amongst once reticent state governments. For example, privatization of power distribution was first introduced by the state of Orissa, which had traditionally not been known to be pro industry or reform. Other states have since introduced or begun looking at this subject.
- There is a shifting of growth momentum to the states as industries are increasingly drawn by their overall attractiveness, especially the availability of a suitable workforce and the necessary supporting services, rather than political pressures or artificial incentives. Investment in the metals industry, for example, is now converging on states such as Chattisgarh and Orissa, where ore and coal reserves are significant. Other examples are IT clusters in Karnataka and Maharashtra, pharmaceuticals in Andhra Pradesh and automobile components in Tamil Nadu and Punjab.

The potential for a true common Indian market exists after the removal of the tax on sales and its replacement by a value-added tax and the abolition of interstate duties. These interstate duties earlier acted as a domestic trade barrier. Over time this could bring about the elusive economic convergence between the states and raise the standard of living in India's most backward states.

Coalition politics has proven to be the best form of governance for a country like India. India's pluralism transcends its politicians and style of democracy now. There is no clear "national party", and it is unlikely there ever will be. The political landscape at present represents the true nature of the Indian people: diverse, with different social and economic agendas, yet having a common enough ground to be able to work through or simply trade-off differences at the national level. The powerful catalyst of economic reform was laid out by a Congress party-led coalition government from 1991 to 1995. And ever since that governing coalition there has been a string of changes for the better, each engineered by different coalition governments, culminating in the latest one.

The five years (1999 to 2004) under the BJP-led NDA coalition proved to be a significant era in coalition politics, where the reform process was taken to such a level that it has proven to be almost irreversible. The communist allies, on whose support the government now survives, seem to have laid out their tactics, which consist of tacit support to the government to keep up the reforms momentum (with some changes in emphasis) within parliament by its MPs but noisy protests in the street by the rank and file to keep its constituents happy. The reform locomotive thus rolls on undisturbed, albeit with a few stops.

DISSECTING THE COMMUNIST REALITY IN INDIA

On the face of it the most unpredictable elements in Indian politics are the communist parties, largely due to their history and the influence their ideology has had on the Indian political landscape. The fear that is omnipresent is one of expropriation of corporate assets by an ideologically motivated government, as happened in the 1970s with grave consequences for India. Several industries were nationalized and numerous foreign companies were forced to leave the country at that time.

But the key factor underlining the reality of communist participation (the consolidated body of four communist parties are known as the Left Front) in governance in India today is that though they have 59 seats (all the various communist formations together) in parliament this represents just 10% of the total number of seats. They also have derived the bulk of their seats from two states – West Bengal and Kerala – and some seats from the eastern region of the state of Bihar. This is by no means representative of the people of India, since all three regions have traditionally been bastions of communist support. Even though they increased their tally of seats dramatically in the 2004 general election it does not represent a mandate to foist a leftist agenda on economic policy-making. Investor confidence has been boosted by the realization that though there will be opposition to reforms it will be muted and designed more for effect.

A good indication of what the communists are capable of will come from observing recent developments in those individual states that are communist ruled and are considered to be their strongholds. These states are a study in contrast with what the communists say at the national level and do at the state level. The two states of West Bengal and Kerala have been the hot beds of labor militancy for decades, which resulted in industries gradually dying out. Now industry is being encouraged back with great fervor as both governments seek to reverse the brain drain from their states and enhance the opportunities within. The government of Kerala, for example, has begun to drive hard towards obtaining foreign investments in manufacturing, including wooing the likes of BMW to set up an assembly plant in the state. It also helps that Transparency International recently ranked Kerala as the least corrupt state in India.

A tiger economy in Bengal?

The state of West Bengal (WB) under a reform-minded chief minister is seeking to recreate its old domination of the Indian economy. West Bengal has followed a torturous path to investment-led growth, but the state is now one of the best poised to achieve rapid industrialization and economic growth. Following the communist parties coming to power in the late 1970s, a unique program of land reform and land redistribution was initiated, where sharecroppers were given a stake in the land they tilled and village self-governance was undertaken. This program of land reform gave WB one of the most productive agricultural sectors in the country. The WB chief minister, B Bhattacharya, has been quoted as saying that they want to transform their success in agriculture into industry. The food processing industry is a logical focus area for the government in trying to attract FDI, and several deals have been announced.

Higher and technical education was always prized in the state, and along with Kerala it has almost 100% literacy, making it a fertile ground for industrialization. The thrust of the current progressive-minded government there is to create as many industries as possible and raise the quality of employment as well as income-generation opportunities. The state has long had an emphasis on scientific and technical education, and with its large concentration of university and engineering graduates the state government has automatically identified information technology as a growth area. Knowing the well-seeded culture of protest in their communist state the government has gone one step ahead and declared IT to be a "public utility service", thus preventing any possibility of labor-related disruptions and enabling the industry to work on a 24/7 basis. It is aiming to be among the top three states in terms of IT revenues by 2009.

Information technology investments are already happening in a significant way, but more structured investments on a dramatically larger scale are also happening with some critical foreign participation. Indonesia's largest conglomerate, the Salim group, has successfully bid to invest $10 billion in building one of the largest integrated townships and industrial parks, the Kolkata International Economic Zone (which will accommodate a host of industries with an emphasis on IT), in south of WB's capital city of Kolkata. This ranks as one of the largest examples of FDI in India, all in communist-run WB! The Indonesians will model the economic zone on the lines of the Batamindo industrial park near Singapore, which was the first such integrated economic zone built in Asia, but it will be significantly bigger.

The state's leadership has emphasized that their growth model is the South East Asian one, where domestic strengths were amplified with active state support. They have gone out of their way to woo companies from Singapore, Indonesia, Thailand and also Japan and China to invest. Mitsubishi Chemicals, which first invested in WB in 2000 in a purified terephthalic acid (PTA) plant, has increased the scale of their operations with another plant and is an example of what is possible for global corporations. The state government has been successful in pulling in a number of Japanese companies, including big names such as Sumitomo Corp, Mitsubishi Heavy Industries, Itochu Corp and Mitsui & Co, to begin operations.

According to the Confederation of Indian Industry (CII) the state is the only power surplus one in the country, and is now able to attract funding from Japanese investors for improving the quality of the power supply and distribution, unlike other states that have struggled with private funding.

Political maturity to count, as reforms enter home stretch

The new communist thinking and degree of reforms exercised in the states they control becomes overwhelmingly important since the only major reform that is left to tackle at the national level is labor, which is something they have sworn to oppose. There is a gigantic need across the political spectrum to understand the need for labor reform. Companies in India have a right to hire workers but not fire them. Plants can be opened but cannot be closed. There is a myriad of regulations that govern labor, and this imposes such a heavy burden on companies that it is the single biggest demotivating factor for really large, intensive manufacturing investments.

The dismantling of the multi-fiber agreement (MFA) in January 2005 was supposed to usher in great opportunities for the Indian textile sector, which until that point faced quota restrictions on the export of manufactured garments, especially to European and US markets. The key input into exploiting this opportunity was an expansion of the domestic apparel manufacturing capacity. At the very least, Indian companies have great strengths in cotton spinning, natural and synthetic yarn manufacture, dyeing and texturising, and also in fabric manufacture and in design and manufacture of clothing. Essentially the textile industry had capabilities straddling the entire value chain, and before IT began to dominate the external sector it was the country's largest export. The manufacturing base was there but it needed to be expanded by a factor of four or five. Every textile company that I spoke with on their level of preparation for this opportunity said roughly the same thing, that the opportunity was there but they feared making the investment due to inflexible labor laws. In order to be competitive, especially with Chinese firms, they would need to set up clothing manufacturing plants with a capability of producing four to six million pieces annually, each plant employing thousands of people. The fear was that should anything go wrong for any reason they would not be allowed to shut shop and retrench workers. This naturally would not be acceptable to anyone. Leading textile companies such as Arvind Mills that did put up large clothing manufacturing capacities did so in offshore locations such as Mauritius, which is not something everyone can pull off. And similar concerns run through numerous other labor-intensive industries, though none of the other manufacturing industries that are making significant investments are as dependent on the external sector for the outcome of their capacity enhancements as the textile sector and so do not face the same level of anxiety. Labor inflexibility, however, remains an issue with them.

Labor reforms thus become very critical and will certainly lead to larger investment in manufacturing and create a larger base of industrial jobs. Creating the right conditions for the growth of Indian industry becomes critical as the working-age population and those still to enter the workforce now forms a significant percentage of the total population and is likely to grow further, with most of the growth occurring in rural areas. There will increasingly be a shift from rural and agrarian work to industrial jobs as the size of the agricultural economy will reduce over time. There is a flickering of understanding of these concepts among the political class and of the need to shift the political emphasis to job creation versus job protection as the economy enjoys unprecedented growth.

The conundrum over labor reforms has been going on for a very long time. The deliberate approach to resolution of a problem filled with debate and delays tends to be repeated for each type of reform that has been undertaken in the past, whether it was banking, insurance, telecom or power. It underscores the notion that things move very slowly in India. Well, it could be argued that better slow than never. But those who want things to move in a hurry have to understand that few things work quickly without government fiat, and for each action there are layers of opposition or oversight from either the legislature or the judiciary. Even the most avid critics of India's reform process accept that the pace of reform is not due to the lack of desire or inaction on the part of the government, rather it is the reality of a democratic political process where public scrutiny is inevitable and an inalienable right.

To an investor looking at foreign markets, political risk also conventionally includes the threat of major disruption in the political process, such as revolution or military coup. As humorous as these concerns may sound to Indians, foreign investors in the past have been concerned about this. But India in that sense has been a beacon for other emerging economies, and remains a model to follow. Stanford University's The Hoover Institution – in an essay marking India's fiftieth independence anniversary – said, "India's success at unifying a diverse secular state through democratic means is one of the great political achievements of the twentieth century. Information disclosure, an important component of any functioning democracy, will enhance economic performance just as it makes corruption difficult to hide. Indeed, corruption is one of India's most contentious political liabilities, causing successive governments to fail. The worst sins of India's political class eventually come to light, and the voters have responded by making politicians pay, unlike Indonesia or China. Once transparency is adopted by India's political parties, India may once again march ahead of its rivals and become a model for Asia."

Despite the rousing commendation of India's free society the report also severely criticized India's endemic level of corruption, saying that the government's inability to check corruption has made it difficult to make the reform process credible to the people. The report specifically said: "Corruption distorts the private sector's response to the opportunities of the emerging liberal order. It underlies the breakdown of service delivery, the intensification of communal violence, the domination of the economy by the black market, and the government's inability to collect taxes effectively."

Their observations and criticisms are still valid today, several years after they were made, though studies since then have shown that people's perception of corruption has changed, especially since the reduction in the extent to which the government is able to interfere with their lives and livelihood has reduced the impact of corruption. Could India's path to reform also be the path to a solution for what is an endemic problem? Global corruption watchdog Transparency International's India chapter studied the issue very closely, and its 2005 report gave a hint as to where the solution could lie. Two sectors – railways and telecommunications – into which corruption was intricately woven over the years have improved considerably by the use of technology and with the removal of state monopoly respectively. For example, the reservation of seats by Indian Railways that almost always was made through a system of "agents" has been replaced by a computerized system that can be accessed over the internet. Privatization and the introduction of competition into what was a state monopoly in telecommunications have eliminated the high level of corruption that once existed even for such mundane tasks like activating a telephone connection. The argument that reforms are good for the nation's moral fiber may be simplistic but is also very realistic.

Most emerging economies have developed without growing the institutions needed to stabilize the development efforts, which eventually dampens their potential, as happened in Russia and in many emerging economies in Eastern Europe and Latin America. India has avoided this problem; all the institutions that are needed to bring in and sustain economic vitality were around long before liberalization even began, and other critical institutions such as independent regulatory bodies have been put into place very quickly. India's problem was the overbearing presence of government-controlled institutions, which has been reduced and replaced with self-governing mechanisms backed by strong laws and a lot more transparency than ever before.

The bottom line is that India's economic destiny has been divorced from its political destiny. And the political class now realizes that they can mess around with the country's investment and growth potential only at their own peril.

Regional instability and risk premiums

While India's domestic polity is undoubtedly stable and secure with political winds blowing towards sustainable reforms, there is only one major question left and that is the economic impact of regional instability. Is a regional instability premium needed when valuing the Indian economy, and is the prospect of war or a major act of terrorism a credible threat to the Indian economic scene?

Unfortunately India is located in a politically unstable region and is in close proximity to what is considered to be the epicenter of global terrorism and sectarian militancy. This fact has often left it vulnerable to perceptions of being a very real target. But in today's global climate, where the dangers of religious radicalism and politically motivated terrorism are better appreciated, there is a clearer understanding of who is really vulnerable and to what degree, and how that translates into investment risk. Mumbai or New Delhi are as likely to be hit by a terrorist strike as the streets of a European capital or an American city, thus putting terrorism-linked political risk into perspective. The considerable number of investors who are already on the ground and who are planning to get here in critical areas such as industrial, engineering and pharmaceutical outsourcing, or those who are establishing global or regional manufacturing hubs in increasing numbers in a post-9/11 world, show investor comfort with the level of risk or the potential for disruption.

The specter of war – especially nuclear war (the region is often referred to as a flashpoint) – is another matter, but one that has been clearly overblown. Foreign governments and investors worry whether or not the nuclear arsenal lying within neighboring countries will be used against India in the event of a fundamentalist coup. The reality is that if nuclear arsenals do fall into the hands of fundamentalists in South Asia then it is not only India but dozens of countries that are at risk of being struck, and for that matter are more likely to be struck.

A GUIDE TO WEALTH CREATION IN INDIA

INVESTING IN INDIA: A BRIEF INTRODUCTION

China as the workshop of the world and India as its back office is now a well-worn cliché. But the depth of opportunity is much greater in India, and in a host of industries other than IT and IT-enabled services for which it has become famous. India ruefully has never been viewed as an industrial economy. But though it is a common enough perception that India's strength is only in services, it is misconstruing the reality, which tells a completely different story.

For example, India is now becoming a hub for the design and manufacture of auto components and for research into and manufacture of specialty chemicals. Semiconductor design has taken off in a big way, with every big global name, including Texas Instruments, Intel and AMD, setting up laboratories – and in the case of AMD a manufacturing facility – with an investment close to $1 billion. Significant opportunities are also emerging in the oil and gas, retailing, apparel manufacturing, pharmaceuticals and computer hardware industries. A vast and increasingly recognized talent pool is not restricted to IT workers but extends to a host of sectors, especially in pharmaceuticals, biotechnology and specialty chemicals, engineering and manufacturing, and design and industrial services. The new composition of exports from India is a testimony to this change, where manufacturing and engineering exports are taking a bigger share from services and many of the above sectors – and others, such as refined petroleum products – are high-growth areas.

The quality of the opportunity in India is something that global investors should pay close attention to. A number of companies have won global manufacturing quality awards consistently. Twelve Indian companies out of only a handful of non-Japanese firms have won the much-coveted Deming Application prize for quality, awarded by the Japanese Union of Scientists and Engineers (JUSE), an award that is the ultimate in recognizing total quality management (see the table below). Companies have to prepare for three or four years before making a submission to be considered for the award. Numerous Indian companies have won other prestigious awards for productivity management too.

Indian companies awarded the Deming Application prize

Year	Company	Sector
2001	Sundaram Brake Lining	Auto component
2002	TVS Motor Company	Motorcycles
2003	Brakes India Ltd (Foundry Division)	Auto component
	M&M (Farm Equipment Division)	Engineering manufacturing
	Rane Brake Linings (India) Ltd	Auto component
	Sona Koyo Steering Systems Ltd	Auto component
2004	Indo Gulf Fertilisers	Fertilizers
	Lucas TVS Ltd	Auto component
	SRF Ltd (Industrial synthetics)	Textiles
2005	Krishna Maruti Ltd (Seating division)	Auto component
	Rane Engine Valves India	Auto component
	Rane TRW Steering Systems (Steering gear division)	Auto component

Source: JUSE

But even bigger opportunities are emerging in sectors that are just opening up and where the government has a strong development agenda: civil aviation, rural agricultural infrastructure (cold chains, storage and processing facilities), food processing, retailing, real estate, health care and media and entertainment. The government's thrust on building the infrastructure that is lacking in India is creating the growth impetus for cement, metals, plastics and petrochemicals, which are the traditional commodity sectors. Many of the bigger companies in the traditional sectors have undergone such dramatic change in terms of production and capital efficiency since the mid-1990s that they are easily amongst the better-managed and more profitable firms in their sector globally.

The auto components sector is particularly revealing, and show-cases how Indian companies went about methodically creating three superb industrial clusters with world-class technology and manu-facturing facilities, and how this has revolutionized the perception of the "Made in India" brand in manufacturing, just as the software companies have done in services. India has the unique distinction of being a developing economy with a large, and in several instances mature, services sector. It is also probably the only country where services or knowledge-based sectors are driving growth, hence the label an intellectual economy. Traditionally it is manufacturing that led the transformation of economies from developing to developed, and that is true for China even today. India is revolutionizing its manufacturing sector to catch up with competing economies, while it has already made giant strides in furthering its services capability.

The outsourcing of business processes to Indian firms has a lot to do with labor cost arbitrage and the fact that the Indians have mas-tered the art of systems management. But India's business process outsourcing (BPO) boom has very little to do with the might of the Indian IT companies and the immense success that those companies enjoy. The ability of educated Indians to speak English and "think" in English is pushing more business process outsourcing business its way, aided by a 90% fall in telecom costs in recent years and an in-crease in the "reliability factor" of the Indian back office. But for the most part this is low value-added work, and essentially will provide employment to people emerging from and competing with the hos-pitality industry, besides providing starter jobs to younger people. The real value addition from human capital is increasingly coming from other sectors of the economy besides IT, with the potential to be very big in the years ahead.

The effort behind the book is to showcase what is right with Indian industry and to showcase the potential in various segments. For eve-ry company that we talk about, we will showcase their strengths and fully reflect their potential in that industry and the economy. The attempt is to identify the key to future sustainable growth and to the unlocking of value across promising sectors. For example, in the case of banks it may be mergers, focusing on high-growth retail as-sets and a relaxation in foreign ownership and voting rights. In insur-ance, it is market penetration and availability of capital; in outsourc-ing, it is companies climbing the value chain in their service offering; in oil and gas, it is overseas acquisitions and domestic consolidation, besides exploration and development of new blocks. In pharmaceu-ticals, it is the introduction of patents in domestic markets and the opportunity to partner multinational corporations in new drug dis-coveries, as well as the ability to innovate processes targeting drugs going off patent. In auto ancillaries, it is the increasing integration that Indian companies are enjoying with global car manufacturers and the unprecedented growth in automobile sales and exports.

We will also look at the larger companies in each industry and reflect briefly on smaller but more promising companies. The idea is not to merely dissect each company but to look at the underlying trends taking root in India and what these mean for the companies concerned, and how this could lead to an opportunity for investors. This book is a guide to investors in India, right from understanding the canvas that is the investment opportunity to understanding the quality of companies and industries that make up that canvas, to the risks and threats that could disrupt or diminish that opportunity. This book neither comments on the appropriateness of current valuations of the individual stocks nor on the market levels. Wherever there has been a reference to the valuation of an individual stock it is to illustrate the underlying trend in market sentiment for that particular stock or as a generic observation.

The common characteristics running through the various companies that I have covered in the book are those of strong, aggressive and focused managements, a global outlook, strong product lines, proven ability to innovate, and growth orientation to the point of obsession. Many of these companies are relatively young, and many of the sectors that are seeing the best quality of growth have come about in the post-liberalization era.

PICKING STOCKS IN INDIA – WHAT TO LOOK FOR

Realistically speaking, given India's long track-record of public companies and established managements, and investor and corporate governance practices that are similar to those in the West, the analytical approach to Indian companies should be done in a manner similar to analyzing companies in more developed markets.

When foreign investors first stepped ashore in India in 1993, the universe of "investable" stocks numbered no more than 50, though at least 150 more would have made the grade on several quality parameters and growth prospects, if not on size (most would have been under $50 million market capitalization). Today there are over 100 companies with a market cap over $1 billion, and the number of companies over $200 million is quite significant, thus offering a large investment pool to tap into. It no doubt makes a lot of sense to look for large cap companies when investing in a rapidly growing and stable market like India, since an investor would get the benefit of high growth and higher returns along with lower risk. But at the same time, looking for smaller or mid-sized companies to complement a portfolio of larger companies could be very rewarding since a small proportion of the corpus invested in high-beta stocks provides a kicker to the portfolio.

QUALITY OF THE OPPORTUNITY

Any investment opportunity should be assessed with an analysis tailored specifically to the conditions in India. It is critical to look at the regulations governing the sector, if any, and whether there are any investment limits. The Indian government has also been known to go from imposing stifling regulations to promoting a high level of competition in various industries, so it is important to understand the degree of competition in an industry.

Valuation is the trickiest component of the investment process. Relative valuation at the best of times is misleading; when applied between companies and when applied to markets with different characteristics it can be disastrous. For example, valuation comparisons are very often made between Indian companies, sectors and markets with those in South East Asia. Relative valuations give no consideration to differences in taxation, accounting quality and the depth of the opportunity. And the evidence of investors bailing out too early or not making investments at all is precisely because of the tendency to benchmark with other markets.

The depth of economic activity in India is unprecedented, with fundamental changes having taken place in the mindset of consumers, companies and regulators. Indian companies are operating at an unprecedented level of competition, yet many are surprisingly focused on their return on capital employed as well, and so considering investments on merit is critical.

QUALITY OF EARNINGS AND FINANCIALS

This is where major differences crop up in evaluating investments in India. The universe of investment-grade stocks is separated from the others by the quality of the financial statements. Indian generally accepted accounting principles (GAAP) are not as comprehensive a standard as US GAAP though there is an attempt being made to close the "gap". However, the stock exchanges and the market regulator do require a number of disclosures that improve transparency and consistency in adopting accounting standards. Companies are required to file numerous corporate governance-related reports with the stock exchange periodically.

There are numerous situations that could be peculiar to the Indian context. For example, sometimes there will be a number of contested liabilities, especially on account of direct and indirect taxes due to the government. This can be potentially debilitating, especially if judicial or arbitration decisions go against the company. Loans or advances given to companies controlled by the same management are a frequent occurrence. Companies very often tend not to provide for diminution in the value of investments even after auditors cast doubts on the recoverability of the investment – which happens too often for comfort. Cross-holdings too tend to be very complicated and common. This can be an especially vulnerable area for investors, and they need to understand the nature of Indian managements.

QUALITY OF THE MANAGEMENT

When looking at any company anywhere in the world, understanding the management quality is paramount, especially so in developing economies. Even choice investment candidates would fall to the wayside if the management is of poor quality or is less than adequate a trustee of shareholder wealth.

The depth of board supervision is an issue in India, as it would be anywhere else in the world, and companies with a strong and independent board of directors do not really exist. Most businesses in India are still family controlled or tend to have one large, dominating shareholder. Nearly 60% of equity in India is held like this. That is why in the not-too-distant past many investors preferred to hold stocks of multinational companies over Indian companies, even though the Indian stocks may be faster growing with better prospects. The greatest issue I have with the investment opportunity in India is the quality of managements. Though many corporate houses have improved their attitudes, I am unsure as to whether a sufficient number of them have truly understood what it means to be a public company and the responsibilities that they bear.

The level of corporate governance-related disclosures, however, has gone up exponentially, and a lot of information is statutorily required to be published by the market regulators. These statements should be scrutinized for consistency and depth. A sign to watch for is whether management compensation has suddenly increased by a significant amount. Are there a lot of outstanding warrants issued to the promoters which can be used to pick up stock on the cheap? This is not a regular phenomenon as it once was, but it does still tend to happen.

The objective of this section is to raise the veil, so to speak. The first section was a detailed sketch of the investment canvas and the changes that have created it; Section 2 is now the manifestation of those changes and represents a detail of the opportunity.

The appendices at the end of the book carry four sets of data that are integral to understanding the depth and quality of the opportunity. For example, one data set ranks companies by return on capital employed and track changes in this measure of capital efficiency over a three-year period. Quantitative details are also presented in another data set of companies from a cross-section of industries covered in the book, besides carrying a ranking based on market capitalization.

PRIVATIZATION: A CAPITAL QUESTION

When the decision was made by the Indian government in late 2004 to allow National Thermal Power Corporation Ltd, the country's largest power-generating company, to offer roughly 10% of its stock to the Indian public, it was a welcome sign that the process of privatizing state-owned corporations was not dead despite the change in the government. This decision was followed by others, such as the one to exit completely from Maruti Udyog Ltd, the country's largest car maker (Suzuki Motors controls 54% of the company) and to offload an additional stake in Bharat Heavy Electricals Ltd, the country's largest power and capital goods maker, onto the equity market (despite immense pressure to do otherwise). The process of privatizing state-owned corporations may have slowed down considerably since mid-2004 but it is not dead. The recent decision taken in principle to reduce the government's stake in public sector corporations, including banks, to 51% is another case in point. It gets a whole lot closer to what is finally needed, which is a complete exit from something that governments are ill-equipped to do; running businesses.

Between 2002 and 2004 a few very significant privatization deals happened, which were enough to give the punctuated process some much needed momentum. All that was required was that the momentum be allowed to continue. After the BJP-led National Democratic Alliance (NDA) was voted out of power in the 2004 general elections it was anticipated that the thrust on privatization would diminish greatly. While there has been no overt attempt by the new government's communist allies to scuttle the entire process of privatization, there has been only guarded momentum to take it forward. For example, the thinking among the leftist parties is that the profitable companies should not be privatized (which they have defined as a complete exit from the concerned company), though there is little opposition to reduce the government's stake in these companies to a minimum threshold level from where it can still retain control. Naturally that attitude is missing the point of privatization, but the important thing is that the process has not been scrapped; while some privatization cases have been shelved others have been taken forward. The pace has certainly changed but not the direction.

The fact is that by holding onto the public sector corporations the government is sitting on some incredibly valuable assets that in reality are of little strategic value to it and serve no concrete agenda. There was a time in the early flush of nation building where the companies undoubtedly had value to the government. Nehru had envisioned these public sector entities as "temples of a modern India". His vision was one where the public sector built the heavy industry and infrastructure and the private sector would do the rest. In reality, the government slowly began doing everything, from building steel and cement plants to running textile factories. They eventually nationalized the banks, entered food processing, automobile manufacturing, ship building, computer maintenance and software, commodity trading, airlines; the list goes on. That age of a government deeply involved in running businesses is long past. In today's world where India is in the midst of liberalization and the economy is open to competition, government ownership is actually detrimental to the long-term health of some excellent companies. In a fast-paced environment companies need to respond to opportunities and challenges the way they think fit, instead of referring key decision-making to bureaucrats sitting in government offices far removed from reality. The joke was that when global metal prices were rising a proposal would be put up to the concerned ministry by a state-owned metals company for a new mining or smelter expansion project, but by the time permission to start feasibility studies was received a few years later the cycle would have turned and prices would be on their way down.

The news in early January 2006 that Air India had finally placed an order worth $11 billion with Boeing for 68 aircraft was a poignant reminder of the environment in which government companies function; Air India had been negotiating this particular deal (that kept getting bigger) for 10 long years before finally being able to act!

It has been demonstrated time and again that corporate assets are better utilized outside of government control, and very significant value can be unlocked if the government follows through with its intention of exiting several – if not all – of these corporations. Thanks to government patronage many public sector entities became giant corporations and very strong national brands. Over the years they also attracted good talent within the country and currently have an outstanding combination of quality managerial manpower and strong balance sheets, making them very attractive to potential private and foreign suitors. The continuation of the privatization process will lead to the unlocking of value in these companies and improve transparency and decision-making, besides providing much needed financial resources to the government.

In general, privatization leads to increased dynamism in the economy since it tends to improve efficiencies in the companies and sectors. In the context of privatization in India this phenomenon has been repeated in each and every industry that has been opened to competition and where the state monopoly has been surrendered to market forces. The leftist parties have raised the specter of large-scale job losses in the aftermath of privatization. So far the evidence in India has been just the opposite. When banking was opened to the private sector in the mid-1990s and insurance a few years later the same concerns surfaced, leading to labor agitation. But in reality there have been significant additions to the banking and insurance workforces. Besides, the labor market in India is tightly regulated and workers cannot be disposed off and businesses cannot simply close overnight.

So far in cases of privatized companies – such as Bharat Aluminum (BALCO) that was taken over by the London-based Vedanta Resources Plc – worker retrenchment has happened through voluntary retirement schemes, which is normal practice across companies in India – including the government-owned ones – and significant compensation is paid if early retirement is voluntarily accepted. In fact, Indian publicly owned banks have conducted one of the biggest voluntary retirement schemes in Indian corporate history, where the workforce was reduced by tens of thousands in recent years, the largest of which was successfully done by the State Bank of India. These legions of former bankers have either been absorbed by private sector banks that are expanding rapidly or by the private sector insurance companies that are in need of a gigantic direct and mature sales force. The moral of the story is that reduction in the workforce is always a possibility when there is a change in ownership, but in a rapidly growing economy like India job losses in one company or sector are more than compensated for by job creation elsewhere. The all important function of the government is to promote growth in the economy with better quality jobs, and not hold onto redundant ideologies and subsume whatever potential public sector companies may have.

PRIVATIZING INDUSTRIES VERSUS COMPANIES

Privatization in the Indian context would encompass more than just shedding entire stakes in companies, but also opening up activities that were once the sole purview of the government. Power distribution, for example, has always been an exclusive state monopoly, until the state government of Orissa decided to experiment and allowed the Mumbai-based power giant Reliance Energy (REL – formerly BSES Ltd) to manage its own distribution. That was not a very satisfactory experience for REL since the task of managing and ensuring compliance among the consumers has been frustrating. However, Tata Power, another Mumbai-based power company, has seen very encouraging results from their efforts to manage distribution of power in the New Delhi region, which was plagued by the theft of power and non-payment of dues. While transmission losses remain unacceptably high in Delhi especially in some pockets, this company found to its surprise that consumers were more than willing to pay for regular and uninterrupted power but would not pay for erratic power. Despite the difficulties in Delhi and Orissa, the experiment is being picked up by other larger states such as Gujarat and Madhya Pradesh.

The Indian telecom sector has seen the single most successful attempt by a government anywhere to bring in private sector investment. As a part of the privatization process in this sector the entire monopolistic structure – in domestic long distance, local subscriber networks and international voice and data – was dismantled. Mobile telephony was introduced on both CDMA and GSM standards. The government-owned long distance carrier VSNL was sold to the Tata conglomerate, raising $300 million for the government, excluding a huge $400 million dollop of cash that the government took out of the company just prior to the sale, as well as commercial land worth nearly $200 million. In hindsight the timing was excellent, since after opening international voice and data to competition, prices have fallen by almost 90%. Domestic long distance prices have fallen to ridiculous levels with the introduction of competition. At the start of

2006, Reliance Infocomm announced a new tariff of one rupee (US 2.2 cents) per minute for domestic long distance calls, showing just how competitive a market it has become, when just a few years ago it was monopolistic and predatory. A big juicy pie in the form of Bharat Sanchar Nigam Ltd – the giant domestic long distance, mobile and local telephony operator – now awaits privatization. (Indian government-owned companies are well known for long-winded names that leave no doubt as to the businesses they are in.)

Insurance is another area where the government has broken its own monopoly by allowing privately owned companies in partnership with foreign insurance companies to compete with state-owned businesses. The colossal growth in the insurance industry has been stunning after allowing private sector investments. At some point the government will have to consider selling its stake in the Life Insurance Corporation of India, the country's largest insurer with over $110 billion in assets and $24 billion in annual revenues (for fiscal year 2004–05), though for the moment that is not on the agenda – and never will be as far as the communists are concerned.

As with telecom, the timing for the government to get out of the two dozen plus banks it owns could not be more propitious. Most of the state-owned banks are in the pink of health following several rounds of capital infusion and bad loan write-offs in the 1990s and the earlier part of this decade. The quality of assets and the lending options of banks have increased greatly too; banks once only chased short-term lending options, often to dubious borrowers. Today, flexibility in pricing and a better understanding of credit risk have improved the quality of borrowers, and have also brought a widening of product offerings. In addition there has been a quantum jump in the retail financing segment. Increasingly as the levels of sophistication amongst consumers rises and people shed traditional inhibitions towards borrowing, and as the cost of borrowing falls, banks benefit from the rapid creation of retail assets. Not surprisingly, given this backdrop, bank equity in India has never been valued higher than it is at the moment.

The government ownership of banks did not come about by great foresight. In the 1970s at the peak of the government's socialist fervor (and in an effort to control vast resources), banks were nationalized. During the peak reform period of the 1990s, most of these banks were allowed to list on stock exchanges and access private capital. There are no publicly traded, state-controlled banks now that they are not profitable. Even simple changes such as mergers between the state-owned banks and the lifting of restrictions on minority voting rights would be welcomed as quasi privatization. Refusing to allow mergers or even takeovers of public sector banks by domestic and foreign banks runs contrary to logic for the simple reason that foreign banks can open branches in India, subject to a cumulative limit of 18 to 20 branches a year (though with a caveat that they focus on under-banked areas). According to media reports, Standard Chartered Bank has plans to open 10 to 12 branches every year in India. Deutsche Bank will open six branches in six different Indian cities; HSBC too has aggressive growth plans in India. Each of these banks, and many other foreign banks, has invested and will continue to invest several hundred million dollars in the process. So if foreign banks can operate, grow and compete with state-owned and domestic banks, why then should the government not benefit by selling out to these and other banks for a handsome profit?

The experiment with the aviation sector – where private sector investments were welcomed in the mid-1990s – was also encouraging, for despite a number of private airlines closing down, two strong private airline companies have since emerged. One of these companies, the recently listed Jet Airways (with a market capitalization of $2.2 billion), is already going global, both with its services and a listing in the United States. The second wave of investments is now happening in the aviation industry, where more privately owned airlines are emerging. IndiGo, a domestic Indian airline co-promoted by former US Airways CEO Rakesh Gangwal, has unveiled very aggressive growth plans involving the acquisition of 100 new aircraft from Airbus for $7.8 billion. And there is a commitment from the government to completely privatize the two state-owned airlines – the domestic carrier Indian Airlines and international carrier Air India – which are in need of a huge infusion of funds for their gigantic expansion plans, especially with the $11 billion order to Boeing.

Even the highly protected agricultural sector will see private investment flowing in over the next few years. There is increased interest from the government to include foreign companies in building up agro-infrastructure such as cold chains and increased food processing facilities. The level of value addition in food processing is minimal right now, and the government has been making efforts in the past few years to bring in private capital.

A FRAGMENTED BUT LUCRATIVE PROCESS

Despite the obvious merits, the entire process of privatization has been fragmented and very slow to get off the ground thanks to relentless political pressure and misguided opposition from trade unions. The benefit of privatization as a means of galvanizing Indian industry was not always obvious, especially within the political establishment. The manner in which India has handled its privatization program could have frustrated even its most enthusiastic supporter. For well over 10 years the politicians struggled with legal and political challenges, until finally the NDA government saw the inevitability as well as the potential of the process and went for some big deals. They also institutionalized the effort by creating a dedicated ministry of disinvestment that forcefully spearheaded the entire effort. The ministry was eventually dissolved with the change in government in 2004.

The renewed specter of uncertainty over disinvestment after all the rewards and potential that it has displayed is unfortunate. As it is, the process has inched forward very painfully, literally deal by deal since it was instituted in the early 1990s, beginning with the transfer of select government holdings to state- and bank-run mutual funds. It was only as recently as 2003–04 that the really big-ticket deals happened, with an additional stake sale for domestic and foreign investors in ONGC Ltd, Gas Authority of India Ltd, Indian Petrochemicals Corporation, Computer Maintenance Corporation and an oil marketing company, IBP Ltd. In March 2004 the disinvestment ministry that had finally gotten its way engineered a second IPO on behalf of ONGC, through which the government raised $2.2 billion, with the other four companies helping raise another $1 billion. The company was formerly the Oil and Natural Gas Commission, a government department responsible for oil and gas exploration and production in India, and its key entity for overseas oil field acquisitions. It was the classic prize holding in the public sector and typified the kind of business the government should be exiting. The value of the company climbed rapidly from a little over $21 billion pre-IPO to $30 billion post-IPO. ONGC now commands a market cap of $37 billion (December 2005), making it the most valuable listed company in India, and the government still holds 74% of the outstanding equity.

The country's largest car maker, Maruti Udyog Ltd, is a good example of the unlocking of value taking place through privatization. The government earned around $250 million from the sale of 27.5% out of its nearly 46% stake in Maruti Udyog to individual Indian investors and foreign institutional investors in July 2003. It held onto the remaining 18.3% in anticipation of a higher price at a later point in time. After just a couple of years that remaining stake is worth close to $800 million, and is being offered to bidders among Indian financial institutions in a staggered manner. This could be a disinvestment strategy that the government uses in the future, leading to further unlocking of value in other companies. The year 2003 can safely be considered the real and serious beginning to the privatization program. Between 1991 and 2003 the government could raise roughly $7 billion through privatization by various means, including dumping stock on state-owned financial institutions. But since mid-2003 until late 2004 it has pulled in nearly $5 billion through the sale of stakes of varying proportions in key companies and hot sectors through strategic or market sales. Thus the building up of momentum in the privatization process has been one of the big opportunities for investors, both Indian and foreign, to invest in some very large, strong and dominating companies.

Greater opportunities continue to be uncovered as the privatization process continues. The possibility of merging the various publicly owned oil companies – including ONGC, Hindustan Petroleum Corporation, Bharat Petroleum Corporation and Indian Oil Corporation – into two distinct entities will lead to the creation of two giant Indian oil companies with cross-border operations that will further yield value when they are privatized.

The results of privatization that we have seen thus far, whether of companies or sectors, have been encouraging. Privatization has broadened the capital markets by listing high-quality companies and raising the capitalization to GDP ratio, and has enabled a larger inflow of foreign investments. A bulk of the $4 billion to $5 billion raised through the sale of portions of the government's holdings in several companies in 2003 and 2004 went to foreign investors. In fact, the reason this effort was a resounding success was precisely because of the enthusiastic response of foreign investors, and this underscores the argument being laid out here that privatization could be the impetus needed for the capital market to better reflect the size and depth of the economy. It stands to reason that there will be a sustained flow of capital from overseas into the Indian economy that will closely correlate with the privatization process.

India has benefited a lot in the last three years from capital flows, through financial investors, foreign direct investment, and from overseas Indians. By some estimates these three sources have pumped close to $75 billion into the economy in this time period. But it has also been argued that these capital flows have come in part due to a global liquidity boom created by falling interest rates. The overriding composition of holdings by overseas Indians and portfolio flows makes the capital flow pipeline vulnerable to interest rates or any financial shock globally or in India. It's not that the capital inflows will reverse as much as incremental capital may not be as forthcoming. The role that privatization can play in enhancing and sustaining capital flows is thus crucial to India's economic boom.

Along with energy and raw materials India's hunger for capital is now insatiable, and the demands are only getting stronger and – as with the other two – its sustained availability from all sources needs to be addressed. There are 48 publicly traded, government-owned corporations with a cumulative market capitalization (as at the end of 2005) of $152.75 billion (see table 5.2). The government's stake in these entities ranges from 51% in Hindustan Petroleum Corporation to 98% in HMT Ltd, and has a cumulative value of $113.86 billion. These unlocked resources (I'm referring only to listed entities and not the dozens of unlisted government companies) could be used to reduce the national debt (see table 5.1) and fund a number of infrastructure projects. The interest saved on the national debt alone can provide the seed capital for a number of projects that would help in improving the quality of the investment canvas.

Table 5.1: Composition of government's total debt (in US $ billion) 2005–06

Central government debt*	State government debt	External debt
492.47	136.19	14.37

* Includes short-term debt of $319 billion.
Source: Reserve Bank of India, Union Budget estimates.

The weighted average rate of interest for the Indian government is 6.11%, so applying the rate across only the central government debt yields an interest outflow of $30 billion (excluding state government interest and external borrowing cost). Using proceeds from the sale of public sector equity to redeem a portion of the debt would save the central government around $7 billion annually.

The large-scale privatization of government corporations promised by the NDA alliance seems to have all but vanished for the moment. But the number of sectors being opened up to competition and to increased foreign investment levels has increased tremendously; this is what we could call quasi privatization.

Power to the states

With their growing political power and clout in national economic decision-making the individual state governments have picked up the momentum of privatization. Certain proactive state governments have begun to make headway in privatization with probably less opposition than the national government has had to face.

Progressive states such as Gujarat and Punjab have led the effort at privatization and have not shied away from the closure of unviable companies. An interesting mix of companies owned by these two state governments are traded on the stock exchanges. Some deals for sales of stock have already happened, while others are expected to take place in due course. The state of Punjab through its industrial development corporation has closed down loss-making units, and sold off its stakes in profitable companies – including a 23% stake in Punjab Tractors Ltd, one of India's best known agricultural equipment brands – to the UK's CDC. The Gujarat government owns sizeable stakes in some very profitable listed companies in the fertilizer, power, mining, oil and gas, and chemicals industries, which it fully intends to sell at some point.

Other states such as Haryana are also looking at privatization, and not only of government-owned corporations but also of services. The West Bengal government too has taken a serious look at privatization of certain services, and has even opted for the privatization of some state-owned companies, while at least two firms were closed during 2005. It is being aided by the UK's Department for International Development as it embarks on a project to restructure 16 loss-making companies.

Water management and distribution is an area that is being looked at seriously by various state governments, despite the controversies that have already cropped up. One of the earliest known cases of privatization of a waterway in India, along the Sheonath river in the State of Chhattisgarh, ran into a lot of controversy over local communities' access rights that snowballed into a major political brouhaha. Despite that episode, water resource management is considered a prime candidate for privatization.

Table 5.2: Public sector companies owned by the central government and traded on the stock exchanges

Public sector company	Sector	Market capitalization	Govern- ment stake	Value of government holding	Foreign institutional investor holding
		(US $ million)	%	(US $ million)	%
Allahabad Bank	Bank	845.18	55.23	466.79	14.65
Andhra Bank	Bank	855.45	62.5	534.66	15.95
Balmer Lawrie	Packaging	204.27	61.8	126.24	0.56
Bank of Baroda	Bank	1,616.89	66.83	1,080.57	16.99
Bank of India	Bank	1,367.89	69.47	950.27	11.25
Bank of Maharashtra	Bank	319.48	76.77	245.26	1.32
Bharat Earth Movers Ltd	Capital goods	835.48	61.23	511.56	8.94
Bharat Electronics	Capital goods	1,653.27	75.86	1,254.17	11.96
Bharat Heavy Electricals	Capital goods	7,939.11	67.72	5,376.37	22.3
Bharat Petroleum Corporation	Oil and gas	2,854.77	66.2	1,889.86	17.25
Bongaigaon Refineries	Oil and gas	331.75	74.46	247.02	1.68
Canara Bank	Bank	2,074.23	73.17	1,517.71	15.24
Chennai Petro	Oil and gas	809.20	67.27	544.35	12.05
Corporation Bank	Bank	1,221.66	57.17	698.42	9.25
Container Corporation	Transport	2,189.86	63.09	1,381.58	27.29
Dena Bank	Bank	210.55	51.19	107.78	8.2
Dredging Corporation	Capital goods	394.16	78.56	309.65	5.78
Engineers India	Project consultancy	873.98	90.4	790.08	1.37
Gas Authority of India Ltd	Oil and gas	5,248.80	57.34	3,009.66	15.08
Hindustan Machine Tools	Capital goods	1,015.64	98.22	997.56	0.05
Hindustan Organic Chemicals	Chemicals	51.20	58.61	30.01	0.09
Hindustan Petroleum Corp	Oil and gas	2,435.66	51.01	1,242.43	21.83
IBP	Oil and gas	292.07	53.38	155.91	18.3
Indian Oil Corporation	Oil and gas	15,708.23	82.03	12,885.46	1.94
Indian Overseas Bank	Bank	1,159.55	61.23	709.99	15.8

IDBI	Financials	1,658.05	52.8	875.45	15.55
ITI	Telecom equipment	483.36	92.98	449.43	0.11
Jammu & Kashmir Bank	Bank	540.89	53.17	287.59	23.79
Kochi Refineris	Oil and gas	560.30	54.81	307.10	6.68
MTNL	Telecom	2,079.00	56.25	1,170.27	14.13
National Aluminum Co	Metals and mining	3,276.45	87.15	2,855.43	1.71
National Fertilisers	Agricultural products	497.25	97.6	485.32	1.73
National Mineral Development Corp	Mining	4,965.00	98.38	4,865.70	0
National Thermal Power	Power	19,995.34	89.5	17,895.83	
Neyveli Lignite	Power	2,995.59	93.56	2,802.67	0.86
Oriental Bank of Commerce	Bank	1,436.32	51.09	733.81	19.87
Oil and Natural Gas Corporation	Oil and gas	37,263.70	74.14	27,627.31	8.79
Punjab National Bank	Bank	3,311.75	57.8	1,914.19	20.06
Rashtriya Chemicals	Agricultural products	559.84	92.5	517.85	0.01
Shipping Corporation of India	Shipping	1,050.59	80.12	841.73	1.63
State Bank of India	Bank	11,030.68	59.73	6,588.63	11.86
SAIL	Metals and mining	5,214.61	85.8	4,474.14	3.6
Syndicate Bank	Bank	1,028.52	66.47	683.66	8.7
Union Bank	Bank	1,262.70	60.85	768.36	19.15
UCO Bank	Bank	475.98	74.98	356.89	1.49
Vijaya Bank	Bank	562.57	53.87	303.06	17.13
		152,756.82		113,867.8	

6

THE OLD WORLD: COMMODITIES AND THE MAKING OF INDIAN BLUE CHIPS

Commodity-linked industries have been the mainstay for Indian investors for the longest time, until information technology, auto components, pharmaceuticals and other "knowledge" sectors took over. Cement, metals, agro-commodities and petrochemicals are the traditional commodity-based sectors that have thrown up most – if not all – of the blue chip names until the last decade or so, and had traditionally been the preferred destination for most private sector investments. The cement and metals industry in particular attracted a lot of investment from premier business houses and corporations. Almost all of India's industrial houses have built their fortunes and honed their business skills in various commodity industries.

The leading companies in these sectors and several new ones have bounced back as market favorites over the last couple of years. Naturally, since commodity-linked industries will benefit not only from the upswing in the commodity price cycle, but also the rapid economic growth that India is experiencing and will follow the country's macro growth cycles, there is a close correlation between consumption, investment and the demand for commodities. The growth and value for various companies in these sectors will be driven variously by increasing capacities, consolidation, and the sustained improvement in their global competitiveness. But a lot of value has already been created in these sectors by the high level of domestic competition, tremendous and sometimes painful restructuring already undertaken, and the relative attractiveness of the Indian commodity sector to foreign corporations.

The factor that really stands out among many Indian commodity companies is the presence of very capable and high caliber managements. High-caliber management is something that is readily associated with more contemporary industries such as technology, or even with some manufacturing sectors such as automobiles or auto components. But the undisputable fact is that Indian companies understand global commodity cycles very well and they are receiving increased international recognition for this, especially since many of them are spreading their wings globally, buying out mines in Australia, wood pulp manufacturers in Canada, smelters in Eastern Europe and downstream processing capacity in Western Europe and South East Asia, especially in metals.

India has a huge and growing pool of these excellently managed commodity companies, where earnings have typically been higher and profitability better than their global counterparts. This is largely due to the domestic demand growth in the Indian economy and the competitive advantages that these companies have succeeded in building over several decades. Many of these companies have invested heavily in modernizing their plants, removing legacy-based systems and bringing in firm-wide enterprise solutions, cutting down on their workforces by increasing automation and squeezing more out of their physical, financial and human assets. The amazing thing about the larger and well-run Indian commodity companies is that despite being constrained by capital cost, environment and labor cost considerations they are very often more profitable than most of their global competitors, and even more so when compared to their Chinese competitors that do not have the same constraints. The emergence of better profitability is evident across various commodity sectors and across different companies with completely different management styles, and has a lot to do with the fact that managements have increasingly adopted global industry best practices. The biggest threat that Indian commodity companies feared before embarking on their major restructuring effort was that because of the liberalized trade environment and the superb economics of agro and industrial commodities today they could see Chinese imports entering the country in a big way. But the reality is that the Chinese producers themselves have been and will largely remain net importers of various commodities, especially metals, until 2008, the year of the Beijing Olympics, thus leaving a very lucrative domestic market all to the companies already entrenched or for those that may invest or acquire manufacturing capability.

GLOBAL GIANTS IN THE MAKING: THE CEMENT STORY

The Indian cement industry is unrecognizable today from what it was just a few years ago. Less than a decade ago it was a fragmented industry, filled with regional players and hampered by operating inefficiencies and plenty of bottlenecks, especially in distribution. Consolidation has happened at a very rapid pace, that too between the larger players, to the point where there are now companies with a strong national footprint and with higher levels of operating efficiency. This change has been triggered largely by the threat of increased competition from foreign cement manufacturers, who were looking to buy up large capacities. So to the local managements it was a far better scenario that Indian companies buy up their domestic rivals and create a national production and distribution footprint rather than see hungry foreign competitors step in and fill the void. While that has worked well in creating larger and stronger Indian companies they have not been able to stop foreign arrivals completely, nor will they be able to do that, much to the benefit of their shareholders since foreign companies will most certainly look actively for companies to acquire.

The dramatic change within cement companies is a great example of how liberalization has worked for Indian industry and what the prospect of increased competition can do. Indian cement companies are among the most profitable compared to their global peers. Less than two decades ago the industry was heavily regulated by the government. Companies such as Gujarat Ambuja Cement, Grasim, ACC, Ultratech (formerly L&T Cement) and others quickly seized on opportunities to expand and improve efficiencies, especially in the pricing of cement, once these regulations began to be relaxed in the mid-1980s and early 1990s. That has culminated into a process of consolidation of ownership that has begun to tilt the balance in favor of manufacturers now that the industry is less fractious and there is more control over pricing. There have been numerous hiccups in the process as big-thinking managements cobble together giant companies through mergers and acquisitions, sometimes biting off more than they can chew and sometimes paying a high price or accepting a difficult operating structure all in the name of staying ahead of the game.

This industry has provided a fair share of India's blue chip names, and these are the very same companies now driving consolidation and growth. The country is the second-largest cement producer in the world with an installed base of over 140 million tons, next only to China. The two dominating business combinations are the Holcim–Gujarat Ambuja–ACC combination – which commands close to 31 million tons in production capacity and has combined revenues of $1.65 billion – and the combination of Grasim Industries and Ultratech Cement. Ultratech had revenues of $620 million in 2005 and a market capitalization of $1.2 billion, while for Grasim – being a diversified corporation – it is difficult to apportion its market capitalization between the different operating businesses, but its cumulative market cap is over $2 billion, with revenues from its cement division totaling $623 million for the fiscal year 2005.

But the story here, as it is in the rest of the Indian economy these days, is one of unprecedented growth and a huge potential re-rating due to the possibility of acquisitions by foreign companies and continuing consolidation by domestic ones. Cement is one sector that tracks the economy very closely. There is a close correlation between macroeconomic growth and growth in the cement industry. The cement industry growth factor is estimated at 1.25 times, so if GDP growth is 8% then the cement industry will grow at 10%. Nearly 60% of the demand for cement in India comes from the housing construction industry, which is one of the fastest-growing sectors in the economy, and around 25% comes from infrastructure, which is also expanding very rapidly. The potential for the Indian cement industry can be measured through its per capita consumption, which belies its status as the world's second-largest producer. According to an assessment done by the Aditya Birla conglomerate (which controls both Grasim and Ultra Tech Cement), the per capita consumption is just 244 lbs of cement in India against a global average of 577 lbs, while in China it is 952 lbs, South Korea consumes 2,111 lbs and even Thailand and Malaysia have a higher consumption of 650 lbs and 1,174 lbs respectively.

But the key to cement industry profitability is not volume growth but price growth, as cement is a high variable cost business, with power and freight accounting for a large part of total costs. The company that can successfully address these two issues, either through better use of technology or better location, is positioned to succeed exceptionally well as India now begins to see supply-side pressures in the industry as most manufacturers are currently operating at near full capacity. And with minimal capacity additions being announced, growth will come inorganically through acquisitions, and greenfield capacities will come about only after a sustained rise in the price of cement. Demand for cement is expected to range between 8% and 10% per annum in volume terms, while capacity addition through expansions or plant modernization will not exceed 5% per annum. Added to this is the expected expansion in realizations by 5% to 7%; we could be looking at an average annual industry growth of 15% to 17% for the next few years. This is probably the only industry that is completely insulated from imports, since there are no facilities at any of the ports (other than those owned by some cement companies) for the handling of cement. So the industry is sitting rather pretty, thinking of all the money they're going to be making over the next few years.

The trend of growth from acquisitions rather than greenfield expansions is one of the key drivers of cement valuations in India. Added to this scenario are the global cement companies that have realized that after China, India is the next great growth market; they are making a beeline looking for cement capacities. After Swiss cement giant Holcim bought a controlling stake in ACC, investing several hundred million dollars in the process, there seems to be a growing interest in standalone cement companies, since the larger ones have already consolidated. Companies such as Mexico's Cemex and Brazil's Votorantim Cimentos have already expressed an interest in becoming active in India through acquisitions. Though many Indian managements have said that they will not sell out, the asking price per ton of capacity is now reported to have climbed to the region of $130 to $150, from the $90 per ton at which the last round of acquisitions was done. This calculation alone gives the entire Indian cement industry an enterprise value of $18 billion to $21 billion, against a cumulative market capitalization of around $8 billion to $9 billion, thus showing the significant value gap that could possibly be exploited in the near future.

It is a fair question to ask under what circumstance the cumulative expected enterprise value of $18 billion holds true. At $18 billion the industry would trade at an enterprise value (which is the market value of both equity and debt) to sales (EV/Sales) ratio of nearly 2.5 times, though the justified P/E would be higher. The larger, better run companies that control chunks of the industry or are capital-efficient currently trade at an EV/Sales ratio of between 2 and 3 times. But the smaller companies that comprise 40% to 45% of the industry by capacity currently trade at an EV/Sales of below 1, and many would be below 0.5. We saw in the case of ACC's takeover – first by Gujarat Ambuja Cement and then by Holcim – and in the other major consolidation between Grasim and Ultratech that the pooling together of capacities pushed up price to sales ratios, since that route more than any other ensures pricing power for the companies concerned, and as the trend gathers momentum it will do that for the industry as a whole. So it stands to reason that consolidation is the single biggest factor that will drive valuations in the years to come since it can be expected to push pricing power, and the expected enterprise value of $18 billion does become achievable, making Indian cement companies very attractive indeed.

A premium stock

Gujarat Ambuja Cement has always been fancied by the stock market not because of its blue chip status or its market liquidity as ACC was but because of its operating performance. Along with Madras Cement, and of late with standalone operator Shree Cement, the stock always traded at a premium to other sector stocks. The company's operating performance on several parameters, not least its ability to keep costs low and high capital efficiency, has set the industry standard, and even a quick look at its operations and profitability justifies its preeminent valuation. Even if it is not the largest by revenues (2005 net sales were $700 million), GACL commands the largest market capitalization at over $2 billion and directly controls about 12 million tons of capacity (31 million tons in combination with Holcim and ACC).

It also compares very well on key relative valuation measures. For cement companies, price to sales is a better relative measure to employ than price to earnings since there are several accounting measures – not the least of which are depreciation and differential effective tax rates – that would distort the comparison. GACL commands the highest price to sales multiple at 3.2 times, while the industry carries an average price to sales ratio of just 1.4 times. Its revenue growth rate is the highest in the industry, and needless to say so are expectations from it. For the latest financial year it reported a 27% growth in revenues, while similar large companies ACC and Ultratech Cement reported growth rates of 19% and 21% respectively. Gujarat Ambuja Cement has the highest operating margin in the industry at 28%, while its net income is the largest in the industry at $116 million, and its net income margin of 16% is around double that of the industry average of 8.2%. It reported a five-year compound EPS growth of 26%, which is truly remarkable for a company in a cyclical industry. One concern that stands out here is its extensive use of leverage, but then its use of leverage is compensated by its constant efforts to bring down its cost of debt and the superb efficiency with which that debt is used (see figure 6.1).

Figure 6.1: 10-year return on equity trend for GACL

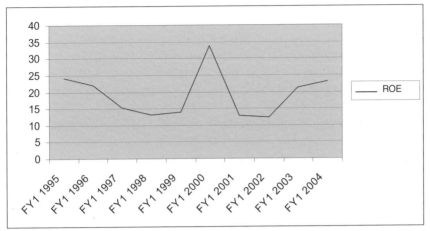

Source: Bloomberg.

This company is a perfect example of the view that Indian managements are good at managing commodity businesses, a fact that has to be seen from what companies such as GACL achieved despite operating in an era of strict government regulation. The management has always come across as very dynamic and very aggressive, probably more so than any of the others in the industry. They were the first to invest in sea-based transportation of cement across India's coastline to a very lucrative southern Indian market, where typically prices were higher, and it avoided costly road transport with all the attendant bottlenecks that India's inadequate infrastructure offered. The access that it created to port facilities also gave it the flexibility to import coal from suppliers in East Asia and Australia if the pricing was right, instead of buying domestic coal hauled from coalfields in central or western India, besides now being able to export cement to various markets, even outside of Asia.

It entered the cement business during the period of deregulation in the industry in the mid-1980s, but has far outpaced its contemporaries, and a few years ago even made a bid to control ACC, the leading company in the industry, which it does partly own today through a company it controls jointly with Holcim. The deal with Holcim is a sweet one for GACL, where it not only is part of a powerful combination that will help it consolidate its already formidable position further but it has a put option under which it can offer its 33% stake in the joint venture company any time until 2008 to Holcim, for which it would receive $300 million.

Playing catch up

Associated Cement Companies (ACC) is the oldest cement company in India and has been the flag bearer for the old-world blue chips in India. The company has a history spanning over 100 years of operations and is still a solid growth story. The price of its stock – as with the rest of the cement sector – has run up considerably in 2005 and early 2006, pushing its value way ahead of itself, but that is not to take away from the fact that it is a quality play on the potential before the Indian cement industry.

It is the largest cement company in India, with 18 million tons of capacity, and it is quite likely that Holcim – its new owner – will merge another two million tons of capacity with it. The company had been in play for quite some time as leading industry players tried to take advantage of the fact that there was no dominant shareholder who had interests to defend and that in one swipe any strategic buyer could dominate India's cement industry. GACL tried that tactic first by buying a 13% stake in the company, but then a stronger acquirer came along in the form of Swiss giant Holcim. Holcim purchased a two-thirds majority in Ambuja Cement India Ltd, the holding company through which GACL controlled its stake in ACC, and then made an open offer to acquire additional shares in ACC, now controlling 34.7%, and it is quite likely that Holcim will continue to seek to raise its stake in ACC until it crosses the majority mark. Though it effectively wields control over ACC this possibility will serve to keep the stock price strong since open market purchases or the buy back of shares are the only meaningful routes for it.

However, due its legacy of over-staffing and relatively inefficient operations its EBITDA margin at just 17% does not do justice to its potential. It is quite likely that the new management will try to address its legacy of high operating costs and push up operating efficiencies further than it already has gone (see figure 6.2).

Southern comfort!

Like most Indian companies from down south, Madras Cement was always low profile and usually let its performance speak for itself. The company, one of the oldest cement producers in south India with a 33-year operating history, was known for its performance, especially on profitability and capital efficiency parameters, even in the mid-1990s when return on capital employed and other equity-linked return parameters did not matter to most Indian companies.

Figure 6.2: Improving sweating of assets at ACC

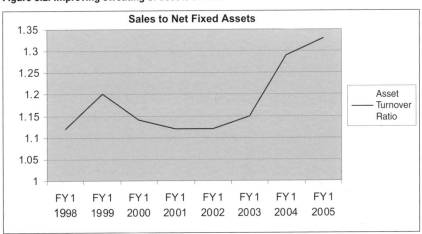

Source: Bloomberg.

In that sense it stood out; however, it went through a lean patch along with the rest of the industry in the south largely due to severe competition, over supply, political interference and tremendous pricing pressure. After going through that lean patch for several years, where its capital efficiency was challenged and it was surpassed by other companies, it has begun to bounce back very well over the last couple of years. Its EBITDA margin is at 21.5%, which is amongst the highest in the industry and is probably bettered only by GACL and Shree Cement. And since 2002 its net income has grown at a compounded rate of 30% annually.

The stock is typically illiquid and so does not attract the same level of market interest as the other cement stocks that have a wider following, but despite its high leverage (probably the highest in the industry) it would easily hold its own among the high-quality stocks available on the Indian investment canvas. The discounting that it typically tends to receive would make it one of the top-ranked stocks in the industry.

The company makes and sells cement largely in the two fast-growing southern states of Tamil Nadu and Andhra Pradesh, and it operates a total of six million tons. This region is seeing rapid development not only from investments by the corporate sector and from housing construction but also from investments being made in rural infrastructure. A large portion of the central government's public investment going into irrigation is also happening in this region. Interestingly, MCL has also entered into wind power generation and owns a wind power farm, selling the power to the State Electricity Board.

Besides the fact that it is located in and caters to one of the fastest industrializing regions in the country, there are two basic reasons why the company has been doing so well and will probably be one of the top-performing cement stories going forward. One, it has a relentless focus on maintaining operating efficiencies, and two, it is constantly striving for self-reliance in power, which will bring down its cost of operation. Its two captive power plants, including a new 18 MW plant, will bring down its power cost substantially, and power is one of the single largest cost items that cement companies have to wrestle with, more so in India where the power supply is unstable and manufacturing units tend to generate their own power. Because it is in the proximity of a fast-growing market and has built-in super efficiencies, it is a difficult competitor to be up against.

Married to growth but once-elusive returns surface

Together with UltraTech Cement, in which it acquired a majority stake in 2004, Grasim Industries controls a commanding 31 million tons of capacity, of which UltraTech controls 17 million tons (just a shade short of ACC's capacity) and Grasim the remaining 14 million tons, making it the ninth-largest cement group in the world. Though they control an equally large capacity between them and are collaborating at the moment the GACL–Holcim–ACC combination does not qualify for the distinction of being among the top 10 cement groups in the world since GACL is independently run.

Grasim Industries is another superbly run corporation, belonging to the Aditya Birla group of companies, a powerful Indian industrial conglomerate. But the company has never enjoyed great valuations. Perhaps the fact that it is the only major cement manufacturer that has diversified into other businesses (it is also the world's largest producer of viscose staple fiber) and for the most part the fact that it has never really managed to beat its cost of capital have held back its valuations. The company has always been a cash cow, and its cash generation and subsequent asset build-up has been a drag on capital efficiency. For example, its balance sheet of $1.5 billion includes investments and cash holdings amounting to $750 million. Naturally its return on capital employed has historically been one of the lowest in the industry, though it has improved substantially in the last three years driven by tremendous improvements in the economics of the cement business, where its EBITDA margins have improved to 20%.

However, the reason it cannot be ignored is that this company, through its acquisitions, is now the largest cement manufacturer in

India. It will, because of its size and the ability to dominate the industry and many regional markets, dictate prices over time. Also by virtue of its ability to generate huge amounts of cash from operations it becomes a formidable force in the industry; for example, its $500 million all-cash acquisition of UltraTech Cement cannot be emulated by any other player in the industry. Its two main operating divisions of VSF and cement throw up a large chunk of the $300 million a year in free cash flow.

Already, with focused efforts, operating and capital efficiencies have improved, and this is one Indian company, if not the only one, with the resources to continue making acquisitions in the domestic market. Grasim controls 12% of the global market and accounts for 98% of India's total VSF production, and it is also India's second-largest producer of caustic soda. There remains the possibility that its steel-making division – which has suffered from high cost of input – may be sold or spun out of the company, thus aiding valuations.

UltraTech Cement was a part of India's preeminent engineering company, Larsen & Toubro Ltd, and had some of the best plants in India, and even has a cement packing plant in Sri Lanka. The company is a relatively recent entrant to the business, despite its size, and has only just started earning profits. Its EBITDA margin at 13.8% is one of the lowest among the large cement companies in India, but that will rise over the next few quarters.

Rise of the pretenders

Another company to impress with its efficient operations is Shree Cement Ltd. But it was always one company that had lots of potential but somehow never really cut the grade to make the leap into the big time. Shree Cement has been and still remains a prime pick for anyone, be it Indian cement companies or foreign manufacturers looking for acquisitions of cement assets in India. It does face some drawbacks, since it operates in a single geographic region where it has several powerful competitors, but in its favor it also operates one of the most modern cement manufacturing plants in the country. It has put up a new plant, adding 1.2 million tons of capacity close to its existing three million ton facility in the state of Rajasthan, which is also one of the most modern cement units in India. This will enable the company to produce very high quality cement of pure limestone without using additives such as fly ash, thus enabling them to price it at a premium. The stock trades at premium valuations, and its price to sales ratio of 2.8 times is second only to that of Gujarat Ambuja

Cement. And with an EBITDA margin of 28% it is on par with GACL. Its new-found profitability makes it even more attractive for acquirers that are also looking for an acceptable size, quality of manufacturing facilities and a captive market.

There are other companies that are well positioned and consequently should be high on the list of potential acquirers, especially those companies that have done well in recent quarters. These companies range from the larger and supremely profitable Birla Corporation to others of varying quality and strategic advantages, such as JP Associates and Prism Cement. JP Associates, for example, has the largest single-location cement plant in India, which is being expanded further from 4.2 million tons to 7 million tons, with improving fundamentals, while Prism Cement has excellent profitability ratios and has shown some fabulous growth in recent quarters.

AT THE CROSS-CURRENTS OF GLOBALIZATION

The metals industry, and steel in particular, is the unrecognized winner of the growth potential in India and the rising clout of Indian industry. Economic growth needs physical investments and steel will be the commodity in most demand since it is a common input into most physical economic activity. All capital investment – such as building manufacturing plants, housing construction, cars, appliances, roads and bridges – requires steel. The building of one new steel plant alone will require upwards of one million tons of steel, and there are greenfield steel plants with huge capacities being planned. But besides steel, other metals such as aluminum, copper and zinc also have tremendous potential. These two industries apart from steel have created some celebrated companies that epitomize the competitiveness of Indian commodity companies and their quest for new and value-added markets. The entire Indian metal industry has been brushed with the need to develop markets and a mining resource base overseas.

The steel industry is now the largest recipient of foreign direct investment in India. Just two global steel corporations – South Korea's POSCO and the world's largest steel company, Mittal Steel Company NV – have committed a total of $21 billion to build two large steel plants in eastern India. The global hunt for sustainable sources of iron ore has now brought international giants to India's doorstep since India has the world's third-largest deposit of coal and iron ore, both of which are basic inputs in steel making. Natural gas is also a basic input in producing intermediate raw materials for making crude steel, and the huge gas discoveries in eastern India could also be a factor in improving the competitiveness of Indian steel companies. Both these global giants have said that their interest is also in the huge domestic market, where growth rates in the steel industry are expected to ratchet up substantially.

But at the same time as global giants are coming to India, Indian steel companies are looking at markets overseas, especially in Asia. Tata Steel, for example, is looking at putting up two steel plants, one in Thailand and the other in Indonesia. This is true for other steel and other metals companies as well. Steel Authority of India Ltd (SAIL) – the country's largest steel company – is planning on sourcing over 40% of its requirement of coal from outside India, mostly from Australia, while Sterlite Industries has acquired copper mines overseas, and Tata Steel is obtaining iron ore reserves from Asia and Australia. Like in the case of energy, Indian metals companies will increasingly acquire mines overseas in order to secure potential lines of supplies, and many will also look at establishing manufacturing units overseas as they seek to become integrated global players.

The biggest threat to steel plants or to any metals business in India is the reduction of tariff protection. Already tariffs are at their lowest ever, and could go still lower. At lower duty levels the margins for Indian producers will definitely be under pressure, and Indian companies have looked at various measures that will boost competitiveness and reduce their dependence on only one market. We have seen that whenever the domestic price of crude steel has risen above international prices there is a flood of imports and a build up of inventory; this was the case during the second half of 2005.

Besides the integrated metals companies, smelters and downstream companies, there are also high-quality companies in the mining of iron ore and in the production of intermediate products such as coking coal. A key risk to the mining companies remains the attempts by the government to interfere in the export of ore – especially iron ore – citing its strategic importance to India. Though this is not done overtly, attempts are made to talk up the threat, which affects investor confidence in these companies that are otherwise enjoying superlative years.

Of the key drivers of the metals industry, the foremost is a significant expansion in the major industries that consume the large volumes of higher value-added products, especially automobiles, construction, appliances and capital goods. The Indian steel ministry has forecast that demand for steel will double in the next seven years – implying growth of 10% compounded every year – and has asked Indian steel producers to prepare for that kind of growth. Aluminum and copper producers also benefit from the same trend, while copper will benefit additionally from the huge rural electrification drive in India. Unlike in cement where consolidation is the key to improving cement prices and valuations, in steel it is a huge increase in demand from consumer industries. Since metals are a high fixed-cost business, increasing volumes and productivity is the key to profitability. The planned public and private capital investment is $150 billion for the next few years, which will trigger a huge increase in demand for metals. The Indian steel producers are at a minimum cumulatively investing $18 billion to double steel-making capacity to 70 million tons in the near future, and over the next decade will push capacity to 110 million tons. This does not include the steel capacities that Indian companies are looking at acquiring or setting up overseas.

The other driver is the restructuring and repositioning that Indian metals producers have already undertaken and the significant level of integration that has been built in, thus paving the way for the next big push to earnings from volume expansion. But a striking development and an undoubted driver of future value is the realization among many companies across the metals spectrum that, thanks to their restructuring, they are globally competitive and in a position to take advantage not only of the opportunities in India but in Asia and the rest of the world.

Integrated steel producers – who control the entire value chain from iron ore mining to producing sponge iron/pellets to crude steel, and hot rolled coils to downstream products – have a singular advantage when steel and product prices are on the rise since they are protected from any raw material price increase. Some companies – such as Tata Iron & Steel (TISCO), which for the moment is the country's largest private sector steel producer, and the public sector-owned Steel Authority of India Ltd (SAIL), the country's largest producer, and others such as JSW Steel – are benefiting immensely, and undoubtedly their recent gains are pushing both domestic expansion and overseas acquisitions. So despite the fact that the Indian steel industry is large and there are a number of good-quality companies – many of which are in specialty areas like coated galvanized steel (used in household appliances), drawn steel or sheets – our focus will be the integrated players, since they are the best positioned to gain from the fact that the steel industry in India is at a major inflexion point, though many other categories of metal companies will benefit also. Of these companies, TISCO and SAIL control 45% of the steel market in India, and though their hegemony will likely be challenged by global giants setting up capacities here, they are very strong growth companies.

Global ambitions

Tata Steel Ltd (TISCO) is one company that cannot be ignored any more, especially if one is looking for a stock that best reflects the opportunity not only in the Indian market but globally. It is not only the world's most profitable steel company but it has been ranked by World Steel Dynamics as the world's best steelmaker. That study was done in 2005 as a comparison with 23 of the world's best steel companies. Aside from these accolades, from the growth plans that it has drawn up TISCO is aiming to be the world's most aggressive growth stock too. To add to its plans to invest $10 billion to $12 billion in expanding its steel manufacturing capacity in India over the next few years it will also invest a like amount acquiring capacities overseas. It currently has five million tons of capacity located in India and by 2010 will have 15 million tons of capacity spread out in India and other parts of Asia.

It has grown revenues – under rather trying circumstances for the Indian steel industry – at a compound rate of 21% for the last five years to $3.6 billion for fiscal 2004–05, with commensurate improvement in profitability and return on capital (see figure 6.3). Corresponding EPS growth has been 55% compounded annually. The coming few years will see an acceleration of this growth rate as, aside from India, it contemplates supplying steel in China, Vietnam, Australia, Thailand, Malaysia and the Philippines, a region that cumulatively consumes over one-third of the world's steel output. It has begun to target this market through Singapore-based Natsteel Asia Pte, its first overseas acquisition that gave it a capacity of two million tons. Natsteel will add $1.2 billion to TISCO's revenues in fiscal 2005–06.

Figure 6.3: Improving growth, profitability and return on capital parameters for TISCO

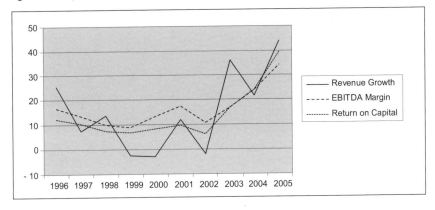

Source: Bloomberg.

The company is also moving to rapidly secure coal from outside the country, mainly by buying stakes in three coal mines in Australia. The way Indian steel companies are expanding and greenfield projects are coming up will see huge pressure on the Indian coal industry, and the fear is that they will not be able to cope.

Not wanting to be stuck for coal, many companies have moved to secure resources even before embarking on full-scale expansion. An important element in efficient steel-making is the use of billets instead of scrap iron ore. The company plans to set up large capacities in countries such as Iran and Russia, which have the second-largest and largest gas reserves respectively, which as we mentioned is a critical input in producing intermediate materials. It is already building a 1.5 million ton billet plant in Iran, which will start production by 2008.

It is hard to imagine that just a few years ago Tata Steel was setting itself up for failure. By virtue of various commitments to the government of the state in which its plant was located and due to pressure from workers, the company was engaged in running hospitals and maintaining a township, roads, schools and other social infrastructure. The company's thinking had become so entwined with its corollary activities that even its corporate advertising emphasized that "they also made steel". That is now history, and steel-making and growth has become its dominant focus. Tata Steel created a record of sorts with the depth of the internal restructuring that it carried out, where it reduced by nearly one-third its workforce and cut back on numerous ancillary and secondary activities without impinging on the quality of the lives of its employees and their dependents. Tata Steel's turnaround was a great achievement and a milestone for corporate India. In the space of a few years the company has gone from being the least efficient producer of steel among major steel companies globally to the lowest cost producer anywhere in the world.

Becoming more responsive to global trends

Unlike TISCO, Steel Authority – the largest of the integrated steel plants in India with 12 million tons of crude and special steel capacity – may not be aggressively looking for markets overseas but it is taking a leaf out of TISCO's book and taking a hard look at its efficiency parameters, and the evidence is that it has worked hard at improving them. It is also looking at how global resource markets can help it better manage cost and product quality. The company has been facing problems due to an inadequate supply of coking coal from its captive mines, which means that since the beginning of fiscal 2005–06 it has been exposed to rising prices of coking coal globally. This has begun to hurt its performance in the short term, especially after a six-quarter uninterrupted growth in earnings. The company's decision to buy mines overseas and ensure supplies while protecting itself from price rises will benefit it as it continues to expand. It plans to have a total of 20 million tons in place by 2010, thus retaining control of one-third of the Indian market.

SAIL is 86% owned by the Indian government and was one of the first creations of an independent India to realize Prime Minister Nehru's dream of building the foundations of a modern India. There is always a possibility that the government may decide to reduce its stake in the company, making it a great catch for any Indian or global steel major. Despite huge inbuilt inefficiencies, the company cannot be ignored; its size, location and domination of the Indian steel scene ensure that. With strong steel prices and improved plant efficiencies the company has become a net cash generator that has helped it pull down debt. The company reported revenues of $7.1 billion and a net income of $1.5 billion for fiscal 2004–05, after growing at a compound rate of 25% for the last few years. It sold half a million tons in 2005 to the Indian Railways, and with the railways looking at a massive expansion over the next few years this single customer could help push volumes greatly. And with the Indian government asking Indian steel companies to increase production by 10% annually, being a largely state-owned corporation means that SAIL will be expected to expand rapidly.

India's first family of steel

The companies in the steel and infrastructure industries promoted by the Jindal family have repeatedly demonstrated their potential and represent some of the better-quality steel companies in India. In the past, the reputation of the Jindal family went against them achieving a better market valuation for their companies. But then they undertook a business and ownership reorganization that brought in some more transparency and has helped in the revaluation of their companies. Some of their companies – such as Jindal Stainless and Jindal Steel and Power – now get premium valuations.

JSW Steel – India's third-largest integrated steel company created after the merger of two Jindal steel companies, the venerable Jindal Iron and Steel Company and Jindal Vijaynagar Steel – is among those Indian steel companies that are investing over $1 billion in expanding their steel-making facilities. JSW Steel will push up capacity in two phases; first ending in March 2006 when it will have a 3.8 million ton capacity, and then to 7 million tons in the next two years. The total cost will be roughly $1.2 billion. The fact that the management has ruled out equity dilution and will instead use debt and internal cash accruals means that existing shareholders will enjoy all the benefits of the expansion. The company has a huge exposure to the construction sector with its large production of galvanized steel. Besides, with an aggressive export initiative it has built markets for itself around the globe.

The company earns $1.5 billion annually in revenues, which should grow to between $3 billion and $4 billion by 2010 simply through organic growth of its capacities, implying a minimum compound annual growth for the next five years of 15% to 18%. It enjoys EBITDA margins of 34%, which it can easily sustain given its focus on maintaining its cost advantage, thus giving it a sustainable high RoCE. It follows a process of manufacturing steel that consumes non-coking coal and considerably less coke, which is very expensive. Additionally, it has proven very adept at producing very low-cost power through its own plants, and can bring this down still further.

Jindal Stainless Ltd too is an integrated producer operating in a very lucrative market, one in which it is a dominant player. The company produces stainless steel, and controls 40% of the domestic market. It is one of the world's leading producers of a premium grade of stainless steel. The market in India for stainless steel is growing at 12%, which is about 60% faster than the market for crude steel. The domestic market for stainless steel has become so attractive that the company has reduced its exports to some extent, though exports still remain a substantial portion of its business. China too remains an integral part of its business, since the rate of growth in the Chinese market for stainless steel will remain roughly twice that of India for the next few years. With the expansions it has planned and with tight supply conditions for stainless steel favoring manufacturers a compounded volume growth of 15% to 20% until 2012 is possible, especially given its cost advantage. Between its operations in India and Indonesia (operations it acquired for $32 million) it has a capacity of 550,000 tons, which will be raised to 2.32 million by 2012, including a brand-new 1.6 million ton plant in eastern India. Further volume growth is possible as acquisitions of steel mills in Taiwan and Korea and ferro chrome mines in South East Asia are being contemplated.

Though it is not one of the integrated steel companies, Jindal Steel and Power is an important growth stock. Its business is producing sponge iron, mining iron ore and power generation. With the availability of scrap becoming increasingly difficult, Indian steel producers are moving towards sponge iron, which also improves the quality of steel. The company has enjoyed an amazing recent record in earnings, with 14 consecutive high-growth quarters, with its EPS compounding by 48% annually for the last five years. Revenues have grown at a compound rate of 52% for the last five years, giving it revenues of $500 million for fiscal 2004–05, and at a price to sales of 1.5 to 1.8 times it does trade at a premium to the sector.

Playing the metals story

Besides the integrated steel players which are demonstrated and potential world beaters, there are numerous examples of other smaller and more specialized up and downstream steel companies – such as foundry grade pig iron maker Tata Metaliks and metallurgical coking coal giant Gujarat NRE Coke – that have shown excellent earnings growth (see figure 6.4) and fantastic return on capital employed in recent years and quarters, and are well positioned to grow profitably in the future. The potential for pig iron closely correlates with the growth in production of automobiles, engineering and capital equipment and electric steel.

Figure 6.4: Sesa Goa's quarterly EPS growth rate between Q1 2003-04 and Q1 2005-06

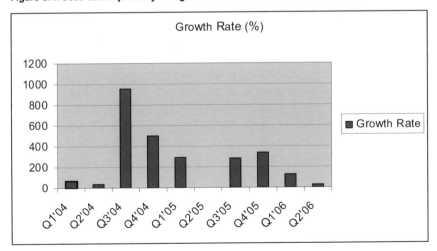

(The quarter corresponding to Q2 2004-05 was a loss, hence the growth rate cannot be computed.)
Source: Bloomberg

Gujarat NRE Coke has emerged from the shadows to become India's largest merchant producer of met coke, producing half a million tons annually. But given the likely demand from the steel industry, it is investing in order to quickly pull up its capacity to 1.4 million tons by the end of 2006. The raw material for met coke is coal, and knowing that the competition for coal in India is rising it has moved quickly to acquire mines and facilities in Australia. It is a good play on the global dynamics of the steel industry as well as the domestic industry. Not only has its net income quadrupled over the last couple of years but the P/E expansion has been spectacular, where the P/E multiple has doubled from five times to 10 times 12-month trailing earnings.

Indian mining companies also offer great growth opportunities. The projected increase in steel-making capacity over the next decade or so will require an annual iron ore output of 190 million tons. India currently produces 145 million tons of iron ore, of which 78 million tons is exported. Though a large portion will come from captive mines owned by the integrated steel producers, the merchant miners will benefit immensely. Sesa Goa Ltd, the largest merchant iron ore miner in India, is superbly poised to profit from the expected growth. It has already seen 10 successive quarters of strong growth, of which the last seven have been triple-digit growth rates, and it currently earns a fantastic return on capital employed. The company annually produces 10 million tons of ore and a quarter of a million tons each of low ash metallurgical coke and pig iron. It controls 12% of the Indian export market in iron ore. The company's fortunes are determined by the price of iron ore, and demand from Indian steel companies will add to the pricing pressure created by Chinese companies. According to Merrill Lynch, the price of iron ore is not expected to return to 2004 levels of $45/ton before 2008. This gives companies like Sesa Goa a minimum of two years of superlative growth and cash flows that will be used to expand mining capacity. It is working on opening a mine in the eastern Indian state of Jharkhand that will push up its output by 50% to five million tons annually. Over the last three years it has compounded revenues by 46% and net income by 207%.

Meet India's leading integrated metals and mining group

The London Stock Exchange-listed Vedanta Resources Plc is the brainchild of Anil Agrawal, the founder of Sterlite Industries, India's largest producer of zinc and copper, and if he has it his way it will be India's largest producer of aluminum too within the next couple of years. He created Vedanta Resources (2005 revenues of £1.02 billion) to give life to his ambition of becoming a diversified and integrated metals and mining company. Vedanta Resources owns mines and smelters in Australia and Zambia, but through four subsidiary companies – Sterlite Industries, Hindustan Zinc, Balco and Malco – it has bet especially heavily on India's rapidly rising demand for metals. It has already commenced investing a total of $2 billion into greenfield and expansion projects in copper, aluminum, alumina and zinc through the four metal companies in India, a lot of which has been completed.

This is one corporate group that has always impressed, and not just by the fact that they are probably the lowest cost copper producers in the world (at just seven cents a pound) and one of the lowest cost producers of aluminum (see figure 6.5). Vedanta Resource's market capitalization stood at over $3 billion on the LSE. Sterlite Industries, with fiscal 2004–05 revenues of $1.01 billion, is listed on the Indian stock exchanges and is valued at $1.76 billion.

Figure 6.5: Declining cost of copper production at Sterlite Industries

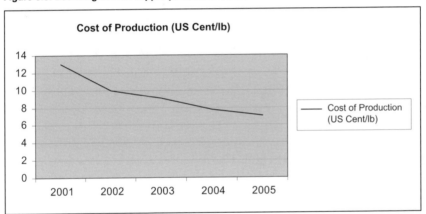

Source: Sterlite Industries

Of its subsidiary companies in India, Balco and Malco are aluminum companies with total production capacity of 136,000 tons, which is being expanded to 400,000 tons per annum by March 2006 with a $900 million investment; Hindustan Zinc (HZL) is a virtual monopoly producer of zinc and lead in India with capacities expanded to 400,000 tons of zinc and 85,000 tons of lead; and Sterlite Industries manufactures copper cathodes and copper rods, producing 40% of India's annual copper output.

Sterlite Industries was the first company to be promoted in the mid-1980s by this family of metal traders that took a small-town copper trading enterprise, moved into manufacturing copper rods for their jelly-filled telecommunication cables business, and successfully turned it into India's first integrated copper company. It spread rapidly from there, including the acquisition of the government-owned Balco, and then of Hindustan Zinc, also a public sector company. Now that Sterlite has increased its copper cathode capacity to 300,000 tons from 180,000 tons and copper rod facilities have expanded to a quarter of a million tons, its revenues could easily double to $2 billion within the next two years. Over the past five years, Sterlite has compounded its revenues by 35% and net income by 32%. Hindustan Zinc, the other listed entity in India, is a brilliant play on the growing demand for galvanized steel (which is needed for construction), since zinc is used as a coating on this type of steel. The demand for zinc is expected to grow by 40% by 2008, and all that growth will accrue to HZL. Over the last four years its net income has compounded by 40%, and conservatively considering the demand growth and its own huge capacity expansion its net income will likely compound by a minimum of 30% for the next few years.

The copper, aluminum and alumina operations were folded into Vedanta Resources, which is essentially a holding company, and the group obtained a listing on the London Stock Exchange. When the group's holding company did its IPO in London towards the close of 2003, the £507 million (€730 million) it raised made it the second-largest IPO in London for that year and the third-largest IPO in the European Union, and it was the seventh-largest mining equity deal ever. The management of Vedanta Resources appears to be limited only by the scope of their own vision and their ability to implement it. Their appetite to grow and integrate operations and fully exploit efficiencies in the metals industry globally can probably only be exceeded by that shown by Reliance Industries, India's largest private sector company, and in some ways they have mimicked Reliance's relentless drive to integrate and grow (see figure 6.6). And, like Reliance Industries and cement giant GACL, its growth strategy has centered around its ability to raise and judiciously manage large amounts of rupee and dollar debt, balanced with timely equity placements at very favorable prices. But they always have been a bit of an enigma, even by the standards of Indian commodity companies, and they were moving towards building an integrated metals business with strong global links long before other Indian companies even knew that was possible.

King of the mines

Bauxite is one of the minerals available in plenty in India and of a very high quality too, and India has the world's fifth-largest reserves of that ore. Indian aluminum companies are the most profitable in the world, with returns on capital that are higher than most – if not all – of their global competitors.

Figure 6.6: Five-year trend in Vedanta Resources revenue and EBITDA growth

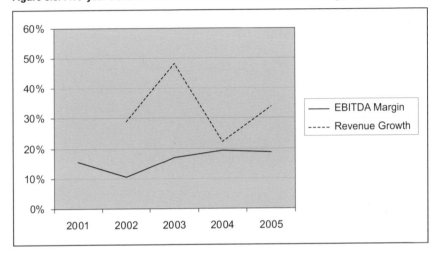

Source: Vedanta Resources Plc

Two companies – Hindalco Industries, controlled by the AV Birla conglomerate, and National Aluminum, whose largest shareholder is the Indian government – dominate the industry in India. There are a few other companies active here, including Vedanta Resources–owned Malco and Balco. The demand for aluminum has expanded in India, and the growth factor is considered to be 1.1 times that of the macroeconomic growth, which is slightly lower than that of steel. But the value addition is higher here and the companies tend to focus on high value-added products. The competition in the sector is likely to increase sharply given the planned increase in aluminum refining capacities. Between Hindalco, Jindal South West and Vedanta Resources a total of $5.2 billion is to be invested in expanding refinery capacity.

Hindalco Industries is the largest aluminum company in India, with $2.25 billion in revenues for fiscal 2004–05. Nearly 55% of its revenue is derived from aluminum and the rest from merchant sales of copper cathode, 60% of which is exported. Being a merchant business, Hindalco's copper business is not stable since it depends on global copper companies sending it copper concentrate for conversion to cathode. So neither the copper sales volumes nor operating margins are stable, and that tends to undermine a superbly run aluminum business for which the company is very well recognized.

National Aluminum (NALCO), on the other hand, concentrates solely on aluminum – it reflects well in its EBITDA margins, which are higher and more stable than Hindalco's. The company reported revenues of nearly $1 billion for fiscal 2004–05, and its return on equity was around 21%, one of the highest among aluminum companies globally and it has demonstrated strong earnings growth (see figure 6.7).

Figure 6.7: NALCO's consecutive EPS growth rate over 11 quarters

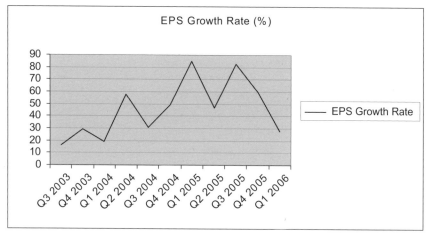

Source: Bloomberg

TURNING ADVERSITY INTO OPPORTUNITY

The Indian petrochemicals and polymers industry has turned out to be extremely globally competitive, despite not having a single competitive advantage, unlike in cement and metals. Despite being located between the Middle East and far eastern regions that either have a natural competitive advantage in raw materials or have built gigantic capacities and hold a cost advantage, Indian petrochemical and polymer companies are racing along the growth and profitability path, driven in part by the expansion in the domestic market and in part by exports, buoyed by some of the world's largest capacities in various petrochemical and polymer segments.

The industry is made up of four large players – Reliance Industries, IPCL, Gas Authority of India Ltd (GAIL) and Haldia Petrochemicals – and a number of downstream manufacturers. The petrochemicals industry in India is large, and is driven by demand growth for polymers (from the plastics and packaging industries), polyester (from the textile industry) and fiber intermediates (from the synthetic fiber industry), and demand from the chemicals industry, all of which are high-growth industries. Imports are a problem for the industry, but then companies such as Reliance Industries have mastered the art of battling competition from low-cost suppliers from countries such as Saudi Arabia and Korea. But no new capacities coming on stream anywhere in the world means higher and sustained prices for the next few years, and strong growth for large integrated players focused on the Indian domestic market.

Baptism by fire!

After acquiring a 51% stake in the Indian Petrochemicals Corporation (IPCL) from the government and minority shareholders, Reliance Industries now controls over two-thirds of the petrochemicals industry in India. The company is India's largest private sector company by revenues ($15 billion for fiscal 2004–05) and assets ($18 billion for fiscal 2004–05), and is the only Indian private sector company on the Fortune 500 list. In 2004 it won the title "Petrochemical Company of the Year" at the annual Platts Global Energy Awards. It is also the largest exporter, selling $3.6 billion worth of its products overseas in fiscal 2004–05. And its market capitalization at $17 billion is the largest among all Indian private sector companies, and only a handful of state-owned corporations have larger market caps (see figure 6.8). The company currently contributes almost 2.5% of India's annual GDP.

Figure 6.8: Reliance Industries expansion in market capitalization over a decade

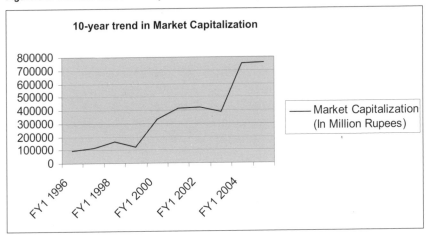

Source: Bloomberg.

Following the split in its management where a number of subsidiary businesses – such as telecom, financial services and energy – were transferred to a separate holding company, RIL is now an oil and gas, petrochemicals, polymers and textiles company. These businesses generate a huge cash pile every year of $3 billion to $4 billion, which gives it a lot of muscle to expand organically and look for acquisitions.

Today it is one of the largest producers globally of polymers, plastics and petrochemicals, and it has set its sights on becoming the largest player globally in a number of petrochemical segments. RIL has already emerged as the world's largest producer of polyester fiber and yarn after the acquisition of polyester manufacturer Trevira of Germany in 2004. Among its anticipated expansions are acquiring polymer and petrochemical assets in Europe and Asia, investing $6 billion to double its crude oil refining capacity, investing in oil and gas exploration, and an investment of $1.1 billion to acquire 25 ships – including chemical carriers, LNG carriers and crude carriers – as it continues to strike gas in its license areas, refinery capacity expands and so does its exports.

No Indian industrial group had striven harder or achieved more in just a couple of decades the way Reliance Industries has. A lot of apocryphal stories surround the company and its legendary founder, the late Dhirubhai Ambani, simply because the company has achieved so much, so fast and so quietly that it seems almost impossible that all this could be done with cold hard logic and old-fashioned hard work. The company's late founder had molded the company in his image; very aggressive, financially savvy, relentless focus on growth and a remarkable feel for the country's equity pulse. Though relentless is the adjective that is most commonly used to describe Reliance Industries and its management, the company has also shown remarkable dexterity in managing growth and change in an environment that was hostile to large enterprise, and deeply entrenched opponents in the textile and petrochemicals industry. They turned a very fragmented industry into a competitive business with global scale and gigantic cash flows.

Their links with the government and the ability to cultivate the necessary patronage is extremely well documented by the mainstream and financial media in India, and was a critical component in the growth story but is much less so today. Though it is easy to fault them there is no other company in India, or maybe anywhere else in the world, that so completely dominates the industries in which it operates in a near monopolistic manner.

Reliance Industries started out in the late 1960s as a trading house, trading in textiles and commodities, graduated to manufacturing textiles in the 1970s, a business that it continued to expand before embarking on a mind-boggling strategy of relentless growth through backward and forward integration, creating the entire value chain from oil and gas exploration, refineries and producing basic petrochemicals to finished textile fabrics, all the while ramping up capacities to meet global operating scales. A key factor in the near monopolistic growth of its petrochemicals business was when in the 1980s and 1990s it engineered a shift from DMT (produced by rival companies) to PTA, which it produced as an intermediate in the production of polyester.

In the mid-1990s, it went upstream by establishing an oil refinery, which is the third-largest in the world with 33 million tons a year of capacity (660,000 barrels per day). They are now setting up an identical refinery next to its existing one, with a 27 million-ton capacity (580,000 barrels per day), to be operational by December 2008, making it the largest refining complex in the world at 60 million tons. It is also one of the cheapest refineries built given that capacities this size usually cost 30% to 40% more. The largest refinery in the world currently is in Venezuela, with a 40 million-ton capacity. At the time of writing, Reliance Petroleum, the subsidiary created to execute the refinery expansion, was preparing for a $1.9 billion IPO, which will be India's biggest ever. Chevron picked up a 5% stake in Reliance Petroleum on the eve of the IPO for $300 million with an option to pick up another 24%.

Reliance could face more exacting challenges now that it has focused its gigantic new refinery on the global market place, so having a partner like Chevron makes a great deal of sense. For the moment the picture is rosy since globally refining capacity has remained stagnant for over 20 years while demand has risen, besides, two-fifths of the world's refining capacity are more than 25 years old and cannot meet current environment standards. However, given the subsequent rise in refining margins, a number of projects have been announced that could add up to 22 million barrels per day of new capacity (it is fair to assume that some portion of that capacity will replace obsolete refineries, though when these capacities will be operational is uncertain). Even though the company has expressed confidence that not more than 4.5 million barrels per day will be added by 2010, it still is a very significant risk factor. In the meanwhile Reliance's refineries will continue to earn a premium over regional refining margins, which at the moment at is $2.5 to $3 over the benchmark Singapore refining margin.

However, despite its proven ability to manage risk and the ability to build some of the cheapest yet state-of-the-art plants, capital efficiency – especially RoCE – has been a consistent concern. These concerns could persist in the future too, as it continues to expand its main petrochemicals business and as it invests heavily in a series of hypermarkets and in retailing of petroleum products through its own network of gas stations, acquiring stakes in infrastructure projects and investing in its life sciences business.

SUGAR, SPICE AND EVERYTHING NICE!

Agro-commodities, always perceived to be a dull industry, has thrown up some great companies in sectors ranging from sugar to tea. Some leading corporate names here have evolved into global players, with businesses running on all the major continents. Several Indian companies have turned staid agro-based businesses into sophisticated operations with significant value addition, strong brands and terrific growth potential, driven largely by a huge domestic market for these commodities and also a gigantic production base. India is the world's largest consumer of sugar and among the top three producers of sugar by volume. It is also the world's largest producer and consumer of tea, accounting for a quarter of all global production. Indian tea producers have been eyeing global markets as they begin to expand aggressively. Ironically (since it was the British that introduced the tea crop to India) two of the top three tea brands in the UK – including Tetley (number 1) and Premier Foods' Typhoo (number 3) – are now Indian-owned by the Tata's and the Apeejay Surendra Group respectively.

Agro-businesses are very difficult to manage, to say the least, and are especially prone to volatile swings in earnings depending on crop yields, not only in India but in global markets.

Brewing the perfect cup

Tata Tea Ltd ($683 million in revenues and $52 million in net income for fiscal 2004–05) went from being one of the largest tea companies – and consequently one of the largest commodity businesses in India – to being the second largest tea producer and marketer in the world, running a very sophisticated global operation. To all those who doubted corporate India's ability to buy out a world class, global scale operation, Tata Tea's £271 million ($470 million) acquisition of the UK-based Tetley Tea half a decade ago was an introduction to what was possible. The Tetley acquisition, which was superbly structured and financed, pushed Tata Tea second only to Unilever's tea business, with operations in Asia, Europe and North America. In late 2005 the company has gone in for another acquisition of a large California-based speciality tea maker FMALI Herb Inc, which holds a sizeable chunk of that market in the United States.

Tata Tea is a superbly managed business in India with an excellent financial and management track record. Despite being fully exposed to the vagaries and cyclicality of a commodity business, it has managed to increase its book value by an annual compound rate of 17% for the past decade and carries an enterprise value of $1.1 billion.

Sweet success

The sugar industry is hardly a typical industry that one would think of as investment-worthy when considering investing in a booming economy. But like hard commodities such as cement and metals, agro-commodities such as sugar are also a direct beneficiary of improving lifestyles. India is seeing a boom in the demand for chocolates, confectionary products and even traditional Indian sweets. This fact alone is driving up the consumption of sugar. The rising demand from India is serving up a bull market in global sugar prices as India is the world's largest consumer of sugar, accounting for 13% of world consumption.

Domestic sugar production has not been able to keep pace with demand for the last few years, and India has had to import between one and two million tons a year, which is a significant quantity for the global markets too. As an example of what Indian sugar producers are experiencing, India is expected to consume around 19.5 million tons in 2005–06, and this figure is expected to rise by 4.5% to 5% at a minimum thereafter, but the production of sugar – despite a huge increase over the previous year – is not expected to exceed 17.5 to 18 million tons, leaving a significant gap to be covered. Though these figures are apt to change, the underlying trend for the future is unmistakable; producers will be pushed hard to meet demand and higher prices could be sustained. As a caveat, sugar production depends on the cane yield per acre and the sugar recovery rate from the crushing process, which currently averages around 10%.

In agro-commodities, even a small demand–supply gap means a huge advance in prices. And sugar mills in India are typically big beneficiaries since many have access to captive production of sugarcane from which sugar is extracted, and thus are protected from raw material price increases but enjoy appreciating end prices. Sugar companies typically also sit on huge stocks of molasses and raw sugar, since the harvest is done only over a short period after the monsoon. So any increase in prices has a positive effect on the value of inventory held. Not surprisingly, businesses as innocuous as sugar companies have been among the top performers in the Indian equity market, despite the fact that the Indian government still partially restricts the companies' ability to freely sell all their sugar in the market. A portion of sugar produced is sold at government-mandated prices, while the rest is sold at market prices. However, what the government takes away with one hand it gives back with the other, since it has allowed the maximum proportion of ethanol that could be blended with petrol to increase from 5% to 10%. Ethanol is a by-product of producing molasses from sugarcane, and could provide a substantial revenue source for sugar manufacturers should the Indian oil retailers decide to go ahead and use ethanol in their fuel mix. For the moment, however, like the trend globally that is by no means certain.

Balrampur Chini Mills is India's largest sugar manufacturer and is led by what is considered to be a very savvy management. The company has managed very well the ups and downs that are all too frequent in the sugar industry, and has moved towards branding its product in an effort to obtain premium pricing. The earnings growth and return on capital employed have been good for the well-managed sugar companies, including Dhampur Sugar (second largest in India) and Bajaj Hindustan (third largest). Balrampur Chini reported an RoE of 33% for fiscal 2004–05, while Bajaj Hindustan and Dhampur Sugars reported an RoE of 47% and 38% respectively. On profitability and return on capital parameters Indian companies tend to lead their global counterparts by a very large margin.

The key driver of profit growth for these companies will now be their ability to rapidly expand cane-crushing capacity. Balrampur Chini has already moved to raise their capacity from 29,000 tons crushed per day (tcd) to 40,000 tcd. And others are implementing similar plans too.

7

THE NEW WORLD:
FRUITS OF LIBERALIZATION

While Indian companies have developed great levels of competitiveness and a previously unseen aggression after going through years of painful restructuring, and are now able to compete effectively in foreign markets, the reality is that the biggest opportunity for them is still in India. Of that there is little doubt, whether it is financing consumption, building water infrastructure, installation of telecom networks, or even the discovery of new drugs. To take this argument further then, for investors too the biggest wealth-creating opportunity lies within those industries that will benefit the most from the expansion and growth of the domestic Indian market. The opportunity created by domestic growth is a result of the same liberalization process that also threw up so many globally competitive sectors and companies in India's external sector. This combined phenomenon is the New World for Indian companies and their investors.

The sectors that have clearly benefited from domestic economic expansion are the banking and financial sector, engineering, capital goods and infrastructure, construction, oil and gas, power, automobiles, textiles and telecommunications. A number of companies in this sector would not have come about but for the deep-rooted change in India. We're seeing companies that have been around literally for decades, that had stagnating revenues without much money being reinvested in their businesses since they could not fathom any potential. But since the mid-1990s companies have instinctively invested heavily in modernization and expansion, and also took great leaps of faith, looking for opportunity. A great example of this leap of faith is found not in IT or in pharmaceuticals – though they have their share of truly great liberalization-era companies – but in the relatively unknown sector of wind energy, and the company that took it is Suzlon Energy. This is Asia's largest wind-power company and the sixth largest in the world. It has been in this business for all of a decade. Suzlon was a textile company, whose promoter, Tulsi R Tanta, decided to go in for wind energy for his textile plant, an exercise that convinced him of the earning power from wind, and he went on to create a great business, literally putting India on the map. India today is the fourth-largest wind-power generator in the world, after the United States, Spain and Germany, producing 4,225 MW by 2005; it is a bigger producer even than Denmark, which is renowned for its use of wind energy. Incidentally, in Autumn 2005 the company began operations in Denmark, which is now the base for Suzlon Energy's global operations.

Moving from being a consumer to an accomplished solutions provider in wind energy, the company even offers (very successfully too!) consultancy, design and manufacturing of wind-power generating equipment, including turbines and maintenance. Suzlon's is probably the only known case of an Indian company outsourcing its R&D outside of India, with that activity being conducted in Germany through a subsidiary company and an R&D facility in the Netherlands for rotor-blade molding and tooling. For fiscal 2004–05 it captured 50% of the total market for wind-power generating capacity, though at a cumulative level it has installed 36% of the total wind-power generating capacity in India, having put up 1,634 MW until December 2005.

A large portion of the growth in wind energy will come from Asia and Australia, with countries such as India and China leading the way. In 2005 India added 1,225 MW of generating capacity from wind, representing 12.25% of the capacity installed worldwide for the year. By 2009 India is expected to grow its wind-power generating capacity by 23% compounded, from an installed base of 4,225 MW in 2004–05 to 8,300 MW, retaining its status as one of the big growth markets for this type of power in the world. The Indian government has estimated the potential from wind energy at 45,000 MW, and Suzlon will likely capitalize well on the growth in India and other countries, making it a great play on India's domestic as well as external segments. The company is establishing manufacturing facilities in the United States and China. The Indian stock market has not missed this opportunity either. When Suzlon went public in late 2005, not only was its IPO oversubscribed 51 times but upon listing the company was valued at almost $5 billion, putting its promoter among the top 10 wealthiest Indian industrialists, with his stake valued at $3.5 billion. Not a bad reward for creating something from thin air! This also goes to show just how much opportunity there really is in India, and that it can be unlocked fairly quickly.

There is a whole category of companies that have benefited during this period of liberalization in the external sector by exploiting India's innate engineering ability, whether it is developing a global delivery model on a previously untried scale by the software services industry, reverse engineering of molecular structures to produce drugs for the global market at a fraction of the cost, or the precision engineering of moving parts for the automobile and automobile ancillary sector.

All these sectors fully reflect the new India and capture its strengths and the advantages of its demographics and the quality of its manpower, besides the rising incomes, rising standard of living and global competitiveness.

"WATCH THE BANKS"

"If you watch a bank like a hawk, you'll see in the pattern of their lending practices a blue print of the macro picture." – Mark Mobius, observing an economic truism in his book *Passport to Profits*.

This observation is strikingly accurate whether in India or in any other economy. Indian banks are mirroring the social and economic trends that are shaping up to drive the economy, and this is one sector that readily identifies with India's status as a top growth economy with a rapidly growing consumerist culture.

Life with leverage; how household spending is driving Indian banks

The Indian banking sector has some amazing growth stories, many of which have been years in the making. The earnings growth profile of most Indian banks now clearly reflects the shift from wholesale to retail lending, especially as Indian consumers begin to lap up mortgages, automobile loans, personal loans and credit card debt. Indian families are clearly overcoming their traditional aversion to household debt as a means to finance improved lifestyles. It is a brand-new trend that is unprecedented for the Indian economy and carries huge economic consequences. India today has one of the lowest levels of household debt amongst any of the world's major economies, and it is almost negligible in comparison even to Asian economies such as South Korea, Taiwan and Japan, which have financed domestic expansion by taking on enormous amounts of debt. India will likely see the benefits of increasing household debt on the economy long before it has to worry about the proportion of that debt to household income and the resultant sensitivity to changes in interest rates of the country's economic growth.

In most major economies a large proportion of household income is needed to service debt, making sensitivity to interest rate changes a major concern. India is very far from this possibility. But already bank loans to individuals is one of the fastest growing banking and economic segments in India, recording a 25% growth to $252 billion in the first half of 2005, according to the Reserve Bank of India. But traditionally credit growth is stronger in the second half of any given year, so the composite growth for the whole year would be much higher (see table 7.1). Indian banks would typically claim that the growth rate in the retail segment is expected to compound between 30% and 40% for the next few years. The evidence is that the cumulative growth in credit has already crossed 30% and the momentum is still building, with a slightly higher growth rate being reported for the first half of fiscal 2005–06. These are average figures, and banks with a strong retail focus that work on sophisticated technology platforms, such as ICICI Bank and HDFC Bank, report growth rates in retail at twice the sector average. So far, Indian households are spending on domestically produced goods and services, and the break up of import figures does not show too much of consumer goods coming from overseas as yet.

Table 7.1: Deposit and credit growth – a snapshot

	Deposit and credit growth			
	Fiscal 2003–04		Fiscal 2004–05	
	Deposit	Credit	Deposit	Credit
State Bank of India	19.7	16.1	15.7	26
Public sector banks	16.2	15.6	15.9	33.6
Foreign banks	28.6	15.3	5.2	24.6
Private sector banks	23.4	23.8	17.8	31.9

Source: Reserve Bank of India

The growth potential for Indian banks is a significant trend that can be capitalized on. There are two aspects to this growth. The first is the expansion in the banking sector as GDP expands. The growth factor in bank assets to GDP growth would be at least 2, so if GDP expands by 8% to 10% the banking sector should expand by 16% to 20% at a minimum (though even in mature economies we have seen a faster rate of expansion in recent years). So in India, a country that is relatively under-banked,15% to 20% annual expansion is significantly on the lower side. The second aspect of the expansion is the proportion of bank assets to GDP; that is, the proportion of the economy that is financed by bank debt but expressed as a GDP ratio. Indian banks represent a small percentage of the Indian economy in comparison with other major global economies, currently accounting for a little over 60% of GDP. The ratio in emerging market economies is about 95%, while for China it is 178%, for South Korea it is 106% and for Malaysia it is 150%. Major European economies have larger proportions of their economy financed with bank debt, with the UK extending to 262% and France at 255% (see figure 7.1). So India does have a long way to go, and banks are gearing up for this kind of growth. It is interesting to note that even though India is the fourth-largest economy in the world (PPP terms) and the eleventh-largest in US dollar terms, there is no Indian bank among the top 50 global banks. The largest Chinese bank is over seven times the size of the largest Indian bank. The problem is the highly conservative nature of Indian banks and the dramatic level at which India is under-banked. But new trends are bringing in change.

Figure 7.1: A country comparison of bank assets

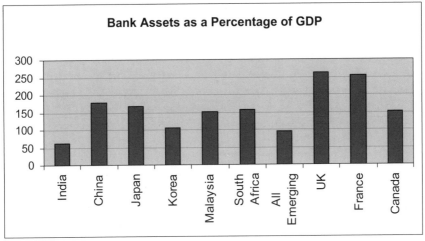

The emerging sophistication in the system is also driving growth; the use of credit derivative instruments, for example. Banks were exposed to it in India once interest rate futures were introduced in 2001. Now there is a growing transfer of credit risk from banks to other asset-rich intermediaries such as mutual and pension funds and insurance companies, especially as retail assets drive growth and banks feel the need to hedge these risks. Essentially credit risk is packaged in two ways; it is bundled as securities backed by fixed or floating receivables and sold to institutions that need to match liabilities, or it is simply insured. This risk transfer is moderate so far but helps in freeing up capital for growth. The introduction of derivative instruments for banks thus becomes a critical component for growth of this sector in India.

Emerging demographics drive values

The interesting and exciting thing about this trend in retail-driven growth within the above framework is that it becomes even more powerful when it is linked to India's emerging demographics. It is typically younger, often double-income, upwardly mobile families that are spearheading this trend. The bulk of these consumers at all levels of the income spectrum, seeking to pay for today's consumption from tomorrow's earnings, are benefiting from higher incomes and seeking to imitate the images of a Western lifestyle thrown at them by consumer marketers. Most importantly for these people, for the economy and for the banks that finance them, they have age on their side and the bulk of their productive working lives ahead of them. So an implosion like the one that happened in South Korea in 2003, caused by high household debt and little room for expansion in household income, is rather difficult to conceive in the foreseeable future.

We have seen that the key emerging trend in Indian banking is the fast rate of growth in credit to the household sector, but small and medium enterprises are a significant growth area too. This growth has been especially pronounced for the public sector banks, followed by the private sector banks. And, more importantly, we seem to be at the beginning of this very powerful consumer trend, coupled with strong interest in financing industrial assets.

The case for consolidation

A key long-term driver of bank valuations will be the possibility of allowing meaningful stakes of public sector banks to be held by

Indian and foreign investors, especially as the rapid growth in assets will push many banks to increase tier I or equity capital. The Indian government's official policy towards banks is to now allow the sale to foreign investors of up to 74% of privately owned banks but state-owned or public sector banks are still off limits. This does offer a window of opportunity for foreign banks, and there could be some consolidation in Indian banking as a result of that, except that the Reserve Bank of India has chosen to delay issuing guidelines on how this can happen.

Indian banking has a myriad of regulations – especially on ownership and voting rights – which are detrimental to foreign investors, or even domestic investors for that matter. For the public sector banks there is a 20% cap in the foreign ownership, and this includes portfolio investors. There is a cap on voting rights to the extent of 10%, no matter what the equity holding or whether the bank is privately held or in the public domain. Currently no domestic bank can acquire more than 10% in another bank, no foreign bank with operations in India can acquire more than 5% of the equity capital, and a foreign bank without operations can acquire no more than 10% in an Indian bank. Whew! Restrictions on voting rights are a huge impediment to unlocking value since they impede mergers and acquisitions. These regulations and the divergence in the will to introduce change between the government and the Reserve Bank has more to do with the bureaucrats traditional passion for control than any regulatory desire to protect Indian banks or depositors. The Indian banking sector seems to be the last frontier in the effort to liberalize the economy, and the irony is that even the defense sector is more open to private Indian and foreign investments than the banking sector. And it has more to do with vested interest than anything else.

Many foreign banks, such as HSBC, Citibank, Deutsche Bank and Standard Chartered Bank, have marked India as a key market for their future growth. In late 2005, Deutsche Bank announced that India will be the first non-European market where they will launch a retail presence. Deutsche Bank is the only one of the major foreign banks active in India that does not have a retail presence as yet, though they have over $2 billion worth of wholesale and high net worth assets (including corporate banking, cash management and wealth management). The stated preference of the foreign banks is to grow organically, but that is because of the tight regulatory regime. Foreign banks have understood that they should not challenge the status quo on ownership issues by attempting to take strategic stakes in existing Indian banks, especially in the public sector. Canada's Bank of Nova Scotia's attempt to take a minor 7% stake in the North India-based Bank of Punjab flew into a regulatory web and the Canadians were forced to withdraw. Despite all the restrictions, foreign banks already account for a little over one-eighth of the banking sector's assets in India. But that effort underscores the kind of intolerant regulatory regime being enforced at present, which proves to be detrimental in the long run as India seeks to finance a rapidly growing economy.

The Indian banking sector today as a whole is also ripe for consolidation, especially the private sector banks. And the government has signaled its intention to back this trend, especially among the domestic banks. But so far the government has not done anything to alter the ground reality that meaningful acquisitions are impossible. Most big banks are looking for as large a distribution network as possible, and acquiring these assets by buying small niche banks is sometimes a lucrative proposition. Second is the ground reality where banks have been growing aggressively but many will be constrained by capital adequacy and will be forced to look for alliances or simply sell out. Most Indian private sector banks have excellent infrastructure that would appeal to foreign banks looking to expand or set up shop in India that could leverage on quality assets. Being the largest stakeholder in the banking industry, the Indian government can easily be a facilitator in the process of consolidation. A total of 27 banks are owned by the central and various state governments and 19 of these are publicly traded. The market value of these 19 banks is close to $30 billion; most of that stock is held by the government. The state-owned banks (including a variety of rural banks, land banks and others) control nearly three-quarters of the banking industry.

The listed public sector banks are one group of stocks that has seen an unprecedented improvement in valuation by the stock market. For years most state-owned banks traded at P/E multiples of 1.5 times and price to book ratios of less than 0.5. That has changed, and the P/E multiple has expanded four or five times – maybe more in some cases – and the price to book ratios have also tripled and quadrupled. There has been a huge expansion in the earnings of these banks, which many banks have used to clean the books of non-performing loans, making India among the strongest in any emerging economy. The growth in the market value too has been unprecedented, making it an opportune time for the government to consider exiting a segment that in reality has no strategic value and which in any case is very closely regulated by the central bank.

The rapid growth rates in retail assets and lending to SMEs has been the main driver, but there are three other factors that have driven the re-rating of these banks. First, since deposit growth is not keeping pace with asset growth, a lot of the cash balances that banks have traditionally held with the central bank over and above statutory requirements and other low-yielding securities are being converted into the loans being made out to the faster-growing, higher-yielding sectors. Second, the public sector banks are the largest holders of long-dated government securities, and with the sharp multi-year decline in interest rates these banks have enjoyed a major revaluation of their portfolios, and in many cases they cashed out of their excess holdings accumulated during decades of slow credit private sector demand, thereby increasing treasury profits. Both these trends have meshed together in a profitable synergy. And third, the Indian government has pushed hard to give banks more teeth in seizing assets of defaulters and reducing the number of loopholes available to large defaulters, which had been a problem in the past. This restructuring will over time release tens of billions of dollars back into the banking system, besides throwing up huge opportunities for those organizations willing to buy into these distressed assets.

The strength of Indian banking and the platform for growth has already come about by the dramatic reduction in the level of net non-performing loans, though in absolute terms the gross NPLs remain. This has been achieved by massive increases in bank provisions for these bad loans, utilizing their excellent profit growth in recent years.

Despite major strides made in cleaning up their balance sheets and improving the quality of their assets, unfortunately many of these banks still trail the industry in efficiency and asset quality. A merger between some of these banks would eliminate overlapping infrastructure since most state-owned banks compete against each other, which makes no sense since they have one common major shareholder, thus improving the case for sustainable valuations. The value of the parts is in reality greater than the sum total, and mergers would only serve to make the government richer.

We will begin our dissection of the industry not with a bank but with a housing mortgage company, since it epitomizes all the right ingredients necessary to maintain high growth with high profitability and to benefit from India's new consumer culture. The housing mortgage market has set a scorching pace of growth and is a result of a combination of rising disposable incomes, availability of high-quality housing and, most importantly, falling interest rates and mortgage costs, both in absolute terms as well as in relation to the earning power of families in India.

Built to last

It is said in Indian investment circles that no fund manager visiting India from overseas can ignore meeting with the management of the Housing Development and Finance Corporation (HDFC), and having met them would leave very deeply impressed. In fact, if HDFC were the only company that they had met their impression of the quality of managements in corporate India would be flattering indeed.

For those familiar with its workings this view comes as no surprise, for HDFC has set very high standards and its operating parameters are the benchmark in an industry not yet very well known for its professionalism. The management is renowned for its business acumen (they dominate the mortgage business in India, with a 50% market share and with an outstanding loan portfolio of one million dwelling units), innovation (they have developed the fastest application turnaround time in the industry), cost control (they have the lowest expense ratio in the business and it is managed with a single-minded focus) and competitiveness (commercial banks with their huge scale of operations have not been able to dislodge them from their market domination). HDFC is probably the only real and very powerful consumer franchise in the Indian financial services industry.

As we have already established, for the commercial banks the retail market is the new growth mantra. And housing mortgages are the centerpiece of the new growth strategy, with banks such as ICICI Bank and State Bank of India (number two and number three respectively in the housing mortgage market) leading that rush. But HDFC's response has been to fight quantity with quality. The point that HDFC hinged its bet on is that in a country where the process of document maintenance and recovery is unsophisticated (it is still done largely in physical form), the importance of well-defined processes cannot be overemphasized. And the importance of understanding the true nature of costs in the business is also critical. HDFC is a master at that game, and has bet correctly that the cost of the mortgage is not the only driving factor in this business. Upon settling their mortgages, many home buyers found to their dismay that their bank or mortgage company had either misplaced their property papers or did not have systems in place to facilitate a quick and painless retrieval. Accepting documents was one thing but managing and closing the loop was a different issue altogether. In hindsight, the decision of the HDFC management not to get too involved in a pricing war seems to be the right one, for despite all the efforts of the competition they have not been dislodged as the market leader (see figure 7.2).

Figure 7.2: So where is the competition?

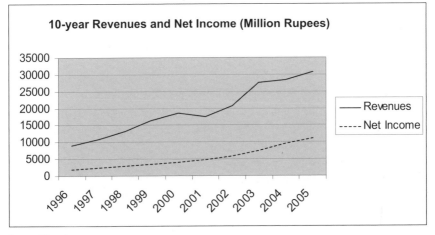

Source: Bloomberg

Banks began competing seriously in the housing mortgage market only a few years ago, and they gained market share very rapidly, largely by under-pricing loans or by adding on huge freebies to attract customers to whom they later hoped to sell other products. But this strategy has not been very profitable, though it has worked brilliantly in enlarging and deepening the housing mortgage market (aided no doubt by record low interest rates). Given the pricing effect of the cut-throat competition between banks and the various housing mortgage companies, a lot of first-time house buyers were emboldened to take on a mortgage and many families found it easy to take on larger mortgages. Though it is difficult to compute the figures for the banks it is widely accepted that despite several years and rapid gains in market share, no-one has turned a profit in housing mortgages yet.

Interestingly HDFC has entered numerous other financial services in association with some big global names. It has a life insurance joint venture with Standard Life, a general insurance venture with Chubb, a business process outsourcing subsidiary with Barclays, and promoted a banking subsidiary (HDFC Bank). Its latest joint venture is with WL Ross, the global turnaround specialist, to invest in distressed assets, particularly distressed debt securities. This opportunity to acquire distressed securities is emerging as banks use their hefty profit growth to begin writing off their non-performing loans.

HDFC is a unique case since it has managed growth profitably without taking recourse to equity infusion to bolster capital adequacy, unlike most of its competitors. It has compounded revenues by 22.5% annually for the past 10 years. But more interestingly, the period between 2001 and 2005, when it experienced unprecedented competition, it compounded revenues by 23%, while in the preceding five years (1996 to 2000) it grew revenues by 22% (see figure 7.3).

Figure 7.3: 10-year asset growth and pre-tax margin for HDFC

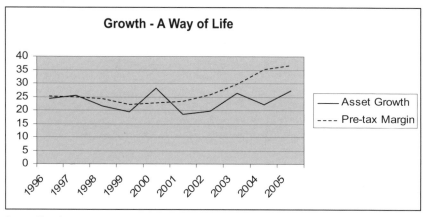

Source: Bloomberg

Dancing with elephants

There is no other sector in the country that has as many large organizations as the banking sector, and most of these heavyweights are in the public sector with 11 banks trading at a market capitalization each of more than $1 billion. The average market capitalization of the big four private sector banks – comprising ICICI Bank, HDFC Bank, Kotak Mahindra Bank and UTI Bank – is $3.5 billion.

The State Bank of India (SBI) – the country's largest bank by assets, market capitalization and profitability, standing at $100 billion (fiscal 2004–05), $10 billion and $1 billion respectively – controls one-fifth of the country's total bank deposits of $413 billion. This bank, along with its seven subsidiaries, would easily hold the world record for the largest number of bank branches in any one country, standing at nearly 14,000, and that number is probably still growing. But the change in SBI from a monolithic relic of India's socialist past to a more responsive and somewhat dynamic organization has been tremendous. The bank has already undertaken some major restructuring of its operations that has included a gigantic reduction in workforce through a voluntary retirement scheme, and the management has undertaken to bring its workforce down further over the next few years.

SBI's entry into the retail market has shaken up both the bank and the retail finance market completely, largely because the brand is widely known and trusted. In just a short while it has come to dominate the credit card business, that traditionally was the purview of multinational banks in India, especially Citibank. It is in a close race with ICICI Bank for second place in housing mortgages, and it is now a force to reckon with in the consumer finance business. These businesses have powered its recent growth. Besides, it has always had a near monopoly over government business, and most public sector companies prefer to route their foreign exchange business through this bank.

There is always the possibility and an expectation from the stock market that the government will one day permit the bank to merge with its various subsidiaries (whose businesses seriously overlap). This could in a single stroke increase SBI's asset base by 50%.

There are others belonging to this tribe of giant government-owned banks, all competing with each other and impressing with their managerial abilities. Listed banks such as Punjab National Bank, Canara Bank, Oriental Bank of Commerce, Bank of Baroda (see figure 7.4) and Corporation Bank, and relatively smaller ones such as Andhra Bank and Union Bank, stand out for their recent consistent performances and very rapid and increasingly profitable growth.

Figure 7.4: Bank of Baroda: Nine-year unbroken trend of asset growth is a good proxy for the sector

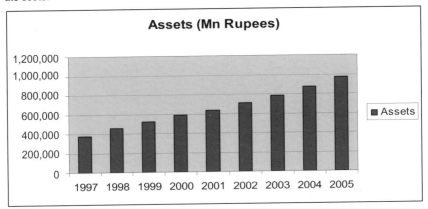

Source: Bloomberg.

Resurgence of a relic

There was a time when the Industrial Development Bank of India (IDBI) was known as the personal pocket book of Indian politicians. A "development financial institution" it most certainly was (as organizations created by the government to lend long-term funds for industrial projects were known, compared with commercial banks which were only supposed to lend short-term or working capital funds), but in the era of state control, rent seeking, especially in the control over public funds, led to some very dubious and poor lending decisions. But we are now seeing the resurgence of what was once supposed to be the torch bearer of India's effort at industrial development but which had faltered badly due to political interference in its lending activities. It competed with two other institutions, the Industrial Credit and Investment Corporation of India (ICICI) and the Industrial Finance Corporation of India (IFCI). While IDBI is in much better shape than IFCI, which has suffered more from corruption and dubious lending, it has not been able to (and probably might never) catch up with ICICI, which has since turned itself into ICICI Bank and is now the second-largest bank in India in terms of both market capitalization and assets, after the State Bank of India.

Despite its best efforts IDBI has not made the shift to a universal bank, even after promoting and recently merging with the IDBI Bank, one of India's new generation banks. But its efforts at restructuring, especially after the government pumped in nearly $2 billion worth of bonds, and refocusing have helped considerably, besides the fact that it holds a diversified industrial portfolio that has recovered well thanks to the last few years of strong industrial growth and is of very significant value in today's prosperous economy. The once-looming threat of overwhelming non-performing assets never materialized, and now there should be no looking back for India's once-premier development financial institution.

The era of universal banking

While IDBI struggled first with the political environment and then the economic environment, ICICI prospered, even as a development finance institution in pre-liberalization India. In the liberalization phase, especially since the mid-1990s, it introduced the concept of universal banking to India, and it embodies that concept like no other in the country. It successfully converted itself from a development institution into a banking giant. HDFC Bank could come close to that, especially since it cross-sells financial products with HDFC Ltd, its biggest stakeholder and promoter. ICICI Bank, as it is now called, has grown at an amazing pace. Its assets in 2005 stood at $40 billion, and it commands a market capitalization of $8 billion. The success it enjoys is largely as a result of the far-sightedness of its chairman, K V Kamath, a banker highly respected in Indian and now even in global banking circles.

This bank has captured the stock market's fancy thanks to its ability to not only grow the fastest in the industry but also to retain above-average profitability. It seems almost incredible that this one time development financial institution that lent long-term funds exclusively on a project-finance basis has turned around almost completely, where over two-thirds of its loan book now comprises retail assets and lending to small and medium enterprises. The bank's management is considered to be one of the best in the entire industry, and has been credited with sparking off several trends in Indian banking; most notable is the shift to universal banking, the identification of the retail segment as a significant growth opportunity and acquisitions as a growth strategy in niche markets.

Not surprisingly, this bank commands sustained premium valuations, streets ahead of its peers and surpassed only by its close qualitative rival, HDFC Bank.

Small is beautiful

There are smaller banks in India that have been goldmines for their investors, and not just for their acquisition value, though this is always a possibility a few years down the line when competition among banks in India becomes more intense and when the artificial barriers are lifted. The inherent quality of some of these smaller banks makes them stand out in the crowded banking space. The common threads that run through these low-profile but highly profitable banks are the sustained and profitable growth through all the change that has happened in the industry, the strong managements often carrying the legacy of the founder, and an unshakable niche market in their home and surrounding states.

A niche actor

Federal Bank has benefited from a market niche that is almost impossible to replicate. The 75-year-old bank is based in the southern state of Kerala, whose most famous export is its people, many of whom are migrant workers in Middle Eastern countries. For the longest time the key foreign exchange inflow into the state was from remittances made by migrant workers. Given the dozens of years of serving the specific banking needs of that migrant population, Federal Bank established itself very clearly in that niche, and even for their other needs it was a bank of choice. Nearly 300 of its 500 branches are concentrated in that one state. It grew with the rising wealth levels of these people, but now has taken its business far ahead in terms of diversity, but without altering its base. The giant ICICI Bank owned 5.76% in Federal Bank but this has been disinvested entirely. And the Federal Bank itself is now on the prowl for acquisitions, and will likely raise funds through an issue of global depository receipts (GDR). It gave up the chase for another southern bank, the Lord Krishna Bank, citing differences over valuation, but its appetite for inorganic growth has obviously been whetted.

An unrecognized performer

One of the more enigmatic banking successes in India is that of Karur Vysya Bank. This is a very low-profile, 90-year-old bank, almost entirely focused in southern Indian states, with just two states accounting for 80% of its branches. It is almost negligible in terms of size compared to the Indian banking giants, with just 200-odd branches and a little over $1.6 billion in assets and just $190 million in market capitalization, but it could teach its larger competitors a thing or two about focus and sustainable growth. When most Indian banks have sacrificed everything, including sustainable RoAs, in the name of market share and growth, Karur Vysya Bank stands out. The bank has one of the highest RoAs – at 1.4% – in the entire Indian banking industry, rivaled only by the highly focused HDFC Bank and more than 60% higher than industry averages. Its high capital adequacy ratio will enable significant growth without disturbing the capital structure. That is a notable achievement since it has grown as aggressively as the rest of the sector. It has also pursued delinquent accounts with a vigor that others would do well to emulate; its recovery rates are the highest in the industry and net accretions to delinquent accounts are the lowest.

However, despite its outstanding fundamentals and financial performance its valuations are modest in comparison with some others. It traded at a price to book ratio of just above 1, when the industry average stood at 1.65. With the market being growth obsessed, and with other banks being more in the news and also more actively traded, as opposed to any fundamental reason, banks such as KVB are less thought of. Interestingly, despite their small size foreign investment funds hold an identical 15% in both Federal Bank and KVB. This level of institutional interest is rarely seen among smaller capitalized companies outside the banking sector, or even among other smaller banks.

The potential for banks in India, given their increasing share of the GDP pie, is only overshadowed by the potential for the infrastructural sector that covers a wide swath of the economy. The creation and expansion of physical infrastructure in India is now being undertaken on a massive scale, given that Indian policy-makers have finally understood the link between growth in manufacturing and the creation of jobs. The service sector is a great growth engine but is not capable of creating the kind of jobs that India needs. For truly meaningful, wealth-creating growth the country needs greater investment in industry, and industry needs gigantic investment in infrastructure, especially power, roads, water, ports, airports and telecommunications.

A HIGHWAY TO HEAVEN; THE EMERGENCE OF INFRASTRUCTURE IN INDIA

As any visitor to India will readily acknowledge the country's infrastructure is woefully inadequate and greatly belies its status as an emerging global economic power. Surface transport infrastructure – such as broad and well-maintained roads, which are taken for granted in developed Asian economies and in the West – is to a large part only an illusion to an Indian. What is currently considered to be a network of "national highways" linking most of the major metropolises is in reality little more than glorified country roads with single lanes clogged with slow-moving traffic.

Having had so much exposure to the abysmal level of infrastructure, it is difficult for me to believe that this was not always the case. It has often been said that when the British left India in 1947, they left the country with the best infrastructure in Asia. One can look at this negatively, and say that the infrastructure that then consisted of a network of railways linking strategic areas, roads and ports, and a few thousand megawatts of power were only meant to facilitate British rule and hasten the export of raw materials and the import of finished goods. But the British did leave, and the base for a potentially fantastic economic infrastructure was already in place. All that was needed was sustainable investment at the right time in order to expand it, but alas that did not come about – not for a few decades, at least. Over time it became a popular misconception in India that the backlog of infrastructure that was left to be created could not be bridged any time soon, at least until the Chinese showed everyone what was possible with their creation of gigantic infrastructure in a short time span. Now the Indian government is thinking that they cannot emulate the Chinese example soon enough.

This awakening has been late in coming but is welcome nonetheless. India, unfortunately, after a little over half a century of independence has the worst infrastructure among the major economies in Asia. I would, however, prefer to take a more positive spin and say that thanks to decades of corruption and neglect that retarded infrastructure creation, India now has the best "potential" for investment in infrastructure, not only in Asia but in the world. And for the companies – whether in the private or public sector – the opportunity to grow and grow fast is unprecedented, thanks to the building momentum in capital spending. Some of the best performers in recent times in the Indian stock market have been infrastructure-related and construction stocks. This buoyancy in investor sentiment is not restricted to those companies that are bidding for government contracts to put up power plants, build roads and ports, and redevelop airports, but extends to companies that are shipping in capital goods, building the trucks and earth-moving equipment, manufacturing compressors to drive drilling equipment, putting up sanitation and water pipelines in Indian cities, and providing the logistics for the movement of vital goods from the ports to the hinterland.

With the forceful initiative of former prime minister Atal Behari Vajpayee, the country is beginning to see the genesis of a modern transport network and the beginnings of meaningful investment in rural infrastructure. India has the second-largest network of roads in the world after the United States, but they are not of a comparable quality. The former government's thrust was to link the four major metropolises in India – Mumbai (in the west), New Delhi (in the north), Kolkatta (in the east) and Chennai (in the south) – with a multi-lane expressway known as the Golden Quadrilateral, which then becomes the nodal framework for a world-class national transportation infrastructure that would link up other major centers. A total of 48 road projects costing $12 billion are currently under construction. But the total investment being anticipated for roads is much higher (see table 7.2).

Table 7.2: Major road projects under construction			
Project	Distance	Cost (US$)	Completion
Golden quadrilateral	5,000 kms	$5.5 billion	2007
North–South–East–West corridor	7,000 kms	$7.5 billion	2008
Interlinking highways	10,000 kms	$7 billion	2008

One reason why so much has happened in road infrastructure is its tremendous impact on economic costs. Freight is one gigantic cost factor that weighs on Indian industry, since raw materials and finished goods are usually shipped across enormous distances, mostly by road. This is a huge mark up over the cost of production. The slow speed of transportation and inefficient load carrying are major problems. Even though the speed limit on Indian highways is 65 kilometers per hour, transporters on average do half that. The cost imposed by inefficient transportation impacts different industries differently, but by some estimates it usually would range between 40% and 150% over the cost of production. Inefficient and poorly maintained road network systems mean smaller vehicles must be used, longer turnaround times, and higher costs of operations for transporters, expenses which are in turn recovered from users.

The earlier government's plan also included putting up or modernizing several brand-new airports and ports, and an expansion of the railway network. The new UPA government has emphasized the importance of and its focus on building up rural infrastructure, including basic structures for irrigation and vital components for post harvest, such as cold storage facilities for farm produce. This investment will yield substantial benefits in enhancing food quality while reducing costs, considering that 30% or more of India's harvest is lost on the farm itself due to both improper handling and a complete absence of modern storage and transportation facilities. The creation of storage and handling facilities at the farm-gate will provide a strong fillip to India's fledgling food processing industry.

With the thrust of providing infrastructure to the Indian industrial and agricultural sectors which have been badly neglected, the government very clearly has been signaling its change of focus from running the economy from a control perspective to managing the economy from a growth standpoint. The finance minister Mr P Chidambaram has repeatedly said at various forums in India and overseas that the GDP growth rate of 7% (between 2002 and 2007) is not enough, and that the sustainable growth has to be somewhere around 10%. That the operating environment has indeed changed and that there is a new, almost missionary zeal within the government to bring about the physical implements to enable growth can be seen in the manner in which it wants to go about it. Gone are the thoughts that infrastructure creation is the sacred duty of the public sector. The message being given to everyone willing to listen is that private investment will be welcomed without too many questions being asked (see table 7.3), though a preferred route may be a public–private partnership (see box "Public-private partnership as a policy").

The investment potential in roads is mind-boggling, with just 2% of the national highway network currently being four-laned while over two-thirds of the network consists of single-lane roads (see table 7.4). The state highways are in even worse shape and badly need upgrading. To add to this endeavor is the effort to expand this network, which has the potential to keep Indian infrastructure companies busy for a very long time.

Table 7.3: Wooing the foreign investor with greater control

FDI infrastructure equity ceiling	
Real estate (townships)	100%
Roads	100%
Power	100%
Airlines	74%
Airport	74%
Banks (private)	74%
Mining	74%
Telecom	74%
Defense	26%
Insurance	26%

Table 7.4: Scope for the road sector – existing roads and highways

Type of road	Km
Total highway length	58,000
Single lane	38,860
Four lane	1,160
Road network	2,500,000
State highways	138,000

Just to give an example of the kind of industrial talent available in India that can be tapped to assist in infrastructure building, one should simply cast a cursory glance at Bharat Earth Movers Ltd (BEML). The company, 60% owned by the Indian government, is Asia's second-largest manufacturer of earth-moving equipment and is India's largest, controlling 70% of the domestic market. Close to two-thirds of its revenues comes from providing almost every conceivable piece of heavy machinery and ancillary equipment to the mining and construction industry (the equipment used by both industries has a lot of overlap since there is a lot of excavating, shoveling, bull dozing and dumping in both). Its performance during fiscal 2004–05 was nothing short of spectacular, though revenues grew modestly by 5% to $417 million, its net income grew 730% to nearly $40 million, which also explains why its market capitalization raced from $230 million to over $700 million towards the end of 2005. The best part is that this earnings result came from a qualitative change in its operations.

Public-private partnership as a policy

The roads sector has seen a lot of cooperation between the government – through its agency the National Highways Authority of India (NHAI) – and various private companies. The partnership has seen the successful completion of 13 projects. The criteria that the government applies for this kind of cooperation is that there should be a minimum of 40% private equity contribution and government support will be up to 20% of the project cost. In addition there is a "viability gap funding" component from the government that will cover any project shortfalls.

The other sectors to which this policy is being applied are airports, railways, seaports, water treatment and sewerage systems. So far road projects have seen the most successful implementation of this policy.

Like most giant public sector companies that were formed and funded by the government, BEML are technology leaders driven by strong in-house research and development. But like most public sector companies, they have also had a checkered earnings history and a management that is predisposed towards ignoring the stock market's views on its operations and fundamentals. There was a time just a couple of years ago when the BEML stock traded at a fraction of the per share value of its cash holdings, as an indication of how poorly the market thought of its prospects, making it a seriously undervalued stock. How much would have changed, both in the company's true fundamentals and in the management's attitudes, in the intervening period is difficult to say. Despite the qualitative change in earnings and the stock market's appreciation of that fact, the business remains a very competitive one with the mining and infrastructure companies being allowed to freely import whatever machinery they need. But there is potential for earnings growth (a further appreciation in the stock is another matter given already steep valuations) because of its strong exposure to the defense sector, which we will visit a little later when we discuss the increasing number of companies catering to India's increased defense needs.

Companies supplying equipment may or may not benefit from the current expansion, depending on how competitive they are on pricing compared to their global competitors. But with between 65% and 80% of the various construction projects going to Indian companies, some of the well-established infrastructure and construction companies with strong project implementation skills – such as Madhucon Projects Ltd – will do exceptionally well. The infrastructure sector more than any other is peppered with very well-run companies, probably because most are managed by technocrats or engineers, so choosing the best among them is never easy. Madhucon Projects lacks the scale of operations of a company like Hindustan Constructions, or the size, depth and complexity of industry giant Larsen & Toubro Ltd, but it stands out as an example of what is possible in India today for focused, efficient and technology-savvy companies. It has been around for 15 years (though longer if one considers the operations of an older company it acquired), and by now has diversified very well with a firm presence across various sub-segments of the infrastructure industry, including roads, highways, water, irrigation, bridges and canals. Less than one-fifth of their revenues comes from the water and irrigation segment but it has cumulatively put up 375 kilometers of irrigation canals, including a number of prestigious projects. They have an unleveraged balance sheet, which is virtually unheard of in this industry, where reliance on debt financing of the balance sheet is the norm, but it also means that growth for the foreseeable future can easily be sustained with incremental debt funding, and no dilution of equity need happen.

They have raised their profile substantially in recent months after winning prestigious contracts for building portions of the Golden Quadrilateral. Highway construction and road building now has become increasingly a growing source of revenues, and highways alone contributed to 70% of its revenues. Over the years the company has built more than 1,000 kilometers of road. It has also developed skills in tunnel building, given some of the challenging terrain these companies come across in India. Among the more prestigious projects it completed was a tunnel cut deep into rock for the Konkan Railway, which is one of the most advanced railway networks in India. Its multi-engineering skill has been amply demonstrated in its management of a variety of coal-handling projects, usually considered to be a test of engineering ability. It has developed technology that enables the extraction of coal involving the loading of large-capacity rakes in perfect synchronization and coordination. But their pioneering technology has not been restricted to coal handling. It has proven its expertise in turnkey projects as well. For example, it has constructed a heavy engineering workshop for the maintenance of 170-ton rear dump haulers and other heavy equipment, which was done for the first time in India. The other major projects involve moving of coal entirely by machinery and stacking and loading of coal in moving wagons. These were noteworthy advances done for an industry notorious for its ancient technology and manual exertions.

We are seeing that roads and highways are a priority for the government and, along with the power sector, today comprise the bulk of the opportunity for companies, especially with the importance being given to private sector participation. So though this is a small company today it really is at the right place at the right time. Companies such as Madhucon Projects fully epitomize the growing clout of private sector companies in infrastructure building, and reflect how strong the growth is likely to be for most companies.

The full extent of private sector participation and their growing role is relatively unknown. According to data from the Indian government-run Central Statistical Organization (CSO), the share of private investments in total investment has accelerated to 72.5% in 2002, from 52.5% in the late 1980s. This involvement has huge implications for Indian industries that have the skills and the access to resources but are looking for unrestrained growth opportunities. A more telling example of private sector participation has been telecommunications. Private companies, both Indian and foreign, have pumped in billions of dollars setting up fixed line and mobile telephone networks, backed by a fiber optic backbone across the country, while government-owned former monopolies had to race to keep up.

Water, water everywhere, but not a drop to...

The energy needs of India are now being discussed all over the globe, and India's efforts at achieving a combination of self-sufficiency and unrestricted access to select global energy reserves is well documented. But its efforts at ensuring water security and the government's plans to enable access and distribution of this most precious of all commodities is relatively unknown. India has survived with major loopholes in its energy policy, but naturally lacks that luxury in the case of access to water. The key thrust of the government's development agenda then is in access and distribution of water and the creation of the necessary infrastructure to ensure water security. Not surprisingly, the government expects an annual investment of close to $6 billion in the creation of water infrastructure, not only largely irrigation and canals but also including bringing in piped water to urban areas and waste water facilities in rural and urban areas. It has been well documented by now that the major threat of instability in India is not border wars or terrorism or energy security but the threat of water wars within the various states and communities in the countries. The Indian finance minister recently referred to these ongoing and potentially large water conflicts as "mini civil wars".

Urban water infrastructure is one of the most pressing needs and suffers greatly from underinvestment and mismanagement. The country's capital New Delhi alone is short of a daily requirement of water by some 4,000 million liters. A World Bank report pointed out that 30% of the country's population is now urbanized, and this trend is only accelerating. So the need is to quickly design and expand the water-, sanitation- and environment-related infrastructure in most urban centers. Preservation of water bodies will begin to see growing investments since most cities are now tapping heavily into ground water reservoirs for their requirement, which has led to the deterioration of the water table levels and represents a trend that needs to be held back.

A very interestingly positioned company is Thermax Ltd, a company based in the Western city of Pune, a region known for its hard-boiled engineering companies. The company was founded by the Aga family, and is still largely family owned but has been professionally run for a long time. The company is not very large by the standards of the capital goods industry, with fiscal 2004–05 revenues at $210 million, but it is positioned in such a way that it is exposed to the growth opportunity in several industries and is almost a microcosm of the opportunity in India. One of its key growth businesses is water management and waste water treatment solutions, a wonderful business to be in today's increasingly environmentally conscious and water-challenged world. That particular division produced just $20 million in revenues, but its size belies the company's clout in the industry and the gigantic opportunity before it. It has productized its waste water treatment system and has focused on implementing waste water treatment for gas stations. It has also begun to get contracts for cleaning and preservation of water bodies.

More funding is expected both from the Indian government and from various bodies such as the World Bank for the conservation of water bodies, given the tremendous pressure being put on them to save ground water. Compared to its other divisions this business is seeing only modest growth rates – in the low double digits – but will likely be a major contributor since the basic issues it addresses surrounding environmental concerns are only increasing and are attracting better funding.

While the issue of ground water management is beginning to be addressed, Indian cities have been forced to address the issue of floodwater in recent years. Several cities in India – Mumbai and Bangalore in particular – were hit by record rainfall in 2005, with over 500 millimeters dumped in a day or two. This brought home even to India's urban residents just how much investment is needed in infrastructure such as storm drains and more and better sewerage.

This realization alone will open up numerous opportunities for several companies with a diverse range of expertise. Our journey to explore the depth of the opportunity before the Indian economy and Indian companies showcases the immense breadth and depth of talent and resources that has been built in India which has so far been kept well hidden. Among the many, many companies that will benefit from the impact of investments in water and related infrastructure are infrastructure players, material and equipment suppliers such as Electrosteel Castings, Welspun Gujarat, Kirloskar Pneumatic, Cummins India and ION Exchange, and water infrastructure builders IVRCL Infrastructure.

The southern Indian states have been proactive in infrastructure building, and especially in creating and improving their water infrastructure. A mid-sized water infrastructure company based in Chennai in South India, IVRCL Infrastructure, has been quietly bagging prestigious projects in quick succession and in increasing size and complexity, ranging from building storm drains in Bangalore to desalination plants in Chennai to a water supply network to the city of Ahmedabad. IVRCL Infrastructure has been awarded over $700 million worth of projects in 2005 alone, making it one of the fastest-growing infrastructure companies in India. It has concentrated heavily on water-related projects, and nearly three-quarters of its $250 million revenues comes from related projects. Though it has begun to get some good projects in road construction as well, this will nicely diversify the revenue stream while it benefits fully from the growth in water infrastructure.

The management has expressed its view that it expects to compound revenues at 25% annually for the next 10 years. If it continues to grow at the rate management envisages, by 2010 it will be producing close to $1 billion in revenues. In the recent past it has compounded revenues at 40%; if this is sustained for the next five years (and this is possible for many companies involved in infrastructure creation in India) its revenues will grow to $1.5 billion. The company has been active in irrigation projects in the southern state of Andhra Pradesh, whose government has plans to invest $10 billion in water infrastructure by 2010, of which the company has pre-qualified for over $2 billion worth of projects, so this kind of growth is readily possible. IVRCL has lined up a $250 million overseas depositary offering to fund its potential growth so investors outside of India can have a clear shot at it.

While there are a number of companies among the existing large players that are looking to benefit from the fast-paced creation or improvement in water and related infrastructure, water management is still a relatively specialized and focused business with very few large players active in that segment. ION Exchange is a small but reasonably well-known player in the water management business. They have been around for four decades operating in India and overseas, but have revenues of just $55 million. Their prime customer base is the industrial segment, to which they offer treatment of water used in production processes, recycling and extraction of elements for reuse. They have an installed base of pollution control equipment and recycling plants worldwide. They have broadened their industrial business globally and achieved good results and name recognition. Now they are expanding into the household market, selling home water purifiers adapted to Indian conditions, making it a play on growing retail awareness and demand for a critical health product, in a country where water-borne disease is a gigantic problem.

The worry over ground water depletion and the fact that nearly 80% of ground water in India may be contaminated is prompting governments to pay more attention to water bodies on the surface and the need to build infrastructure that can bring in piped water and distribute it in major and minor urban centers. This growing need for pipes is a bonanza for companies such as Electrosteel Castings Ltd and Welspun Gujarat Stahl Rohrer Ltd. Both are very high-quality companies that have proven their competence over several decades in operation. Electrosteel Castings, a 50-year-old company, is in a league of its own, being India's largest maker of ductile iron pipes, with 200,000 tons of capacity. Ductile pipes, as opposed to regular cast iron pipes, are far more versatile for Indian conditions since they are highly resistant to corrosion as well as being resistant to fatigue.

The ductile iron technology, which involves adding magnesium to molten iron, has been around for a long time but its application is just being appreciated in India now. Thus the company's solutions to India's water problems are cost-effective since these pipes require minimal inspection, fewer replacements and are safer as the water is protected from ground contamination. With Indian cities now prone to flooding and the seepage from sewers causing major health challenges, the shift to ductile pipes and away from cast iron pipes is a certainty. The company has also positioned itself as an integrated water and waste water solutions company, with the ability to implement turnkey projects, taking full advantage of emerging trends to forward integrate. The engineering business now provides 15% of its annual revenues and this will likely increase, improving profitability along the way since it generates high margins. Even in this case, though the company is based in eastern India, the bulk of its value-added work is coming from projects in southern India. ECL's business understandably was never known for its growth, since the product was not widely used as it is beginning to be and the company even today has no foreign institutional holdings, probably because of extremely low liquidity and small size (market cap at less than $200 million).

The overall macro spending requirement on hard infrastructure such as power, highways, sea ports, airports and railways has been estimated by the Indian government and pitched at the highest level to foreign investors at a minimum of $150 billion by 2012, while some government estimates point to a far greater investment requirement of up to $250 billion over the next five to seven years (see figure 7.5). To add to this will be the private sector's demand for capital creation as companies expand, which by some estimates could be around $50 billion in the next few years but could easily surpass that figure since the expansion in the steel industry alone will absorb nearly 70% of that amount and the expansion in refining capacities would account for another 15%, while the rest of Indian industry appears hungry for capital expansion too, pushing up the total anticipated capital investment.

The companies involved in this capital creation effort are likely to grow, and for certain a lot of global and overseas corporations will increasingly be involved, especially in joint ventures, and many already are. But the major thrust will be on domestic companies and locally available capability, though funding may be sought through ADRs and GDRs in US and European capital markets. The effect of large-scale orders pouring in on the companies concerned will understandably be huge, and this process has already begun. Most of

Figure 7.5: Scope of investment required in infrastructure in different sectors (5 to 7 years)

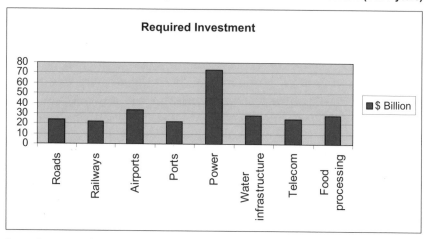

Source: Government of India

the engineering, construction, consultancy and procurement companies are reporting an unprecedented growth in orders and an all-time
high in order backlog. Many of these companies have between three
and six years' worth of backlog piled up. So it is almost a given that
some of the best quality of growth will be seen in those companies
involved in meeting the important physical infrastructure needs of
India.

The boom in equities in India in 2005 stood out due to the leadership role played by infrastructure and construction stocks, which is
almost unprecedented since each of the earlier liberalization-era stock
market booms was led by commodity, manufacturing or information
technology companies. Many of these infrastructure companies have
been widely recognized in 2005, but in reality they have been stellar
performers for a decade or more, providing shareholders with strong
capital appreciation, irrespective of whether they participated in past
booms or not. Nagarjuna Construction Company Ltd is one that easily comes to mind due to its rapid – and more importantly profitable
– growth for at least a decade. I first came across this stock in 1993
when it was relatively unheard of outside a few circles. At that time,
companies such as these were on the fringes of stock market consciousness since they were in an industry where nothing much was
expected to happen. But despite the challenges of operating in a difficult business environment in the 1980s and 1990s, the company has
rewarded its earliest shareholders superbly and continues to do so.
Today it is a market favorite, and that is a well-deserved accolade.

The company rivals industry leaders in the breadth and depth of
construction services that it offers, which include for the main part

highways and roads but also include water-related infrastructure, commercial buildings, townships, industrial structures and transmission lines. NCCL too is a south India-based company, but even though capital formation is taking place at a faster pace in the south and NCL is at the forefront, it has spread out in several other regions of India. It has shown sound judgment in going for large projects in collaboration with its main rivals (in one case it teamed up with Hindustan Constructions for a river project – the Godavari Lift project). This could turn out to be a very viable growth strategy. It has close to $1.2 billion in outstanding orders; this comprises as much as 4.3 times its 2005 revenues and nearly three times its expected revenues of $400 million for 2006. The stock has been one of the top performers in the Indian equity markets in 2005, gaining almost four times in one year. In November 2005, *Forbes* Asia included the company on its list of the 200 best Asian companies with under $1 billion in revenues.

The construction sector in India is a fragmented one even though it comprises nearly 6% of the economy and is roughly sized at $25 billion. The size of many of the companies is small by global standards, and they have not grown all that rapidly largely because many are still privately held, and those that are publicly traded typically have a large dominating shareholder (usually family controlled), where dilution is not looked upon favorably. It is the presence of these companies that makes the business very competitive, since there is a lot of undercutting in order to win contracts. Construction and infrastructure companies in general face challenges imposed by rapid growth, and it will be interesting to see how they cope, though some of these companies have shown signs of business maturity and the ability to cope with rising capital needs and growth. Their ability to raise capital is critical since a large portion of the industry's attention is shifting to housing which is among the fastest growing segments of the economy and which has been dominated by small local companies. According to the Building Material and Technology Promotion Council the level of urban housing stock is likely to increase from 78 million units to 115 million units by 2011.

Energy and infrastructure

As in construction, in energy too India has traditionally not been renowned for its prowess. The problem has been that decades of state ownership of oil-producing and marketing companies, inadequate investment in oil and gas exploration and the use of older technology have made extraction of oil very slow and difficult, which was fine when the economic engine was chugging along at a slow pace. It was only from the 1990s that the demand for oil began to pick up momentum, and the growth rate in oil consumption now has grown to around 7% to 8% annually, keeping pace with GDP growth, and it is likely to exceed that figure as macroeconomic growth rates begin to accelerate. As a result, India imports around two-thirds of its oil and one-third of its natural gas requirements. Indian refiners, with an annual capacity of 137 million tons, consume nearly three million barrels of oil per day, making it one of the bigger consumers in the world, though by all indications this is just the beginning as the industry is heading for a major expansion. Despite this growth rate and the increase in demand the per capita consumption of energy is still miniscule.

Knowing that it is just a matter of time before the per capita demand for fuel picks up, the government threw open oil exploration to the private sector in 1999 by inviting bids for exploration blocks, bringing in new technology from the global oil industry and also opening the oil infrastructure to private sector investment, including transportation, pipelines, refining and retailing of fuel and other products, whether through gas stations or piped gas to homes. The opening up of the sector throws open opportunities, not only because of the billions that will be spent in discovery and exploitation of India's hydrocarbon assets but also in the import and distribution of energy from overseas.

In just a few years after the award of the first set of exploration licenses in 2000, India has become associated with some of the most spectacular discoveries of hydrocarbon reserves anywhere in the world. The bulk of these discoveries in the form of natural gas have been made since October 2002, when Reliance Industries Ltd made the world's biggest gas discovery for that year off India's east coast, with estimated reserves at 13 to 14 trillion cubic feet (tcf). Since then a number of other discoveries have been made, including one in mid-2005 of a giant offshore gas field by Gujarat State Petroleum Corporation (GSPC), with estimated reserves of 20 tcf. Including other discoveries, the total reserves from new discoveries are estimated to yield close to 40 tcf of natural gas, making India one of the most exciting places to be in the oil exploration world, and it has begun to attract a lot of attention from major oil companies. The fifth round of bidding held in mid-2005 attracted 64 bids for 20 exploration blocks. Even though five rounds of bidding for licenses have been completed, only a fraction of the blocks allotted have been explored and already spectacular discoveries have been made. ONGC Ltd, the country's largest exploration and production (E&P) company, has taken 57% of the oil blocks awarded so far, while Reliance Industries, the private sector oil giant, has taken 26% of the blocks. As an indication of how serious this has become, ONGC, a company that currently controls the bulk of India's domestic production of oil and gas, will be investing $2.5 billion a year for the next several years in its domestic oil exploration program. The momentum is building for the rest of the sector too, with the Reliance Industries gas field of the east coast likely to come into production in 2008, and GSPC's giant field will be able to bring its field into production sometime after that.

But there is anticipation in the energy industry that even these discoveries may not be enough to meet future demand, keeping in mind the growth rates of consumption from industries, particularly power generators and fertilizers manufacturers. Thus the demand for imported energy from a hungry and fast-growing nation is a major catalyst for creating a network of specialized ports, plants, pipelines and retail outlets. The investments that are currently being made, and those being contemplated, in the transportation of fuels by surface and by pipelines and the generation and distribution of power have come as a windfall for a number of companies involved.

Though currently most of the inflow of fuel is in the form of crude oil, increasingly it is natural gas. India will import liquefied natural gas (LNG) in ever-larger quantities as it has suddenly been awakened to its potential, especially to fuel its power plants. Even some old thermal power plants are to be converted to gas-based plants over the next few years. With delays expected in extracting gas from newly discovered Indian gas fields, the Indian oil ministry has estimated that by 2012 India's total imports of LNG will equal 60 million tons (roughly the quantity that Japan imports today). That is a lot of growth in imports in a very short period of time, since India imports less than 10 million tons today. India's current consumption of natural gas is around 150 million standard cubic meters per day (mscmd); this is expected to rise to 313 mscmd by 2012 and 391 mscmd by 2025. The current domestic availability of natural gas is under 100 mscmd, and by 2012 is expected to be about 150 mscmd from domestic gas fields. Even if large gas finds still happen in the domestic market, commercializing the fields and the building of infrastructure to evacuate the gas is a long, drawn-out and complicated process, especially since a lot of the finds have been in offshore, deepwater blocks. We have already seen some examples of scheduled production dates being postponed by a year or so by large gas field operators such as Reliance Industries due to the complexities involved, including the final utilization of that gas.

The companies that are in one way or another involved in the effort to facilitate the availability of gas and its utilization include Petronet LNG Ltd, Gas Authority of India Ltd, the country's largest shipping company Shipping Corporation of India (SCI), and a bunch of companies providing infrastructural services. SCI (with revenues for fiscal 2004–05 at $825 million) is now investing heavily in energy transport, particularly in the acquisition of LNG carriers and crude oil tankers. The Indian ministry of shipping has estimated that by 2012 India will require at least 25 LNG carriers in operation, and by 2025 the fleet strength will have to grow to a minimum of 34 carriers. SCI owns just two Maltese-registered LNG vessels (in a joint venture with various other public sector companies), so a gigantic expansion is now being planned and this company will very likely lead the effort. The capital requirements of this business are huge since LNG carriers are complex vessels, and in all likelihood acquisitions will continue to be through joint ventures with companies such as Petronet LNG Ltd (the re-gasification and pipeline company, and currently the other major investor in the two LNG subsidiaries). An added advantage is that India will source a large chunk of its LNG requirements from nearby Qatar, making it a short-haul route for SCI and others, thus improving turnaround time and operating efficiencies.

The future of Indian shipping has shifted towards the energy sector, and this is more pronounced for Shipping Corporation of India, which is the first mover not only in LNG but earlier also in crude oil transport and in the transport of refined products. It owns 83 vessels, largely comprising crude oil tankers, petro products tankers and dry bulk carriers. GE Shipping, the second-largest shipping company in India with 41 vessels, on its part has traditionally devoted a large chunk of its fleet to the transport of bulk commodities and dry cargo but is looking to expand into crude oil tankers. There is a tendency, especially by the public sector oil companies, to charter cargoes through Indian flag carriers, though the government officially withdrew that sole privilege for SCI in 2002 to allow more competition. There is also a desire by the Indian government, especially the shipping ministry, to import the bulk of the LNG requirement using Indian-owned vessels. Thus there is the making of a great monopoly for Indian shipping companies in India's future energy transportation, probably making it the only sector to have one. The Indian ship-owning industry naturally loves the idea, and they bolster their case citing the examples of Japan and South Korea, the other two large importers of natural gas who overwhelmingly use national flag carriers to import their fuel.

Eighty per cent of SCI is owned by the Indian government but it is finally heading for partial divestment in 2006, with the shipping ministry looking to sell 15% of the stock.

In the past, a number of global shipping companies were interested in SCI but a lot of controversy has dogged the SCI disinvestment with the government worried about foreign ownership over India's energy transportation, but it has begun to show encouraging signs of relenting. SCI could have higher growth rates than its domestic competitors, considering the investments it is currently making in acquiring newer very large crude carriers (VLCCs) of a significantly large tonnage, where the average size is over 300,000 dead weight tons (DWT), and it is scrapping a lot of its older, smaller crude tankers.

In order to transport natural gas it has to be liquefied (a process that greatly reduces its volume, thus more of the product can be carried in a single cargo making it more economical), loaded onto LNG carriers and then brought to re-gasification terminals, where it is converted back into gas and then transported by pipeline to its final destination. In India so far it is Petronet LNG that owns the two re-gasification terminals. One LNG handling terminal is on India's west coast and is able to handle five million tons of the liquefied gas (roughly about 19 million standard cubic meters per day), though it is being doubled to 10 million tons, while another port of 2.5 million tons has also been built by the company on the southern coast which is being doubled as well. So if the 2012 import level of 60 million tons of LNG is to be matched with handling capacity, then a few billion dollars will need to be poured into that infrastructure, with Petronet LNG capturing a large chunk of it. It has been estimated that at least eight LNG handling terminals will be needed across the country by 2010.

Petronet LNG (Gaz de France owns 15% of its equity) then becomes the focal point of any discussion on LNG usage as the fuel to drive India in the future, since it is capitalizing on that need to build a network of handling terminals and pipelines to carry re-gasified LNG to various bulk consumers across the country. They've managed to notch up a record of sorts with RasGas, the Qatari state-owned gas producer that is emerging as India's main supplier. Petronet LNG has guaranteed to lift 7.5 million tons of LNG from Qatar annually for 25 years, and this represents the largest such contract entered into anywhere in the world. In just a couple of years it has revenues nearing $1 billion (expected for fiscal 2005–06 based on annualized numbers), and will progress from a cash profit of $10 million in 2005 to a net income of around $40 million to $45 million in 2006, only its second year of operations (the wonders of high energy prices!). In recent quarters it has been doubling its revenues, and it already has a market cap in excess of $1 billion. And in just a couple of years it has already doubled its gas handling capacities and is moving to create a solid cargo port at the site of its Dahej terminal on the western Indian coast, thus creating a base for faster growth. The business model works well since its buyers of gas are the three oil and gas marketing companies that also control a large chunk of its equity and with whom it has a back-to-back off-take agreement for 25 years, thus matching its commitment to RasGas with a commitment from its buyers.

Gas Authority of India Ltd (GAIL) is a great play on the emerging importance of natural gas in India's energy mix. It has positioned itself very rapidly as an integrated energy player from investing in exploration of natural gas fields overseas and in India, running LNG terminal to building new pipelines to carry gas across the country. The company is the dominant player in the transportation of gas through pipelines in India, with an 84% market share, carrying 72 mscmd of gas. It has also moved into downstream activities setting up petrochemical plants to produce ethylene and polymers as well as marketing gas in major Indian cities. The transportation of natural gas, supply of LPG, and a derivative petrochemicals business produced revenues of almost $3 billion in fiscal 2005. GAIL will see a lot of growth ahead as it aggressively seeks to add to its pipeline capacity besides expanding its other businesses such as power. It is one of the companies that now holds an equity stake in Enron's former mega power project in western India.

Though LNG as a fuel source has been around from the mid-1960s it is viewed as the new energy source for India since it was first imported into the country only as recently as 2004. ONGC is the lead investor in India's efforts at uncovering its natural gas and oil assets. Besides being the largest exploration company in India, ONGC is also one of India's largest by revenues ($13 billion for fiscal 2004–05) and market capitalization ($32 billion). It is also India's lead investor in the future of its drive to secure sources of energy from outside the country. The company currently owns a network of oil and gas fields across the globe and is hotly pursuing more such opportunities. In recent times they have launched the world's largest seismic data acquisition program, which is a prelude to the drilling of test wells and is an indication of what is going to happen.

Since other Indian domestic oil exploration companies too are going to invest heavily, and by all indications the bulk of India's oil and gas discoveries lie offshore in deep water blocks, for SCI and also for Great Eastern Shipping the opportunity lies in capitalizing on the huge exposure to India's offshore exploration activities. GE Shipping controls a large fleet of offshore supply vessels (OSVs) and a couple of oil rigs that are being fully utilized given the tight supply conditions for OSVs and offshore production and supply assets globally. The division contributes to roughly one-fifth of its total revenues of $480 million for fiscal 2004–05.

Sharing the bounty

The $120 million IPO in late 2005 of Punj Lloyd Ltd would probably never have happened but for the huge boom in infrastructure construction in India, that pushed even normally high-growth companies such as this to shore up their balance sheets still further in anticipation of what is to come. The company, a specialist in building energy infrastructure, mainly gas pipe networks, was privately held for a long time and had produced over $300 million in annual revenues by the time of its IPO. In industry circles it is considered a potential rival to the best infrastructure companies in the world. The company's own ambitions are to be a cross-border provider of energy infrastructure, and it has completed some prestigious projects globally and in India, thus basing its ambitions on solid foundations.

Energy in retail

The whole world is watching India's domestic consumption of oil and gas. This has been growing steadily, and the growth rate will likely pick up in the months and years ahead. The automobile sector alone will drive demand for energy since in a few years it is anticipated that one in every six cars in the world will be bought by an Indian. There is a concerted move to convert all vehicles in the public transportation system to use compressed natural gas (CNG). The CNG experiment has been successful in China, and India has made rapid strides towards this. India is already the world's largest market for motorcycles, and growth in the utilization of motorized agricultural equipment – including tractors and in public transportation – will add to that demand significantly. Growth in domestic consumption of LPG as a cooking fuel is another major factor driving demand for an expansion in the sourcing, refining and marketing infrastructure of petroleum marketing companies in India.

GAIL, for example, has built a great amount of expertise in this business and was the first company to recognize and move quickly into the retail space for gas. Household gas in India has traditionally been consumed after being packed into iron cylinders. GAIL, in a joint venture with British Gas and the government of the state of Maharashtra, has begun to sell piped gas across Mumbai, where it already has over 130,000 retail and several hundred commercial and industrial establishments as customers. It has a similar joint venture in New Delhi with Bharat Petroleum Corporation; that venture – though not as successful as the one in Mumbai – is nonetheless becoming a significant operation. GAIL is now actively pursuing supply of piped gas across a number of northern and eastern Indian cities, each of which has a population of over a million, and will also market 40% of the LNG imported into India to industrial users and to power plants as per a government mandate.

The drive to find oil and gas in India is now at a feverish pitch, and Indian refineries and marketing companies are investing billions of dollars in expanding refining and distribution capacities. Indian Oil Corporation Ltd, India's largest company by revenues ($30 billion for fiscal 2004–05), is investing $6 billion in expanding its refining capacity, building pipelines and expanding its retail marketing base. Hindustan Petroleum Corporation Ltd is spending $2.5 billion largely to expand its retail presence, while teaming up with British Petroleum to set up a $3 billion refinery in northern India and another $3 billion for a refinery in Vishakapatnam, for which it will involve Total SA of France, while Bharat Petroleum Corporation Ltd will invest $1.75 billion to expand the number of gas stations, besides expanding refining capacity. These companies together will add 14.5 million tons of refining capacity by 2007, and could go over 30 million tons by 2010–11. Even private sector giant Reliance Industry will spend a few billion dollars in setting up a few thousand gas stations across the country, and $5.8 billion to double its refining capacity. The smaller refining companies with single refineries and regional marketing niches are all up for grabs and are being eyed by these bigger companies. Even upstream giant ONGC Ltd is looking at setting up downstream capacities in oil marketing and has already purchased Mangalore Refineries & Petrochemicals, a nine million ton refinery on the west coast that was once owned jointly by Grasim Industries and HPCL.

ONGC's interest in the refining and marketing of fuels to the domestic, industrial and retail markets is understandable; it is a great fit and offers huge scope for value addition. But the competitive layers being created within India's energy marketing sector are not all that healthy, and could undermine the long-term profitability of most companies involved. Like in banking, the fact that all the public sector oil giants have the government as their largest shareholder makes things worse, not better. Foreign oil companies are already beginning to invest in the Indian domestic energy scene, and giants such as Shell are looking to get into the retailing of gas, LPG and other products. So there is a strong argument for consolidation within these large public sector players. A worthwhile exercise would be to fold the existing companies into two large integrated organizations, each with a very significant balance sheet. For example, ONGC is entering downstream activities and IOC is seeking to become an upstream player by investing in exploration. These two companies are the natural fulcrums of two giant competing organizations, since they have already begun acquiring other oil refining and marketing companies in India (IOC has absorbed IBP Ltd, a standalone marketing company that had no refineries, only a network of gas stations), and smaller refineries and marketing companies such as Kochi Refineries, Bongaigaon Refineries and Chennai Refineries are also up for grabs. It makes sense to consolidate the larger refining and marketing companies such as HPCL and BPCL, as well as the smaller one, into one or the other of these two organizations. This creation of two large competing organizations becomes very important when considering that a sizeable portion of India's future energy will come from overseas, and muscle power will determine just how successful India is in that endeavor.

While competing in the various markets for gas may be the purview of the big boys, companies catering to their requirements for equipment and containers are emerging as sizeable and attractive players too. Everest Kanto Cylinders is one such company that has ridden the trend of marketing gas in cylinders to various consumers – including industrial, retail and automobile sectors – very well and is now in a position to cash in. At the writing of this book it was going for an IPO, which by early indications was being anticipated eagerly; its bankers were confident of selling the stock at a forward multiple (based on fiscal 2005–06 earnings) of between 10 and 12 times. The company is a great play on the automobile sector, where an emerging trend is seeing a lot of public transit vehicles, including taxi cabs, shifting from petrol to compressed natural gas-powered vehicles. Now its revenues are small, at under $50 million, but with manufacturing bases in India and the Middle East from where it caters to consumers in other countries in South and South East Asia, as well as some countries in the Middle East, and the fact that all its plants are increasing capacity and it will continue to grow in its markets, its revenue base will expand exponentially.

Power-packed returns

One of the reasons for the rise in global energy prices is the demand for it from China and India, as we've seen. And India just cannot get enough of energy. Consider these statistics: India has an installed base of 113,000 MW of power (utilizing all types of fuel including coal, gas, diesel, nuclear and hydro), which is a very significant installed power generation capacity, but even then there is a huge shortfall between generating capacity and peak demand. The gap according to The Energy and Resources Institute (TERI) is about 8%, which is quite significant. The reason is that for decades demand growth has been outpacing supply growth by at least 2% a year. This gap widened in the 1990s while the government dithered over opening up the power sector to private investment. Demand growth is likely to pick up faster as prosperity trickles down. According to TERI, 60% of Indian households, comprising the bulk of the rural consumers, use traditional sources of energy such as firewood, crop residue and animal wastes; the explosion in demand once these households start wanting their share of energy is driving feverish additions to capacity. An added impetus will come from the increase in the per capita consumption of power, which at just 350 kilograms per oil equivalent is far below the global average.

So far the country has managed to move along without adequate power by rationing it out to industries. It did not matter so much when India was insulated from the external sector and was largely a subsistence economy, growing in low single digits annually, and industry did manage to get by. The picture is different now. Not only is power essential but high quality and uninterrupted power is a critical need.

In 2001 the Indian government's Planning Commission put in place a plan to achieve zero power deficit by 2011–12. To achieve this, the government has to facilitate the creation of around another 100,000 MW of power. Essentially, a generating capacity equal to the entire base installed in the five and a half decades since independence will be created in the span of a decade. The potential for power equipment manufacturers and the project contractors is explosive. The official expectation of investment in power is around $73 billion, but if the target is to be achieved then the realistic investment required will be $100 billion, not including the investment in additional transmission and distribution equipment, which could be between $20 billion and $50 billion. These investments are not that difficult to organize when one considers that China alone will invest between $65 billion and $70 billion a year in creating additional power-generating capacity. India's investment in comparison looks modest. The investment terms, especially for foreign investors, are quite liberal since 100% foreign ownership is now permitted but the risks are enormous.

In a worrisome aspect, crucial problems have been overlooked by the government in their hurry to get mega power projects off the ground. By early 2006, 8,000 MW of new capacities have been announced. All these capacities are located along the coastline and are to be fueled with imported coal or natural gas since domestic fuel availability is an issue. So a critical factor is the availability and cost of imported fuel. This leaves the generators exposed to volatility in fuel prices which have risen sharply in recent months as compared to domestic fuel prices. The expected delay in commercializing various gas fields in India only compounds the fuel availability problem. It will not be easy to pass on price increases since generators are dependent on the individual state electricity boards (SEBs) for distribution to the consumer and the collection of dues. The poor financial health of a majority of the SEBs could potentially be a barrier to sustained investments in the power sector. Power to residential consumers is subsidized and is free to agricultural consumers, the burden of which is carried by the SEBs. There has been no clear policy direction on pricing of power and on the solvency of the state electricity boards, which will determine whether power generators will be able to protect themselves adequately from price shocks and be able to earn an adequate return on investment.

Despite these challenges the order build up for companies such as Bharat Heavy Electricals Ltd (BHEL), ABB, L&T, Engineers India Ltd and a host of others, including smaller companies such as Emco Ltd, and even for American companies such as GE and Bechtel, has been unprecedented during 2004-05 with the momentum expected to continue.

BHEL is the undisputed heavyweight champion of the Indian power equipment industry. Its operations and product and service offerings straddle the entire range of possible activities, from manufacturing boilers, steam turbines and generators up to 1,000 MW capacity for thermal plants and 500 MW for nuclear plants, hydro power and gas-based power plants, to producing diesel generator sets and setting up captive power plants for Indian industry. It just so happens that coal-fired plants (thermal plants) will remain the mainstay of the Indian power industry, but BHEL seems to be well prepared for the emerging potential in gas-fired plants as well, especially since there have been huge, commercially viable gas discoveries in India. But even a company as large and dominating as BHEL faces considerable risk from imported equipment, more so today than ever since India is one of few spots in the world where there is a major expansion taking place in the power sector; in most other places besides China, capacity addition has reduced, forcing equipment makers to seek new markets aggressively. Despite a competitive scenario, BHELs response has been to scale up its capacity from being able to produce 6,000 MW in 2005 to 10,000 MW annually by 2007.

Its activities make it the largest engineering company in India, with fiscal 2004–05 revenues at $2.3 billion, and it has cumulatively installed 65% of India's power-generating capacity over the years. Like it was for the rest of the Indian capital goods industry, the size of orders received by BHEL was unprecedented at over $4 billion received in 2004–05, and the total outstanding orders to be executed was $7 billion, with most of the growth coming from the power sector. They received contracts to set up 5,518 MW of power, which is the most aggressive ever. So the target set by the government is actually translating into orders on the ground, probably marking 2005 as the turning point for the Indian capital goods and infrastructure industry. The orders usually translate into revenues and profits in subsequent financial years, depending on the gestation period for these projects, so the impact on growth is still to come.

But anyone looking at Indian infrastructure cannot overlook Larsen & Toubro, which is almost an icon for the success of Indian engineering, not just in India but globally. It has done numerous landmark projects in India and overseas, including airports. All these have contributed to the company's near cult-like status. Its diversification into cement in the 1990s made little sense to anyone familiar with both industries, other than to speculate that the enlarged balance sheet size would help in bagging larger projects, but that too was a far-fetched argument. Its involvement with cement as a business is now history, and the company can once again focus on its very lucrative engineering franchise.

These companies and others like them will share the $100 billion plus pie that will throw up demand for a host of equipment and services. The demand for transformers for example will be huge, since every MW of generating capacity requires seven MVA of transformer capacity. This kind of demand will put manufacturers like EMCO Ltd, that derive a large portion of their income from transformers, on the investment map. EMCO's compounded revenue growth has begun to pick up substantially, especially over the 2004 and 2005 fiscal years. Its order book is already worth nearly twice its annual sales, and the company is actually in a position to pick and choose whom it supplies its product to, since credit terms and financial viability of the power generator (typical consumers of its product) are critical factors. A disproportionately large portion of its balance sheet comprises of dues owed to it by various state-run electricity generators.

A potentially significant growth area could come from executing projects where it sets up substations for various state electricity boards and from selling meters to measure power consumption. This can be a great growth area provided the government's policy of measuring the power consumption of individual customers (which incredibly has been neglected so far, largely due to populist considerations) is properly implemented. This business grew four times in 2005, though from a small base. Interestingly, the management chose to list a GDR on the Luxembourg Stock Exchange, after it raised a small amount of money. But some red flags on management quality are certainly warranted, especially on issues such as management compensation and transfer of funds to other entities, besides the huge amount of indirect and direct tax liabilities whose levies have been contested by the company. These are unfortunately some typical issues that investors will run into while assessing smaller Indian companies or companies where the promoting family's shareholding is very large.

Investment in power generation and distribution also means investment in raw material infrastructure such as coal mining. It is anticipated that the demand for coal will grow to 263 million tons by 2012, which will need an investment of $6 billion in mining infrastructure, not including the additional infrastructure such as railways. Revathi Equipment, a small Hyderabad-based manufacturer of blast hole rigs and other heavy duty coal mining equipment, thus becomes an indirect beneficiary of the expansion in power and steel, two of the biggest consumers of coal anywhere.

Power play

One of the most solid franchises that any company can hope to have is a monopoly over supply of a most vital commodity to those who need it at any cost. Well, Reliance Energy Ltd comes as close to that as possible, with a mandate to supply power to the Mumbai suburbs. The company has moved fast into other areas, notably being the first non-state company to get into power distribution in the eastern state of Orissa (where it has still to see profits) and in New Delhi, where it has been successful along with Tata Power, another superbly run Mumbai-based power company. Reliance Energy has very serious growth plans (more plants, integrated with gas finds) and is cash rich with a strong, visionary and aggressive management.

But the big daddy of them all is National Thermal Power Corporation Ltd (NTPC), with close to 20% of the installed base of power-generating capacity under its belt, revenues of over $5 billion and a market cap of $20 billion. It intends to maintain its market share, so it will have to increase its installed generation base to 46,000 MW by 2012, requiring an investment of over $20 billion. Its seven gas-fired power plants, representing 18% of its installed base of 21,000 MW, run at a poor 70% capacity (known as plant load factor), due to poor gas availability, which is why it has begun to buy into existing gas fields, as well as investing in gas liquefaction plants in India. The expected improvement in the availability of gas alone will drive revenue growth by an estimated $350 million to $400 million but a substantial equity dilution is expected through convertible bonds and equity placements which could dampen enthusiasm for the stock.

Observing their growth plans, especially given their cash flow and balance sheet strength, this giant actually resembles a growth stock rather than a staid utility. It is also one of the key stocks to watch in the big disinvestment tussle in New Delhi within the ruling coalition. Currently, only 10.5% of the stock is held by the investing public, which was offloaded to it in a $1.2 billion IPO in November 2004, the rest being held by the Indian government.

Private industry joins the party

Indian private sector industry has come to some decisions of its own with regards to its capital spending cycle. Since the mid-1990s, when

Indian industry last went on a major capital spending spree aided by large dollops of liberal equity funding raised from a booming market, until 2003–04 there had been little talk of major capital expenditure. But the Indian manufacturing sector is already running at near full capacity after several years of strong industrial growth, taking up all the production slack, and capacities in several sectors will need to be augmented soon. We have already seen the kind of demand that is emerging from the metals industry, particularly in steel, where production capacity will triple in the seven years to 2012. Similarly, large expansions are being seen in the petrochemicals and oil refining sector, and in textiles, pharmaceuticals, automobiles and consumer electronics.

Praj Industries is a maker of equipment for sugar manufacturers, and is unbelievably well positioned to ride the investment boom in sugar. Sugar companies are investing very heavily in raising their cane-crushing capacities substantially, given the rapid growth in consumption of sugar (see Chapter 6). As sugar companies expand their cane-crushing capacity they simultaneously also expand their co-generation capacity for producing power. Co-generation of power by sugar manufacturers is a bio-thermal process where bagasse, a by-product of the cane processing, is burnt to produce power. This power is used to run the plant, and the excess is fed into the power grid. Talk about eliminating waste!

We talked of Thermax Ltd in relation to its waste water treatment business and also commented on how it is positioned to grow thanks to its multi-industry exposure, which includes steel, cement, oil refining, foods, pharmaceuticals, textiles and water management. One of its most active businesses is energy conservation systems, where it installs waste heat recovery systems for the iron and steel industry. Energy conservation was not an issue when crude oil traded at $18 a barrel, but it becomes a great business with oil at $60 a barrel, especially for a company that is considered to be a market leader. This business is already beginning to see annual growth rates of 50% as Indian industry begins to clamp down on energy costs. The company's main business is selling packaged boilers and heaters, worth $50 million in fiscal 2004–05, and growing at 30% a year. Two of its fastest-growing divisions are its environment division that makes air pollution control equipment (once again for the cement, steel, power and sponge iron sectors) and the cogen division that sets up captive power plants using alternate fuels such as petroleum coke, biomass and waste heat, with both these divisions growing in excess of 100% a year and having combined revenues of nearly $60 million for 2005. Overall it grew 2005 revenues at 62%, driven by some businesses with great future potential, while the capital goods industry grew at 12.8%. Thermax could easily compound its revenues at 50% for the next couple of years. Its market cap towards the close 2005 was around $325 million.

GOOD MEDICINE

If the size of a market opportunity is an indication of the potential before any industry, and if the companies within are competent enough to grab that opportunity, then the Indian pharmaceutical industry has to be considered very seriously as a vehicle for achieving long-term capital appreciation. Before 2010, patents on $80 billion to $100 billion worth of branded drugs will be expiring globally, while $21 billion to $30 billion worth of patents will expire by the end of 2006. And Indian, Canadian, Israeli and Brazilian generic pharmaceutical companies among others are salivating at the thought of the market opportunity this presents. Even though the price of drugs coming off patents drops dramatically, the opportunity can still be extremely large, especially for the generic companies with a robust product pipeline.

And this development is only one of the opportunities before the Indian pharmaceutical industry. The domestic Indian pharmaceutical industry is quite large too. According to consulting firm McKinsey & Co, the Indian pharmaceutical industry is the fourth-largest in the world in volume terms – and fourteenth in value terms – after the US, EU and Japan, and is worth $7 billion in revenues annually, which they expect to grow to $25 billion by 2010. The industry also exports nearly $4.5 billion worth of drugs annually.

India had been heckled for a very long time by the multinational pharmaceutical companies and their industry associations, especially in the US, for the absence of a tighter regime for respecting patents on pharmaceutical products. A new patent regime, compliant under the WTO rules, finally came in force in India in April 2005. Despite the challenges the new regime brings about for the domestic Indian industry that had thrived without it so far, stocks of pharmaceutical companies did participate to a certain extent in the 2004–05 boom in Indian equities, reflecting some optimism that though drugs patented worldwide after 1995 cannot be reverse engineered in India, other big opportunities are being presented and the domestic industry is protected from the brutal tactics of the big pharmaceutical multinational corporations (MNCs). Most MNCs try hard to extend the life of the patent by making some changes to the product or by introducing a new drug delivery system. The Indian patent regime does not recognize the patentability of those developments, thus paving the way for Indian generic companies to take advantage of drugs going off patent. Besides, few major drugs have actually been patented globally after 1995, and if the drug development cycle is normally taken at 15 years then we're really looking at 2010 or so before some major patented product hits the domestic market.

Industry giant Ranbaxy Laboratories, however, lost nearly 40% of its market capitalization between year end 2004 and year end 2005 (even then its market capitalization was a formidable $3 billion, making it India's largest pharmaceutical company). The market seemed to sit up and take notice of some high-profile reversals that Indian pharmaceutical companies have suffered in their strategy of challenging existing patents of global pharmaceutical giants, which had brought significant rewards in recent years. There are plenty of doubts how successful this strategy will remain, and questions abound as to how well these large Indian pharmaceutical companies are geared towards their future. Several Indian companies have already finely tuned the strategies that they will use to exploit the emerging opportunity, besides the opportunity that is perennial in the global and Indian pharmaceutical industry.

Over the last several years, or decades in some cases, Indian companies quietly used the leeway given to them by the domestic regulatory environment that explicitly recognized only process patents to build strong research processes and product development capability. As a result, patented and branded drugs introduced by the large multinational pharmaceutical companies in India could be copied and reproduced with a few changes either in the manufacturing process or by tweaking the molecular chemistry. This strategy does not take away anything from Indian pharmaceutical companies, since they still had to demonstrate product development skills and fight bitter battles with the entrenched MNC pharmaceutical companies in India before they could establish themselves. But that was in a past era. Indian companies have now grown substantially, not only in terms of revenues and profitability but also in stature and confidence, to expand at home and in global markets too. For example, in fiscal 2004–05 Ranbaxy Laboratories derived a little over 20% of its $1.2 billion in revenues from selling generics in the US market alone, including products under its own brand name and selling its products in dozens of other nations manufactured in its plants spread across the globe. In the US market, Ranbaxy has 111 product approvals and 47 pending approvals. Dr Reddy's Laboratories (fiscal 2004–05 revenues of $450 million) is the other homegrown Indian pharmaceutical company that has grown large by first beating the MNCs at their game in India and then taking the fight to their home turf by challenging existing product patents in US and European courts. It is also one of the priciest stocks in the sector in terms of its high P/E multiple.

Ranbaxy Laboratories and Dr Reddy's Laboratories are not alone. Though no other Indian pharmaceutical company derives as large a share of its revenues from the US as Ranbaxy does, other companies have a huge exposure to markets outside of India with manufacturing plants and subsidiary companies, with a significant focus on the US and European markets, and are also equally active in relatively unregulated markets in Asia and Africa. Interacting with any of the managements of any of these companies – especially the likes of Sun Pharmaceuticals, Cipla and Zydus Cadila – one gets the sense of latent, and in many cases overt, aggression, where even acquiring companies globally is a credible option to expand their marketing presence.

Indian pharmaceutical companies have all the hallmarks of becoming truly great multinational companies in the years ahead, though they have some challenges to overcome, especially in the area of developing new drugs (new chemical entities, as they are referred to in the trade). They otherwise have the product and revenue base, have built strong research and product development capability, and have proven that they have the ability to take their product successfully to the market under very competitive conditions. There are three broad categories that have emerged among pharmaceutical companies in India based on their different strategies and priorities. The first kind would be the very large companies like Ranbaxy and Dr Reddy's that have evolved an operating model based on challenging existing product patents and walking away with rich pickings when they win, since they get to share the market with only the original patent holder. The second would be companies that work in tandem with the MNC pharmaceutical companies in either aiding product development or in post-developmental work where they supply the bulk chemicals (the active ingredients) used in production of formulations. And the third are those companies that are pure formulators that try to sell branded products largely in the domestic Indian market, though they are also increasingly looking for opportunities overseas, especially in markets that are not as tightly regulated as the US or the European markets.

Very few of the major Indian pharmaceutical companies have an overlapping growth strategy, each of them having followed a more or less distinct path yet fully capitalizing on the key talents available in India. The Indian pharmaceutical industry has always been strong in chemistry and process synthesis, and they have leveraged this strength with an increasing quantum of investment in R&D. And as the Indian pharmaceutical model matures, Indian companies will straddle a whole range of activities, from new drug discovery and new drug delivery systems to patent challenges to molecular synthesis and contract manufacturing. But despite the obvious signs of maturity, Indian companies are still essentially generics players and not originators or innovators. Many Indian companies are working on a number of new molecules, but in the past that effort has ended up with them doing a lot of the spade work and then licensing out the product to the big MNCs to fund further development work.

The alternate strategy of mounting a patent challenge is a difficult and time-consuming process that only companies such as Ranbaxy and Dr Reddys Laboratories, with their strong balance sheets, can do consistently. As the larger and more established companies moved up the value chain and began to compete effectively on the home turfs of numerous giant pharmaceutical multinationals, their basic approach seeded a culture of research and development-based activity, where even small companies now think it is imperative to first have strong research teams and do not shy away from making the required investments and going through the grind. Research-led growth is now a way of life with Indian pharmaceutical companies, and the result has been a host of high-quality success stories.

The response by leading Indian generic companies to the recent scare over avian flu drove home this point. Cipla Ltd quickly marshaled its resources to produce the generic version (oseltamivir phosphate) of Tamiflu, the influenza drug that is the only known one to fight the avian flu. There is only one manufacturer globally of this drug and that is the innovator, Roche. Ranbaxy Laboratories too moved quickly and entered into talks with Roche for producing both the bulk drug from its facilities in India as well as the capsule from its facilities in the United States. Brian Tempest, Ranbaxy's CEO, made it a point to say that they could produce 100 tons per annum within 12 months of ramping up, enough to produce 1.3 billion 75 milligram tablets, which basically would be enough to provide a course for 100 million people.

This type of response demonstrates the incredibly strong R&D and product development capability, as well as the manufacturing and organizational skills, of Indian pharmaceutical companies, and these are not the only stories. Other companies too have demonstrated an ability to target the most complex blockbuster drugs and introduce them to global markets at a fraction of the cost. Dr Reddy's patent challenge mounted to Eli Lily over the anti-depressant Prozac was quite momentous, especially when it won the legal battle and could introduce the generic version of Prozac (fluoxetine) in the US markets. This strategy – called a para IV abbreviated new drug application (ANDA) – has been used to great effect by companies such as Dr Reddy's and Ranbaxy Laboratories, but has not been actively replicated by the other Indian pharmaceutical companies, even the larger ones.

In a para IV filing the challenger to the patent holder states that either the original patent is invalid or that the generic version of the product does not infringe upon the original product. In the case of a win the generic company is awarded a 180-day exclusive window to market the drug, during which time they enjoy high margins. After that period, assuming that there are no more competing drugs on the market their high margin earnings tend to continue. This is a route used by generic drug companies to grab a share of the market created by a blockbuster drug when the innovator's product patent is still in force. The odds against a successful patent challenge are daunting but the rewards are great. In the numerous cases where the Indian companies have succeeded it has come after very lengthy and detailed legal battles with the patent-holding MNC drug companies. DRL's success with Prozac for example came after numerous legal fights with Eli Lily over two and a half years from 1999 to 2001. But these companies have been successful with this high risk, high reward strategy in the past, and the result is that the market for that particular drug is shared only between the innovator and the successful challenger. But it is increasingly a difficult strategy to pursue since the large pharmaceutical MNCs themselves have research pipelines that are nearly empty of new blockbuster drugs and will fight hard to extend the life of their existing patents. Ranbaxy has been exceptionally successful with this strategy, and has literally dozens of para IV ANDAs pending in the United States. The company expects its US business and other markets, including India, to provide sales of $2 billion by fiscal 2006–07.

The recognition of product and process patents by India is a huge leg up for the Indian patent regime and could usher in good tidings for both Indian and the MNC companies. With pressures that MNC pharmaceutical companies are facing, outsourcing of both research and manufacturing work to Indian pharmaceutical companies is a viable option now that there is patent protection in force and they need not worry about their products being replicated.

India has the largest number of US Food and Drug Administration (USFDA) – approved manufacturing plants in the world, and more companies are joining the queue for approval for new plants or are upgrading older plants to USFDA standards. Despite the stiff regulatory environment worldwide and especially in the United States, which is still the most attractive pharmaceutical market in the world, and even stiffer challenges from the patent holders, the number of ANDAs being filed by Indian companies is increasing, both with US and European regulators. The objective of the pharmaceutical industry, as well as the Indian government, is that Indian pharmaceutical companies now take their huge cash flows and earning power and convert them into investments in original research, which the new patent regime is designed to encourage.

Even companies such as Nicholas Piramal (they bought out Rhone Poulenc in India) and Wockhardt Ltd, which are exceptionally strong and dominating drug companies and powerful marketing machines in the domestic market, are looking to leverage their product development strengths by developing new molecules. Nicholas Piramal had decided against going in for ANDAs since it would rather concentrate on contract manufacturing as one growth strategy. A very lucrative avenue for NPL to deploy its research capability is in new drug delivery systems (NDDS), where companies search for new methods to deliver the same or similar molecules, overcoming barriers within the body to the drug and enhancing targeting of the drug to the affected area. This is a niche area that generic companies and even innovator companies are focusing on as a strategy to compete when a large number of drugs go off patent between now and 2010. According to various studies done by global pharmaceutical industry research groups, the total market for NDDS-based technologies is between $50 billion and $67 billion. This is over and above companies gearing up to bring out generics to compete with blockbuster drugs facing an expiration of patent protection and the growth in the bulk drugs market. An interesting trend is the number of Indian companies that are now discovering new processes for producing active pharmaceutical ingredients (APIs) or for existing formulations.

Many of the smaller companies, such as Aurobindo Pharma and Matrix Laboratories, have used a different approach to that of their larger and better experienced industry counterparts. Because of their size and the growing complexity in the business, smaller players have had to pick out an area and focus on developing a viable business model. All drug manufacturers, whether branded or generic, require active pharmaceutical ingredients, better known as bulk drugs, which are critical inputs in the manufacture of formulations. Many Indian companies have chosen to develop and supply large global multinational drug companies with cheaper variations of the bulk drugs currently in use in formulations, especially ones that have come off patent. Off-patent drugs attract competitors, and there is a drastic need on the part of the former patent holder to reduce costs by sourcing bulk actives from low-cost countries such as India. Besides supplying bulk active ingredients for drugs coming off patents, some companies also target drugs where the product patent has expired but has a process patent in force. Indian companies are involved in every aspect of the game, from challenging existing innovator patents to devising alternate process routes to catering to the same big pharmaceutical companies' research and production needs.

Matrix Laboratories was a singular success story, with its initial focus on process development in bulk actives for a specific product, Citalopram. This particular patent was held by a Danish pharmaceutical company, Lundbeck. Knowing the ever-present possibility of a process patent infringement, Lundbeck held a large number of process patents on that one single product. But Matrix Labs managed to produce a different process and effectively scooped the market from under Lundbeck. The Danish company was so disturbed by the loss of its monopoly over this bulk actives market that it made a standing offer of $50 million to Matrix, which could be cashed at any time and was basically equivalent to buying it out of the business. But Matrix saw greater value in staying the course rather than selling out, and it did very well with that decision, growing revenues to $150 million with a 16% net income margin commanding a $250 million market cap, having expanded its portfolio to include anti-retrovirals (ARVs), which has become a major growth area for the company.

The company that once was nearly defunct (before the current management took over) now has a pipeline of products and is a force in its chosen field of operations, including anti-AIDs drugs and producing active bulk ingredients for anti-retrovirals. Matrix has aggressively stepped up acquisitions and joint ventures with overseas companies, largely looking to add layers of expertise to complement and compensate its own. Its latest acquisition was DocPharma, a Belgian pharmaceuticals firm, for which it paid $263 million. Its other acquisitions have included a very small Swiss company, Explora, that will enable it to enter the contract research business as well as contract manufacturing for MNCs; a Chinese company with specialization in APIs; and a couple of joint ventures with Aspen Labs of South Africa to produce APIs for oncology substances and the anti-AIDs effort funded by the US government presently on in sub-Saharan Africa. These acquisitions will push its marketing boundaries and include new technology streams.

The pharmaceutical industry estimates that by 2010 India could attract 20% of the global spend on contract research (including pre- and post-drug discovery work as well as clinical trials of the drug), especially after the recent regulatory changes. The inherent strengths in research and data management and the availability of high-quality medical and research personnel could prompt a lot of the shift. Besides, one of the requirements of the clinical trial process is to screen an ethnically diverse set of people, which India is blessed with. The four phases of clinical trials (post the studies done on laboratory animals, which is the first step) are conducted on healthy volunteers and then on patient volunteers in order to test drug efficacy, toxicity and tolerance levels. This is one of the lengthiest and most expensive portions of the entire drug discovery and commercialization spectrum, usually spanning from eight to 10 years, and maybe even more after the discovery of a new chemical entity. The cost reduction that shifting these vital processes to India entails alone could prompt the emergence of a lot of business for Indian companies.

Pre-drug discovery contract research is a major and very high value -added segment that the Hyderabad-based Divis Laboratories is exploiting fully. Divis belongs to that category of companies that work in the product development stage with MNC pharmaceutical companies. This is not an area that too many pharmaceutical companies are looking at because of the complexities involved, especially since often products are in the development stage and very small quantities of molecules may be ordered, and the level of skill required to do molecular synthesis is demanding. Divis Laboratories is carving out an enviable reputation for itself in this field, and the management has often been referred to as being fanatical about their research-driven approach and their business model.

Clinical research, which also forms a part of contract research, is a growth area for Indian companies and will attract more players in time, but there are companies that are already solidly established. Vimta Labs Ltd is one of the better known names in contract research, having been in business since 1984, and it more or less provides the entire gamut of services – including pre-clinical, clinical and bioequivalence studies – to a number of global names, including six Fortune 500 pharmaceutical companies and three of the top 10 global generic drug companies. The company has been around for a while, but its revenues are small at $12 million, though it is exceptionally profitable with a 27% net income margin. If it continues to compound revenues at its recent rate of growth it should have $50 million in revenues within the next three years.

AN EMERGING PLAY IN CLINICAL RESEARCH

There is an interesting play among unlisted companies involved in the outsourcing of clinical research in Veeda Clinical Research (Veeda CR), a young company based in the western Indian city of Ahmedabad, with operations in Plymouth, UK and India (as a result of a merger with a UK-based clinical research unit). Promoted by a group of technocrats, their operational presence is in all areas of clinical research, including phased trials, bioavailability and bioequivalence. It is a small company with just $7 million in revenues, but it epitomizes the opportunity before enterprising companies that have the technical resources, experience and the guts to go global.

Effectively what these varied examples show is that the Indian pharmaceutical industry took a very strong and abundantly available skill set in chemistry and leveraged it into other areas, notably process and knowledge management. These are incredibly powerful foundations that the industry has been built on, and the Indian pharmaceutical industry would rank right there with the information technology businesses that have greatly enhanced the reputation of Indian scientific and managerial ability and enabled acceptance of the "Made in India" label.

ARRIVAL OF THE DIGITAL AGE

Pharmaceuticals is undoubtedly an area where Indian companies have earned recognition and a reputation for competitiveness overseas, and clinical research has the potential to become another key industry in which India can dominate global trends. But it is the information technology (IT) sector that completely changed the way the world looks at India. And for all practical purposes, given its potential and the natural advantage that India possesses, despite the rapid growth the industry has enjoyed in recent years, it is still in its infancy. Just $12 billion in exports for 2004 grew to revenues of $17.2 billion for 2005, according to a study by consulting firm Gartner. It is one of India's biggest recent success stories and its largest export industry. The National Association of Software and Services Companies (NASSCOM), the Indian IT industry's trade body, has estimated in a joint study with McKinsey & Co that Indian software services export revenues could reach $60 billion by 2010, with Indian companies capturing over 50% of the market for services sourced to offshore corporations. NASSCOM has estimated the total current size of the

Indian IT industry at $22 billion including domestic sales and services. There are numerous estimates that indicate a rapid growth for the entire industry powered by exports, where annual growth rates typically exceed 25% for the industry as a whole.

India's potential in information technology was brought to world consciousness first by the global drive to recruit Indian programmers (who were jocularly referred to in the Western media as techno-coolies) to comb through millions of lines of code to fix the Y2K problem, and second as Indian software companies rapidly became favorite outsourcing destinations for global corporations shopping for large-scale software development services. Their operating models and technical competencies convinced multinational corporations to allow their programs to be coded in India or by Indians sent specifically for the task overseas. India since then has produced some exceptional companies in this field, names that are well known such as TCS Ltd, Wipro and Infosys Technologies, Asia's first-, second- and third-largest software services and systems integration companies respectively. Besides the big three, there are several other lesser-known companies with similarly strong balance sheets and great operational depth. The strength is evident from the fact that the bulk of global IT companies that have been certified as SEI CMM Level 5 (which is considered to be a significant level of competency within the industry) are from India.

The Indian software story is perhaps the best known globally of all the sectors, and is reasonably well tracked and understood in global markets. If one looks at the valuation appended to the software services companies by the stock market in India and of their ADRs in the United States, it would seem as if all the potential that the country offers is embedded in this industry. IT stocks have the largest concentration of foreign institutional investor holdings, reflecting a great degree of understanding and optimism. The growth rate in the industry is powered by a constant expansion in domain expertise, as well as an expansion in the relationships that exist between Indian software services companies and their clients. A large number of Fortune 1,000 companies now either regularly source their requirements from Indian companies or have established IT subsidiaries in India. The cross-country study done by Gartner to understand India's competitiveness in IT said that India was the clear winner on all parameters in the software development, IT outsourcing and business process outsourcing game. Studies done by other consulting firms arrived at similar conclusions as to the high levels of global competitiveness of Indian companies.

The IT industry has fully capitalized on India's abundant availability of well-trained human capital. And several conscious efforts are being made by the companies concerned, as well as by the government, to increase the flow of quality manpower to the industry. Since the mid-1990s several privately funded engineering institutes have been established, and currently account for 80% of the 340,000 IT engineers produced each year by India. Information technology is undoubtedly the flagship for the opportunity in India, since the skills required for it are something that Indians are best recognized for overseas. The UK, for example, has 400 software and information technology companies owned by people of Indian origin, forming a large part of that community's business contribution.

The industry has seen well over 66 consecutive quarters of unbroken growth rates, most of these in double digits, and the best part is that the momentum continues uninterrupted. According to statistics compiled by the University of Manchester's Institute for Development Policy and Management, Indian software exports began with $4 million in 1980, rising to $105 million in 1989–90, before reaching current levels. According to Dr Richard Heeks, who wrote the first analytical book on the Indian software industry in 1996, the first export revenues from the industry really began way back in 1974. Everything that has been achieved was without the active support of or any interference from the government. What is even more interesting, as Dr Suma Athreye pointed out in a very well-argued paper (titled *Multinational firms and the evolution of the Indian software industry*, published by the East West Centre), is that the early development (in the 1980s) of the Indian software industry was catalyzed by investments made by multinational corporations. Indian companies came along much later and made significant modifications and improvements to the then operating model.

She argued that the reason Indian companies were able to build robust businesses is because they could imitate best practices of these multinational corporations yet at the same time did not have to compete with them. The only time they competed with the MNCs was for access to the labor pool (her hypothesis is that it was a tight market then) and not for services, since the MNC's Indian subsidiary catered only to the parent organization overseas and did not offer services to other corporations. Far more competitive pressure was exerted by firms set up in India by expatriate Indians to take advantage of the wage arbitrage. Her contention is that it was the competition in the labor market that galvanized a lot of the process innovation that has made Indian companies unique. The software services model as used by Indian companies today evolved after a lot of trial and error, which even included an early focus on the domestic market for software products.

TCS Ltd is a company that pulls its weight in the global marketplace for software services and systems integration. It was always an industry leader in India and also had a reputation of being a trendsetter. The fact that Indian companies evolved a model of outsourced services is really thanks to early process innovation from TCS. Today it is the largest Indian IT company, with $2.2 billion in revenues (fiscal 2004–05), with 60% of those revenues being earned from services provided to US corporations. It operates in software services, business process outsourcing and product development, mainly for the banking and financial services industry. Its 2004 IPO, through which it raised $1.2 billion from the domestic equity market, made it one of the top Indian IPOs ever, especially considering that its offer of shares received bids worth nearly $7 billion from foreign institutional investors who scrambled over themselves to get at the stock.

TCS embodies the attempt by the top tier Indian companies to move up the IT value chain. Along with Infosys Technologies and others it has been making progress in the consulting space, which provides higher value addition and holds immense potential for Indian companies thanks to the competencies already built in. TCS aims to have a major development presence in the United States by recruiting directly from US campuses in a big way, which is an unusual development for Indian companies and signals a growing belief that they are capable of competing on the home turf of the biggest technology companies in the world.

The Indian government had nothing to do with the success of the Indian software industry, due more out of ignorance rather than design. But that worked to the advantage of the sector since they were allowed to seed and evolve on their terms. Now the government is getting into the act, but in a very positive way by providing the infrastructural and institutional framework that will push growth and create jobs even faster. The government, through a brand-new ministry for communications and information technology (effectively a convergence ministry) and the National Task Force on IT, seeks to expand the human resource base. The government's policy is aimed to alleviate a genuine worry for the industry: a potential shortage of engineers in a few years. The government also intends allowing easier access to capital overseas and has begun to implement a national plan to push the use of IT in India. The government is also pushing hard to develop the IT hardware manufacturing base in India, which has had beneficial impacts on countries such as Israel and even China to some extent. The rapid computerization of Indian public sector banks as well as the large-scale computerization effort by local, state and the national government offers a huge opportunity for Indian hardware and software firms (see figure 7.6).

Figure 7.6: Expenditure on information technology infrastructure

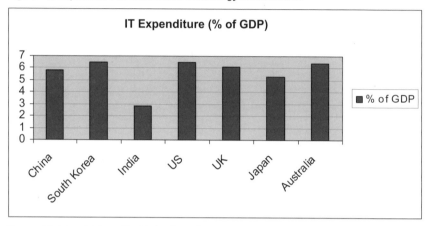

Source: Ministry of Information Technology, Government of India

The government's intervention to boost human capital and update laws and its measures to boost IT hardware manufacturing are timely since there are increasing signs that the Chinese government has decided to push hard for Chinese companies to challenge India's reputation as a country of choice for IT outsourcing. China has a huge domestic market for software services (which Indian companies have begun to tap into) but that can be turned into a globally competitive weapon over the next decade or so.

A key strength that has made the Indian IT industry hard to compete with is the unique global development and delivery model that has been perfected (the blend of marketing, finance, technology platforms and HR). In fact, Indian companies are so accomplished that Canadian, US and European IT companies now send their promising young recruits to India to study how the industry works and to learn best practices. But Indian companies are beginning to face two sets of challenges: from global IT corporations that have already begun to establish a presence in India in order to take advantage of its IT infrastructure and high-quality manpower directly competing with Indian companies in the global market for services, and from other countries that are trying hard to emulate India's success.

This trend will lead India to the next level of activity, where like the pharmaceutical industry it now needs to use its strong cash flows, balance sheet strength and understanding of the global industry to focus on innovation, which – as several CEOs of Indian IT companies have begun to point out – centers around innovation in the business model as well as in knowledge, that is, new development efforts. Though Israel has a much smaller IT industry their firms are much more advanced in terms of product development and original development. Indian companies have focused almost entirely on providing services, though several of the bigger companies have developed product suites catering to specific domains such as the global banking industry. Flexcube®, a core banking solution from I-Flex Solutions Ltd, is the largest selling product in its category globally. Infosys Technologies too has similar product suites such as Finacle (a banking suite), as does TCS. But there is an increasing tribe of companies – such as the Chennai-based Ramco Systems Ltd, one of the earliest to break into the market for ERP applications – that have dedicated themselves to product development.

The banking industry worldwide is one of the biggest consumers of IT products, especially software, hence there has been much development work in this domain. Indian companies' exports of baning products is just $700 million, or a fraction of its total IT exports. The Indian Institute of Management, Bangalore (one of India's premier management institutes), has estimated that given the investments now being made in product development by both multinational companies and domestic companies, Indian product exports could rise to $7 billion by 2010, implying 60% compounded growth for the next five years. In the recent past, product exports have been growing at 30% annually, which is not too different from the average industry growth rates in service exports, but the profit margins are roughly 40% to 50% higher than in the service business. For example, if the service companies enjoy margins between 30% and 35%, a product business would earn between 45% and 55%. Obviously the investment and risks are far greater in developing products, which is why many Indian companies are working jointly with MNCs in building suites. Indian companies have proven proficient at cracking the services market, which is much smaller than the global market for software products and is estimated to be between $300 billion and $350 billion. And it also explains why multinational companies are looking to invest in Indian product companies.

When Oracle Corporation decided to step up its domination of global banking after its acquisition of PeopleSoft and Siebel Systems by going beyond its already-dominating ERP applications, offering greater functionality (what is known as vertical banking technology), it chose as its partner Indian financial software specialist I-Flex Solutions Ltd. In August 2005 Oracle bought Citigroup Venture Capital's entire 41% equity stake in the company for $600 million, and spent another $300 million to acquire an additional 20%, a compulsion under Indian takeover laws. This is the largest acquisition of an Indian company ever. I-Flex (2006 annualized revenue of $285 million) has always been a trailblazer in the products space, having built over the years a very exciting and comprehensive suite of products for the global banking industry. Like everything with I-Flex, this deal could also herald a new era for the Indian IT industry, where acquisitions by global corporations could become a trend and also a major value driver.

On the other hand, Ramco Systems Ltd epitomizes the pitfalls of the product development business and shows why this is one of the most difficult routes to fortune in the IT industry. For much of the mid- to late 1990s until the present, the company struggled with its Ramco VirtualWorks® enterprise-wide solutions framework, piling up development costs and losses. That framework has evolved into a software product incorporating unique, breakthrough features, many of which have been patented. It has piled up losses and a stream of negative cash flows, but with substantial financial support from the promoters and other investor groups it has grown to an operating presence in 40 countries, catering to the ERP requirements of industries such as retailing, aviation, manufacturing, asset management and healthcare, with over 1,700 employees. Its product development legacy has left it with large accumulated losses, largely due to unabsorbed research and development costs and a still erratic earnings profile.

These two companies, I-Flex Solutions and Ramco Systems, are really examples of operations at two ends of the spectrum. One company chose an industry segment well and went about dominating it globally with outstanding products, and the other instead went for a brilliant but complex framework with a universal application and huge inbuilt flexibility but one that has still to make a major financial impact.

Polaris Software Laboratories adopted a more flexible model that oscillates between I-Flex Solutions and Ramco Systems, using the best of what Indian industry offers, with its ambition of becoming a recognized product developer. Its business has been integrated to include services such as application development and maintenance, along with business process outsourcing services that complement its product development capability.

Essentially Indian companies ran away far and fast with a clear opportunity that was presented to them in offering services to global corporations. Four clear segments have evolved within the Indian IT service industry. The first is the large top tier systems integration and services firms that have completely integrated operations, and their service offerings include process outsourcing or back office/call center solutions (usually offered through subsidiary companies such as Infosys Technologies' ITES subsidiary or HCL Technologies' subsidiaries). They have expertise across a number of domains. Their client focus is almost exclusively the Fortune 1,000 companies, and a significant portion of their growth has come from a ramp-up of services offered to existing clients.

The second tier of companies are those that offer standalone but equally high-end IT services and that have significant domain expertise across a few segments. A third category comprises companies that provide application development services and maintenance services, which is not a very high end activity but then it is very scalable. And a fourth category of companies is the business process outsourcing companies that handle back office processing jobs such as credit card applications, insurance claims processing and call center operations.

Animation: The new game in town

Companies such as Hyderabad-based Pentamedia Graphics Ltd have made a name for themselves by providing Hollywood with the animation and special effects for some top-grossing movies over the past few years. Today PGL is one of the bigger animation and services companies in the world, having expanded into markets in Europe and the Far East. While animation is obviously lucrative for Indian companies given the labor and skill intensity of the work required, a greater opportunity exists in video game software. There are a large number of unlisted companies that are developing original programs for game consoles that are being distributed in the global market. Industry studies have shown that developing game software in India can be done for between 10% and 50% of what it would cost in the United States. The possible revenues from this segment of the industry have not been factored in yet in arriving at the growth potential for the Indian technology, outsourcing and product development industry as a whole. Many of these up-and-coming companies have been funded by companies such as Cisco, Macromedia and other big global names.

Information technology as a growth enabler

IT-enabled services (ITES), or outsourcing of process work of both voice and data to India from high-cost centers, is another high-growth story. For fiscal 2004–05 the ITES segment reported export revenues of $5.2 billion, growing by 44.5%, while for fiscal 2005–06 another 40% growth is expected, taking industry revenues to $7.3 billion. The size of the opportunity for Indian companies in this industry could range between $21 billion and $25 billion by 2010.

Even within ITES, companies have demarcated themselves into offering high-end engineering solutions, which Infosys Technologies has decided to focus on (this is a much harder market to break into since the service is customized and not commoditized, but there is much less competition), and companies that offer business process services. The new trend in ITES is knowledge process outsourcing (KPO), which is a combination of data processing and analysis. The key knowledge segments that are being addressed by select Indian companies are market research and business intelligence. The critical skill requirement is mathematical and pattern recognition. This is an exciting growth area for Indian outsourcing companies and high-end software services companies. According to various industry sources the total market size available globally is over $50 billion and could be as much as $100 billion, with over a quarter consisting of spending on market research. Though less glamorous, a far more attractive segment is human resources outsourcing to Indian companies. The total segment size is estimated at $11 billion with a value of $5 billion worth that can be sent overseas, of which Indian companies did $165 million in 2005, but with a segment revenue growth of 120%.

But with the exception of the new trends in knowledge process outsourcing, ITES is the only service activity that begins to resemble manufacturing in terms of its impact on GDP and scalability, besides the fact that it requires specific skills such as language compatibility with higher education levels, a combination that is readily available in India. It has a huge impact on the economy simply because of its potential to absorb significant numbers of India's English-speaking graduates at a fraction of global cost while providing a quality wage to income-earners in India. A previous NASSCOM–McKinsey study has estimated that by 2008 the ITES sector alone will require 1.1 million workers, up from the 350,000 that it currently employs, making it one of the largest such industries worldwide.

The really big players in ITES are not the Indian publicly traded companies but the Indian subsidiaries of global companies. For example, the Indian arm of GE is the single largest ITES player in the country, with a staff strength of over 15,000. The largest Indian-owned (third-party outsourcing) company is WNS, with a workforce of 10,000 people. The US banks and securities firms have established back office operations centers and call centers in India in a fairly big way. JP Morgan, Morgan Stanley and others have also established portions of their securities research facilities in India.

8

THE FUTURE WORLD: OPPORTUNITY UNBOUND

There are numerous sectors that will capitalize on the emerging trends in India, both social as well as economic. India's rising recognition as an outsourcing destination for multiple industries, favorable demographics, rising income levels, consumer confidence, separation of joint families and growing national economic clout are all previously unseen influences. Some of the sectors that are influenced by these trends are seeing an immediate opportunity being reflected in current growth, while others are only being seeded.

Sectors such as automobile components, specialty chemicals, engineering design, biotechnology, retailing, lifestyle products (including home improvement products), real estate, media, entertainment and communications, asset management, food processing and agro-industry, civil aviation, infrastructure logistics, insurance, alternate energy (including agro-based) and defense are but a cross-section of the emerging opportunity. Some of the future opportunity may be out of bounds for retail investors but would very much be in the realm of investment possibility for institutional investors since many companies are not even publicly traded yet, especially in the biotechnology, insurance, retailing and real estate sectors. Some established retail stores, such as Shoppers' Stop and Pantaloon Retail, are already market favorites and trade at lofty multiples. Others in entertainment and media, such as Zee TV, TV 18 and Balaji Telefilms, have great promise of years of profitable growth ahead, and have shown startling aggression and recent growth. The common trend among an overwhelming number of these companies is that they have been built by first-generation entrepreneurs who have had the flexibility of seeding their businesses in a liberalizing India and have had improved access to capital and knowledge pools. Many of these businesses come without the baggage that the old industrial conglomerates carry, and in fact would not have been around but for the amazing fundamental changes that have taken place from the early 1990s.

AUTOMOTIVE MANUFACTURING, A NEW MANTRA

There is life beyond India's formidable information technology and IT-enabled services companies. The "Made in India" tag is being given a whole new dimension, where products requiring high-end engineering and design expertise are increasingly being outsourced to Indian companies. Automobile component manufacturing and some parts of automobile designing are strong examples of the new outsourcing trend.

There are a number of factors that are shaping outsourcing policies of the global automobile companies and the tier I component manufacturing companies. Loss of pricing power in automobiles is now an accepted fact in the global automobile industry, while development, marketing and compliance costs have been skyrocketing. The cost of mechanical parts is the only area where companies can exert any degree of control. And companies in countries such as India hold the key to the competitiveness of the global automobile corporations since they can deliver these mechanical parts thanks to their high-quality engineering and manufacturing expertise at a relatively low cost. Some of the auto component companies in India have indicated in past interactions that the average cost saving on the parts outsourced to India is 25%, which makes a huge difference to the buyer. Also, the structure of automobile manufacturing has changed; auto companies have converted themselves from vertically integrated manufacturers to assemblers and marketers of vehicles. So the industry's future is now hinged on its ability to outsource. While countries such as China, Taiwan and especially Mexico are ahead of the auto component outsourcing game, India has emerged as a strong challenger in recent years. And evidence shows that though the cost saving is formidable it is not the only factor to drive demand for Indian products. It is the established capability from conceptualization and design to production and delivery – what is known in the trade as a full service supply capability – that is helping establish India as a credible supplier of critical components.

In the early 1990s the Indian government changed what was then a highly restrictive automobile policy and permitted foreign investment in the sector, including in automobile component manufacturing. There were numerous riders put on the companies coming in, including stiff export and localization norms. Despite the stiff conditions, several billion dollars in FDI came into the Indian auto component industry. But the operating conditions and the over-capacity in the domestic market pushed these companies, unlike anything else could have, to become highly competitive. Many of these companies had foreign partners that began to source products for their other markets. The resulting success that Indian automobile component companies have enjoyed since then is only the tip of the iceberg given the economics of the business and the recognition of Indian design, engineering and manufacturing strengths. Nearly 60% of the export of auto components from India go to the United States and Europe, which are considered to be very demanding and competitive markets.

According to estimates made by McKinsey & Co and other consultants and trade associations, India's share of outsourcing in automobile components will increase over the next few years. India is exploiting this strength in engineering in two ways: one, Indian companies have sourced initial technology and are now competing very well on their own (Bharat Forge Ltd and Sundram Fasteners are two of the best examples) or as joint ventures with top global technology and manufacturing names (for example Tata Auto Components); and two, the exclusive R&D and manufacturing shops being set up by global auto companies (Toyota, GM and DaimlerChrysler) and global auto component manufacturers such as Denso, Bosch and Visteon that have made India a hub for specific components or markets. Toyota Motors has made India its hub for manufacturing transmission systems, while Volvo has started sourcing truck parts, exporting trucks to South Korea, and more recently has sourced engineering services to support its expansion in Asia.

There is a strong emphasis on the domestic automobile market too (which is the fastest growing in the world) as much as there is a desire or demand for these engineering and manufacturing services overseas. For example, Sona Koyo Steering Ltd has a near monopoly on selling manual and hydraulic steering columns to India's largest automobile manufacturer, Maruti Udyog Ltd (Suzuki Motor's Indian subsidiary).

Sona Koyo Steering has also grown from being a small manufacturing entity to an important global partner to Koyo Seiko Company Ltd of Japan, producing nearly 1.2 million mechanical and hydraulic steering systems for the Indian and global markets. The progression has come about more due to its proven technological ability and stature, since in revenue terms it is a small company by global standards, with under $100 million in annual revenues. It is making the leap from producing mechanical steering columns to producing hydraulic columns to now embedding electronic components into its steering columns. The shift from being a producer of mechanical parts to electronic parts is a value-added shift and has been the route used by several successful global automotive component makers. Once the electronic column plant starts operations in mid-2006 its exports could rise significantly since there is a large overseas market for this. Sona Koyo is one of those Indian companies that has successfully made the leap to engineering and design outsourcing, by designing a new platform for off-road vehicles for an American manufacturer.

The really successful and valuable automotive component companies in the future will be those that are able to demonstrate sufficient technological capability that will see them actually partnering global tier I companies in their development efforts, very similar to what Indian pharmaceutical companies are doing and what Indian IT outsourcing firms have done. Sona Koyo has identified with that thinking, and its development effort surrounding electronic power steering systems is a case in point besides its already-proven vehicle platform design capabilities. This company also has executed another significant strategy that could increasingly become the norm among Indian automotive companies, which is establishing a presence near a targeted overseas market through an acquisition. The purchase of a 21% stake in a European maker of steering columns nearly two and a half times its size is a bold but crucial step. Sona Koyo will bring its strengths in low-cost manufacturing and design capability to its new investee company, besides starting a joint product development.

While companies like Sona Koyo Steering are slowly increasing in number there are few names in the auto component sector that can match a company like Bharat Forge Ltd in its scale of operations. BFL is now the country's and Asia's largest and the world's second-largest manufacturer of castings and forgings for the automobile sector, after Germany's ThyssenKrupp. The bulk of their revenues (over 60%) come from exports of these parts and from their global subsidiaries supplying crankshafts and axle beams. It is widely considered to be a trendsetter in the industry. It turned itself into a full-service supplier and was growing its business globally long before other companies could begin to find a foothold domestically. Its manufacturing facilities are now spread out, with two plants in India, three in Germany – including its second-largest forgings company – and one each in Sweden and Scotland, which it acquired with its purchase of Swedish forgings company Imatra Kilsta for $58 million.

It also has the largest consolidated revenues at $600 million and the largest market capitalization among Indian auto component companies at nearly $2 billion. It is also among the fastest-growing companies, with recent revenue and net income growth compounding in excess of 30% annually. Their strategy has been to either set up or acquire large capacities located close to their targeted market, and they have done this to perfection. The acquisition of a stake in FAW Forgings Ltd is further testimony of that fact. In an interview with *Forbes* magazine, Chairman Baba Kalyani said that his intention is to have a technology front end in the developed world and a manufacturing end in the low-cost destinations. They are now looking at raising additional capital along with a GDR/ADR listing in order to enable further inorganic growth.

But the strategy adopted by some of these companies of expanding overseas for strategic reasons is a clear risk factor that is different from anything Indian companies would have faced in the past. Proper integration of the acquired company and the pressure to spread management resources across borders will test Indian companies' skills greatly.

A differentiated approach

One of the more sophisticated players in the Indian automobile component space is an unlisted company, Tata Auto Components Ltd (TACO), the closest that India has to a tier I auto component maker. TACO (consolidated revenues have been estimated at $330 million for 2004–05) functions as a holding company promoting subsidiaries for different auto component products with different technology partners, rather than basing their business model on a single product or on the dictates of a joint venture partner, which is the way many other companies went. They offer products including radiators, seating systems, plastic component systems and sheet metal components, in conjunction with 13 technology partners from the United States, Europe and Japan. It started operations in 1995, and since then has established 14 plants, three engineering and design centers and several units dedicated to exports.

They evolved their business model based on emerging trends in the global automobile industry. TACO has positioned itself as a technology company providing design, engineering and manufacturing services, and offers these services to Indian companies as well, and has been very successful as a one-stop-shop for all the requirements of global tier I component companies and vehicle manufacturers. They have helped component makers in Europe relocate entire plants to India, besides providing total procurement solutions to overseas vendors that may involve securing qualified Indian suppliers for some specific parts. The operation is very sophisticated and is unlike any other in the industry in India, though similar operating models have sprung up in China and Taiwan.

In their manufacturing activities they are going for more value addition by moving into system assemblies rather than just producing components. For example, Tata Auto Plastics Ltd is a 100%-owned subsidiary that produces dashboards, bumpers and interior parts. Nearly 70% of TAPS business comes from Tata Motors, India's largest heavy vehicle manufacturer, but it has expanded its client list to include other automakers to whom it is looking to supply entire dashboard assemblies (by sourcing the components it does not manufacture) and also interior assemblies, in a similar manner that a global tier I entity would operate. Other subsidiaries and joint ventures have focused on similar upgrades by providing fully assembled engine cooling modules, seating systems and braking system.

Sundram Fasteners Ltd, part of the $3 billion Chennai-based TVS group and a leading manufacturer of high tensile fasteners and radiator caps, was the first Indian engineering company to establish a manufacturing presence in China, in Haiyan about 100 kilometers south of Shanghai, in 2002–03. It is reported to be negotiating its second corporate acquisition in Europe, this time of a fastener company in Germany, following a 2003 acquisition of a bevel gear manufacturer in the UK. It already has one joint venture in Germany.

Interestingly, many of these companies being taken over are similar in size or maybe a bit bigger but have been victims of severe competition from emerging companies from India, China and other low-cost manufacturing centers. Thus, using the newly acquired companies as a base to grow further is a logical extension of what the Indian companies are doing. Being well-recognized in India is now clearly not enough, and the importance of being global players is not lost on any of these companies.

The combination of high-quality promoters and joint ventures and a fiercely competitive domestic market has produced an industry that most global names want to collaborate with. According to the industry association, the Automobile Component Manufacturers Association (ACMA), the feedback from their members (they represent 480 companies in India) is that the industry could expect to compound growth at 16% to 17% annually, which will see it doubling its size to nearly $18 billion by 2009–10 and to $35 billion to $40 billion by 2015. But in reality that growth estimate is on the lower side, since not only is the domestic automobile market growing faster than ever before, so are exports. Between 2002–03 and 2004–05 the industry has grown at 25% compounded annually. Assuming that this rate of growth can be sustained for the next few years the industry will reach a size of $27 billion by 2010. The ACMA expects that export growth will continue to outpace domestic growth rates at 30% compounded until 2015, by which time export revenues will climb to a level between $20 billion and $25 billion and form a larger proportion of the industry than it does today. The recent export growth rates have been around 31% compounded annually and the current export level is around $1.4 billion.

Indian automobile manufacturers are building themselves up to make a gigantic impact on the global auto manufacturing scene by leveraging strong skill sets in engineering and manufacturing and their equally strong balance sheets to build new markets. The Indian auto industry boasts the world's fifth-largest medium and heavy truck maker, some of the most profitable auto companies anywhere, the world's fourth-largest makers of tractors and a rapidly growing global hub for small cars. In the midst of all this the domestic automobile industry too is witnessing rapid growth, and car manufacturing has crossed the one million mark in annual production and sales, and continues to grow at over 20% annually (see table 8.1).

Table 8.1: Indian auto sector – 2005 growth rates

Type of Vehicle	%
Motorcycles	16
Passenger cars (including SUVs)	22
Medium and heavy trucks	27
Light trucks	28
Auto components	29

Pint-sized cars but king-sized growth

Pint-sized cars but king-sized growth would sum up the past and present for Maruti Udyog Ltd, India's largest car maker in both volume and revenues ($2.2 billion for fiscal 2004-05). It controls 50% of the domestic passenger car market share, selling half a million cars a year, with the bulk of its offerings comprising the smaller compact vehicles. But it may look a lot different in the future, as it has begun to seek an increased share of the market for premium vehicles.

The seed of India's dramatic emergence on the auto component scene was planted thanks to the Indian government's joint venture with Suzuki Motors in 1983 (the government has started the exercise of selling its stake in phases, and will completely exit by 2006) to produce compact cars for the common man. That venture catalyzed the moribund Indian automobile industry that had only two players and an extremely expensive and shoddy car market when Maruti entered, and also created the opportunity for building a strong vendor base since many of Suzuki's global suppliers also came in as joint ventures. Since inception, Maruti positioned itself with the right technology and products for a small and highly price-conscious market, where buying a car was a major decision (it is becoming less so) and thus their products had to be everything to everybody.

The Indian car market today, just over 20 years after Maruti became the country's third automaker, has a base of several million vehicles, five million of them comprising Maruti customers. Several of these customers are now beginning to think of upgrading or acquiring a second or third car. Future growth is dependent on the company swinging these customers their way despite the vast choice now available to premium buyers, without diluting focus on its prime market of first-time consumers who eight times out of 10 would opt for a Maruti-made starter vehicle, also known as the A1 segment. The real fight is in the A2 and A3 segments and in the premium segment (the C segment). There are numerous global auto makers, such as Ford, GM, Honda, Mitsubishi, Toyota and DaimlerChrysler, that have concentrated their resources here, since competing with Maruti in the lower segments is next to impossible. However, Hyundai and Tata Motors have begun to make some inroads into the segment that Maruti dominates. But neither of these companies has the sales reach or complex marketing apparatus that Maruti possesses. Demographics and societal changes also may play in its favor. Both younger buyers as well as increasing numbers of women buyers continue to be attracted to the brand and the small zippy models that they turn out. And it is these two market segments that are increasingly driving automobile sales in India.

The future also involves becoming closely interwoven with Suzuki's global plans, which could mean becoming a compact car production hub for its regional markets. This export segment alone could be a significant growth driver for Maruti in the near future, and exports could rise significantly from the 30,000 vehicles it sent out in 2005.

The company has shown a remarkable ability to manage costs, especially raw material and marketing and distribution costs, even in recent quarters when most auto makers have suffered both due to rising input costs and rising fuel costs. A look at its financials would leave doubts as to the keen competition in the Indian auto space, since it consistently improves profitability along with revenue growth. It is also one of the most profitable auto makers anywhere in the world and contributes one-quarter of Suzuki's global profits. It went public in late 2003, as part of the government's exit strategy, to an enthusiastic response from the stock market that currently values the company at over $4 billion.

Tata Motors (NYSE: TTM), the country's largest and the world's fifth-largest medium and heavy truck and utility vehicle maker, did in the late 1990s and in the earlier part of this decade what Maruti did in the early 1980s, which is redefine the Indian auto space. Tata Motors introduced for the first time a completely Indian-designed and manufactured automobile that it christened the Indica in 1999–2000. An entire secondhand assembly line was stripped from an unused European plant and brought to India, which is why the cost could be kept low enough to take market share very rapidly. Its early years were a little erratic as it had to iron out technical glitches and bring the car to par with other global models available, but today it sells over 10,000 cars a month and has several variants out.

The decision to do the Indica was a gamble on the part of its management since no Indian company had the expertise to build a car from scratch until that point, and that too at a price low enough to make it appealing to a mass market. Initially it seemed as if that gamble may severely damage the company as cash losses piled up. But the low fixed cost meant that break even would happen at just 60,000 vehicles, which it managed to do within a couple of years. Today the car division is a major contributor to revenues and profitability, making Tata Motors India's largest integrated automobile company in India with revenues of $4.7 billion in 2005. Recognizing that a significant market for cars exists at a lower price point, $2,200 to be exact, the group has been pushing to develop a "people's car", in the words of chairman Ratan Tata. This price point knocks 70% off the low price established by the Indica, at which point the Tatas believe they can do a volume of one million cars a year.

Tata Motors has a reputation for being an aggressive marketer, and not only dominates the heavy vehicle market in India but has a presence in Europe, East Asia, the Middle East, Africa and Australia. In 2004 it acquired 100% of the equity in the heavy truck manufacturing subsidiary of Daewoo Korea (now called Tata Daewoo Commercial Vehicles), which is the second-largest manufacturer of heavy trucks in Korea with products sold in 50 countries. It also assembles vehicles in South Africa, Ukraine, Malaysia, Bangladesh and Russia. In 2005 it purchased a 21% stake in Spanish bus and coach maker Hispano Carrocera SA, with effective management control and with an option to purchase the remainder. Tata Motors will easily improve the financial health at Hispano as it did with Daewoo Commercial. These ventures coupled with its own assembly and marketing infrastructure give it a reach in 60-odd countries, besides giving it collaborators for incremental product development.

Other companies – such as utility vehicle and farm equipment maker Mahindra & Mahindra Ltd, and component makers Omax Auto, Amtek Auto and Sundram Fasteners – are expanding with acquisitions overseas. Mahindra & Mahindra has expressed its vision of becoming the largest tractor maker in the world through acquisitions. It already produces 110,000 tractors annually, making it one of the largest farm equipment makers in the world, with two manufacturing plants in the United States (where it has had a presence since 1994) and a marketing presence in 10 countries. India incidentally is the largest tractor market in the world, and Mahindra is the dominating brand there. Like Tata Motors it has developed R&D capabilities and the capability to design and manufacture an automobile from scratch. Its SUV Scorpio is all the rage in India, with its stylish look and excellent performance, and it is understandably building a market for itself overseas.

Ashok Leyland Ltd, the other major heavy vehicle manufacturer in India, has increased its spending on R&D to 2% of revenues from less than a quarter of a percentage point a few years ago, with close to 350 scientists and engineers engaged purely in research and development, which they plan to increase by another 400 engineers. Though they are a low-profile company with a presence largely in the southern regions of India, the product quality is usually rated the highest in India and they are reputed to have the best technology. They have also seen a major improvement in capital efficiency (see figure 8.1). Ever since the UK-based Hinduja family took over control of the company in partnership with IVECO (the commercial vehicle subsidiary of Fiat of Italy), the company's access to the latest technology improved, but of late it has been developing specific technologies in-house. For example, it spearheaded the conversion of buses in the public transportation sphere to run on compressed natural gas instead of diesel beginning in 1997, and is the largest manufacturer of CNG buses in the world.

Figure 8.1: Improving returns

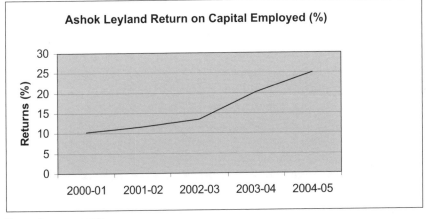

Source: Company reports.

Even in the motorcycle segment, though Hero Honda is the dominating company, companies such as Bajaj Auto and TVS Motors that were once dependent on technology from their former joint venture partners are more assured with their own product development capabilities than ever before. The best-selling motorcycle model from TVS Motors was conceptualized and designed entirely in-house. Since breaking up with Suzuki Motors, TVS has launched new models very rapidly, with advanced design and styling and top of the line technology.

Competitiveness drives the opportunity

Once again when investing in India or in Indian companies investors look at competitive strengths and supporting government policies, in that order. There is a clear understanding that opportunities in industries ranging from IT outsourcing to engineering and manufacturing investment have come because of the availability of specific strengths that meet business requirements. The Indian automobile component manufacturing industry is a very clear example of this. Complete infrastructure has come up in three regions of the country to support auto component manufacturing. Tamil Nadu in Southern India is one of the three major clusters for auto component manufacturing, the other two being Gurgaon in the north of the country and Pune in the west.

Chennai, the capital of Tamil Nadu state, is also considered to be the automobile capital of the country. According to research done by Dr Paul Swamidas of Auburn University, the Chennai region produces 46% of the country's motorcycle output, well over one-third of the value of automotive components, and 21% of auto assemblies. One of the conclusions of his studies is that the depth and structure of the auto industry around this region would rival that found in only very developed countries, indicating just how formidable a cluster has evolved in just over a decade.

A significant number of global and Indian automotive names have factories here, including South Korea's Hyundai Motors, with a plant capable of producing a quarter of a million vehicles a year (which is currently being raised to half a million), 40% of which is exported. Hyundai's Chennai facility is also its hub for engine transmissions for its assembly plants in South Korea and Turkey. Other global names there are Ford, Mitsubishi and Caterpillar, and the latest entrant is BMW which has chosen Chennai for its car manufacturing plant though several other states were vying hard for that investment. There are several of these companies' component suppliers also present, including Visteon, Siemens and a dozen Korean auto component companies that followed Hyundai into the state. Among the big Indian automobile names are Ashok Leyland, the TVS group (the country's third-largest manufacturer of motorcycles and one of the most respected names in the automotive component space), and MRF Ltd (the country's largest maker of a very popular brand of tires).

An industry's commitment to quality and its recognition of the same globally is a testimony to its competitiveness. Mahindra & Mahindra's farm equipment division is the first tractor maker in the world to win the Deming Application Prize, but is only one of many Indian companies to have won this coveted award since 2001. Out of 12 Indian companies to have won this award, 10 are either automobile companies or auto component manufacturers, reflecting a sector-wide commitment to outstanding quality and rigor in maintaining manufacturing best practices. Sundram Fasteners, which supplies radiator caps to GM, has been rewarded with a best supplier award for five consecutive years, also winning the TPM Excellence award from the Japan Institute of Plant Maintenance.

The Indian government policies are exceptionally clear and proactive in this industry. There are actually no restrictions whatsoever surrounding foreign investment in auto component manufacturing, making it one of the most liberal FDI regimes anywhere, which is not surprising considering the tremendous impact the change in policy in the early 1990s had in creating a really great industry segment.

To sum up, growth in income, whether it is due to exceptional earnings in the external sector or expansion in the domestic sector, has improved people's ability to upgrade their lifestyles, and there has been no better way to do this than to buy a house and a car. Indians today are buying more of both than ever before. Car and motorcycle manufacturers have never had it so good, but automobile component companies are faring even better, having had a head start in the global marketplace. Both these segments of Indian industry are in a unique position since they are benefiting both from significant domestic expansion as well as a better recognition of brand India and a consequent increase in export demand.

GOOD CHEMISTRY

Specialty chemicals is another area where India scores high in the global outsourcing market in terms of having the right skill sets and attracting a lot of investment from multinationals. Specialty chemicals are a broad set of chemicals that basically enhance performance or strengthen a variety of basic consumer goods and industrial products, including textiles, plastics, paper products, home and personal care products, automobiles and buildings. The manufacturing process is very skill intensive, and as we've seen in our dissection of the Indian pharmaceuticals industry, the country has strong chemistry and process synthesis skills which are critical elements in manufacturing specialty chemicals too.

The skill sets available to this industry in India are only beginning to be recognized outside the country. Like in IT and pharmaceuticals 25 to 30 years ago, the prime moving force to uncovering India's innate abilities in this industry is the multinational corporations. Numerous chemical manufacturing MNCs have established a combination of R&D centers, as well as global manufacturing hubs, using greatly improved productivity and remarkably low cost as scoring points. The presence of MNCs catering largely to an overseas market is the ideal situation for the development of the industry, since Indian companies tend to emulate best practices and build strong operating models as a result. Indian-listed entities – such as printing and specialty ink maker Micro Inks, and adhesive and chemical company Pidilite Industries – are great examples of the sophisticated levels Indian companies have already risen to in terms of both creating technology barriers and building a dominating local market presence, while also selling successfully in a global market.

Micro Inks Ltd built itself up from scratch beginning in 1991, and by 2005 has become the largest printing ink manufacturer in India with a 35% market share and revenues of $150 million. What strikes most analysts and investors who have visited their facilities, as well as with the management in Mumbai, is their dedication to building in-house technical capability and their vision to build world-scale manufacturing plants (which they have already done), while also developing a unique integrated operation that included developing technologies to manufacture the chemical raw materials themselves.

It was taken over by German ink manufacturer Huber Group, the world's fifth-largest printing ink manufacturer, in October 2005, in a deal that valued the company at $375 million. Like most European and North American printing ink companies the German company needed to address an exploding market in Asia but lacked a sophisticated-enough base from which to do that. Micro Inks was a compelling candidate, primarily because of their technical sophistication, vast product range and low-cost integrated manufacturing base located in the midst of one of the fastest growing markets in the world and close enough to other key markets in Asia. Micro Inks can easily replicate its operating model in plants around Asia and globally too.

This acquisition comes at an interesting time in the company's development, after they had generated a significant amount of technical capability. After dominating the Indian market for printing inks they have set a goal to rise to the ranks of the top five ink manufacturers globally. Despite the fact that they had a committed presence in the United States and exported inks and intermediates to five dozen countries, marketing capability overseas was a stumbling block that could be erased with the new strategic partner.

Manufacturing trends in the global specialty chemicals industry are once again influencing the degree of outsourcing to Indian companies. There was a time until recently when the United States was the center of the global specialty chemicals trade and there was little that was imported into that country. Then profit considerations pushed specialty chemical manufacturing out of the US and into low-cost areas, especially Asia. This move in turn has triggered a big outsourcing boom in this segment, which in turn has begun to push Indian capabilities into the consciousness of chemical manufacturing MNCs, many of whom had a presence in the Indian market. McKinsey & Co has estimated that India has the potential to become one of the top two centers for the manufacture of specialty chemicals, with the other being China. The consulting firm has also estimated that the potential for export of specialty chemicals from India is $15 billion by 2015, from just a couple of billion dollars currently.

These may only be very intelligent estimates but the Indian government, along with several determined individuals and corporate groups, has put into action a plan that could result in much larger export numbers for the chemicals industry. A concept of a special economic region (SER) has been floated which is similar to the gigantic industrial regions or zones in China, where companies are encouraged to set up world-scale manufacturing facilities and are given everything they need to do that. Each of these regions or groups of regions will focus on specific industries where India has strengths that can quickly be leveraged. The government will assist in the infrastructure creation but will not offer any fiscal incentives to companies locating in these regions. Two or three such SERs are to be established by 2008–09, focusing on specialty chemicals, pharmaceuticals, chemical intermediates and petrochemicals, which are essentially interlinked industries. The total investment envisaged in these SERs is around $25 billion to $30 billion, and a large number of MNCs have already expressed interest, including German chemical giants BASF and Bayer and Mitsubishi Chemicals of Japan, as well as oil and gas companies British Petroleum and Exxon Mobil and Indian oil and gas and chemical companies.

COMMON MAN, UNCOMMON POTENTIAL: HARVESTING THE DOMESTIC ECONOMY

While India's true potential in manufacturing is being unleashed, the business of retailing is taking on a new and formidable shape as a mega industry. The size of the retail industry in India comprising all its forms has been variously estimated at $210 billion to $220 billion with an intrinsic annual growth rate of 5% to 10%. There is not much certainty to these numbers, even though they have been estimated by various credible Indian and global business consultancy firms, including AT Kearney, PwC, KSA Technopak and McKinsey & Co. On its part, McKinsey & Co has estimated that the retail market will grow to a size of $500 billion to $600 billion by 2009–10.

Roughly 97% of the retail industry in India is unorganized and represents sales from 10 to 12 million individual retailers, with average space per store of 50 square feet. India obviously has the lowest level of organization in its retail industry as compared to any emerging economy, and consequently has the greatest need. The mushrooming of malls throughout the country is the newest investment trend in India and represents an offshoot of the organization and modernization of the traditional retail trade. The share of organized retailing is expected to rise to 20% by 2010–12 though there is no unanimity on this estimate. Business consultancy firm KSA Technopak (the Indian arm of US consulting firm Kurt Salmon Associates), which has devoted significant time and resources to understanding the retail market in India, has estimated that the share of the organized sector will be 9% of the total retail market by the end of the decade. Global consultancy firms have estimated, and once again this is an average estimate, that growth in Indian retailing is powered by the shift to organized retailing which is growing by 35% to 40% annually.

Unfortunately, since the first mall appeared in 1999 the concept of selling consumer goods to the household segment through the mall format has become so popular among real estate developers and several big corporations – attracting investment enthusiasm and over-concentration in certain high-density pockets – that it has come to resemble a bit of a bubble. Nearly 20 million square feet of mall space will be operational across India between 2006 and 2007. These bubble-like conditions are more evident in some areas in the northern region of the country, especially around New Delhi and its commercial satellite town of Gurgaon, but the undisputable fact is that there is a rising trend towards consumerism and that is matched with rising expectations of a complete shopping experience, which in turn is driving the growth of modern mall- or superstore-based retailing in India. This trend is actually good news for several consumer industries in the country.

The demand for consumer and branded goods and for entertainment, as well as the emergence of several powerful retail brands in the clothing, accessories and consumer goods space, has pushed the mega and multi-store retailing format into the forefront of the consumer boom, largely due to the better understanding of the economics of housing a number of multi-product brands under one roof and of the changing consumer psyche. Currently 30% of average household expenditure is non-food related, compared with just a few years ago where less than 25% was spent on items other than food. The growth in non-food expenditure is a direct result of increasing incomes and aspirations, and the ratio will increase substantially towards non-food items in the years ahead. A shift by even 1% means an added market size of over $2 billion.

Many business groups saw the potential for this from the late 1990s, and retail chain mega stores such as Shoppers' Stop (a chain of department stores created by the Raheja group, a leading Mumbai-based construction conglomerate), Piramyd Retail (mall and private label owners controlled by the Piramal family, who also run pharmaceutical company Nicholas Piramal), Trent (department store chain from the Tata conglomerate), Pantaloon Retail (the largest of Indian chain stores that moved from apparels to food and consumer items),

Wills (the retail lifestyle brand owned by leading tobacco company ITC) and the Lifestyle Malls, among others, were seeded. In bigger cities like Mumbai there is a clear shift in consumer preference towards shopping in malls and in department stores (where the bulk of branded goods are to be found, which is the core driver of the boom in retailing), and even in other urban centers, where the conversion from footfalls to sales is less than 10%, the trend towards organized retailing is irreversible.

Piramyd Retail introduced the concept of the mega store in India with a gigantic signature store in the heart of south Mumbai's upscale residential district opening in 1999. It was a farsighted move from the Piramal family to utilize the real estate lying with Nicholas Piramal (though it generated a fair amount of controversy at the time) to build a mall, which was a novelty when no-one else was doing it. However, the innovation overtook the innovator and other groups that were already looking at similar mass retail formats quickly capitalized on the demand, first within Mumbai and its immediate suburbs and then in various cities where it has begun to have an impact on the economic landscape. Piramyd Retail is now only one of many big-name owners of mall chains and department stores. Competitor Shoppers' Stop, considered to be India's best-managed chain store company, is now 50% bigger, with 20 stores across the country (by the third quarter of 2005), against Piramyd's 12 stores, and Trent Ltd also has 20 stores across the country. Piramyd Retail's hugely successful late-2005 IPO will provide it with the resources it needs to expand its own operations by 50% by 2007, but the others too have extremely aggressive growth plans.

Shoppers' Stop is on a very powerful growth trajectory and scores very high on nearly every key parameter in the trade, such as like-to-like store sales growth, which is what the business really should be all about, and on per-square-foot sales, which is one of the highest in the industry. The management is unique because it is focused on delivering value additions. In their interactions with analysts they make no apologies for preferring optimal utilization of assets over quarterly store accretions. Their customer loyalty program has set industry benchmarks: they have well over half a million customers enrolled in their loyalty program and customer additions to the program are happening at nearly 18,000 per month. They have found that over 60% of their business comes from customers in the loyalty program. They are also the only major retail business with a strong focus on the book trade, with their takeover of India's best known chain store bookseller Crossword, a business that they have added to substantially after buying it out in 2005.

The concept of a huge network of mega department stores with a strong emphasis on cost leadership has been perfected by Pantaloon Retail Ltd, whose founder is often referred to as the Sam Walton of India. Pantaloon Retail incidentally is also the most valuable retailing company in India, with a market capitalization of around $900 million, with well over one-quarter of the stock being held by foreign institutional investors. Its brand of apparels has been around for a long time, and they have a fairly strong standing in India. It has evolved into a very focused, highly growth-oriented and very technology savvy bouquet of retail brands that now include food, lifestyle and discount store segments. The company is very well regarded both in the industry and in investment circles. The management has stated its intention to be a domestic Indian retailing giant in preparation for the inevitability of foreign retailing names eventually being allowed to set up shop in India. Their confidence can be seen from their expectation of doubling revenues every year until 2007–08. By 2006–07 they expect to earn nearly $1 billion in revenues, based largely on tripling the number of stores catering to the various segments they operate in, which they are capable enough to do.

Provogue India Ltd operates at the other end of the scale, but in a few short years beginning in 1998 has climbed to the top of the branded apparel market in India. Though it has partnered with several of the big-name department stores such as Shoppers' Stop and the Trent Ltd – promoted Westside chain of department stores, it has also followed Pantaloon's model and created a network of its own exclusive stores spread across the country, selling their own brands. They have been quiet performers with small revenues and, in stock market terms, would be considered a micro cap stock, but they are very strongly associated with India's fashion industry.

Most of the first movers into organized retailing were Mumbai-based groups with interests in real estate, and the first experimental malls and new-age retail formats were all tested in Mumbai. But the epicenter of the retail experience has shifted to New Delhi, where most of the investments are happening and most of the space additions are taking place, though Mumbai still has a large share of the action and rapidly growing cities such as Bangalore, Hyderabad and Ahmedabad are witnessing huge levels of investment in organized retailing.

Despite the bubble-like conditions in the large-store retailing format the fundamentals are very attractive indeed. The core requirement for retailing or any consumer business to survive is of course the market size. That is difficult to quantify, but statistics available on the qualitative economic clout of Indian families helps in building the argument. The rich households have been estimated to be at over five million in number by 2006–07 with 30 million people, the middle classes (the group that is really the consuming class driving the explosive growth in India) at about 75 million households comprising over 430 million people, and the "aspiring classes" comprising another 81 million households representing 470 million people and the next emerging wave of consumers (see table 8.2). According to the assessment by the National Council for Applied Economic Research (NCAER), the top level of society and the upper level of the middle class segment are increasingly spending a significant portion of their income on discretionary expenses such as entertainment, leisure, books, music and consumer goods. This is a new phenomenon for Indian consumers and those gearing to cater to them. In earlier years the upper crust would usually spend their discretionary funds outside the country, while the next levels either sought to emulate that or were bereft of options. Now that latent expenditure is finding an outlet in India.

Table 8.2: Size of Indian households by profile (million)

Class	2006–07*	2001–02	1995–96
Rich	5.2	2.6	1.2
Middle class	75.5	46.4	32.5
Aspiring	81.7	74.4	54.1

* Projected
Source: NCAER.

Like the bubble in mall building the stocks of listed retailing companies too are very expensive. But the bursting of the mall-building bubble could prove to be very beneficial to these well-capitalized players with very well-established brand recall. Also, the compounded growth rates seen in the top players is very heartening, and for several of them it is reasonable to believe – knowing their inherent strengths – that the growth momentum can be sustained. But there is the distinct possibility that the government will relax foreign investment norms for this industry and there will be a lot more competition from giant MNC retailing companies. This is a risk factor that could skew the operating environment for many of the current retailing giants.

Retailing is one of the last protected bastions of the Indian economy. Government regulations are holding up genuine growth in investment in retail versus some of the speculative kind happening in northern India, since this is still one sector where foreign direct investment is barred, which makes very little sense. Currently foreign brands can only directly sell in India using the franchisee route, which companies such as Benetton and Tommy Hilfiger have used brilliantly, and they have received quite a good consumer response. The reason for the government's reticence towards allowing investment is the political pressure being applied on it by small traders who are extremely vocal constituents. Their logic is that some of the biggest companies in the world are retail chains such as Wal-Mart, that sell every conceivable product under one roof and who could easily dominate the industry if they entered, jeopardizing a lot of their livelihoods and putting millions of jobs at risk. While that is the normal politicizing of an economic event, the reality is that India greatly needs a huge dose of investment into organized retailing. All the growth in retailing is coming from the organized players where growth is three or four times higher than the industry average. But there are just about a dozen companies that run department stores and only a handful that run supermarkets. That number has to increase, and fast, since it holds considerable growth potential as well as serious economic consequences.

Reliance in retail

A mega assault on the retail marketing industry will happen when Reliance Industries launches its chain of retail stores, or hypermarkets, as it moves to exploit the significant growth potential in this business. Reliance's entry will undoubtedly shake up the market as nothing else will, simply because of the scale at which it will unfold its hypermarkets. How much the company really intends to invest is a mystery but the industry has anticipated an investment of $6 billion to $7 billion by 2010 and that the company has targeted $20 billion in revenues in this time frame. But they have also indicated their preference to avoid the metros and big cities and begin in smaller centers first. This kind of scale is unprecedented in Indian retailing, but then everything that Reliance has done in India has been unprecedented.

Real estate

The growth of organized retailing and the mega store format that it is using, in tandem with the development of next-generation IT and industrial parks, is spurring the demand for high-quality commercial space. For example, each mall being built means that the development of several hundred thousand square feet of space is opening exciting new investment opportunities for investors in real estate in India. Each large IT park too can easily absorb a couple of hundred million dollars.

Foreign investors can participate fully in real estate, assuming that the government is serious about fulfilling its intention of allowing foreign direct investment in all forms of real estate in India, especially in mall construction. Currently foreign investment is allowed in integrated townships, which are basically privately owned mini-cities. Foreign investment is also permitted in establishing IT parks, subject to export norms. Both these categories have not done too badly in attracting overseas capital or at the minimum a very high level of interest and a commitment to invest. But allowing foreign investment in purely commercial real estate developments such as malls or office buildings will spur the real estate market on greatly and for that the government's decision-making needs to rise above vested interests determined to disallow competition. Global real estate and consulting firms have estimated that demand for commercial space is doubling annually since 2002 and that prices for quality properties have increased by 20% to 50% between 2004 and 2006. Real estate development and related activities is one of the cornerstones of the immense growth unfolding in India and the lifting of restrictions on capital formation now will swing the growth momentum faster, which is something to encourage.

From 45-odd malls in operation in 2005–06 the Indian landscape will be dotted with a minimum of 250 more functioning malls before 2010, with some of the biggest malls still to be built. Commercial real estate with malls as the crown jewels is typically what investors look for. And observing the recent impact of mall development in markets like China, the lesson is that a successful large mall tends to improve the real estate potential in outlying areas and usually drives prices higher, besides aiding the development of suburban areas. The partnership between the big retailers and real estate developers is underscored by a statement made in an interview by Kishore Biyani, founder Chairman of Pantaloon Retail; he said that he spends more time with real estate developers and investment bankers than with anyone else.

The demand from organized retailers has encouraged real estate development companies to invest significant amounts into commercial real estate. At the same time there are a number of investment pools that are being organized in a big way overseas, especially in the United States, that are looking for high-quality projects. A large portion of the Indian real estate market is unorganized, and once again educated guesstimates abound, but the market is roughly worth $50 billion in annual revenues and is growing at 25% to 30%. But in reality it could be and probably is much larger than that figure.

Funding increasingly does not seem to be a problem for highly regarded real estate developers engaged in mega residential cum commercial projects, who are increasingly being able to access investment pools. By some estimates real estate can capture 18% to 20% of all investment flowing into India. Two of the largest funds organized for the real estate sector are one with ICICI Bank and Tishman Speyer LP for $600 million and the other for $350 million organized by Savills Plc, the UK's largest real estate agency. Smaller venture capital funds such as Kotak Mahindra's Kotak India Real Estate Fund-I, successfully raised $160 million. Global corporations such as GE have made an entry into India's IT parks. GE invested $63 million through its property investment arm in an IT park being set up in Bangalore by a Singaporean company.

The opportunity for real estate investment in India, especially since the ban on foreign investment has been lifted, is clearly in favor of institutional investors. Individual investors outside of India seeking to participate in the gigantic opportunity being created by real estate developers seeking to cash in on the demand for high-end condominium housing, top-quality commercial space and the ubiquitous malls can partake of the growing pie by buying into real estate investment pools or REIT-like (real estate investment trust) structures heading into India. HDFC will launch the first fund for overseas Indians by June 2006 attempting to raise $200 million. That is the best way to do it since buying property directly, whether residential or commercial, is still cumbersome despite systemic improvements, and could turn out to be risky. For Indian investors, buying into regional opportunities or even into different projects of interest is impossible since there are no REITs in India at the moment, but that development is probably not too far off.

SERVICING THE INFRASTRUCTURE BOOM

At the 2005 World Economic Forum, which is the annual stock-taking of opportunities and returns across the globe, many of the delegates present expressed surprise at how India was growing "faster than expected". It did not go unnoticed that for the past several quarters the industry and services sectors were beginning to fire up in tandem. Industry is being driven by the gigantic construction boom, while within services it was not the high-profile sectors that were the center of attraction but sectors such as trade, transport, hotels and communications. This segment of the Indian services sector has been consistently recording double-digit growth rates in recent quarters; in fact, in the two fiscal years of 2003–04 and 2004–05 the growth rates were 11.5% and 12.4%.

Catering to the growth in domestic and cross-border trade is one of the biggest emerging opportunities. For example, the Indian container trade is expected to grow by 18% between 2005 and 2010, according to the National Maritime Development Program. Only 50% of trade from India is containerized currently, compared to an average of 85% globally.

A company such as Gateway Distriparks Ltd – which provides facilities such as inland container depots at major ports such as the JNPT, the country's largest port – fully epitomizes the growth potential even for relative newcomers, and reflects the impact of the shift to containerization. Specifically the surge in the import and export of textiles and automobiles has helped companies like this. The increase in the share of higher value manufactured products has greatly increased the demand for logistics and port services. Gopinath Pillai, the Chairman of Gateway Distriparks (in which Temasek Holdings, a company owned by the Singaporean government, has a stake), says that the company's excellent recent financial performance is a reflection of the tremendous growth in the container port sector, and is only the beginning of the story for companies in this space. It also has plans to run freight train services from ports to inland container terminals. Indian ports handle 90% of the country's trade volume. The company is expanding capacity at all locations and is looking at tapping foreign markets. Its second quarter 2005–06 net income rose fourfold to $5 million while revenue doubled to $9 million. The company is a new entrant to the stock market, having listed only in March 2005, but with a current market cap of over $400 million. Valuations seem to track rising investor interest in this sector. In January 2006, All Cargo Movers (India), a privately held company and a leading private sector logistics service provider, placed 6% of its equity with an institutional investor at a price that valued the company at $225 million, over four times its fiscal 2004–05 revenues of a little over $50 million. Here, too, the management has identified a national network of container freight stations as the route to rapid growth. The opportunity before companies in this sector is significant and the potential for capital appreciation is quite palpable.

India's export break up (see table 8.3) reflects its growing manufacturing base and the fact that it is moving away from traditional sources of export revenue, such as gems and jewelry (though this is still a significant sector), leather and agricultural commodities. Nearly half of India's physical exports come from automobiles and other engineering sectors, chemicals, electronics and petroleum products. These are also the fastest-growing segments and are in need of immense support and logistic services.

Table 8.3: India's export break up for 2004–05

	Growth %	Weight %
Plantation products	2.53	0.78
Agro-commodities	9.12	7.61
Marine products	-6.72	1.6
Minerals and ores	**73.1**	**5.29**
Leather goods	3.49	2.89
Gems and jewelry	**26.75**	**17.29**
Sports goods	-3.12	0.12
Chemicals	**24.45**	**16**
Engineering goods	**35.83**	**18.41**
Electronic goods	-2.27	2.28
Textiles	-3.72	15.16
Handicrafts	-32.79	0.43
Carpets	-0.44	0.75
Petroleum products	**86.12**	**8.57**
Others	8.6	2.64

- Automobile exports are included in "Engineering goods" and comprise 3.5% of total exports.
- Iron ore forms two-thirds of mineral exports growing at 128% and comprising 3.3% of total exports.

Source: Ministry of Commerce & Industry, Government of India

Probably the best positioned logistics company in India is Container Corporation of India (Concor as it is popularly known). It was fully owned by the Ministry of Railways before being partly offloaded to investors and listed on the stock exchange. It was specifically created in 1988 to promote containerization. By virtue of being a government-owned entity the company was given a lot of leeway in expanding and building valuable container hubs in critical locations, which makes it a formidable competitor in today's liberalizing environment. In under two decades it has built itself up to nearly $500 million in revenues (see figure 8.2) and $2.2 billion in market capitalization. Until recently, Concor had a monopoly on the use of Indian Railways' (the sole railway operator in India) freight network but that has changed with private logistics companies being allowed to own and run container freight trains. Competition has reared its head and 14 companies have applied for licenses including formidable ones, such as Reliance Infrastructure, thus greatly increasing the risk to future revenues. However, the size of the pie itself is growing since pricing of container transportation over long distances is much more competitive via a rail network as compared to transport via roads, giving Concor and now the others an edge.

Figure 8.2: Revenue acceleration at Concor (10-year trend)

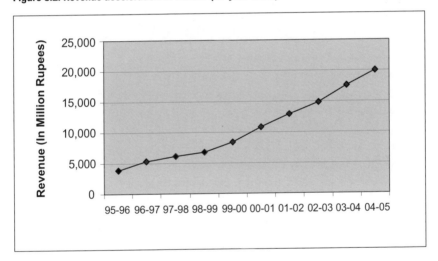

Another really big opportunity awaits the container logistics and transportation trade, and Concor in particular, in the form of the domestic container trade. Concor has a network of 51 container terminals, of which 44 are focused on international trade, while only seven are focused on domestic trade. One could almost argue that the containerization of domestic trade (which is larger than the external sector) has been ignored even by the government.

The quality of the road network and limited spare capacity on the railway networks is a primary reason why container transport has not picked up in India. Even truck manufacturing companies are only just beginning to look at producing larger numbers of multi-axle vehicles as the quality of major trunk roads improves. As India's road network develops it will push the growth of container transportation.

The change in composition of exports means that shipping companies too are witnessing a qualitative change in the opportunity for them. We looked at shipping companies from the energy transport perspective in the previous chapter, and like all crude oil carriers globally Indian shipping companies have benefited from the huge increase in the World Scale index (which shippers use to benchmark charter rates) between 2004 and 2005. Shipping companies globally see a lot of cyclicality in both charter hire rates as well as volumes carried annually. Indian shipping companies, though following much of the same cycles, are cushioned by India's rising share of world trade.

The growth rate for Indian shipping will be significantly higher than domestic macroeconomic growth rates (with a factor of 2× or 3× GDP growth) since it will correlate very significantly with growth in trade and in the external sector. So far Indian industry has been growing its merchandise and manufacturing exports at 24% to 25% a year, and import growth is similarly keeping pace. India has become a major exporter of refined petroleum products, which is the single fastest-growing segment, growing at 86% in 2004–05 to $7 billion (from almost nothing just five years prior). Petroleum exports are primarily driven by Reliance Industries' refinery output, especially the export of aviation fuel, which is very lucrative. It is looking to buy 25 product tankers over the next few years to help integrate this key activity. This trend in petroleum exports will see a further increase as other refiners have begun to expand capacities. Shipping Corporation of India (SCI) has geared up well for the increased export potential of specialized products, with its huge fleet of product carriers.

India is now getting to be a big player in steel. The cross-flow of steel from India to China has grown, and the import of intermediates such as met coke and coal has brought in and will continue to bring in large volume growth for SCI as well as GE Shipping and Mercator Lines (which has proven to be a very dynamic company). There are other Indian shipping companies too that will benefit, but the scale will be significant for these companies. Great Eastern Shipping, the country's oldest and largest private sector shipping company, is building its strength in the crude oil and dry bulk market so it is evenly exposed to growth in both the Indian energy market and the Chinese demand for hard commodities.

SCI's exposure is larger in the energy trade and it has less exposure to the dry bulk segment, where charter price rises have not kept pace with that of crude and energy carriers. But its container business could very well push growth rates and margins. The improving ratio of containerization in Indian trade will drive SCI's growing container transportation business. Containerized shipping typically grows at twice the GDP growth rate under normal conditions, but in India not only is GDP accelerating but there is a lot of catching up happening with the container trade, so the overall market for this type of transport will grow faster. China is a good example of the speed with which containerization can happen, and one could superimpose that growth to the Indian context.

IT'S TIME TO ACT RICH; THE LIFESTYLE STORY

Changing lifestyles and changing tastes are cornerstones of the emerging economic potential in India. Several surveys have shown Indians are growing in consumer confidence. One of the more interesting surveys I've seen was conducted by Synovate Pax, which does what they call an annual Pan-Asia Pacific Cross Media survey that looks at the lifestyle and spending habits of affluent Asians in 11 key markets, including India, Hong Kong, Singapore, Taiwan and Australia. The result in late 2005 showed a further upswing in growth rates of big-ticket items such as PCs, laptops, DVD players, flat screen televisions and digital video cameras, with some product categories showing annual increases of 90% to 100%. In an interesting observation made in this survey, leisure travel by air until mid-2005 increased by 71% in India as against a 19% increase in business travel.

Though the survey looks at a particular segment, it does ring true for the country as a whole and reflects the ability to satisfy aspirations. The acquisition of products such as televisions, cell phones, computers, consumer electronics, appliances and a variety of gizmos is naturally on the rise as incomes rise and availability increases. And the key outcome from that particular survey, and others that track broader market segments in India, is that not only is demand for consumer products on the rise but it is growing at a faster rate than ever.

A great play on India's newly emerging consumer market is the country's largest and the world's sixth-largest watch maker. Titan (2005 revenues of $250 million), controlled by the Tata conglomerate, is not only a very powerful consumer brand in India but it has an excellent distribution and product presence in several markets outside of India. Titan made a huge impact with its watch business in India, since it brought world-class manufacturing and distribution standards to the Indian consumer (they were among the first to use an exclusive store format). Its products are as diverse as the Indian marketplace, ranging from the mass-market Sonata brand to the high-end Nebula brand, where it retails watches at $1,200 to $1,500, making it the most expensive sub-brand in the country, targeting India's very lucrative wedding gifts market.

They were the first corporate house to venture into jewelry manufacture. They stumbled initially since their focus was on Western-style jewelry which used a lower carat gold, instead of the traditional Indian preference of a higher carat gold. Besides, Indians traditionally bought their jewelry and gold ornaments from their family jeweler whose services would have been used for generations. But they completely revamped their jewelry product portfolio a few years ago and have created a strong clientele, even amongst the world's pickiest gold buyers. They are the only jeweler in the country that certifies the purity of the gold, and precious metal purity is a big issue with consumers in India. Today they distribute across 53 Indian cities using 63 exclusive showrooms.

But its real growth story is in watches, and Titan – in tune with the Tata conglomerate's new-found philosophy of creating gigantic new markets at incredibly low price points (they've done it in cars and hotels) – is looking to make low-priced, high-quality watches for the vast Indian market. Its current value-brand Sonata, for example, which is manufactured with its same exacting standards, retails between $9 and $35 and does an annual volume of well over three million pieces.

Red, red wine ...

Improving lifestyles and more Westernized spending habits have pushed companies and businesses that were once on the fringe into the mainstream of India's investment canvas. The news late in 2005 that a Singapore-based fund took a 10% stake in Champagne Indage Ltd, India's largest wine maker with the capacity to produce 3.5 million liters annually, was a sign of the times. The company is one of a small but growing breed of companies that have identified wine making as a high-growth industry in India and are pushing hard for wine to be accepted by mainstream consumers. The equity placement by the Singaporean fund marked the mid-point of a remarkable few months in 2005, when the stock raced up four times to a market cap of over $110 million from the time it made a preferential placement of equity to Reliance Energy Investments in April 2005, equivalent to 9% of its equity to the end of the year.

According to the wine industry, the Indian wine market is expanding at 30% every year, even though it has traditionally been viewed as an elitist drink. But given the complexities involved and the long gestation period, the existing producers are relatively insulated from competition and can enjoy the benefit of a fast-growing market relatively undisturbed for the near future.

What is even more interesting is that India is the only Asian country to not only produce high-end wines but also export them to countries that have very strong wine making industries in Europe, and even to the United States. And Champagne Indage, with a few international award-winning wines in its portfolio of 35 brands, is the leader in this effort.

McDowells India from the United Breweries group is India's largest maker of spirits by volume. The United Breweries group has seen some very rapid growth in the last few years. The spirits industry is heavily regulated and heavily taxed. In fact, interstate regulation is at such a level that spirits manufactured in one state cannot be imported into another. Despite all these restrictions and the presence of foreign brands in increasing numbers, Indian companies have done very well, led by the consumption of beer.

Confectionary and candy bar manufacturers Cadbury India (the management repurchased all outstanding stock and was subsequently de-listed from the Indian stock exchanges) and Nestlé India too will testify to the improving discretionary spending power in India. Like wine (though on a much larger scale), candy consumption in India has always been viewed as a luxury and was more of an urban phenomenon, but that is changing too. The innovation that these companies – and other consumer and staple food companies like Hindustan Lever (the Unilever subsidiary), which is the largest consumer marketing company in India – introduced was to reduce the size of their products into a single serve or single use, thus reducing the price point and increasing affordability. This has served to greatly expand the consumer market.

All of these packaged food and beverage segments constitute a value-added part of the processed foods industry that is seeing the full growth impact of a modernizing India with changing habits and tastes. Marketing studies (including a recent one by AC Nielsen–Confederation of Indian Industry (CII)) have drawn a link between the new retailing format and growth in packaged food and beverages. The packaged foods and beverages industry is worth about $22 billion (according to the Ministry of Food Processing). But the total size of the processed food industry is around $69 billion to $70 billion and growing at 10%, thus underscoring the immense potential.

India certainly has the base to build a significant value-added food processing industry. According to the ministry, it is the world's second-largest producer of fruits and vegetables, the second-largest producer of milk, 30% of the world's spices are grown in India, and it has 20% of the world's cattle. But just 2% of the vegetables and fruits are processed, and just 1% of the meat product sees any value addition. A lot of proposals have been made in recent years, including foreign direct investments, which should lead to a gradual transformation and increasing value addition, throwing up attractive investment opportunities in the process.

There's no biz like showbiz...

The wealth effect and consumer confidence seem to have blossomed into a magnificent growth opportunity for the media and entertainment sector, including television, films and radio. This sector has benefited tremendously from the synthesis of various trends, the rise of consumerism, the rise of brand power, rising disposable incomes, demographics and urbanization, the proliferation of satellite and cable television in India, and the demand for a larger range and better quality of entertainment content both in film and television. The interesting thing about the Indian entertainment industry is that besides large untapped domestic potential, it has a very significant market in the 20 to 25 million persons of Indian origin living outside the country, with five million living in the US, UK and Canada. This group has been estimated to have a disposable net worth of $330 billion. In the Indian film industry, as well as the satellite television industry, this market segment is considered to be a key homogenous distribution segment.

Television entertainment, especially cable- and satellite-based broadcasting, is something households have in common. The television penetration rate in Indian households is about 50%, with 108 million television homes against a total of 200 million households. Of this number, 61 million homes have access to cable television, with an intrinsic growth of 15%. Since the late 1990s a number of quality plays on this industry have gone public, each with solid business models and earning profiles. The leader by a long shot in this industry is Zee Television (fiscal 2004–05 revenues of $300 million; market cap of $1.5 billion) (see figure 8.3), whose chairman, Subhash Chandra, is considered to be a visionary who had the foresight to

Figure 8.3: Zee TV: Strong EBITDA margins

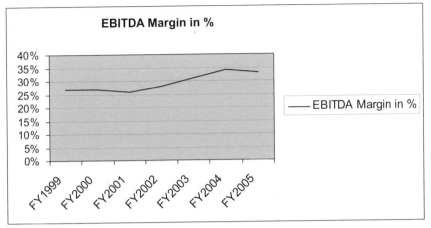

Source: Company reports.

position his company for the convergence of media. The company that began with a television channel in the early 1990s when the industry was in its infancy is now the largest and most successful of Indian broadcasters, owning some of the most popular channels, besides content production including film and television and a cable network. It has also exploited the demand from overseas Indians for entertainment with a selection of channels beamed via satellite. Their entry into direct-to-home broadcasting in India is expected to consolidate its hold further.

Convergence worked well for Zee Telefilms for over a decade but shareholders were flustered with less than satisfactory growth in enterprise value, largely due to difficulties in the cable business and due to increasing competition in news programing. The management responded in March 2006 by splitting its news and regional language channels and the cable TV and direct-to-home business into two companies and listing them separately since these businesses will likely require an infusion of funds sooner or later. Zee Telefilms will thus be a focused producer of TV programs, music and movies.

Cable TV is the largest revenue earner for the entertainment industry, where Zee TV and companies like Hinduja TMT are solidly entrenched in key markets. The other top revenue categories are television broadcasting, film production and television content. There are no authoritative statistics available on the industry that is still unorganized in bits, but for 2005 cumulative television media and cable subscription revenues have been estimated at $4.6 billion. Television advertising revenues have been estimated at $1 billion spread over 130 channels with an intrinsic growth of 8% to 10%, while cable subscriber revenue growth is higher at 15%. The Hindi film industry's revenues have been estimated at $1 billion, though in reality that figure should be much higher.

While convergence was the way to go for industry leader Zee TV, others such as TV-18 have made a huge impact on news content production and broadcasting (see figure 8.4). TV-18's recent growth rate has been almost unparalleled thanks to its content tie-up with CNBC India, where it produces very popular stock market programing, including live market coverage and other investment-related content. It has cleverly leveraged its branding as a business/news channel by setting up a consumer channel (positioned as the voice of the Indian consumer) which has paid off superbly and is ranked as the fastest-growing news channel in India.

Figure 8.4: Market share of English news broadcasters

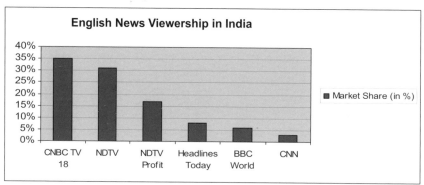

Source: Surveys, company reports

Differentiation in content production has been the key to success, especially for firms like Balaji Telefilms, whose approach to programing has been very in tune with the popular mood and has led to the creation of several genre-defining television serials in four Indian languages. Its size (just $55 million to $60 million in revenue) belies the clout it carries in the world of Indian television content or the impact it has made on increasing television viewership.

Flying high

Flying high may be a cliché but it describes the Indian aviation sector very well. According to an estimate by global aviation journal *Aviation Daily*, India's domestic air travel volume is expected to grow by 25% between 2005 and 2010.

A number of airlines have commenced operations in the space of just two years, and many have begun with very significant plans. Indigo, one of the new airlines, for example, has commenced with plans to induct 110 aircraft over the next few years.

The cost of air travel has plummeted. A frequent air traveler in India recently mentioned to me that Indian airports have now begun to resemble public bus terminals, with similar large crushes of people waiting to board planes. Despite low fares, of the airlines in the public domain Jet Airways is very profitable and SpiceJet is expected to reach profitability in 2006.

The aviation sector is seeing more competition than ever before but Jet Airways has become the dominant carrier in India after its $500 million all-cash takeover of Air Sahara in January 2006, excluding its liabilities. The combined entity now has 80 aircraft as compared to 55 aircraft with Indian Airlines (the state-owned carrier). They also account for nearly half the total number of seats flown per day, spread over 434 flights a day.

This transaction also highlights over-capacity as the key risk in Indian aviation since both Jet Airways and SpiceJet were losing market share to new entrants. This is the same risk factor that undermined a number of airlines in the mid-1990s and remains a key threat to existing airlines and new entrants alike.

SHOW ME THE MONEY

Speculation is the lifeblood of any financial market and apparently of a great many Indians too. After a very long hiatus, the number of Indians flocking to the stock market – and now that some really great trading platforms are in place, even to the high-tech Indian commodities markets – is increasing. The spurt in volumes in both segments – equity markets as well as commodities – has been stupendous over the last couple of years, and these segments trade cumulatively $6 billion to $7 billion worth of securities every day.

A very interesting play on the boom in speculation and trading volumes, thanks to increased retail participation in India's financial and commodity markets, is Financial Technologies (India) Ltd. The company has developed the electronic trading platform and associated settlement and operating systems that are used by an overwhelming number of National Stock Exchange (the country's largest stock exchange) dealer terminals across the country. A large number of brokerage houses, asset management companies, banks and other institutions use the FTIL trading solutions. Their systems are used by a total of 35,000 terminals, and it receives an annual user fee from each of these, thus constituting something resembling an annuity. Its volume and revenue growth in the last year or so has been amazing, with over a 100% increase in trader terminals. The trading solutions offered are integrated in the sense that trades can be conducted across exchanges and segments, and the user front end ranges from desktops to PDAs.

That is not all; they are the company that, in tandem with the National Stock Exchange, State Bank of India and HDFC Bank among others, set up the Multi-Commodity Exchange of India, which has developed into the second-largest commodity exchange in India, garnering 43% of the total traded volume. It may be the second-largest exchange but it is by far the most innovative, having introduced gold and crude oil futures, besides a large number of metals, agro-commodities and even petrochemical futures, being one of only a handful globally to do so. The FTIL solution powers the trading engines at this exchange as well. They have forged close and formal relations with key commodity associations in the country that enhance the viability of the exchange. The company has aimed to grow faster by recognizing the potential in the commodity business. FTIL has two subsidiary companies and a joint venture company now engaged right from running and growing an exchange and trading systems to warehousing capabilities and building a price aggregating and disseminating platform aimed at the actual participants in the agricultural business, including farmers, processors and traders. The commodity exchange and ancillary businesses will be a key driver for FTIL in tandem with its equity-trading solutions.

The company's fortunes are linked with the volumes in the market and the flow of household savings into the equity and commodity markets, and the growth of the brokerage and asset management businesses. India has around 40 million equity investors, representing just 4% of the population. This is an incredibly low figure and is bound to increase. Additionally, the estimate of annual household savings is around $200 billion to $225 billion, a great portion of which is underutilized from an investment perspective. If even 10% of this figure flows into the financial markets the growth rates will be phenomenal, and one of the biggest beneficiaries will be FTIL.

THE DARK HORSE: INVESTING IN THE DEFENSE SECTOR

We've seen the level of innovation and growth that privatization or even private sector participation can bring to an industry. The supply of equipment to the Indian defense sector has for all practical purposes been opened up to private companies in an unparalleled manner. Over the last few years there has been an increasing trend in allocation towards acquisition of capital equipment and development, but since the 1990s there have been changes in India's procurement policy and the emphasis has gradually been on increasing domestic sourcing of weapons as well as technology.

India has long had an excellent network of government-run defense laboratories which has been a fertile ground for developing scientific talent. As a result of the government's policy to open up the defense sector to private sector participation, the trend is that a number of scientists are leaving the government-run laboratories and joining the Indian private sector, either in R&D or establishing their own companies. These companies are now increasingly supplementing the cutting-edge work done by the government laboratories and will benefit substantially from the increased allocation to defense spending as well as from the trend of outsourcing critical technology development to the private sector. For many of these companies the technologies being developed for the defense sector have spillover applications for other sectors as well. For example, the companies that specialize in microwave communications technology primarily developed for defense application have a huge market elsewhere. There is also potential with the development of different types of fuel cell battery technologies by High Energy Batteries Ltd (revenues under $10 million), a dividend-paying micro cap company working for the Defense Research and Development Organization (DRDO) and another government lab. Some of these technologies have helped this company develop markets outside the country. The nickel cadmium batteries it has developed have been approved by the Indian military for use in aircraft, helicopters, missiles, torpedoes, battle tanks and military communications. Its products have also been approved by the Indian Space Research Organization for use in satellite launch vehicles. Its projected growth rates make it an exciting company to watch.

The companies that are created by ex-scientific personnel from the Indian defense industry have certain advantages. The sector itself is very difficult to break into, and, especially after a procurement scandal hit in 2001, access to decision-makers has become difficult. The procurement process itself can be very cumbersome, so those companies that have the necessary links are advantageously placed and are relatively insulated from competition.

The companies catering to the Indian military establishment could easily be among the fastest growing in the country, given the growing level of military outsourcing to private industry. One of this breed of companies riding the new wave is Astra Microwave. It perfectly reflects the potential for the entire spectrum of companies that are now becoming a part of the public–private partnership in building defense technology. Astra was created by a group of former scientists from the country's premier defense laboratory, the Defense Research and Development Organization, and has been in existence since 1992–93.

Astra Microwave has been one of the best performing Indian stocks in 2005. Its revenues for fiscal 2005 stood at barely $15 million but its market capitalization by the beginning of 2006 was $250 million, making it one of the most expensive listed stocks in India by a long shot. But the company has had a remarkable trend of very high earnings growth in recent quarters. For 2006 its revenue growth will easily exceed 100% to $30 million; obviously expectations are running high for subsequent growth (see figure 8.5). Though it has exposure to the telecom industry and to the Indian Space Research Organization (ISRO), its growth is being driven by the supply of military hardware, notably radar surveillance equipment and components for the various missile programs.

Figure 8.5: Astra Microwave

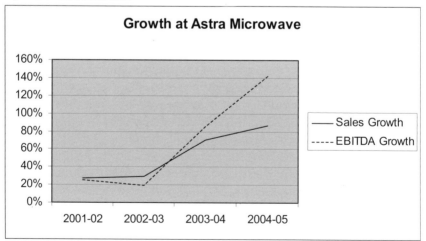

Source: Bloomberg

Other interesting small companies that cater to the military's need for specialized equipment, include Zen Technologies. This company specializes in developing training simulators for the armed forces and police services in India, which considerably reduces the cost of training personnel. Dynamatic Technologies ($20 million revenues and $110 million market cap) produces for the military-aerospace industry. Like the other companies it also has significant expertise in civilian areas and supplies hydraulic pumps for tractors and cars, with a very strong export market.

Bharat Electronics (fiscal 2004–05 revenues of $730 million) is the largest player in the market for military equipment, and the stock has done exceedingly well in recent times, giving it a current market capitalization of $1.8 billion. It took the market a very long time however to warm up to BEL's potential, and for the longest time it was available at a fraction above its cash holdings. Nearly 90% of its revenues come from the Indian army and air force. It supplies products such as air defense guns and systems, 3D static radars for the air force, battlefield surveillance systems, electronic warfare systems for the navy and land navigation systems which are fitted on main battle tanks. Other major corporations such as Mahindra & Mahindra, the utility vehicle and farm equipment maker, also produce armored vehicles for the military, a major growth area, and engineering giant Larsen & Toubro also has a division that caters to the military.

A POWERFUL GROWTH VEHICLE – THE INSURANCE SECTOR

The Indian insurance industry is really the only genuine virgin industry in the country. Five years after opening up the insurance industry the penetration rate is between 2% and 3%. The industry can visualize very rapid growth, and that too for a long time – at least 15 to 20 years. No wonder that, unlike in other industries, almost every major global insurance company is either already there or on its way. Companies like AIG, the world's largest insurer, Allianz, Europe's largest insurer, and several others including Chubb, New York Life, SunLife of Canada, Prudential Plc, UK, and ING are already in the thick of the battle to capture market share, and their joint ventures are among the fastest growing in the country. The Indian government estimates that between 2000 and 2010 annual insurance premiums will rise to $80 billion from $8 billion, an expected compound rate of growth of 25.8% over a decade. This is a fantastic rate of growth and is very realistic. Before the coming of the private sector and foreign players, life insurance in India was viewed as a quasi savings instrument and the emphasis on risk mitigation was minimal. That mindset has changed, largely due to a change in perception and awareness of the benefits of insurance and, more importantly, the tremendous increase in choice.

At present there are three financial-listed companies that have insurance subsidiaries: ICICI (Prudential ICICI), HDFC (HDFC Standard Life) and Kotak Mahindra Bank (OM Kotak). But there are other industrial groups with strong insurance businesses; Tata AIG, Bajaj Allianz and Birla Sunlife are the key players among them. And there will be individual companies that will do fabulously. For example, Allianz AG CEO Michael Diekmann has forecast that his joint venture in India will grow at 44% compounded for at least three years until 2007–08, at which point it would make over a billion dollars in annual revenues.

Today there is not much that an individual or institutional investor can do to participate in the tremendous boom in insurance in India, but the steps that the Indian government is taking could change that. Despite a lot of opposition from political parties and from the public sector employee unions, the government has begun to relax a lot of the restrictions that were in place when the sector first opened up. This could eventually lead to a higher stake in these insurance companies by the non-Indian partners, by either buying out the Indian partners or bringing in additional capital. The Indian groups, banks and corporations that have partnered these global majors will eventually look for a listing as both a possible exit route and also in order to unlock the tremendous value that is being created by the rapid growth and increased insurance penetration. To add to this is the possibility that some or all of India's public sector insurance giants may eventually be partially or fully privatized. There is a lot of opposition to this idea, but there is also an understanding that other than protecting jobs and vested political interests there is no fathomable logic for the government to be in the insurance business.

The growth in demand for insurance and the funds mobilization that it entails could not have come at a better moment in India's growth story. India's greatest need is for investment in infrastructure, which, given their long gestation, requires long-term investment funds, the kind that patient equity holders can provide or can be obtained from long-term debt holders. By nature of their business where liabilities are long term (that is, the typical payoff comes way in the future), insurance companies and pension fund companies need to create assets that are similarly long term in nature and are suited to fund infrastructure creation.

OPPORTUNITIES AND THREATS

9

INDIA AND ITS APPROACH TO ENERGY SECURITY

Within the global energy industry, the year 2005 was marked by a growing recognition that India, already the world's fifth-largest energy market, and China will be battling it out for the control of global energy assets. State-owned oil companies belonging to each country are desperately trying to outwit each other in the fight over oil assets though they have also cooperated in acquiring some. China's CNOC won the fight against India's ONGC Ltd for the Toronto Stock Exchange-listed Petro Kazakh, while ONGC and the China National Petroleum Corporation collaborated successfully in the bid for some of PetroCanada's oil assets in Syria. Earlier in the year, ONGC, through ONGC Videsh, its overseas acquisition subsidiary, went one step ahead and cobbled together an unprecedented deal with the government of Nigeria. In association with Mittal Steel NV, ONGC agreed to spend $6 billion in building a refinery, a railway network, an oil pipeline, schools, hospitals and other infrastructure in the oil-rich but otherwise impoverished Nigeria, in exchange for the right to potentially produce 650,000 barrels of oil per day and ship it to India. That level of production will add nearly 30% to India's daily oil availability.

At present, India imports around 70% of the 2.4 to 2.8 million barrels of oil it consumes per day, nearly two-thirds of which comes from the Middle East. According to the International Energy Agency (IEA), India will import over 90% of its oil requirements by the year

2020, despite the considerable efforts being expended in the domestic oil exploration program. As of now India has just about 0.5% of the world's proven oil reserves, and how the exploration program will turn out is anybody's guess. India's daily oil demand is expected to double to 5.6 million barrels per day long before 2020, as the per capita consumption level increases and a large number of consumers using traditional fuels are brought into the conventional energy fold. ONGC has now undertaken one of the most extensive international seismic data-gathering programs as a prelude to what could be an international acquisition binge. One of the key elements of India's strategy is to reduce its dependence on Middle Eastern oil thereby reducing the risk of supply disruptions. India is not alone in doing this, which adds to the pressure to act fast in grabbing assets elsewhere.

One more reason why diversifying away from the Middle East makes sense is that most of the asset acquisitions overseas have been by way of oil equity, which is advantageous to India. What this means is that companies like ONGC and GAIL will make a one-time capital investment to buy a stake in a block and develop it; the oil or gas that is pumped out is taken away in a ratio determined by its stake in that field. Thus there is no subsequent cash outflow except for transportation costs, and the country is protected from fluctuating oil prices. This becomes a significant strategy, for according to the IEA a sustained $10 per barrel rise in the price of oil leads to a 1% contraction in India's GDP and a 2.5% rise in inflation, with a lag of a year. The results from these deals could show sooner rather than later. The Sakhalin I oilfield in Russia, where ONGC Videsh has a 20% stake, began production in October 2005 and reports from the companies involved in that effort indicate that India could get its full share of oil flow of 100,000 barrels per day from the end of 2006 or early 2007. From April 2006 to the end of the year it expects to get 50,000 barrels per day and with this output its investment of $2.8 billion could be recovered within two years or less from its share of the oil.

India appears to be single-minded in its approach to securing oil assets overseas as much as the Chinese are. There has been veiled criticism of India's approach in the West, especially of the type of deal that was done with Nigeria and the possibility that India may do more of such deals with other countries, thereby undermining Western oil companies' efforts at growing their own reserves. Western oil companies are specifically barred from offering these kinds of deals to win contracts. China's experience with US oil company Unocal has shown that a global hunt for assets only leads to confrontation with global powers. India could be going down that path as it forges links with numerous countries whose international reputation is not very palatable, such as those in Central Asia and around the Caspian Sea region, which is the hottest new destination for oil investments, or even countries such as Iran or Sudan where it has already made large investments. India has been maintaining a military base for the past several years in the Central Asian region, and it has been speculated upon that this is to guarantee stability in what is now becoming a crucial area for it. ONGC has also picked up assets in Venezuela, Egypt, Libya, Russia (Sakhalin, in Siberia) and Vietnam. Reliance Petroleum on its part had enough foresight to calibrate its gigantic refinery to process a range of crude, including heavy crude, and has been importing it from Venezuela from the beginning. Other Indian oil refiners are expected to do the same. The Venezuelan President Hugo Chavez's distaste for the United States and his attempt to reduce dependence on them for crude offtake has come as a blessing for India. He emphasized the point that he felt that India was not benefiting from Venezuelan oil assets enough and urged more investment from India during a visit to New Delhi in March 2005.

The Americans in particular have taken affront to India's oil dealings with "unacceptable" regimes, Iran in particular. India is working on a gigantic gas deal with Iran, where a pipeline is to be laid under the Arabian Sea to India's west coast. But India has no reason to accommodate any criticism or anyone else's interests. Western oil companies have already saturated the world's oil-producing assets and control oil assets completely, even in places like Nigeria, leaving emerging nations like China and India to scramble and grab assets wherever they can be found. Politics and pressure from activists at home has forced some Western oil companies out of certain countries, where human rights may be an issue or corrupt regimes prevent oil wealth from trickling down to the people or where the governments support religious extremism. Sudan and Syria are two countries where ONGC Videsh has picked up the stakes of Canadian oil companies Talisman Energy and PetroCanada.

According to the Federation of Indian Chambers of Commerce and Industry (FICCI), a pan-Asian gas grid is a very real possibility, spanning from Iran and the Caspian region in the west to China and Myanmar in the east to Siberia in the north. India becomes a key player here with three possible pipelines flowing to it, including the pipeline from Iran through Pakistan into India, the Central Asian pipeline and a pipeline from Myanmar through Bangladesh into India.

While scouting for oil assets overseas has become a cornerstone of India's strategy to ensure its energy security, there are alternatives available that will be a lot less costly. One alternative is to ensure a steady supply of coal, a fuel which has become even more important in India's energy mix, especially since India's power industry is the key driver of projected energy consumption (including gas-fired plants), along with growing demand for automotive fuels of course. In chapter 7 we discussed the investment plans being implemented by India's power industry where generating capacity will be increased by over 100,000 MW by 2012, a large portion of which will be coal and gas fired. India has made significant infrastructural preparations to ensure the flow of coal and natural gas from abroad.

The availability of fuel is not the only major risk to India's energy security, the price of that fuel is critical too especially for power generation. Ensuring adequate supplies of domestic coal thus becomes imperative. India is sitting on the third-largest coal reserves in the world and needs to push hard to exploit this. A lacuna in India's energy policy is that while imported coal-fired power plants is considered a viable option, not enough is being done to dramatically increase domestic coal production, which would be a much cheaper option. At the present coal mining is a monopoly controlled by Coal India Ltd and other public sector entities but the task of increasing production is clearly beyond them. A key element of the plan to ensure energy security should therefore be to bring in as much private sector investment into coal mining as possible. Captive coal mines are being handed over to integrated steel producers; this policy needs to be broadened to include merchant coal miners too. If domestic coal production is increased then mega power plants can be set up at the coal pithead thus eliminating haulage costs. If the interlinked national power transmission grid can be expanded, there can be greater cohesion between power generated by mega plants run on domestic coal with power from coastal plants using imported fuel, then the blended cost of power will be substantially lower.

Though India has significant coal reserves that must be exploited the quality of coal is poor with large ash content and by some estimates only 20% of this coal is actually recoverable. As a result there is a concerted move to use coal gasification technology – or what is known as clean coal technology – for energy extraction. Accelerated development of coal bed methane gas is also a strong possibility. GAIL is the only known Indian energy company trying to commercialize surface coal gasification technology. It has also invested $20 million and teamed up with a Canadian company to commence underground coal gasification projects. A small Indian company called Great Eastern Energy Corporation Ltd (GEECL) is actively developing a market for coal bed methane in West Bengal. It recently raised

£10.9 million in London's Alternative Investment Market (AIM) to develop 20 wells producing this gas. This is the first project of its kind in India and the enthusiastic reception that the company got in the London market in mid-December 2005 shows that there is no shortage of global funding for developing clean energy sources for the Indian market.

The second alternative towards enhancing energy security is to increase domestic oil and gas exploration efforts, and to that extent the privatization of the exploration program has been a welcome move that has already begun to pay off handsomely with large offshore gas discoveries. A few more discoveries like that, especially of oil, can change the picture significantly. The major issue with the newly discovered gas fields is that they are deepwater blocks, where extraction is a delicate and complicated task, and therefore the timing of production is by no means certain. Production schedules at a couple of major new gas fields have already been pushed back by a year or so. ONGC alone is pumping $2.5 billion a year into its domestic oil exploration program. A major oil discovery was made recently in the north western state of Rajasthan by Cairn Energy of the UK. Bringing in private players has increased the depth of the exploration efforts besides bringing in much needed new production technology. Use of new technology has helped revive production from once abandoned fields.

There are other alternatives too. The government used to maintain an elaborate machinery doling out subsidies to shield domestic consumers from rising oil prices. Fuel subsidies formed a very large part of the government deficit and played a great role in distorting true demand and supply patterns, and consumption would be reasonably inelastic irrespective of where global energy prices were. Subsidies have now been greatly reduced, except for cooking fuel used by very poor families. The role of reversing subsidies in order to encourage restraint in the use of fuels could prove to be significant in enhancing India's energy security. This logic should be applied to the power sector too. Until all categories of users, especially urban residential and rural agrarian consumers are made to pay for their power consumption, India may never achieve self-sufficiency in power generation. Pricing power to reflect its true cost may actually serve to improve availability and reduce cost in the long run.

A key element to having reliable power will be increasing the share of nuclear energy. The government's long-term plan is to eventually generate 25% of the country's electricity from nuclear sources. At present the share of nuclear energy is 2.7% or just 3,000 MW. According to the World Nuclear Association (WNA) India is reasonably self-reliant in nuclear technology but has not been able to pursue large scale power generation largely due to the fact it does not have adequate uranium deposits within the country. The WNA feels that by 2020 India should be able to produce 20,000 MW of nuclear-based power. The Indian atomic establishment is developing technology using thorium as a fuel since there are large deposits in the country. India has about 54,000 tons of inferred uranium reserves and an additional 23,000 tons of reserves are estimated. In the case of thorium it has 290,000 tons of inferred reserves, representing one-quarter of the world's total.

There is uncertainty over the United States' proposed nuclear co-operation with India, despite the enthusiasm shown by the two governments. If the deal passes legislative scrutiny in the US, it will enable access to additional technology and nuclear materials by India. Countries like Russia, France, the UK and Japan have also welcomed nuclear co-operation with India as has the International Atomic Energy Agency (IAEA). This deal basically puts India on par with China as far as access to nuclear materials is concerned. Whatever direction Indo–US nuclear co-operation takes the underlying logic is undeniable – that India needs to generate nuclear energy in tandem with energy from other non-fossil fuels.

The experience of Suzlon Energy has shown that India can harness alternate energy sources, especially wind power, very successfully. There are already fiscal incentives available from the government to establish commercial wind energy farms and there should be adequate resources made available to push this form of clean energy. India is already the fourth-largest producer of wind energy. Between 2002 and 2005 the generating capacity from wind grew by 35%. Still, by 2012 the contribution of wind energy to India's power spectrum will be less than 7%, but there is no reason why this renewable energy source cannot be tapped in a bigger way.

The sugar industry widely uses bagasse, a by-product from the sugar extraction process, to generate power. This co-generation of power has become a very lucrative revenue source for the sugar companies, which sell over 600 MW of surplus power to the state grids, though the potential is for seven to 10 times that.

The sugar industry has also been actively pushing for the increased use of ethanol blended with petrol as a viable automotive fuel. There have been some issues that need to be resolved with the use of 10% ethanol blended with petrol, especially issues with engine compatibility. India being a price-sensitive market, this issue has not yet become a priority with automobile manufacturers. Essentially, though calibrating fuel delivery systems and making engines robust enough to handle the significantly higher levels of vapor and oxygen may take a bit of time and cost, it would be well worth it. The oil refining industry has expressed willingness to speed up the blending process and increase fuel availability but has fretted about the consistent availability of ethanol within the country to start with. A similar effort is being made to develop bio diesel, which is a blend of an acid extracted from virgin or used vegetable oils or animal fats and petroleum diesel. In the case of bio diesel the automotive engines require no modification since the properties of the two fuels are the same. In France, using a minimum of 5% bio diesel in petroleum diesel is mandatory, and the United States has high rates of bio diesel usage. India is making efforts towards a 10% bio diesel ratio.

Brazil has demonstrated technology for using 100% ethanol as an automotive fuel extracted entirely from sugarcane or molasses. All vehicles in Brazil use fuel with a higher ratio than the artificial 10% limit on the ethanol blend with petrol. India too has had rich experience in experimenting with the use of ethanol-based fuel systems, even those using 100% ethanol. Prestigious institutes such as the Indian Institute of Science, Bangalore and other national institutes and universities have conducted research on ethanol use for decades. But it was the lack of a clear government policy towards alternate automotive fuels and lack of funding from industry, even the sugar industry which stood to benefit the most, that derailed the research effort. The environment in the country is different today, and there is no reason why India cannot race ahead with the necessary research, or even collaborate with countries like Brazil, and develop the technologies needed to commercialize this renewable fuel source.

Brazil has calibrated itself towards using ethanol as a substantive automotive fuel. And the Brazilian sugar industry is dedicated in its production of ethanol, unlike in India where only a marginal portion of the molasses derived from sugarcane crushing is used to produce ethanol. Even China and the United States produce more ethanol (the US produces it from corn) than India, and India has the world's second-largest sugar industry after Brazil.

India's dependence on oil and fossil fuel can be substantially reduced by using a mix of alternate fuels especially for power generation and by going green in the automotive sector. These are viable alternatives that could very well change the dynamics of India's growth over the next decade or two.

10

INDIA AND CHINA: CREATING A SUSTAINABLE ADVANTAGE

The creation of the East Asia trading bloc in 2005–06 is a significant and weighty event in world trade, and in geopolitics for that matter. The inclusion of India, Australia and New Zealand in the ASEAN + 3 trading block (that is, ASEAN nations plus Japan, China and South Korea) has created the world's most powerful trading bloc after the EU, covering one-fifth of global trade. In some ways it becomes more powerful than the EU, since it encompasses the fastest-growing regions covering half the world's population, and is powered by Asia's largest economies. The economy that most of the ASEAN nation's have significant trade relations with is China. And the fact that the de facto leader of the block is China and not Japan or India has not been lost on anyone. There is a lot at stake here since the East Asian bloc may have started out as an economic partnership bloc but may well blossom into a free trade zone backed by political and military alliances, which will easily make it the dominant alliance in world politics, superseding the EU and most certainly APEC.

Added to this scenario is the possibility of an India–China free trade area (FTA), as proposed by the Chinese Prime Minister Wen Jiabao during a visit to India in early 2005. Despite the potential to cooperate, India versus China remains the perennial debate. The reason there is a debate on the potential in India and China is that these are the two biggest growth opportunities the world has seen in a long while, and probably will ever see again. Both these economies dominated world trade for a long time before the rise of Western Europe, and both hope to regain that power quickly, hence the interest. *The Economist* magazine once equated the emergence of India and China to the emergence of Germany and the United States in the previous two centuries and the impact those developments had in the world. But the two Asian giants have adopted entirely different approaches to their economic growth. The question that is really being asked is which of the two approaches will work and where do the relative and specific advantages lie.

China has had a head start, with reforms beginning in 1978 (a full 13 years ahead of India), and it has accomplished a lot. That India has a lot of catching up to do is undisputed. The points on which China scores over India are well known: the state-of-the-art infrastructure, the labor pool designed for an industrializing economy, a population stronger in basic education, and a focused political leadership undisturbed by opposition. But a look at the annual Global Competitiveness ranking for 2005–06 from the World Bank tells a different story; India stands just one rank behind China, and more importantly (from India's perspective) China dropped three places while India rose five places from the previous year. The World Bank's methodology for the competitiveness rankings includes an assessment of factors, institutions and policies that drive productivity, which in turn is used to assess the level of prosperity and the growth potential. The interesting point made in the report is the high level of technology absorption in India, but the factors holding back both India and China are inherent weaknesses in public institutions, notably political ones. Official corruption is a major problem in both countries. The other major drawback would be public finances; the high fiscal deficit and public debt, largely in India's case, work against long-term productivity. For example, the Indian government spends close to 35% of its revenue on interest payments while the Chinese government spends 15% on the same account. Thus the Indian government has greatly reduced economic flexibility and has less to use for development initiatives as opposed to China. As a result, macroeconomic stability is another gap that India needs to close with China.

According to another set of rankings developed by the World Bank, called the Governance Index, India scores better on control of corruption, the rule of law and regulatory effectiveness, but in terms of political stability and government effectiveness China is ahead.

However, relative political stability in China has come at a frightful price over the decades, which included forcible relocation of millions of people and the events at Tiananmen Square, where the Chinese government killed hundreds of its own people in June 1989 to beat back a "counter revolution".

Despite inherent weakness in political decision-making the qualitative edge that India holds over China is understated and not well understood. India does have genuine advantages over many, if not all, emerging markets, making the quality of the opportunity rather difficult to match. The real argument is not whether India has been able to put up gleaming new airports and gigantic networks of expressways, because as each of the tiger economies of Asia has shown, that is something that will come in due course, and in many parts of the country the building is already well under way. And corruption and quality of governing institutions is a serious issue in all of the Asian tiger economies in varying degrees, including China, but despite this they have all seen robust investment-led growth for a long period of time. The real arguments are whether India has a sustainable advantage over other emerging markets, and whether it can attract the investments it needs from global capital in a new world whose investment spectrum is dominated by China, and as a consequence, whether India can offer greater and more stable long-term opportunity.

A HUGE POOL OF MANAGERIAL AND ENTREPRENEURIAL TALENT

Ask any multinational company that has been in India long enough what they think is the greatest asset they have in India and the answer in most cases will be their managerial personnel. For example, British multinational Unilever Plc has been exceptional at exporting its management personnel from India to its various subsidiaries around the world, and was also amongst the first major global corporations to have one of its Indian CEOs sit on the Unilever board of directors. Citibank is another example of an MNC utilizing its Indian personnel globally. Quality managerial talent is a key difference in India's favor.

This well-developed managerial talent plus the entrepreneurial drive and now increasing access to capital makes India an exciting opportunity. The Indian IT industry may have been created by an entrepreneurial spark ignited from outside the country but it was built to current levels by some exceptional managerial talent developed inside it. In the case of pharmaceuticals, both the entrepreneurial spark and managerial talent were home grown. In China, though there is ample entrepreneurship it is the government that decides which industry needs to be promoted and which company gets the funding and who eventually survives and grows. That is a significant difference between the two systems, where one is completely immersed in an entrepreneurial free-market system driven by self-interest and self-preservation and the other is still in a controlled economy driven by directives from a central authority.

India probably has the unique distinction of being an economy developing rapidly without any direct financial or directional push from the government, unlike the Chinese and other East Asian economies. Even Japan had the powerful Ministry for International Trade and Investment (MITI) that drove selected predetermined industries to great heights. The Indian IT miracle happened because the sector was left alone to do what it had to do. The success that Indian companies enjoy and the competitive edge developed is purely a testimony to the management strength, the level of entrepreneurship and their innate resourcefulness. This is reflected in the competitive edge developed even in sectors where India has no known competitive advantage: for example, in petrochemicals, where India has the world's largest petrochemical complex and the world's third-largest grassroots petroleum refinery; and in copper, where Sterlite Industries has created the lowest cost copper producer in the world on a conversion cost basis. Hindustan Aluminum's products trade at a premium to aluminum prices on the London Metal Exchange, while Tata Steel has gone from being the world's most inefficient steel producer to the lowest cost producer (on a per ton basis). These are but a few examples of what Indian managerial excellence is able to achieve, and not because of the government but despite of it. India's development is being driven by strong and competitive managements that have access to the best of the country's highly developed talent pool.

Indian companies are also making a small but rising number of global acquisitions, and these are increasing in value. Unlike Chinese companies that have hit the headlines with attempts to bag big-name US corporations and other assets in Asia and Europe, Indian companies have made acquisitions to primarily complement the skills they have with the ones they don't, and to access technologies and grow their markets simultaneously. *BusinessWeek* magazine compiled a list of Indian overseas acquisitions and found that over a period of a few months in 2005, 62 acquisitions worth $1.38 billion were made. This is an interesting phenomenon where Indian companies want to leverage a low-cost production base by acquiring various types of companies and moving some part of the production or processes to India, thus increasing profitability, while also obtaining new markets all in one stroke.

The Indian IT and technology outsourcing industry has not yet gone on a major acquisition spree, and almost all the deals are originating from other sectors such as pharmaceuticals, auto components, chemical and electronics. For the Indian pharmaceutical companies global acquisitions have become a desperate need since they have to accelerate their technology development spectrum by working on new molecules, and acquisitions can help both R&D and distribution. Medium-sized companies like Sun Pharmaceuticals and Matrix Laboratories have made bold moves in this direction. Most of these companies are typically cash rich, have room to raise debt and equity, and have a history of competing globally. As this book was being written, reports surfaced that Ranbaxy Laboratories and Dr Reddy's Labs – the top two Indian generics companies – had bid for Betapharm, Germany's fourth-largest generics company, which Dr Reddy's won with a €550 million bid. The oil and gas sector is already becoming a major source of global acquisitions, and they have only begun to scratch the surface in terms of opportunity as India's energy security needs move into higher gear.

The severe cost-cutting exercises that almost all Indian companies went through in the 1990s and the complementary drive to develop efficiencies to survive in a liberalizing economy flooding with competition has given them the confidence that they can add value to any situation and in any market. Many have embarked on a strategy of acquiring loss-making companies and turning them around. A number of companies have now realized that there is a good fit between what they're doing in India and what is happening elsewhere, and making acquisitions is a good way to capitalize on this.

CORPORATE GOVERNANCE AND MARKET RESPONSIVENESS

Indian companies have become very aware of the link between corporate governance practices, understanding investor expectations and value. A strong institutional market now exists for financial assets and there has been a rising institutional holding of major asset classes, especially in equities. Though equity in India is still largely held by corporate founding families (nearly two-thirds) or the government (around one-sixth), the rising proportion of financial and individual investors is igniting greater transparency. That Indian companies are more responsive to their operating environment is very apparent. A Deutsche Bank survey showed that Indian companies were more commercially driven than Chinese ones and that explained why, despite huge capital inflows and higher rates of growth, Indian companies enjoyed higher profitability and superior return on capital employed as compared with their counterparts in China. *The Economist* survey of India and China (5 March 2005) said much the same thing but with a macro perspective, where India has invested 22% to 23% of its GDP for a decade and has seen an average economic growth of 6% a year in real terms, while China has invested at twice that rate but its average growth is just 50% higher.

ROBUST BANKING AND FINANCIAL SYSTEMS ARE A STRONG EDGE FOR INDIA

If one accepts the logic that the long-term trend in the stock markets is a good proxy for a nation's economic potential, then India should really win hands down. Since 2000 the Chinese stock market (represented by the Shanghai A and B share indices) has fallen sharply, while the Indian stock market indices (represented by the BSE Sensex and the NSE 50) have been among the top-performing markets globally since 2003. Despite the multi-year correction in stock prices in China, the price earning ratios (of the index) are much higher than that in India, on average by 40% as of late 2005. But the Chinese market is not properly regulated and rampant speculation exists, reducing the reliability factor, so adequate inferences cannot be drawn.

The Indian equity markets on the other hand are among the most sophisticated in the world. A Goldman Sachs managing director visiting India a couple of years ago said that the systems in use on the stock exchanges in India would make the NYSE look primitive. The change from the open outcry system and the adoption and development of high technology has led to the creation of a national market system trading on one gigantic satellite-based platform linking 240 cities and towns across the country and thousands of trader workstations. The two major national stock exchange systems now trade nearly $14 billion worth of equity volumes every day including equity options and futures. India is also unique in the sense that it is one of the few countries where individual stock futures have done very well, even with a fairly advanced stock lending mechanism in place.

The well-regulated domestic capital market is the first choice for listing for most Indian companies. It is only those companies with a large business presence or with significant expansion plans overseas that are looking for an overseas listing, but in addition to a domestic listing and not in isolation. China lacks a transparent and well-functioning securities market, which means that many of its companies are heading for markets outside of China without a corresponding domestic listing. This may be fortunate for the companies since they are able to access capital, but not so for the domestic economy that could have benefited greatly from the wealth effect created by successful public companies. That is not all. The absence of a well-functioning securities market compounds capital allocation inefficiencies since the bulk of economic decision-making remains in the hands of the government.

In fact, India's problem if any is that it lacks a critical mass of its securities listed on exchanges overseas, which can significantly increase the investor base and can help build investor appetite. An overseas listing of ADRs makes it easy for even individual investors to buy into Indian companies that they otherwise may not do directly. Besides, having cross-border listings diversifies the capital resource base. This anomaly will be addressed over time. Numerous companies in the IT, biotech and pharmaceutical industries and public sector companies are looking to list on the NASDAQ. Currently there are just around a dozen Indian companies listed on the NASDAQ and the NYSE and a handful listed in London and Luxemburg. Given the importance attached to this potential flow from India, Bangalore is one of a few cities in the world where NASDAQ now has a representative office. And as it's been understood from press interviews given by senior NASDAQ executives, there seems to be an IPO pipeline from Indian companies that stretches into 2007–08, which will seriously increase the investment choice for those investors looking to benefit from the India story.

Since 2001 we've seen a lot of regulatory convergence in the major global financial markets and India has very much been a part of that process, where compliance requirements have been tightened. Tightening domestic compliance is turning out to be useful for Indian companies since it facilitates a quicker response time whenever the companies decide to go for a cross-border listing, besides raising institutional investors' comfort levels in participating directly.

Numerous studies have shown the Chinese financial system to be vulnerable to internal collapse thanks to large non-performing loans and inadequate supervision of its banks. The level of non-performing loans within the Chinese banking system has been estimated at 15% of total assets (though some estimates put out by US investment banks peg it much higher), which is more than three times the level in India. Banks in South East Asian economies are known to have non-performing loans of up to 30% of assets, and it would be realistic to assume that the real level of Chinese non-performing loans would be somewhere around that level. Not surprisingly, one of the awaited key developments is the clean up of China's shuttered banking and financial sector. Indian banks have already expended considerable efforts at using recent profit growth and capital infusion from the domestic equity and international debt market to reduce non-performing loans and raise capital adequacy. Besides, rapid economic growth has revived the fortunes of a number of ailing sectors and improved loan recoverability, whereas China's banking system has accumulated this gigantic level of non-performing loans despite higher economic growth rates.

EDGE IN SERVICES, A SEGMENT THAT WILL IMPACT THE WORLD ECONOMY TO A GREATER EXTENT

China and most other East Asian economies have built strengths in manufacturing. The trend has been that the innovations of one of these economies have been quickly picked up by another since there are similar structures, education levels and skill sets in each country. The South Korean electronics industry is a case in point, where 40% of the country's economy is made up of this sector, especially the manufacture of semiconductors and entertainment electronics. Over the years Samsung Electronics, the country's leading conglomerate contributing 10% of South Korean GDP, has located 29 factories employing nearly 50,000 people in China, in order to benefit from lower cost. This network of factories – along with several other Korean, Chinese and Taiwanese factories – has now begun to outpace Korean exports in electronics, threatening the very country that spawned them. Though the Korean industry and economy may not wilt due to their huge emphasis on R&D and innovation-based development of electronics, this example underscores the nature of competition in manufacturing that is widespread in East Asia. India can easily aspire to this level of intensity in manufacturing over the next decade or so, given its huge R&D infrastructure that can be scaled up and skill sets that can be quickly mobilized. The Indian economy invests 0.85% of its GDP in annual research expenditure compared with China's 1.22% of GDP. The Indian corporate sector has begun in earnest to invest in innovation- and R&D-based development, so the percentages can be leveled over time.

Manufacturing is not only highly competitive it also accounts for a relatively smaller portion of global GDP. Services, on the other hand, that form a larger portion of the world's GDP is where India has numerous advantages and where its companies are poised to deliver significant value addition. For example, services comprise 75% of the US economy, while industry and manufacturing comprise less than a quarter. And the global market for systems and business processes has only begun to be tapped.

In the dozen years starting from 1990, the influence of agriculture on the GDP of both China and India dropped substantially, from 27% of GDP to 15% of GDP in China's case and from 32% of GDP to 22% in India's case. But the interesting thing is that industry and manufacturing took up the entire slack in China, growing to 53% of GDP, while in India the services sector took up the entire slack, growing to 56% of GDP in the same time frame.

A HUGE COMMODITY POOL, BUT BULLION IS THE WAY TO GO

The impact that China has had on the world's commodity markets in recent years is unprecedented. Even a rising Japan and East Asia in recent memory have not had an equivalent impact. It is dependent on imports for most of its commodity requirements. As a measure of its status as a global economic engine, it consumes 8% of the world's oil and 22% of the world's copper, and is the largest producer and consumer of coal. In metals like copper and silver it is becoming an important trading center, with price changes in Shanghai being reflected across global markets. India's share of world oil demand is roughly two-fifths that of China, and demand for copper is at one-eighth of Chinese demand, though its coal reserves are the third-largest in the world and its global consumption share is 7%. A realistic comparison has to be seen in the context of growth. For a large part of its reform and growth process China did not dominate world trade in commodities nor set the pricing and production agenda. It is only a climax of demand in China over the last half a decade or so that has seen such a rise in domestic consumption and impact on world commodity prices. Rising demand from India is also contributing to higher commodity prices (especially for gas and oil), and its real impact on other commodities will be felt over the next few years, as economic growth sustains and then accelerates.

The fact that India is a huge producer of a variety of agricultural and industrial commodities – unlike China, Japan and other East Asian nations – means that even though it will rise to be amongst the largest consumers of commodities in the world it may not have as great an impact on global prices as China. Since India has established modern commodity exchanges that trade derivative instruments on a variety of commodities, this rise in consumption and domestic production could turn into a significant and unique opportunity that goes beyond being able to set commodity markets on fire, and instead allows India to become a key arbiter of commodity prices.

The country has 25 commodity exchanges, which is one of the largest collections anywhere in the world, ranging from cotton and oil seed exchanges to those trading in coffee futures and spices such as pepper. Most of these exchanges trade single commodities, though there are three world-class, multi-commodity exchanges: the National Commodity and Derivative Exchange (NCDEX), which in 2005 captured 55% of the total domestic commodity traded volume and is the best regarded of the exchanges trading derivative contracts in 44 commodities; the Multi Commodity Exchange of India (MCX), which is the second largest with a 43% market share; and the National Multi Commodity Exchange (NMCE). NCDEX introduced gold and rupee-denominated Brent crude oil futures in collaboration with the International Petroleum Exchange (IPE) in September 2005, making it one of only a handful of exchanges worldwide to trade these commodities. It has now started trading furnace oil contracts and is finalizing the introduction of natural gas contracts too. MCX too trades gold futures contracts and crude oil futures linked to Brent crude, and offers futures contracts for several agro-commodities, base metals and petrochemicals.

The dominating commodity trading on Indian exchanges and one that would be of immediate interest to any investor is gold. Indian commodity exchanges trade over $1.5 billion worth of bullion futures contracts every day. It is in gold that India makes a significant impact globally, accounting for over one-fifth of the world's demand. Indians buying gold acts as a major price stimulus and offers key support to this important market. According to unofficial estimates collated by the NCDEX, Indian households currently store 13,000 tons of gold worth $150 billion.

But foreign investors are not yet allowed to participate directly in the Indian commodity exchanges, though that is something that will be rectified sooner rather than later, especially if there is any desire to be a global player in the commodities market. Global investors are always on the lookout for properly functioning markets and India can exploit this sentiment by allowing them in, which will also help create and develop an important trading hub in select commodities like bullion, oil seeds and cotton, and probably even in metals such as aluminum, considering that 10% of all known bauxite deposits are in India and supposedly are of very high grade, and in gold. If the restrictions on the participation by foreign investors are lifted and India's share of the global commodity consumption increases, then not only will India be among the top natural resource producing and consuming nations but it will also be a major trading center. India already possesses a formidable domestic institutional framework and established trading systems that will significantly aid the development of these markets.

The difference between the approaches to exploiting their natural wealth is evident since China has developed a very strong physical infrastructure to exploit its natural and agro resources. India, on the other hand, needs to sharpen its edge and go one up by offering investment alternatives along with the efficient development of its natural resource market. Iron ore, coal, bauxite, zinc, natural gas and a host of minerals lie deposited in various parts of the country and have not been adequately explored. The price level that commodities trade at makes even remote and smaller projects viable, thus further guaranteeing India's industrial security.

The impact that China's development is having on global commodity markets is a lesson for India to learn as it rapidly expands and begins to rival China in its demand for natural resources. Right now slow but steady progress is being made towards the full-scale exploitation of India's mineral wealth. The government has quietly introduced reforms that will allow foreign investors to participate in this effort and in some cases have full control over the mining venture. This is a great trend to build on.

AN OPEN AND LIBERAL SOCIETY THAT THE WEST CAN EASILY RELATE TO

A perceptible difference between China and India lies in the quality of systems in place that could drive India's capitalist and free market ambitions. Its political system, demographics, systems of judicial oversight and penchant for free market economics are crucial factors that could help it derive significant long-term advantages over China and other emerging markets, where the institutions needed for the successful evolution of a free market have not fully developed. Expropriation of assets in Russia and developments in other markets underscore the importance of having a strong and independent judiciary, independent regulatory bodies and a free press.

On numerous quality, political and economic governance parameters developed by the World Bank and other global bodies and research institutes, India and China come out marginally ahead of each other in different areas. But on one crucial parameter used by the World Bank Governance Index, which is on the freedom to voice an opinion, India's score is three times that of China's.

India has rigid labor laws, but so do numerous European and Asian nations, but the rigidity does pose some severe challenges to industry, and the negative impact on the Indian economy in terms of lost investment has already been discussed in relation to the textile industry. But on the other hand, commercial contracts have vastly greater sanctity, and respect for the rule of law is an undisputed and critical component of economic life in India.

CAPITAL FLOWS: COOKIES AND CRUMBS

Unfair comparisons have been made between capital flows into India and China. Skeptics point to China's level of annual foreign direct investments at $50 billion versus India's lowly $7 billion to $8 billion. This argument is facile and does not reflect the qualitative difference in the nature of capital flows. First is the difference in the methodology used to calculate the FDI received by the two countries. The Chinese method includes the reinvestment of profits and dividends, which the Indian method does not include. If the two methodologies are harmonized then the picture looks very different and the gap, though still large, is less disquieting from India's point of view. And it has been well documented that there is round-tripping of investments from China to Hong Kong and back. A large portion of the investment has also come from overseas Chinese. Second is the fact that China receives no portfolio investment. The great chunk of Chinese-listed equity is in Hong Kong, with the stock market on the mainland considered to be very speculative and unreliable. India receives a large chunk of its foreign interest through portfolio flows. The total FDI and portfolio flows for India come to nearly $20 billion a year. So if investment flows from all sources are reckoned and if the methodology for calculating FDI is harmonized then China probably receives double what India gets, and not the daunting six or seven times that is commonly referred to. More importantly, FDI is growing at 40% a year in India, and assuming that the pace sustains, in three or four years India could be looking at $25 billion in FDI and a similar amount in portfolio investments, which would then make it the largest recipient of foreign investment in the world.

To sum up, China's advantage over India is its infrastructure and the government's determination to excel. But these are advantages that can be eclipsed. India's edge in its systems, governance practices, corporate history and talent pool are a little harder to eclipse. It is almost like China has the hardware to succeed and India has the software. The country and system that will succeed over the long term is the one that can create both the hardware and the software, and each nation has embarked on creating what it lacks.

It is easy to be drawn into comparisons that distract from the fact that India and China have a lot to gain from each other. Mani Shankar Aiyer, India's petroleum minister, put forward an idea that the two countries seek out oil and gas assets globally, together, but the possibilities of co-operation go significantly beyond that. It is inevitable that over the next 15 to 20 years India and China will once again be the dominant economies of the world. And both can participate in each others growth; China by helping India build up its physical infrastructure quickly, and India by helping China build its systems and knowledge-based economy.

11

A COMPASS
FOR THE FUTURE

There is a huge opportunity awaiting institutional, corporate and other investors looking at the Indian market, whether it is as FDI or as portfolio investors. The changes that India has witnessed – both political and economic – over the last one and a half decades are both fundamental in nature and permanent, and we're seeing the future beginning to take shape. The country is now brimming with opportunity, with a government that is emphasizing the right mix of economic dynamism with social responsibility.

There are multiple ways in which investors outside the country can take advantage of the economic rise of India. There are a large number of mutual funds available to investors in the Far East, United States and Europe that invest between 1% and 100% of their assets in India. A detailed list of these funds is available on my website www.midastouchglobal.com. Each of these funds has registered as a foreign institutional investor (FII) with the Securities and Exchange Board of India (the Indian equivalent of the SEC). Obviously the exposure that an investor wants to take will determine which one of these funds is best for him or her. But investing in India as we have demonstrated carries far fewer risks than most other emerging markets, and risk is lower than what it is conventionally believed to be.

Indian companies have become dominant issuers from the Asia Pacific region in the global market for convertible securities. The demand from institutional investors globally has prompted an ever-growing number of Indian companies to tap the convertibles market to fund capital expansion on very attractive terms. In the first two months of 2006, for example, Indian companies raised $1.4 billion through foreign currency convertible bonds (FCCBs) or convertibles as they are popularly known, accounting for nearly three-quarters of the amount raised by companies from the Asia Pacific. Convertibles offer an excellent entry opportunity for global investors looking to build an exposure to the Indian economy. The companies issuing these securities are generally mid- to large caps with an excellent operating track record and generally with a strong competitive position within their respective industries.

American Depository Receipts (ADRs) of Indian companies are traded on the NYSE and NASDAQ and represent very high-quality Indian corporate names; unfortunately, only about a dozen ADRs are currently available, and around 40 Global Depository Receipts (GDRs) are traded in London and Luxemburg. However, this is likely to change as several dozen Indian companies are looking to raise capital and their profiles by listing in the US and in the UK by 2008.

London's Alternative Investment Market (AIM) has the potential to become a major source of capital for smaller Indian companies. In Chapter 9, I mentioned Great Eastern Energy Corporation Ltd, a company developing coal bed methane wells in the state of West Bengal. GEECL was the first Indian company to list on the AIM in December 2005 and upon listing commanded a market capitalization of £110 million. The unusual part of the story is that it is unlisted in India. It could herald a new trend where younger Indian companies could opt to raise capital using specialized global exchanges like the AIM or Canada's Toronto Venture Exchange or the US OTC Bulletin Board. Even Indian public sector companies are looking at raising capital this way. The Noida Toll Bridge Company Ltd, a public sector infrastructure operator that is currently listed on both the Indian stock exchanges, raised $42 million through the AIM in March 2006, through an issue of GDRs. According to investment bankers involved in cross-border issues, the number of Indian companies looking at the AIM is growing substantially and that market could provide a large chunk of equity funding in the years to come.

India too once had an OTC market that was conceived to provide liquidity to investors in very small and young companies. Unfortunately the exchange was over-regulated and all speculation was discouraged, which robbed the exchange of liquidity and eventually led to its demise by the late 1990s. There is a need to revive this exchange, since the demand from small companies is very much there and there is an investor risk appetite to match.

There is also a growing breed of stocks listed on exchanges in the US, Canada and the UK that are essentially companies domiciled in these countries but which derive the whole or a large part of their revenues from operations in India. This presents an interesting way to gain exposure to the Indian market by simply investing in these companies and letting them do all the work. This strategy has worked well for investors in companies such as Niko Resources (TSX: NKO), GeoGlobal Resources (AMEX: GGR) and Hardy Oil (AIM). GeoGlobal Resources is a classic example of the returns that could come to investors in newly opened up sectors. The company was a part of the consortium led by Gujarat State Petroleum Corporation that in early 2005 hit a mega gas field off India's east coast, with gas reserves "unofficially" estimated at 20 trillion cubic feet, and it was reputed to be the largest find of the year globally. The GeoGlobal stock blasted from an average price of $0.95 per share in April 2005 to $10, even though the company had only a 5% stake in the field.

There are other smaller companies such as Canoro Resources Inc (TSXV), which has managed to bid successfully for the right to explore in a couple of blocks. There are also a number of smaller Indian companies in the oil and gas sector that are looking to list in Canadian markets such as the Toronto Stock Exchange and the Toronto Venture Exchange, where there is a significant concentration of high-quality oil stocks. This will increase the complement of options available to investors.

The returns earned by GeoGlobal's shareholders are a rarity and the story has only been used to illustrate a point. The best investment results from investing in India will come to those looking for long-term value and to those willing to grow with the next generation of world-class Indian companies and sectors.

A lot of the foreign investor interest in India is reflected largely in listed equity. But a really great opportunity exists in unlisted companies, a number of which are truly undiscovered gems. Quality companies exist away from public scrutiny in exciting industries – including specialty chemicals, biotechnology, IT products, apparels, retailing, housing construction, dairy farming, food processing and engineering – that have been in existence for many years, in several cases for a couple of decades or more. I've seen cases where many of these companies have had a track record of profitability for several years and are financially extremely conservative. A number of these companies are looking to expand and are especially open to takeovers outside India since this brings technology and new markets, besides giving them an inbuilt opportunity to outsource some processes to their units in India. Most of them would rather look for a strategic financial investor to hold a portion of either their stock or some hybrid instrument than conduct an IPO at what they still consider to be early stages in their growth. Many are small, with revenues typically ranging between $5 million and $25 million, but growth rates are significant in all cases. The opportunity for private equity funds is enormous. Usually private equity investments are targeted towards younger, poorly capitalized firms or struggling firms where timely capital infusions are essential. The private equity market has also become more sophisticated with the creation of secondary funds. In essence these funds create liquidity for the early institutional investors in a private equity fund by allowing them to lock in gains and exit. The first such fund dedicated to India was a $35 million fund organized by the London-based Coller Capital. In India, conventional opportunity exists for private equity funds, and for certain there are many significant success stories waiting to be tapped into.

The number of global private equity houses that have already invested or committed to invest sizeable sums – in many cases a billion dollars or more – in India is rising, and includes names like Blackstone, Carlyle and General Atlantic Partners. The tremendous success that Warburg Pincus enjoyed with its investment in Bharti Televentures – it managed to sell two-thirds of its holding in the company for over a billion dollars by 2005, as compared with its total investment of around $300 million made between 1999 and 2001 – only serves to underscore the potential of private equity in India and the speed with which that potential can be unlocked.

A lot of work has been done to unshackle the opportunity for the Indian private sector companies, in terms of financial reforms, privatization, deregulation, creation of platforms for private–public partnership, investment in rural infrastructure and investments in vital segments such as airports, ports and expressways. But while some of the things that needed to be done have been enthusiastically tackled, several times that effort now needs to be put in to address various deficiencies, including fiscal balancing, official corruption, energy security and creating sorely needed infrastructure. The new political dispensation has realized that all of the above is urgently needed and is doing all it can to address these issues. There is also a clear recognition that there has been a neglect of some very basic issues – primary education is one and health care is another. Only when the basic needs of all segments of Indian society are taken care of can there be a push for true social equality, by which I mean everyone is presented with equal opportunity to pursue economic fulfillment. This will serve to improve the quality of the investment opportunity in India substantially.

The risk of fiscal profligacy on the investment canvas cannot be overemphasized. India's central government runs a budget deficit that is estimated to be 4.3% of GDP for 2005–06, down from 4.5% for 2004–05. If lumped with the deficits run by the various state governments the cumulative deficit is estimated to be 10% of GDP. While high budget deficits are no strangers to investors even in developed countries – Japan for example has a consistently high budget deficit at 7% to 8%; France and Germany have had consistently high budget deficits; since 2000 the United States too has been experiencing a period of high deficits – it is the level of national debt in India that is a worry. The national debt (the bulk of it is to domestic investors so the risk of external instability is greatly reduced) is so large, at nearly 80% of GDP, that almost all the budget deficit is accounted for by interest payments. By 2009 however the government is compelled by a fiscal responsibility law to reduce the revenue deficit to zero and bring the budget deficit down to 3%.

Any economist will agree that merely having a budget deficit is no crime, even a sizeable one; it is the composition of that budget deficit that matters. If the bulk of the deficit is on account of servicing the national debt and the debt is incurred to subsidize the economy rather than to invest in it then it is nothing but a vicious, unproductive and negative cycle. Today more than ever the Indian economy needs fiscal flexibility from the government, which unless government revenues improve substantially it will not be able to offer.

The issue of explicit and implicit subsidies given by the government to various segments of society remains unresolved. This is a festering sore that needs to be fixed before it poisons the system, since it is the root cause of high fiscal deficits, unsustainable levels of government borrowings and diversion of government revenues to debt servicing rather than development. India has to improve its savings to GDP to bring it on par with the other East Asian nations and China, and more importantly improve its investments to GDP ratio substantially if it is to create sustainable growth. China and other Asian economies do one and a half times better than India on domestic savings and public investment ratios. For the moment the change that India saw in its savings and investment rate for 2005–06 shows those ratios to be improving, though India needs to improve its savings rate to well over 30% (it is almost there) and sustain it at higher levels if the current rates of GDP growth are to accelerate.

The introduction of the value-added tax on 1 April 2005 – in lieu of the sales tax that each individual state levies – will go a long way towards rationalizing internal trade and improving the tax to GDP ratio. We saw in Chapter 10 just how much better China is doing on fiscal issues than India. A government with fiscal flexibility is one that can add fuel to the economic engine, as the Chinese and other East Asian governments have demonstrated. This is important; if the government is unable to sort out this mess, sustaining reforms and more importantly passing on the benefits flowing from improvements made to the economy down the various layers of society, may not happen quickly enough, leading to frustration and feelings of alienation among those left out. A McKinsey & Co study indicated that if India is able to grow at 10% per annum, by 2010 75 million new jobs will be created outside of agriculture and the unemployment rate will drop by more than half. This is precisely what needs to happen.

Other risks too may not be easily mitigated in the short term. Infrastructure deficiency and cost of services remain high. Economic productivity is a natural casualty of this, and though gains have been steadily made a lot still needs to be done. Size matters too, and this understanding has come a bit late but is welcome both within government and industry. The government on its part has dismantled a lot of the regime that discouraged size. One of the last few things that it is doing is a faster reduction in the number of products that are reserved for the small-scale industry. Indian industry is reciprocating, and the thinking has gone from "small is beautiful" to "bigger is better".

But it is technology that is the key to India's fortunes in the future, and not only the scale of operations or labor cost arbitrage. The companies and sectors that understand this – like those in pharmaceuticals, auto components, specialty chemicals and increasingly in electronics – are already producing world beaters. Companies such as Bharat Forge have shown that even in older companies and industries the focus on technology, R&D and productivity-led growth can be a great enabler and can provide a lasting competitive edge besides being a great source of value. But this has to happen on a broader front in many other sectors and companies. The Chinese miracle is one led by both investments and by a leap in labor productivity. India with its inherent strength of exceptional managerial talent, mature industry and science and technology base needs to leapfrog the learning curve and deliver productivity gains while growing its manufacturing base. It is economics 101 that only a real increase in labor productivity can guarantee an increase in real wages and thus purchasing power over time. India will have to utilize its vaunted intellectual talents and hard-built industrial assets to raise productivity and thus its standard of living. Studies done by some academics and consulting firms have shown that the potential exists for Indian industries to on average triple their levels of productivity over the next few years.

The combination of improving labor and capital productivity, lower indirect taxes on goods, lower customs duties and lower transportation and communication costs will contribute to a sustainable consumption boom, driving domestic demand higher and faster, and can quickly erase the stigma of mass poverty. India has made progress with efforts to remove poverty over the last couple of decades, even with all the hiccups it has experienced. According to the Reserve Bank of India overall poverty levels have declined from 51.3% of people living below the poverty line in 1977–78 to 26.1% in 1999–2000. But there are still a great many people, numbering over 260 million, living in great poverty. This is a travesty that India needs to reverse quickly if it is to count itself amongst the great nations in this world.

There is no doubt that India has first-world institutions and attitudes that developed quietly in the decades of isolation. Yet it was able to study the best practices of the West through its greatest export: its high-quality manpower. These institutions and attitudes are now coming through as the country prepares for the next generation of reforms and true competition with the rest of the world. The bottom line is that India does need faster reforms and more investments; it does not matter whether that investment comes from within or from outside. From India's perspective the color of the money does not matter, only the quantum.

BIBLIOGRAPHY

Ashish Arora and Alfonso Gambardella, *The globalization of the software industry: perspectives and opportunities for developed and seveloping countries* (NBER Working Paper 10538, National Bureau of Economic Reserch, Inc, 2004)

"Assessing India's potential for accelerated economic growth", Strategic Insight (New Delhi, World Economic Forum, 2004)

Augusto Lopez Claros, *Global competitiveness rankings* (World Economic Forum, 2005)

Bibhutibushan Datta and A N Singh, *History of Hindu mathematics* (New Delhi, Bhartiya Kala Prakashan, 2001)

Charan Wadhwa, *Economic reforms in India and the market economy* (New Delhi, Allied Publishers, 1994)

Chikako Mogi, *Japan Inc. wakes up to India's allure* – (Reuters, July 12, 2005)

Don M Chance, *Essay's in derivatives* (New York, John Wiley 1998)

Dr David Gray, *Indic Mathematics: India and the scientific revolution* (Educational Council on Indic traditions)

Dr Sumla Athreye, *Multinational firms and the evolution of the Indian software industry* (East West Center, Working Paper No 51, January 2003)

"Global wind power continues expansion", Global Wind Energy Council (Brussels, 2004)

Hilton L Root, *"India: Asia's next tiger?"* Essays in Public Policy (Stanford CA, Hoover Institution Press, June 1998)

India: are the skeptics right? (IMF Survey – December 1, 2003 Vol 32, No 21)

India corruption study 2005 (New Delhi, Transparency International India & Center for Media Studies, 2005)

"India, China and NPT", World Nuclear Association (March 2006)

India: E-readiness assessment report, Department of Information Technology, Government of India & NCAER (September 2004)

India's quest for higher growth, (IMF Survey – February 21, 2005 Vol 34, No 3)

"Interview with Yasukoni Edeki – Japanese ambassador to India" (Financial Express, April 29, 2005)

IT spending: potential and prospects for Indian states, India: E-readiness assessment report 2004 (Ministry of Information Technology, 2004) chapter 5

Jairus Banaji and Gautam Mody, *Corporate governance and the Indian private sector* (QEH Working Paper Series 73, May 2001)

James Heitzman and Robert L Worden, *India: a country study* (Division 5th edition, 1996)

Jawaharlal Nehru, *The discovery of India* (New Delhi, Jawaharlal Nehru Memorial Fund, Twenty-second impression, 2002)

Jaya Prakash Pradhan, *Rise of service sector outward foreign direct investment from Indian economy: trends, patterns and determinants* (New Delhi, Research and Information System for the Non-aligned and other Developing Countries, 2003)

Montek S Ahluwalia, *Economic reforms in India since 1991: Has gradualism worked?* (Journal of Economic Perspectives, Summer 2002)

N Vittal, *Issues in corporate governance* (5th JRD Tata Memorial Lecture series, 2002)

Omkar Goswami, David Dollar, et al, *Competitiveness of Indian manufacturing: results from a firm level survey* (Confederation of Indian Industry, The World Bank, 2002)

Ranjit Pandit, *Fulfilling India's promise - 2005 Special Edition* (The Mckinsey Quarterly)

Sir P C Ray, *History of chemistry in ancient and medieval India* (Indian Chemical Society, 1956)

APPENDIX

ROCE RANKING

Large, medium and small cap companies with strong operating performance and capital productivity

Company Name	Year	RoCE %	5-yr CAGR Revenue %	EBITDA Margin %	Financial Leverage Ratio	Year	RoCE %	Year	RoCE %	Sector
Nestle India Ltd.	2004/12	127.39	8.94	20.69	1.02	2003/12	133.72	2002/12	125.13	Food processing
Sesa Goa Ltd.	2005/03	126.79	42.73	46.13	1.02	2004/03	78.75	2003/03	39.33	Mining
Tata Metaliks Ltd.	2005/03	117.96	27.21	37.18	1.20	2004/03	81.08	2003/03	51.67	Steel-Intermediate
Gujarat N R E Coke Ltd.	2004/09	113.39	56.80	47.12	1.41	2003/09	46.28	2002/09	33.61	Metallurgical coke
Bongaigaon Refinery & Petrochemicals Ltd.	2005/03	100.26	29.96	15.27	1.08	2004/03	77.73	2003/03	74.60	Refineries
Swaraj Mazda Ltd.	2005/03	86.27	25.97	7.37	1.42	2004/03	97.74	2003/03	58.33	Commercial vehicles
Praj Industries Ltd.	2005/03	84.75	37.11	12.85	1.00	2004/03	42.86	2003/03	29.13	Heavy engineering
Vimta Labs Ltd.	2005/03	79.24	66.25	51.63	1.36	2004/03	83.54	2003/03	51.45	Clinical research
Colgate-Palmolive (India) Ltd.	2005/03	77.51	-0.31	18.57	1.02	2004/03	57.94	2003/03	56.27	Personal care
Hero Honda Motors Ltd.	2005/03	75.64	30.73	15.95	1.14	2004/03	85.03	2003/03	94.06	Motorcycles
Shoppers' Stop Ltd.	2005/03	73.49	26.96	14.40	1.93	2004/03	53.73	2003/03	36.49	Retailing
Tata Elxsi Ltd.	2005/03	70.06	9.63	20.50	1.00	2004/03	49.85	2003/03	42.79	Computer hardware
Mercator Lines Ltd.	2005/03	69.45	78.01	68.32	2.54	2004/03	103.68	2003/03	26.00	Shipping
Astra Microwave Products Ltd.	2005/03	65.28	53.03	46.84	1.44	2004/03	35.95	2003/03	32.29	Defense
Tata Steel Ltd.	2005/03	63.25	17.40	38.35	1.40	2004/03	37.53	2003/03	21.31	Steel
Munjal Auto Inds. Ltd.	2005/03	62.31	48.01	20.39	1.85	2004/03	63.96	2003/03	54.19	Auto ancillary
Aventis Pharma Ltd.	2004/12	58.02	8.89	28.29	1.05	2003/12	46.42	2002/12	34.57	Pharmaceuticals
Procter & Gamble Hygiene & Health Care Ltd.	2005/06	57.47	9.07	19.43	1.00	2004/06	54.87	2003/06	42.91	Personal care
Abbott India Ltd.	2004/11	56.82	9.64	21.20	1.01	2003/11	52.89	2002/11	53.26	Pharmaceuticals
National Mineral Devp. Corpn. Ltd.	2005/03	56.26	23.05	55.64	1.00	2004/03	34.55	2003/03	27.53	Mining
Automotive Axles Ltd.	2005/09	56.02	24.14	15.16	1.82	2004/09	46.05	2003/09	45.81	Auto ancillary

Company Name	Year	RoCE %	5-yr CAGR Revenue %	EBITDA Margin %	Financial Leverage Ratio	Year	RoCE %	Year	RoCE %	Sector
Alfa Laval (India) Ltd.	2004/12	53.17	21.96	21.02	1.03	2003/12	44.06	2002/12	37.36	Heavy engineering
Castrol India Ltd.	2004/12	52.83	5.36	15.34	1.01	2003/12	58.17	2002/12	66.10	Lubricants
Infosys Technologies Ltd.	2005/03	52.26	50.68	34.52	1.00	2004/03	49.71	2003/03	48.84	Software services
Glaxosmithkline Pharmaceuticals Ltd.	2004/12	52.14	10.88	28.55	1.00	2003/12	45.10	2002/12	35.06	Pharmaceuticals
Dabur India Ltd.	2005/03	51.85	4.01	16.06	1.15	2004/03	30.04	2003/03	22.54	Personal care
Siemens Ltd.	2005/09	51.68	20.81	10.12	1.00	2004/09	41.35	2003/09	37.31	Instrumentation & process control
Greaves Cotton Ltd.	2005/06	50.38	1.52	14.60	1.56	2004/06	51.38	2003/06	25.66	Diversified
Bharat Electronics Ltd.	2005/03	48.57	16.49	21.43	1.01	2004/03	44.09	2003/03	42.35	Electronics
Astrazeneca Pharma India Ltd.	2004/12	48.44	15.50	25.36	1.00	2003/12	43.31	2002/12	23.15	Pharmaceuticals
Merck Ltd.	2004/12	47.75	8.34	28.14	1.00	2003/12	51.88	2002/12	38.66	Pharmaceuticals
Nava Bharat Ferro Alloys Ltd.	2005/03	47.21	14.35	31.58	1.68	2004/03	36.18	2003/03	22.47	Diversified
Bharat Forge Ltd.	2005/03	46.55	18.04	27.14	1.95	2004/03	43.50	2003/03	34.52	Forgings
Kochi Refineries Ltd.	2005/03	45.68	21.11	9.50	1.30	2004/03	43.65	2003/03	40.51	Refineries
Motor Industries Co. Ltd.	2004/12	45.57	11.64	24.03	1.12	2003/12	44.67	2002/12	30.47	Auto ancillary
Oil & Natural Gas Corpn. Ltd.	2005/03	45.35	18.90	62.14	1.21	2004/03	38.39	2003/03	54.57	Oil and Gas
ZF Steering Gear (India) Ltd.	2005/03	45.19	28.41	21.02	1.46	2004/03	39.44	2003/03	25.87	Auto ancillary
Hindustan Lever Ltd.	2004/12	44.91	0.06	14.91	1.70	2003/12	62.21	2002/12	63.26	Personal care
Havell's India Ltd.	2005/03	44.89	44.54	10.63	3.01	2004/03	46.25	2003/03	39.56	Electrical equipment
Asian Paints Ltd.	2005/03	44.70	11.33	14.92	1.15	2004/03	42.16	2003/03	45.06	Paints
Balkrishna Industries Ltd.	2005/03	44.51	30.38	23.25	2.08	2004/03	33.68	2003/03	28.12	Tyres
Motherson Sumi Systems Ltd.	2005/03	43.84	28.82	19.12	1.41	2004/03	43.52	2003/03	31.63	Auto ancillary
Britannia Industries Ltd.	2005/03	43.59	6.72	10.88	1.06	2004/03	34.00	2003/03	27.09	Food processing
National Aluminium Co. Ltd.	2005/03	42.98	15.32	56.34	1.00	2004/03	27.05	2003/03	20.12	Aluminum
Wipro Ltd.	2005/03	41.39	25.26	25.68	1.01	2004/03	31.34	2003/03	31.09	Software services

Company Name	Year	RoCE %	5-yr CAGR Revenue %	EBITDA Margin %	Financial Leverage Ratio	Year	RoCE %	Year	RoCE %	Sector
Divi's Laboratories Ltd.	2005/03	40.92	18.07	33.35	1.23	2004/03	50.96	2003/03	47.62	Pharmaceuticals
Opto Circuits (India) Ltd.	2005/03	40.42	33.87	28.15	1.30	2004/03	34.21	2003/03	26.67	Medical accessories
Jaypee Hotels Ltd.	2005/03	40.29	17.99	54.58	1.50	2004/03	36.65	2003/03	21.07	Hotels
Marico Ltd.	2005/03	39.93	8.00	8.84	1.24	2004/03	35.97	2003/03	26.93	Personal care
Cranes Software Intl. Ltd.	2005/03	39.69	65.35	64.76	1.76	2004/03	43.47	2003/03	82.83	Software services
Vesuvius India Ltd.	2004/12	39.48	31.41	22.76	1.00	2003/12	35.22	2002/12	33.67	Refractories
Bosch Chassis Systems India Ltd.	2005/03	39.43	22.41	17.68	1.49	2004/03	41.76	2003/03	28.11	Auto ancillary
Container Corpn. Of India Ltd.	2005/03	39.30	19.15	31.26	1.02	2004/03	39.85	2003/03	41.50	Logistics
Vishal Exports Overseas Ltd.	2005/03	38.82	23.19	2.73	2.23	2004/03	42.25	2003/03	40.76	Trading
Shanthi Gears Ltd.	2005/03	38.81	27.94	34.41	1.78	2004/03	30.29	2003/03	20.58	Engineering
Rico Auto Inds. Ltd.	2005/03	38.78	22.99	12.24	2.49	2004/03	49.74	2003/03	44.22	Auto ancillary
ABB Ltd.	2004/12	38.72	25.82	10.12	1.00	2003/12	29.80	2002/12	26.43	Electrical equipment
Foseco India Ltd.	2004/12	38.54	7.85	20.32	1.29	2003/12	32.95	2002/12	24.41	Organic chemicals
Hindustan Zinc Ltd.	2005/03	38.30	12.18	37.98	1.27	2004/03	49.25	2003/03	25.29	Metals
ITC Ltd.	2005/03	37.94	10.28	38.93	1.03	2004/03	40.14	2003/03	40.97	Cigarettes
Bombay Rayon Fashions Ltd.	2005/03	37.90	53.05	11.24	1.60	2004/03	50.91	2003/03	54.17	Textiles
Blue Dart Express Ltd.	2005/03	37.61	17.46	18.42	1.33	2004/03	28.53	2003/03	25.95	Couriers
Gujarat Gas Co. Ltd.	2004/12	36.97	24.62	21.15	1.22	2003/12	34.59	2002/12	34.72	Industrial gas
Suprajit Engineering Ltd.	2005/03	36.94	33.24	18.00	1.87	2004/03	38.20	2003/03	36.83	Auto ancillary
Blue Star Ltd.	2005/03	36.56	14.20	5.86	1.26	2004/03	31.54	2003/03	29.34	Consumer goods
NRB Bearings Ltd.	2005/03	36.36	12.08	24.79	1.24	2004/03	32.48	2003/03	23.12	Bearings
Emami Ltd.	2005/03	36.34	8.82	17.39	1.44	2004/03	33.48	2003/03	32.65	Personal care
3M India Ltd.	2004/12	35.98	18.51	18.33	1.00	2003/12	42.00	2002/12	42.83	Diversified
Jindal Steel & Power Ltd.	2005/03	35.81	52.51	35.49	2.13	2004/03	27.94	2003/03	20.77	Steel
Matrix Laboratories Ltd.	2005/03	35.73	71.60	27.32	1.07	2004/03	69.76	2003/03	104.17	Pharmaceuticals

Company Name	Year	RoCE %	5-yr CAGR Revenue %	EBITDA Margin %	Financial Leverage Ratio	Year	RoCE %	Year	RoCE %	Sector
Berger Paints India Ltd.	2005/03	35.59	13.42	9.68	1.31	2004/03	33.61	2003/03	27.51	Paints
Apar Industries Ltd.	2005/03	35.21	18.52	7.02	2.70	2004/03	35.82	2003/03	31.81	Rubber products
IVRCL Infrastructures & Projects Ltd.	2005/03	35.11	37.77	9.65	1.97	2004/03	34.27	2003/03	23.37	Construction
Balaji Telefilms Ltd.	2005/03	34.36	57.81	35.23	1.00	2004/03	65.09	2003/03	104.11	Entertainment
Easun Reyrolle Ltd.	2005/03	34.31	11.62	16.43	1.58	2004/03	26.88	2003/03	20.01	Electrical equipment
Thomas Cook (India) Ltd.	2004/10	34.25	11.54	36.51	1.11	2003/10	31.82	2002/10	34.89	Travel
Goodlass Nerolac Paints Ltd.	2005/03	34.08	11.18	14.85	1.27	2004/03	27.92	2003/03	20.43	Paints
Dynamatic Technologies Ltd.	2005/03	33.97	3.58	19.14	3.02	2004/03	25.97	2003/03	24.95	Hydraulics
FAG Bearings India Ltd.	2004/12	33.65	14.94	17.33	1.00	2003/12	27.06	2002/12	28.49	Bearings
Atlas Copco (India) Ltd.	2004/12	33.53	27.72	18.57	1.59	2003/12	40.05	2002/12	26.88	Compressors
Machino Plastics Ltd.	2005/03	33.51	10.43	30.35	1.77	2004/03	39.26	2003/03	24.95	Auto ancillary
Sundaram-Clayton Ltd.	2005/03	33.44	21.72	15.53	1.45	2004/03	33.91	2003/03	27.88	Auto ancillary
Unichem Laboratories Ltd.	2005/03	33.23	15.50	17.21	1.24	2004/03	31.00	2003/03	28.24	Pharmaceuticals
Cipla Ltd.	2005/03	33.00	25.47	22.17	1.13	2004/03	35.52	2003/03	31.43	Pharmaceuticals
Ind-Swift Ltd.	2005/03	32.98	26.33	11.61	2.19	2004/03	29.47	2003/03	35.41	Pharmaceuticals
Tata Motors Ltd.	2005/03	32.83	18.36	11.14	1.61	2004/03	37.03	2003/03	21.32	Automobiles
Spanco Telesystems & Solutions Ltd.	2005/03	32.47	81.84	27.55	1.68	2004/03	29.07	2003/03	20.64	IT-enabled services
Macmillan India Ltd.	2004/12	32.44	18.21	36.51	1.00	2003/12	28.20	2002/12	25.76	Printing and publishing
HCL Infosystems Ltd.	2005/06	32.21	11.99	6.91	1.19	2004/06	31.82	2003/06	29.96	Computer hardware
Rane Engine Valves Ltd.	2005/03	32.11	10.81	17.69	1.30	2004/03	42.10	2003/03	24.61	Auto ancillary
Maharashtra Seamless Ltd.	2005/03	31.99	35.12	16.72	1.35	2004/03	33.02	2003/03	36.82	Steel tubes
Ahmednagar Forgings Ltd.	2005/06	31.45	14.12	18.52	1.84	2004/06	26.57	2003/06	22.16	Forgings
Pidilite Industries Ltd.	2005/03	31.26	13.99	16.82	1.17	2004/03	31.35	2003/03	33.09	Specialty chemicals
Shah Alloys Ltd.	2005/03	30.83	23.69	7.82	2.31	2004/03	30.03	2003/03	28.52	Steel alloys
Sundram Fasteners Ltd.	2005/03	30.40	19.15	14.51	2.14	2004/03	33.91	2003/03	36.65	Fasteners

Company Name	Year	RoCE %	5-yr CAGR Revenue %	EBITDA Margin %	Financial Leverage Ratio	Year	RoCE %	Year	RoCE %	Sector
Crisil Ltd.	2005/03	30.38	21.06	40.53	1.00	2004/03	26.94	2003/03	32.61	Credit rating
GAIL (India) Ltd.	2005/03	29.93	10.86	26.65	1.23	2004/03	33.00	2003/03	33.57	Oil and gas
Elgi Equipments Ltd.	2005/03	29.62	15.23	12.79	1.08	2004/03	46.94	2003/03	24.66	Compressors
Clariant (India) Ltd.	2005/03	29.51	7.15	8.51	1.07	2004/03	33.53	2003/03	31.15	Specialty chemicals
Era Constructions (India) Ltd.	2005/03	29.42	25.21	9.20	2.29	2004/03	21.37	2003/03	20.19	Construction
Navneet Publications (India) Ltd.	2005/03	29.23	13.76	20.96	1.23	2004/03	32.40	2003/03	39.38	Printing and publishing
Bajaj Hindusthan Ltd.	2004/09	29.21	11.98	18.91	3.34	2003/09	26.77	2002/09	33.32	Sugar
Biocon Ltd.	2005/03	29.07	NA	29.19	1.11	2004/03	40.01	2003/03	36.64	Biotechnology
Heritage Foods (India) Ltd.	2005/03	29.05	20.01	7.77	1.19	2004/03	55.30	2003/03	58.75	Food processing
LG Balakrishnan & Bros. Ltd.	2005/03	29.03	18.85	13.93	2.56	2004/03	29.08	2003/03	23.52	Engineering
Bilcare Ltd.	2005/03	28.95	34.98	24.83	1.75	2004/03	21.02	2003/03	22.12	Paper
Geometric Software Solutions Co. Ltd.	2005/03	28.83	24.33	25.64	1.01	2004/03	22.99	2003/03	21.27	Software services
Donear Industries Ltd.	2005/03	28.52	18.86	19.08	1.36	2004/03	34.31	2003/03	37.68	Textiles
Nectar Lifesciences Ltd.	2005/03	28.42	14.57	10.75	2.29	2004/03	35.17	2003/03	27.32	Pharmaceuticals
Gateway Distriparks Ltd.	2005/03	27.92	46.86	57.37	1.48	2004/03	25.08	2003/03	20.76	Logistics
Shasun Chemicals & Drugs Ltd.	2005/03	27.71	12.37	19.90	1.65	2004/03	27.20	2003/03	25.01	Pharmaceuticals
Indoco Remedies Ltd.	2005/06	27.62	12.00	21.36	1.31	2004/06	36.31	2003/06	26.23	Pharmaceuticals
Omax Autos Ltd.	2005/03	27.58	29.30	8.80	2.21	2004/03	32.39	2003/03	46.07	Auto ancillary
Monnet Ispat Ltd.	2005/03	27.57	41.14	34.68	2.60	2004/03	23.71	2003/03	25.11	Sponge Iron
Radico Khaitan Ltd.	2005/03	27.38	NA	11.91	3.36	2004/03	29.14	2003/03	37.63	Distilleries
Ipca Laboratories Ltd.	2005/03	27.32	14.77	18.34	1.65	2004/03	36.47	2003/03	35.90	Pharmaceuticals
Gammon India Ltd.	2004/12	27.20	21.57	12.56	1.93	2004/03	42.45	2003/03	38.53	Construction
Godfrey Phillips India Ltd.	2005/03	27.10	3.75	15.81	1.19	2004/03	27.58	2003/03	29.94	Cigarettes
India Nippon Electricals Ltd.	2005/03	26.93	12.24	18.57	1.04	2004/03	43.42	2003/03	53.48	Auto ancillary

Company Name	Year	RoCE %	5-yr CAGR Revenue %	EBITDA Margin %	Financial Leverage Ratio	Year	RoCE %	Year	RoCE %	Sector
Savita Chemicals Ltd.	2005/03	26.64	25.72	8.93	1.13	2004/03	27.87	2003/03	24.48	Petrochemicals
Ind-Swift Laboratories Ltd.	2005/03	26.56	28.36	18.84	2.58	2004/03	23.03	2003/03	23.11	Pharmaceuticals
Ranbaxy Laboratories Ltd.	2004/12	26.32	17.77	15.37	1.05	2003/12	43.05	2002/12	40.26	Pharmaceuticals
DCM Shriram Inds. Ltd.	2005/03	26.30	15.16	11.09	3.43	2004/03	34.35	2002/09	30.92	Diversified
Adlabs Films Ltd.	2005/03	26.12	18.27	41.79	1.21	2004/03	26.69	2003/03	28.65	Entertainment
FDC Ltd.	2005/03	26.12	19.16	17.92	1.01	2004/03	40.40	2003/03	27.75	Pharmaceuticals
Nagarjuna Construction Co. Ltd.	2005/03	26.03	40.56	9.82	1.82	2004/03	31.67	2003/03	26.32	Construction
Carborundum Universal Ltd.	2005/03	25.84	5.84	17.65	1.21	2004/03	20.63	2003/03	20.52	Abrasives
Shri Lakshmi Cotsyn Ltd.	2005/06	25.52	28.05	7.75	2.48	2004/06	23.93	2003/06	25.01	Textiles
Monsanto India Ltd.	2005/03	25.48	28.63	23.56	1.01	2004/03	28.87	2003/03	25.04	Chemicals
Jubilant Organosys Ltd.	2005/03	25.43	19.72	13.76	1.75	2004/03	25.50	2003/03	23.75	Petrochemicals
Jindal Stainless Ltd.	2005/03	25.42	NA	15.72	2.73	2004/03	29.61	2003/03	42.39	Steel alloys
KPIT Cummins Infosystems Ltd.	2005/03	25.10	50.77	13.82	1.33	2004/03	28.43	2003/03	27.73	Software services
I-Flex Solutions Ltd.	2005/03	25.00	35.52	28.97	1.00	2004/03	25.50	2003/03	32.38	Software services
Madhucon Projects Ltd.	2005/03	24.84	25.5	14.21	1.44	2004/03	25.18	2003/03	27.82	Project consultancy
Rajshree Sugars & Chemicals Ltd.	2005/03	24.81	9.81	21.26	2.72	2004/03	21.69	2003/03	21.10	Sugar
JB Chemicals & Pharmaceuticals Ltd.	2005/03	24.79	16.32	20.74	1.23	2004/03	27.76	2003/03	29.65	Pharmaceuticals
Ucal Fuel Systems Ltd.	2005/03	24.63	16.68	17.00	1.08	2004/03	34.32	2003/03	38.03	Auto ancillary
Zandu Pharmaceutical Works Ltd.	2005/03	24.52	0.75	13.69	1.02	2004/03	30.62	2003/03	26.26	Pharmaceuticals
Avaya Globalconnect Ltd.	2005/03	24.46	12.32	13.79	1.01	2004/03	45.43	2003/03	34.51	Telecom equipment
Aarti Industries Ltd.	2005/03	24.21	22.98	13.32	2.10	2004/03	25.86	2003/03	27.64	Organic chemicals
D-Link (India) Ltd.	2005/03	24.18	29.26	12.94	1.01	2004/03	27.39	2003/03	23.58	Computer hardware
Wyeth Ltd.	2005/03	24.16	2.06	23.93	1.01	2004/03	32.79	2003/03	31.34	Pharmaceuticals
Wockhardt Ltd.	2004/12	23.97	0.25	27.13	2.32	2003/12	27.81	2002/12	32.45	Pharmaceuticals
Punj Lloyd Ltd.	2005/03	23.92	27.68	16.65	2.21	2004/03	44.30	2003/06	41.19	Engineering

Company Name	Year	RoCE %	5-yr CAGR Revenue %	EBITDA Margin %	Financial Leverage Ratio	Year	RoCE %	Year	RoCE %	Sector
Exide Industries Ltd.	2005/03	23.60	9.58	14.53	1.68	2004/03	29.08	2003/03	25.09	Auto batteries
Finolex Industries Ltd.	2005/03	23.20	8.97	20.85	2.10	2004/03	21.13	2003/03	21.25	Petrochemicals
TVS Motor Co. Ltd.	2005/03	23.00	16.59	7.42	1.31	2004/03	37.24	2003/03	42.20	Motorcycles
Andhra Sugars Ltd.	2005/03	22.87	10.43	22.09	2.65	2004/03	23.36	2003/03	21.86	Sugar
Hindustan Construction Co. Ltd.	2005/03	22.77	24.12	11.18	2.21	2004/03	24.13	2003/03	23.69	Construction
Eicher Motors Ltd.	2005/03	22.50	44.48	6.11	1.59	2004/03	35.60	2003/03	58.07	Automobiles
Asahi India Glass Ltd.	2005/03	22.28	25.60	20.29	3.45	2004/03	21.43	2003/03	20.35	Glass
CMC Ltd.	2005/03	22.04	10.85	5.94	1.47	2004/03	40.04	2003/03	45.81	Software services
Man Industries (India) Ltd.	2005/03	21.95	41.31	8.59	2.75	2004/03	65.33	2003/03	28.15	Steel tubes
Revathi Equipment Ltd.	2005/03	21.05	4.91	31.68	1.51	2004/03	28.46	2003/03	28.66	Compressors
Hindustan Petroleum Corpn. Ltd.	2005/03	20.98	14.34	3.38	1.26	2004/03	38.35	2003/03	35.03	Refineries
Glenmark Pharmaceuticals Ltd.	2005/03	20.88	29.93	24.74	2.53	2004/03	23.35	2003/03	25.99	Pharmaceuticals
Nicholas Piramal India Ltd.	2005/03	20.83	23.28	12.84	1.65	2004/03	38.76	2003/03	49.24	Pharmaceuticals
Indian Oil Corpn. Ltd.	2005/03	20.82	10.47	5.19	1.67	2004/03	38.66	2003/03	43.38	Refineries

The list comprises companies with a minimum return on capital employed (ROCE) of 20% for the latest reported financial year, being either March 2005 or December 2004. In a few cases there may be a different year ending. The ranking has been done on the basis of the latest year's ROCE. ROCE for three years have been provided.

The list was filtered on additional criteria of strong revenue growth, profitability and conservative financing; capital productivity was a ranking criteria and not the sole determinant for inclusion. A number of companies with high capital returns have been excluded if one or more of the other criteria were less than satisfactory.

Source: Prowess (Center for Monitoring the Indian Economy)

Micro cap companies with strong operating performance and capital productivity *

Company *	Year	RoCE %	5-Yr CAGR Revenue %	EBITDA Margin %	Financial Leverage Ratio	Year	RoCE %	Year	RoCE %	Sector
Tata Sponge Iron Ltd.	2005/03	88.06	16.33	40.48	1.01	2004/03	67.39	2003/03	35.01	Sponge iron
Nagarjuna Agrichem Ltd.	2005/03	82.07	43.31	16.11	1.68	2004/03	64.54	2003/03	37.20	Pesticides
Orient Abrasives Ltd.	2005/03	57.55	16.70	18.58	1.58	2004/03	61.32	2003/03	45.56	Abrasives
Pitti Laminations Ltd.	2005/03	54.97	19.02	19.11	2.02	2004/03	57.59	2003/03	72.27	Engineering
Teledata Informatics Ltd.	2005/03	54.76	154.57	41.34	1.05	2004/03	23.72	2002/12	36.30	Software services
National Peroxide Ltd.	2005/03	54.21	6.42	33.66	1.00	2004/03	33.07	2003/03	22.93	Inorganic chemicals
Gujarat Reclaim & Rubber Products Ltd.	2005/03	53.71	25.52	19.04	1.66	2004/03	56.43	2003/03	36.36	Rubber processing
Steelcast Ltd.	2005/03	52.78	26.58	13.30	2.18	2004/03	21.43	2003/03	23.16	Castings
Hind Rectifiers Ltd.	2005/03	52.49	22.00	11.82	1.69	2004/03	23.78	2003/03	26.13	Electronics
Jay Bharat Maruti Ltd.	2005/03	52.25	23.09	10.49	2.56	2004/03	39.18	2003/03	31.14	Auto ancillary
Carnation Nutra-Analogue Foods Ltd.	2005/03	52.06	NA	14.68	1.00	2004/03	43.76	2003/03	24.27	Edible oils
Bhagiradha Chemicals & Inds. Ltd.	2005/03	51.80	33.07	11.84	2.37	2004/03	46.22	2003/03	38.76	Pesticides
Investment & Precision Castings Ltd.	2005/03	49.89	25.15	25.39	1.11	2004/03	47.35	2003/03	52.63	Castings
Fem Care Pharma Ltd.	2005/03	49.33	12.20	18.46	1.22	2004/03	45.25	2003/03	34.24	Personal care
Kitex Garments Ltd.	2005/03	47.87	35.46	8.46	3.11	2004/03	28.15	2003/03	35.38	Apparel
Swaraj Engines Ltd.	2005/03	44.85	-2.34	22.45	1.02	2004/03	33.18	2003/03	31.98	Engines
Talbros Automotive Components Ltd.	2005/03	43.99	15.48	12.20	2.79	2004/03	28.77	2003/03	22.78	Auto ancillary
Gandhi Special Tubes Ltd.	2005/03	43.74	11.13	37.57	1.04	2004/03	33.83	2003/03	27.13	Steel tubes
Wendt (India) Ltd.	2005/03	43.72	18.69	32.28	1.02	2004/03	45.81	2003/03	37.42	Abrasives
Sarla Polyester Ltd.	2005/03	43.60	19.24	16.21	1.50	2004/03	39.56	2003/03	35.42	Textiles
High Energy Batteries (India) Ltd.	2005/03	42.82	9.45	13.30	1.82	2004/03	51.51	2003/03	41.20	Dry cell batteries
Shivalik Bimetal Controls Ltd.	2005/03	42.70	24.08	16.49	2.03	2004/03	39.31	2003/03	38.20	Steel
Hercules Hoists Ltd.	2005/03	41.62	22.71	16.40	1.13	2004/03	29.87	2003/03	22.66	Engineering
Shilpa Medicare Ltd.	2005/03	39.64	16.99	14.57	1.35	2004/03	49.85	2003/03	29.39	Pharmaceuticals

Company *	Year	RoCE %	5-Yr CAGR Revenue %	EBITDA Margin %	Financial Leverage Ratio	Year	RoCE %	Year	RoCE %	Sector
Sulzer India Ltd.	2004/12	38.63	9.99	14.94	1.00	2003/12	37.19	2002/12	40.07	Engineering
Alpha Geo (India) Ltd.	2005/03	38.10	77.53	37.30	1.13	2004/03	38.45	2003/03	21.61	Oil & gas exploration
Yuken India Ltd.	2005/03	37.73	21.80	14.93	2.50	2004/03	37.57	2003/03	54.61	Hydraulics
Orissa Sponge Iron Ltd.	2005/03	35.19	19.75	20.28	3.30	2004/03	27.07	2003/03	22.00	Sponge iron
TIL Ltd.	2005/03	34.78	6.44	11.19	2.95	2004/03	32.15	2003/03	32.99	Engineering
Plastiblends India Ltd.	2005/03	33.68	18.63	14.16	1.15	2004/03	42.06	2003/03	41.54	Plastics
Genus Overseas Electronics Ltd.	2005/03	33.08	43.17	11.70	2.57	2004/03	24.37	2003/03	25.05	Electronics
Enkei Castalloy Ltd.	2005/03	32.71	31.86	24.30	3.57	2004/03	25.41	2003/03	21.52	Castings
Sundaram Brake Linings Ltd.	2005/03	32.60	11.45	15.18	1.61	2004/03	35.49	2003/03	26.93	Auto ancillary
Ador Fontech Ltd.	2005/03	32.52	10.43	9.61	1.46	2004/03	20.90	2003/03	21.79	Welding equipment
Universal Luggage Mfg. Co. Ltd.	2005/03	31.42	-0.72	6.72	2.86	2004/03	38.57	2003/03	56.53	Luggage
Poly Medicure Ltd.	2005/03	31.08	44.79	18.52	1.76	2004/03	33.17	2003/03	41.68	Medical accessories
Aro Granite Inds. Ltd.	2005/03	30.99	28.23	21.50	1.47	2004/03	28.14	2003/03	31.51	Granites
Magna Electro Castings Ltd.	2005/03	30.94	21.07	17.68	1.66	2004/03	33.35	2003/03	35.48	Castings
Surya Pharmaceutical Ltd.	2005/03	30.71	21.07	17.80	2.03	2004/03	22.89	2003/03	21.58	Pharmaceuticals
Bihar Caustic & Chemicals Ltd.	2005/03	30.64	12.27	45.62	1.73	2004/03	21.98	2003/03	20.90	Inorganic chemicals
Kalyani Forge Ltd.	2005/03	29.70	22.29	16.02	1.52	2004/03	38.37	2003/03	25.07	Forgings
Triton Valves Ltd.	2005/03	29.44	7.68	19.09	1.00	2004/03	38.50	2003/03	39.99	Auto ancillary
Precision Wires India Ltd.	2005/03	29.17	37.97	10.05	1.14	2004/03	26.28	2003/03	27.10	Copper alloys
Flex Foods Ltd.	2005/03	28.95	15.38	40.73	1.70	2004/03	54.70	2003/03	41.95	Food processing
Impex Ferro Tech Ltd.	2005/03	28.94	NA	9.80	1.62	2004/03	22.80	2003/03	24.06	Ferro alloys
Sterling Tools Ltd.	2005/03	28.46	24.59	14.55	1.73	2004/03	28.08	2003/03	25.04	Fasteners
Classic Diamonds (India) Ltd.	2005/03	28.01	22.49	6.84	3.17	2004/03	38.80	2003/03	40.56	Diamond jewellry
Avery Cycle Inds. Ltd.	2005/03	27.87	38.23	7.14	2.60	2004/03	25.94	2003/03	24.40	Engineering
Bayer Diagnostics India Ltd.	2004/12	27.24	8.68	16.35	1.08	2003/12	28.23	2002/12	35.93	Medical equipment
Banco Products (India) Ltd.	2005/03	26.62	7.18	14.20	1.24	2004/03	27.33	2003/03	21.90	Auto ancillary

Company *	Year	RoCE %	5-Yr CAGR Revenue %	EBITDA Margin %	Financial Leverage Ratio	Year	RoCE %	Year	RoCE %	Sector
Shrenuj & Co. Ltd.	2005/03	26.56	21.62	7.39	3.26	2004/03	24.20	2003/03	20.04	Diamond jewellry
RTS Power Corpn. Ltd.	2005/03	26.44	10.41	6.30	2.31	2004/03	21.50	2003/03	22.50	Electrical equipment
Harita Seating Systems Ltd.	2005/03	26.30	17.91	7.96	1.09	2004/03	29.43	2003/03	27.90	Auto ancillary
Menon Bearings Ltd.	2005/03	26.16	12.87	23.90	2.00	2004/03	23.10	2003/03	24.03	Auto ancillary
Lanxess A B S Ltd.	2004/12	25.72	19.63	11.71	1.00	2003/12	32.19	2002/12	34.49	Petrochemicals
Anuh Pharma Ltd.	2005/03	25.26	22.50	11.01	1.01	2004/03	39.68	2003/03	32.12	Pharmaceuticals
Hi-Tech Gears Ltd.	2005/03	24.33	17.46	13.56	2.71	2004/03	23.30	2003/03	31.35	Auto ancillary
Pokarna Ltd.	2005/03	23.95	31.89	18.85	2.13	2004/03	30.37	2003/03	54.47	Granites
Om Metals Ltd.	2005/03	23.53	8.95	19.73	1.72	2004/03	22.91	2003/03	22.83	Steel tubes
MM Forgings Ltd.	2005/03	23.50	18.18	19.27	1.96	2004/03	20.25	2003/03	20.19	Forgings
Sambandam Spinning Mills Ltd.	2005/03	23.28	8.06	22.01	4.83	2004/03	25.47	2003/03	21.52	Cotton spinning
Visaka Industries Ltd.	2005/03	23.26	13.91	17.45	2.68	2004/03	22.93	2003/03	22.60	Diversified
International Conveyors Ltd.	2005/03	23.00	48.06	11.24	1.79	2004/03	33.99	2003/03	28.28	Engineering
Greaves Morganite Crucible Ltd.	2005/03	22.99	8.48	21.25	1.00	2004/03	30.10	2003/03	23.58	Abrasives
Rajratan Global Wire Ltd.	2005/03	21.92	18.40	10.89	2.01	2004/03	22.76	2003/03	21.67	Steel tubes
Super Sales India Ltd.	2005/03	21.68	21.21	14.23	2.02	2004/03	28.58	2003/03	22.09	Cotton yarn
Pioneer Embroideries Ltd.	2005/03	20.36	24.07	19.25	2.50	2004/03	22.17	2003/03	24.29	Hosiery
Kaira Can Co. Ltd.	2005/03	20.21	10.58	2.53	2.50	2004/03	21.55	2003/03	24.41	Metallic packaging

* Micro cap companies have been defined as having a market cap less than $50 million.

The list comprises companies with a minimum return on capital employed (RoCE) of 20% for the latest reported financial year, being either March 2005 or December 2004. In a few cases there may be a different year ending. The ranking has been done on the basis of the latest year's RoCE.

The list was filtered on additional criteria of strong revenue growth, profitability and conservative financing, capital productivity was a ranking criteria and not the sole determinant for inclusion. A number of companies with high capital returns have been excluded if one or more of the other criteria were less than satisfactory.

Source: Prowess (Center for Monitoring the Indian Economy)

INDUSTRY AGGREGATES

Agro-based industry

Company Name	Revenue (Million $)	5-yr CAGR (%) Revenues	Net Income (Million $)	5-yr CAGR (%) (Net Income)	RoCE (%)	P/E Ratio	1-yr Stock Return (%)	Market Cap (Million $)	Economic Activity
Tata Tea Ltd.	202.96	-0.45	29.30	0.69	15.24	33.60	107.22	1,210.26	Tea
Rei Agro Ltd.	192.05	45.58	8.60	69.69	29.73	12.80	29.81	141.95	Rice
Satnam Overseas Ltd.	115.20	14.97	3.52	18.34	25.03	8.72	-9.17	40.51	Rice
KRBL Ltd.	114.77	18.07	3.70	1.65	20.57	9.78	23.36	52.72	Rice
Lakshmi Overseas Inds. Ltd.	92.66	17.08	5.25	22.94	45.16	13.32	501.22	99.78	Rice
Jay Shree Tea & Inds. Ltd.	48.74	0.80	1.43	-14.00	5.36	11.69	12.32	26.20	Tea
Tata Coffee Ltd.	45.16	-1.63	6.52	-0.44	13.63	11.84	23.03	91.55	Coffee
Goodricke Group Ltd.	44.08	1.79	0.73	-23.89	7.09	18.14	13.13	34.95	Tea
Williamson Tea Assam Ltd.	42.37	-0.56	1.91	-22.06	10.89	44.61	11.80	53.83	Tea
Vikas WSP Ltd.	38.18	-7.03	6.33	-17.36	16.63	0.61	-85.43	15.98	Guar gum
Agro Dutch Inds. Ltd.	32.83	17.64	2.62	-7.52	20.95	16.91	56.97	29.63	Mushroom
Harrisons Malayalam Ltd.	32.45	-3.63	10.83	NA	21.39	2.28	48.57	41.99	Tea
Warren Tea Ltd.	28.39	-2.54	1.10	-22.2	6.86	-18.70	-16.59	21.34	Tea
Assam Co. Ltd.	26.44	-4.75	1.18	-1.65	10.22	19.52	311.52	98.24	Tea
Parry Agro Inds. Ltd.	19.33	-1.12	2.83	19.19	11.23	37.02	224.08	111.31	Tea
Dhunseri Tea & Inds. Ltd.	13.73	-2.03	1.03	-13.36	9.34	45.46	-7.79	10.64	Tea
Rossell Industries Ltd.	9.38	-9.06	-2.58	NA	89.20	505.95	130.77	48.30	Tea
Nath Seeds Ltd.	8.99	-4.93	-0.54	NA	1.22	-5.24	53.00	6.01	Oilseeds
Diana Tea Co. Ltd.	6.76	9.66	0.41	4.83	9.77	18.63	183.24	14.23	Tea
Flex Foods Ltd.	5.67	15.38	1.82	NA	28.95	4.39	45.89	6.33	Mushroom

Source: Prowess (Center for Monitoring the Indian Economy)

Airlines industry

Company Name	Revenue (Million $)	5-yr CAGR (%) Revenues	Net Income (Million $)	5-yr CAGR (%) (Net Income)	RoCE (%)	P/E Ratio	1-yr Stock Return (%)	Market Cap (Million $)	Economic Activity
Jet Airways (India) Ltd.	991.93	17.11	89.09	107.58	27.70	24.44	-7.23	2,369.28	Airlines services
Jagson Airlines Ltd.	1.34	7.74	0.20	17.75	-1.01	86.56	148.87	5.31	Air transport services
Spicejet Ltd.	0.45	NA	-6.52	NA	-50.93	NA	208.38	300.95	Airlines services

Note: The bulk of the airline companies in India including the state-owned ones are unlisted.
Source: Prowess (Center for Monitoring the Indian Economy)

Auto ancillary manufacturers

Company Name	Revenue (Million $)	5-yr CAGR (%) Revenues	Net Income (Million $)	5-yr CAGR (%) (Net Income)	RoCE (%)	P/E Ratio	1-yr Stock Return (%)	Market Cap (Million $)	Economic Activity
Motor Industries Co. Ltd.	597.18	11.64	85.18	28.79	45.57	24.46	41.57	1,894.35	Automobile engine parts
Bharat Forge Ltd.	299.21	18.04	36.71	28.66	46.55	43.37	95.60	1,877.65	Automobile ancillaries
Sundram Fasteners Ltd.	235.72	19.15	15.77	10.23	30.40	21.68	35.58	365.10	Automobile ancillaries
Subros Ltd.	164.67	8.37	4.60	7.83	26.76	9.36	27.45	40.83	Automobile ancillaries
Rico Auto Inds. Ltd.	161.88	22.99	8.01	21.68	38.78	31.76	80.89	285.71	Wheels for automobiles
Omax Autos Ltd.	152.09	29.30	4.61	24.71	27.58	15.72	35.13	74.35	Other automobile ancillaries
Sundaram-Clayton Ltd.	145.49	21.72	12.14	18.69	33.44	26.99	29.83	359.50	Suspension & braking parts
Motherson Sumi Systems Ltd.	144.95	28.82	14.11	31.87	43.84	30.42	55.24	464.71	Wiring harness & parts
Jay Bharat Maruti Ltd.	142.90	23.09	2.35	22.17	52.25	10.70	81.90	26.85	Other automobile ancillaries
Munjal Showa Ltd.	138.63	20.91	1.78	-9.74	19.06	30.77	99.89	79.36	Shock absorbers
Pricol Ltd.	121.23	17.00	9.59	22.97	40.39	10.29	1.38	93.27	Automobile equipment
Goetze (India) Ltd.	116.68	20.42	5.01	16.97	18.84	23.75	33.23	126.81	Piston rings
Amtek Auto Ltd.	115.61	50.60	11.83	51.15	20.03	29.60	55.83	649.87	Automobile ancillaries
Gabriel India Ltd.	109.66	14.45	4.07	47.30	16.94	11.55	63.69	42.02	Shock absorbers
Kalyani Brakes Ltd.	95.60	22.41	7.37	31.30	39.43	23.77	49.60	187.48	Suspension & braking parts
Denso India Ltd.	86.61	14.08	3.71	62.75	23.04	16.15	37.22	57.38	Electrical automobile parts
Amtek India Ltd.	78.93	56.39	9.28	50.37	26.11	11.77	102.59	154.99	Automobile ancillaries
Lumax Industries Ltd.	78.58	10.03	1.64	12.42	19.07	15.04	31.67	23.66	Auto head lights
Ucal Fuel Systems Ltd.	72.55	16.68	6.05	22.18	24.63	14.71	39.36	75.95	Carburettors
Automotive Axles Ltd.	69.53	21.81	5.14	31.51	46.05	23.79	138.38	199.29	Axle shafts
Amforge Industries Ltd.	67.59	7.77	-3.02	NA	3.99	NA	68.58	69.93	Automobile ancillaries
Munjal Auto Inds. Ltd.	65.01	48.01	5.91	56.85	62.31	15.17	115.72	102.41	Automobile ancillaries

Company Name	Revenue (Million $)	5-yr CAGR (%) Revenues	Net Income (Million $)	5-yr CAGR (%) (Net Income)	RoCE (%)	P/E Ratio	1-yr Stock Return (%)	Market Cap (Million $)	Economic Activity
Ennore Foundries Ltd.	59.35	14.03	2.97	21.16	42.76	17.99	120.38	56.75	Automobile ancillaries
GKN Driveline (India) Ltd.	56.73	14.40	7.25	48.36	41.66	7.36	260.34	15.43	Drive transmission & steering parts
Minda Industries Ltd.	51.46	25.66	2.32	35.35	28.78	17.87	123.87	55.39	Electric horns
Rane (Madras) Ltd.	51.26	NA	0.96	NA	NA	16.19	-7.18	22.70	Steering gears
Phoenix Lamps Ltd.	46.08	14.54	2.80	6.52	23.27	12.36	155.70	49.70	Auto head lights
ZF Steering Gear (India) Ltd.	45.99	28.41	4.66	44.43	45.19	11.36	58.76	63.88	Steering gears
Lakshmi Auto Components Ltd. [Merged]	43.91	42.67	4.63	19.84	39.88	8.46	112.24	39.17	Other automobile ancillaries
India Nippon Electricals Ltd.	40.99	12.24	4.20	9.19	26.93	12.56	-6.45	50.86	Flywheel magnetos
Hi-Tech Gears Ltd.	40.84	17.46	1.78	9.91	24.33	26.08	97.61	43.33	Drive transmission & steering parts
Rane Engine Valves Ltd.	39.97	10.81	3.79	34.71	32.11	15.91	17.75	58.37	Engine valves
Automobile Corpn. Of Goa Ltd.	38.76	26.35	3.28	NA	80.82	13.31	169.89	44.27	Other automobile ancillaries
Bharat Gears Ltd.	38.65	4.60	0.99	6.72	22.93	21.44	24.61	10.87	Gears including crown wheels
Rasandik Engineering Inds. India Ltd.	38.54	27.85	1.24	24.44	65.47	16.81	338.95	23.04	Automobile ancillaries
Bharat Seats Ltd.	37.85	12.25	0.55	9.93	19.81	16.00	21.80	6.33	Auto seating systems
Rane Brake Linings Ltd.	36.81	10.10	4.34	19.02	15.21	8.15	26.94	37.17	Brake linings
Kalyani Forge Ltd.	33.64	22.29	2.34	30.01	29.70	15.65	98.24	38.52	Automobile ancillaries
Steel Strips Wheels Ltd.	33.01	24.39	2.79	19.99	30.88	16.71	38.40	35.10	Wheels for automobiles
Banco Products (India) Ltd.	31.46	7.18	2.36	-0.12	26.62	10.94	29.35	26.97	Automobile engine parts
Shanthi Gears Ltd.	31.38	27.94	4.35	30.56	38.81	21.29	70.74	102.33	Gears including crown wheels

Company Name	Revenue (Million $)	5-yr CAGR (%) Revenues	Net Income (Million $)	5-yr CAGR (%) (Net Income)	RoCE (%)	P/E Ratio	1-yr Stock Return (%)	Market Cap (Million $)	Economic Activity
Harita Seating Systems Ltd.	31.10	17.91	1.04	9.55	26.30	12.80	40.44	14.05	Auto seating systems
Talbros Automotive Components Ltd.	26.70	15.48	1.07	22.41	43.99	17.90	9.66	25.75	Gaskets
Siemens VDO Automotive Ltd.	26.07	25.41	0.82	NA	18.09	42.66	180.09	44.98	Automobile equipment
JMT Auto Ltd.	25.49	31.60	1.65	13.58	29.87	19.75	116.67	30.70	Drive transmission & steering parts
Suprajit Engineering Ltd.	24.34	33.24	2.23	37.28	36.94	17.15	143.42	46.03	Automobile equipment
Clutch Auto Ltd.	24.10	2.44	1.30	23.84	25.18	16.42	287.93	39.38	Drive transmission & steering parts
Jai Parabolic Springs Ltd.	23.72	7.08	-3.89	NA	4.87	285.25	140.06	12.97	Leaf springs (automotive)
JBM Auto Ltd.	23.33	44.10	1.20	NA	25.93	11.85	31.33	17.39	Automobile ancillaries
Lumax Automotive Systems Ltd.	21.75	NA	0.61	NA	31.86	20.22	85.33	12.96	Filter elements, inserts
Jay Ushin Ltd.	21.53	7.38	0.54	108.60	28.85	10.39	43.98	5.29	Automobile locks
Ceekay Daikin Ltd.	21.50	8.80	0.50	20.33	14.11	10.81	136.28	9.19	Drive transmission & steering parts
Samkrg Pistons & Rings Ltd.	21.38	9.82	1.53	0.30	26.06	12.50	27.41	23.32	Pistons
EL Forge Ltd.	21.16	16.84	0.31	NA	28.06	12.27	-8.00	16.12	Automobile ancillaries
Bimetal Bearings Ltd.	20.94	5.58	2.49	6.53	17.36	9.70	13.13	24.11	Thickwall, thinwall bearings
Ramkrishna Forgings Ltd.	19.24	NA	1.51	NA	27.65	14.64	57.60	27.25	Automobile ancillaries
Yuken India Ltd.	17.01	21.80	1.45	62.00	37.73	15.35	185.95	23.17	Fuel pumps
Menon Pistons Ltd.	16.68	1.17	0.66	NA	25.55	12.08	58.77	9.55	Pistons
Perfect Circle India Ltd.	16.65	-3.39	1.28	-3.50	19.18	19.09	21.04	17.01	Automobile engine parts
Rane Holdings Ltd.	15.93	-13.94	1.62	27.82	15.29	26.46	20.44	43.06	Steering gears
Hindustan Composites Ltd.	15.48	-1.09	0.33	7.20	10.71	42.88	93.11	11.01	Brake linings
Vybra Automet Ltd.	11.83	36.45	0.97	NA	126.81	13.90	112.75	12.13	Automobile ancillaries
IP Rings Ltd.	11.71	9.34	1.14	9.13	17.67	17.97	16.14	21.45	Piston rings

Company Name	Revenue (Million $)	5-yr CAGR (%) Revenues	Net Income (Million $)	5-yr CAGR (%) (Net Income)	RoCE (%)	P/E Ratio	1-yr Stock Return (%)	Market Cap (Million $)	Economic Activity
Pradeep Metals Ltd.	8.07	5.11	2.24	NA	116.37	2.07	45.74	4.70	Automobile ancillaries
Gajra Bevel Gears Ltd.	8.03	1.36	0.10	NA	7.11	NA	177.04	5.65	Gears including crown wheels
Harig Crankshafts Ltd.	6.66	18.19	54.76	NA	-0.83	0.51	5.95	29.08	Crankshafts
Menon Bearings Ltd.	6.08	12.87	0.70	6.51	26.16	18.17	81.06	12.02	Other utomobile ancillaries
Denison Hydraulics India Ltd.	4.58	21.48	0.60	44.32	43.99	11.46	140.76	12.19	Hydraulic pumps

Source: Prowess (Center for Monitoring the Indian Economy)

Automobiles

Company Name	Revenue (Million $)	5-yr CAGR Revenues (%)	Net Income (Million $)	5-yr CAGR Net Income (%)	RoCE (%)	P/E Ratio	1-yr Stock Return (%)	Market Cap (Million $)
Tata Motors Ltd.	4,608.31	18.36	281.13	77.00	32.83	17.71	27.24	5,293.92
Maruti Udyog Ltd.	3,063.36	7.36	194.00	20.93	30.49	19.23	44.82	4,318.88
Hero Honda Motors Ltd.	1,956.05	30.73	184.20	33.37	75.64	19.48	71.93	3,844.21
Mahindra & Mahindra Ltd.	1,738.53	12.11	115.02	13.95	27.27	20.09	93.17	2,686.52
Bajaj Auto Ltd.	1,516.63	12.10	165.72	2.81	18.78	24.25	98.95	4,872.10
Ashok Leyland Ltd.	1,115.57	12.74	61.68	28.16	19.62	11.78	57.19	898.73
TVS Motor Co. Ltd.	754.83	16.59	31.59	10.15	23.00	17.82	21.91	538.79
Eicher Motors Ltd.	505.65	44.48	13.38	29.98	22.50	3.18	9.67	157.29
Hindustan Motors Ltd.	307.30	-5.69	13.91	NA	-21.50	5.95	82.59	113.37
Force Motors Ltd.	227.26	8.05	0.62	NA	3.17	33.05	33.25	105.25
LML Ltd.	158.24	-1.02	-21.89	NA	-64.67	NA	-5.25	44.90
Swaraj Mazda Ltd.	153.85	25.97	5.51	53.56	86.27	16.15	27.70	89.01
Kinetic Engineering Ltd.	54.17	-4.06	-11.74	NA	-19.82	NA	97.04	16.01
Kinetic Motor Co. Ltd.	52.02	-6.55	-4.85	NA	-24.11	NA	41.42	21.49
Atul Auto Ltd.	26.15	48.25	0.69	11.40	23.88	30.21	682.44	23.07

Source: Prowess (Center for Monitoring the Indian Economy)

Banks

Company Name	Revenue (Million $)	5-yr CAGR Revenues (%)	Net Income (Million $)	5-yr CAGR Net Income (%)	RoCE (%)	P/E Ratio	1-yr Stock Return (%)	Market Cap (Million $)
State Bank of India	8,827.49	8.65	978.30	15.98	59.90	10.55	60.05	11,036.73
ICICI Bank Ltd.	2,807.96	63.79	455.73	80.28	18.12	22.82	63.44	11,630.16
Punjab National Bank	2,301.38	11.45	320.48	28.14	61.99	10.01	30.62	3,310.68
Industrial Development Bank of India Ltd.	2,059.93	3.87	105.68	-18.06	15.72	15.17	7.41	1,657.24
Canara Bank	1,990.33	9.89	252.16	36.28	69.64	10.49	17.29	2,073.76
Bank of Baroda	1,709.41	5.62	153.83	6.13	54.58	12.07	12.92	1,608.63
Bank of India	1,568.36	5.38	77.28	14.50	39.56	13.88	62.98	1,361.95
Union Bank of India	1,266.73	9.35	163.42	48.01	58.55	9.25	20.20	1,260.62
Indian Overseas Bank	1,062.76	11.24	148.04	74.43	86.81	7.30	41.88	1,160.80
Syndicate Bank	952.77	9.44	91.57	13.32	97.88	8.37	86.26	1,027.92
Oriental Bank of Commerce	922.50	8.78	165.02	21.11	74.22	10.99	-21.13	1,434.63
Uco Bank	896.53	12.97	78.56	56.65	92.80	10.19	15.77	475.98
HDFC Bank Ltd.	865.92	36.46	151.26	40.85	43.18	28.89	46.66	4,967.70
Allahabad Bank	864.24	12.59	123.13	50.86	106.91	6.53	34.46	845.18
Andhra Bank	644.64	11.77	118.20	33.95	63.14	7.86	27.35	854.55
Bank of Maharashtra	629.93	11.12	40.25	14.46	74.12	11.10	2.24	318.98
Corporation Bank	605.65	7.74	91.40	11.49	41.29	10.78	14.25	1,220.71
State Bank of Travancore	540.73	12.06	56.17	30.05	116.59	6.36	69.28	336.82
Vijaya Bank	532.14	12.81	86.49	48.42	60.06	7.89	-8.61	563.08

Company Name	Revenue (Million $)	5-yr CAGR Revenues (%)	Net Income (Million $)	5-yr CAGR Net Income (%)	RoCE (%)	P/E Ratio	1-yr Stock Return (%)	Market Cap (Million $)
UTI Bank Ltd.	524.29	32.15	76.04	45.64	47.90	19.02	64.46	1,812.61
State Bank of Bikaner & Jaipur	498.71	10.43	46.74	11.30	55.07	9.36	49.16	330.97
Dena Bank	444.32	1.87	13.86	-11.50	58.60	-5.89	2.71	210.23
Jammu & Kashmir Bank Ltd.	365.92	10.76	26.15	-0.86	58.90	10.73	42.93	539.56
State Bank of Mysore	343.04	9.70	46.65	33.59	69.52	6.92	114.15	328.17
IFCI Ltd.	327.01	-12.60	-100.77	NA	3.56	NA	-17.32	146.17
Federal Bank Ltd.	307.29	6.26	20.48	14.20	71.73	8.09	25.31	266.15
Indusind Bank Ltd.	286.54	10.54	46.71	50.22	44.31	9.48	12.10	382.87
ING Vysya Bank Ltd.	258.12	2.44	-8.68	NA	36.67	37.23	-67.52	337.69
Karnataka Bank Ltd.	239.44	10.22	33.44	29.30	72.62	8.52	70.63	311.09
South Indian Bank Ltd.	176.88	7.96	1.98	-19.42	76.44	8.71	5.74	70.81
Infrastructure Development Finance Co. Ltd.	164.40	20.22	69.10	15.29	9.75	20.36	2.01	1,809.96
Karur Vysya Bank Ltd.	156.24	7.99	23.94	8.17	55.13	8.44	35.85	222.48
Bank Of Rajasthan Ltd.	128.20	5.29	7.96	23.72	54.18	96.91	2.59	118.93
Kotak Mahindra Bank Ltd.	127.45	14.95	19.29	6.44	35.57	80.57	127.97	1,703.46
Centurion Bank Of Punjab Ltd.	92.91	-4.73	5.71	-6.06	29.86	40.59	52.13	509.15
City Union Bank Ltd.	71.56	9.11	10.53	18.22	94.12	4.54	22.29	51.19
Nedungadi Bank Ltd.	49.98	22.08	0.29	-21.35	660.66	NA	-62.73	3.80
Dhanalakshmi Bank Ltd.	46.27	1.91	-4.91	NA	47.54	NA	15.81	22.15
Tourism Finance Corpn. Of India Ltd.	18.39	-11.03	3.23	-6.79	11.22	7.80	0.64	26.28
Yes Bank Ltd.	10.93	NA	-0.85	NA	NA	36.95	14.8	428.32

Source: Prowess (Center for Monitoring the Indian Economy)

Cement

Company Name	Revenue (Million $)	5-yr CAGR Revenues (%)	Net Income (Million $)	5-yr CAGR Net Income (%)	RoCE (%)	P/E Ratio	1-yr Stock Return (%)	Market Cap (Million $)	Economic Activity
Associated Cement Cos. Ltd.	1,033.85	10.91	86.00	NA	17.58	17.63	70.36	2,249.80	Cement
Ultratech Cement Ltd.	712.88	NA	0.65	NA	7.54	104.50	47.11	1,283.00	Cement
Gujarat Ambuja Cements Ltd.	688.57	18.38	106.43	1.82	18.49	23.89	58.55	2,460.33	Cement
Birla Corporation Ltd.	327.33	6.96	19.74	NA	23.08	20.95	56.78	407.12	Cement
India Cements Ltd.	315.23	-0.28	1.04	-25.67	3.88	35.18	99.28	411.54	Cement
Madras Cements Ltd.	202.23	11.43	12.71	8.12	10.70	28.72	50.38	408.44	Cement
Shree Cement Ltd.	164.33	10.29	6.61	37.90	9.26	35.12	107.22	395.13	Cement
OCL India Ltd.	129.75	12.29	6.40	37.20	15.81	13.02	99.22	102.60	Cement
Prism Cement Ltd.	120.68	8.74	5.87	NA	17.74	24.06	20.28	138.28	Cement
Dalmia Cement (Bharat) Ltd.	118.41	6.89	7.33	8.82	9.14	18.14	193.09	155.08	Cement
Chettinad Cement Corpn. Ltd.	114.08	16.71	6.35	34.13	16.30	17.41	81.54	138.31	Cement
Ambuja Cement Eastern Ltd.	107.33	14.41	10.24	102.31	22.69	23.17	20.85	254.78	Cement
Roofit Industries Ltd.	103.70	62.15	9.47	44.20	29.45	1.36	-76.59	1.67	Corrugated asbestos sheets
JK Cement Ltd.	96.24	NA	1.43	NA	11.68	49.54	10.65	189.16	Pozzolana portland cement
Hyderabad Industries Ltd.	94.54	8.55	2.21	NA	31.40	18.00	266.79	90.08	Asbestos-cement products
Mangalam Cement Ltd.	83.19	25.04	3.81	NA	18.08	12.22	35.99	46.58	Ordinary portland cement
Narmada Cement Co. Ltd.	63.10	4.98	4.65	NA	49.04	NA	107.81	34.24	Cement
Ramco Industries Ltd.	57.72	7.01	6.55	12.75	22.66	16.75	119.92	125.07	Asbestos-cement products
Everest Industries Ltd.	51.77	8.81	4.36	24.89	27.82	13.91	69.30	70.13	Asbestos-cement products
Saurashtra Cement Ltd.	50.94	1.77	-11.71	NA	-3.52	NA	48.63	24.13	Ordinary portland cement
Visaka Industries Ltd.	48.90	13.91	3.26	22.28	23.26	8.88	2.80	34.72	Asbestos-cement products
Gujarat Sidhee Cement Ltd.	45.45	4.49	-4.42	NA	-6.87	NA	27.64	39.90	Cement
Indian Hume Pipe Co. Ltd.	45.41	15.92	5.76	46.18	14.85	9.39	42.63	30.20	Cement products.
Andhra Cements Ltd.	43.88	7.48	0.55	NA	15.61	NA	241.90	54.89	Cement

Source: Prowess (Center for Monitoring the Indian Economy)

Construction & infrastructure

Company Name	Revenue (Million $)	5-yr CAGR Revenues (%)	Net Income (Million $)	5-yr CAGR Net Income (%)	RoCE (%)	P/E Ratio	1-yr Stock Return (%)	Market Cap (Million $)	Economic Activity
Jaiprakash Associates Ltd.	686.15	NA	47.19	NA	17.97	10.36	89.89	1,348.75	Roads, bridges, tunnels etc.
Hindustan Construction Co. Ltd.	344.36	24.12	16.82	52.08	22.77	24.16	326.38	638.90	Roads, bridges, tunnels etc.
Nagarjuna Construction Co. Ltd.	270.11	40.56	12.96	21.58	26.03	32.40	210.76	558.04	Roads, bridges, tunnels etc.
IVRCL Infrastructures & Projects Ltd.	239.43	37.77	12.89	45.06	35.11	23.12	115.75	344.29	Roads, bridges, tunnels etc.
Punj Lloyd Ltd.	233.65	26.84	9.22	14.04	49.47	NA	NA	1,311.82	Civil engineering works
Simplex Infrastructures Ltd.	227.06	25.35	5.72	38.84	16.60	20.67	497.82	201.77	Construction allied activities nec
Engineers India Ltd.	206.85	15.62	25.60	-2.25	20.89	27.03	100.02	871.12	Civil engineering works
Gammon India Ltd.	198.18	21.57	8.67	30.67	27.20	40.09	218.40	677.78	Construction & allied activities
ITD Cementation India Ltd.	126.10	7.83	-9.44	NA	1.92	NA	157.29	69.25	Civil engineering works
Unitech Ltd.	115.76	18.92	6.80	20.35	16.50	30.63	213.84	241.24	Construction of buildings
Patel Engineering Ltd.	106.22	18.31	8.85	21.69	17.56	30.82	290.74	320.96	Civil engineering works
Madhucon Projects Ltd.	69.65	25.50	3.70	32.05	24.84	37.73	275.73	141.30	Roads, bridges, tunnels etc.
Aban Loyd Chiles Offshore Ltd.	65.94	31.93	11.75	58.08	16.32	24.65	119.76	411.24	Offshore drilling services
Ansal Properties & Infrastructure Ltd.	44.02	6.00	3.10	11.97	16.73	23.91	661.67	149.53	Construction of buildings
Era Constructions (India) Ltd.	35.51	25.21	1.24	21.36	29.42	20.44	114.84	44.59	Construction allied activities nec
Valecha Engineering Ltd.	33.07	26.64	1.42	7.58	19.81	22.29	108.11	27.06	Construction allied activities nec
Shiv-Vani Oil & Gas Exploration Services Ltd.	30.84	19.44	3.37	16.88	22.33	27.75	186.32	100.27	Offshore drilling services
Dolphin Offshore Enterprises (India) Ltd.	30.77	15.59	1.41	13.72	36.85	24.35	604.08	53.35	Offshore drilling services

Company Name	Revenue (Million $)	5-yr CAGR Revenues (%)	Net Income (Million $)	5-yr CAGR Net Income (%)	RoCE (%)	P/E Ratio	1-yr Stock Return (%)	Market Cap (Million $)	Economic Activity
Techno Electric & Engg. Co. Ltd.	26.18	11.18	1.11	9.95	24.32	22.86	355.28	33.46	Construction of power plants
Stewarts & Lloyds Of India Ltd.	25.25	17.50	0.84	27.23	48.45	15.56	88.62	14.99	Civil engineering works
Ansal Housing & Construction Ltd.	18.13	2.38	1.38	12.56	20.42	16.26	604.42	38.65	Construction of buildings
MSK Projects (India) Ltd.	17.91	NA	1.05	NA	17.62	16.90	102.36	28.39	Civil engineering works
Morarjee Realties Ltd.	14.14	-26.84	-2.16	NA	-1.01	9.17	511.69	119.94	Construction of buildings
DS Kulkarni Developers Ltd.	7.86	32.74	0.83	12.56	9.80	18.01	632.74	41.91	Construction of buildings
Noida Toll Bridge Co. Ltd.	7.00	NA	-3.75	NA	4.28	NA	145.75	96.77	Roads, bridges, tunnels etc.
Arihant Foundations & Housing Ltd.	6.50	17.23	0.13	-21.29	3.55	40.63	1,193.36	25.85	Construction of buildings

Source: Prowess (Center for Monitoring the Indian Economy)

Data processing

Company Name	Revenue (Million $)	5-yr CAGR Revenues (%)	Net Income (Million $)	5-yr CAGR Net Income (%)	RoCE (%)	P/E Ratio	1-yr Stock Return (%)	Market Cap (Million $)	Economic Activity
Tata Consultancy Services Ltd.	1,829.80	NA	416.23	NA	NA	36.35	37.68	18,752.30	
Wipro Ltd.	1,653.68	25.26	339.73	43.81	41.39	37.82	15.71	14,232.60	
Infosys Technologies Ltd.	1,560.93	50.68	432.81	45.35	52.26	37.52	41.80	18,518.23	
Satyam Computer Services Ltd.	787.32	38.61	170.51	41.99	31.59	27.57	72.20	5,293.14	
HCL Infosystems Ltd.	450.41	11.99	30.18	12.69	32.21	31.87	68.68	996.79	Mini/micro Computers
HCL Technologies Ltd.	328.87	29.33	74.83	10.50	11.65	52.90	60.08	3,942.14	
I-Flex Solutions Ltd.	205.20	35.52	44.92	23.33	25.00	43.07	63.32	1,799.56	
Hewlett-Packard Globalsoft Ltd.	185.75	67.04	25.06	39.51	22.37	22.06	31.76	640.20	
Tata Infotech Ltd.	176.74	13.01	18.24	45.75	34.98	15.26	125.64	344.08	
CMC Ltd.	176.42	10.85	5.16	12.93	22.04	41.33	-33.03	162.86	
Patni Computer Systems Ltd.	159.56	NA	52.40	NA	25.34	30.02	29.54	1,504.43	
Polaris Software Lab Ltd.	152.04	35.61	12.14	7.50	10.37	38.06	-15.16	306.62	
GTL Ltd.	123.75	-2.72	24.04	-14.31	8.55	16.19	-10.89	201.11	
Flextronics Software Systems Ltd.	108.27	34.69	24.58	23.46	33.82	22.39	32.22	577.05	
Igate Global Solutions Ltd.	98.10	43.26	6.08	111.61	4.55	22.81	-9.49	168.51	
Rolta India Ltd.	78.63	14.28	23.49	11.41	18.74	12.06	164.80	301.31	
TVS Electronics Ltd.	78.47	119.09	0.97	NA	21.73	NA	6.78	29.86	Peripherals
PCS Technology Ltd.	77.03	13.69	0.73	13.10	14.28	25.01	-7.99	16.71	
D-Link (India) Ltd.	67.07	29.26	6.50	33.07	24.18	15.31	18.13	97.04	Peripherals
Zenith Computers Ltd.	64.90	5.21	1.06	-1.82	18.05	10.59	83.34	17.33	
NIIT Ltd.	64.50	-13.26	3.63	-35.50	14.65	33.83	82.36	129.32	

Company Name	Revenue (Million $)	5-yr CAGR Revenues (%)	Net Income (Million $)	5-yr CAGR Net Income (%)	RoCE (%)	P/E Ratio	1-yr Stock Return (%)	Market Cap (Million $)	Economic Activity
Hexaware Technologies Ltd.	58.36	-6.87	9.85	-3.24	17.28	22.60	16.72	353.35	
Mastek Ltd.	58.05	22.38	10.77	9.99	36.53	14.71	61.21	164.95	
Mphasis B F L Ltd.	56.31	15.41	11.40	157.88	11.46	42.43	1.36	533.60	
Teledata Informatics Ltd.	52.73	154.57	17.16	137.00	54.76	2.03	-50.77	52.16	
Sasken Communication Technologies Ltd.	50.97	24.19	4.93	7.87	23.14	49.18	-13.48	253.95	
3I Infotech Ltd.	50.85	39.79	4.00	10.86	9.51	25.55	62.80	189.04	
Silverline Technologies Ltd.	47.00	21.65	-50.48	NA	-1.03	-20.59	-4.23	23.11	
Mascon Global Ltd.	46.77	28.33	5.76	19.13	9.79	13.79	-38.87	56.16	
Tata Elxsi Ltd.	44.54	9.63	5.98	31.41	70.06	21.96	47.94	154.35	
KPIT Cummins Infosystems Ltd.	44.29	50.77	5.15	46.49	25.10	21.26	30.47	114.89	
Prithvi Information Solutions Ltd.	43.80	NA	4.72	NA	50.46	14.84	19.20	138.25	
Visualsoft Technologies Ltd.	42.77	22.58	6.44	-0.02	13.56	18.47	84.39	109.07	
Zensar Technologies Ltd.	40.07	NA	8.54	122.46	15.65	14.35	18.57	100.30	
Infotech Enterprises Ltd.	34.95	35.59	5.07	16.67	17.35	32.49	149.77	157.56	
Aftek Infosys Ltd.	31.58	56.88	10.76	50.56	18.59	15.58	36.97	228.30	
Hinduja T M T Ltd.	31.34	79.89	15.92	34.08	13.45	31.29	39.96	374.62	
Cranes Software Intl. Ltd.	29.97	65.35	10.20	275.65	39.69	22.04	24.31	272.68	
Subex Systems Ltd.	26.49	30.15	5.75	38.14	24.21	24.54	125.60	197.19	
Ramco Systems Ltd.	26.25	-0.11	-9.54	NA	-0.28	-8.64	-27.81	91.37	
Sonata Software Ltd.	24.55	-9.13	3.73	-6.86	13.16	18.46	97.15	81.74	
Spanco Telesystems & Solutions Ltd.	23.72	81.84	2.21	74.51	32.47	29.39	169.39	79.62	
Geometric Software Solutions Co. Ltd.	21.69	24.33	4.70	0.44	28.83	32.94	45.45	143.20	
RS Software (India) Ltd.	18.57	5.30	-0.34	NA	34.23	18.61	100.35	9.68	

Company Name	Revenue (Million $)	5-yr CAGR Revenues (%)	Net Income (Million $)	5-yr CAGR Net Income (%)	RoCE (%)	P/E Ratio	1-yr Stock Return (%)	Market Cap (Million $)	Economic Activity
Gemini Communication Ltd.	16.13	46.72	1.06	10.82	25.89	10.74	274.68	17.16	Peripherals
Nucleus Software Exports Ltd.	15.23	54.36	3.60	86.58	26.81	23.76	143.56	143.18	
Helios & Matheson Information Technology Ltd.	14.87	42.51	2.87	35.87	28.28	15.38	434.40	98.07	
Datamatics Technologies Ltd.	13.86	18.63	6.90	26.48	19.35	14.81	-27.02	85.79	
PSI Data Systems Ltd.	13.59	-0.06	-0.47	NA	-7.08	-30.70	-0.66	18.14	
Orient Information Technology Ltd.	13.53	6.49	1.75	-5.09	7.54	10.93	-19.93	13.69	
Kale Consultants Ltd.	11.20	15.75	0.03	-54.41	7.74	85.29	16.04	23.65	
Geodesic Information Systems Ltd.	9.15	NA	4.34	198.91	42.08	48.08	234.33	315.34	
SSI Ltd.	8.07	-15.79	-9.87	NA	3.18	-80.05	123.86	39.48	
Visesh Infotecnics Ltd.	8.06	35.80	0.44	2.19	7.71	16.96	305.18	21.09	
KLG Systel Ltd.	7.99	20.45	0.58	-1.79	9.99	20.54	93.87	18.02	
Vakrangee Softwares Ltd.	7.73	10.52	0.64	-21.16	3.45	16.95	540.47	25.58	
Financial Technologies (India) Ltd.	7.26	145.26	2.12	NA	15.16	184.05	806.90	1,294.22	
Megasoft Ltd.	6.55	83.92	-1.67	NA	-16.61	33.38	149.37	74.50	
Micro Technologies (India) Ltd.	6.08	26.06	1.57	55.96	14.70	26.14	201.13	64.04	
Zenith Infotech Ltd.	4.98	4.30	0.81	-2.19	12.72	17.77	348.64	23.99	
ICSA (India) Ltd.	4.89	75.01	0.82	70.48	61.34	38.38	573.83	76.15	
Onward Technologies Ltd.	4.38	-11.70	0.81	30.80	9.00	35.39	7.37	23.17	
IT Microsystems (India) Ltd.	4.13	204.02	1.98	193.56	15.93	16.55	158.18	29.01	
Telesys Software Ltd.	0.67	NA	-0.18	NA	-3.37	-3.32	43.65	1.37	
Moschip Semiconductor Technology Ltd.	0.53	NA	-2.20	NA	-23.62	-27.44	5.88	40.79	
Websity Infosys Ltd.	0.01	NA	-2.26	NA	-7.78	198.04	931.00	27.90	

Source: Prowess (Center for Monitoring the Indian Economy)

Defense

Company Name	Revenue (Million $)	5-yr CAGR Revenues (%)	Net Income (Million $)	5-yr CAGR Net Income (%)	RoCE (%)	P/E Ratio	1-year Stock Return (%)	Market Cap (Million $)	Economic Activity
Bharat Electronics Ltd.	733.65	16.49	100.70	32.64	48.57	15.69	42.54	1,653.45	Electronics
Astra Microwave Products Ltd.	17.28	53.03	3.88	64.88	65.28	30.81	342.35	262.06	Communication equipment
High Energy Batteries (India) Ltd	7.20	27.39	0.48	NA	28.76	15.43	207.00	7.36	Dry cells
Dynamatic Technologies Ltd.	4.55	3.58	0.31	16.03	33.97	65.10	324.25	23.40	Hydraulic pumps
Zen Technologies Ltd.	4.32	NA	1.46	NA	69.59	29.97	162.66	28.60	Computer simulation

Source: Prowess (Center for Monitoring the Indian Economy)

Engineering companies

Company Name	Revenue (Million $)	5-yr CAGR Revenues (%)	Net Income (Million $)	5-yr CAGR Net Income (%)	RoCE (%)	P/E Ratio	1-yr Stock Return (%)	Market Cap (Million $)	Economic Activity
Larsen & Toubro Ltd.	3,049.63	12.52	223.60	23.56	29.65	30.18	74.79	5,158.28	Turnkey projects
Bharat Heavy Electricals Ltd.	2,454.73	9.09	216.68	9.73	21.70	28.82	99.48	7,925.22	Prime movers
ABB Ltd.	555.86	25.82	35.07	32.92	38.72	41.85	108.50	1,853.62	Switchgears, nec
Crompton Greaves Ltd.	512.76	6.26	26.09	NA	26.74	28.67	183.21	886.66	Motors & generators
Siemens Ltd.	438.68	11.92	34.40	33.94	41.35	45.93	177.15	2,659.13	Switching apparatus
Suzlon Energy Ltd.	435.80	65.79	82.15	66.36	56.50	99.55	33.80	6,037.50	Wind turbines
Bharat Earth Movers Ltd.	424.89	7.03	39.84	64.41	40.27	19.31	194.15	831.43	Earth moving machinery
Exide Industries Ltd.	339.81	9.58	17.56	9.59	23.60	18.52	35.45	389.06	Storage batteries
Cummins India Ltd.	299.26	9.47	31.19	6.09	27.55	21.36	38.52	739.80	Internal combustion engines
Kirloskar Oil Engines Ltd.	293.52	8.72	39.52	16.23	20.64	6.08	150.47	395.52	Internal combustion engines
Escorts Ltd.	286.01	0.60	-71.26	NA	-6.83	NA	10.05	127.64	Tractors
Lakshmi Machine Works Ltd.	260.24	20.95	3.30	-6.82	34.16	26.29	130.64	514.59	Textile spinning machines
Videocon Appliances Ltd.	251.08	12.23	4.86	-7.86	17.50	2.91	5.45	20.88	Domestic appliances
Whirlpool Of India Ltd.	248.94	1.94	-22.68	NA	-20.98	NA	53.98	86.36	Refrigerators, freezers, etc.
Thermax Ltd.	220.85	18.70	12.57	11.32	21.75	28.76	78.36	506.28	Steam boilers
Punjab Tractors Ltd.	214.20	-4.68	14.30	-13.94	19.48	10.03	16.61	295.29	Tractors
Blue Star Ltd.	209.67	14.20	8.90	11.00	36.56	22.16	116.41	218.73	Air conditioning machines / systems
Areva T & D India Ltd.	198.84	15.99	4.82	65.07	29.40	42.95	316.29	321.64	Switching apparatus
Alstom Projects India Ltd.	194.17	54.74	10.89	NA	12.28	34.11	46.16	329.48	Turnkey projects

Company Name	Revenue (Million $)	5-yr CAGR Revenues (%)	Net Income (Million $)	5-yr CAGR Net Income (%)	RoCE (%)	P/E Ratio	1-yr Stock Return (%)	Market Cap (Million $)	Economic Activity
Kirloskar Brothers Ltd.	172.41	15.35	11.53	32.36	33.59	23.58	489.33	641.44	Pumps
Eveready Industries (India) Ltd.	169.48	-2.20	10.53	40.33	8.62	9.96	64.37	169.26	Dry cells
Greaves Cotton Ltd.	165.96	1.52	14.11	NA	50.38	21.49	203.91	317.71	Diesel engines
SKF India Ltd.	158.76	15.82	12.87	41.96	34.69	20.94	97.53	330.78	Ball or roller bearings
Bajaj Electricals Ltd.	153.69	14.14	3.10	58.17	27.47	17.15	243.26	76.47	Electric appliances
Havell's India Ltd.	151.55	44.54	6.94	55.85	43.26	19.29	231.33	203.79	Miniature circuit breakers
Finolex Cables Ltd.	148.50	3.82	6.99	-15.32	7.58	24.55	82.83	204.70	Cables & other conductors
Sandvik Asia (India) Ltd.	125.73	24.84	19.80	46.38	57.70	29.40	13.11	37.08	Machine tools for drilling, boring, etc.
Alfa Laval (India) Ltd.	119.75	21.96	17.84	29.76	53.17	24.64	42.39	401.60	Food & beverage machinery
Ingersoll-Rand (India) Ltd.	113.76	3.14	25.41	15.94	8.95	33.03	28.26	243.43	Compressors
Atlas Copco (India) Ltd.	99.85	27.72	5.25	27.60	33.53	27.88	76.80	305.44	Compressors
ABG Shipyard Ltd.	85.60	34.36	10.17	99.67	121.05	30.99	-0.04	315.14	Ships, boats, etc.
FAG Bearings India Ltd.	84.54	14.94	7.02	33.84	33.65	15.22	141.70	147.93	Ball or roller bearings
Sterlite Optical Technologies Ltd.	84.24	NA	2.32	NA	6.11	39.94	20.58	114.47	Jelly filled cables
Flat Products Equipments (India) Ltd.	81.52	28.75	0.36	NA	11.24	NA	-2.60	9.83	Other industrial machinery
KSB Pumps Ltd.	75.94	10.15	6.97	17.17	35.98	19.00	88.79	155.88	Pumps
HBL Nife Power Systems Ltd.	74.04	17.14	4.19	6.81	23.98	28.44	139.00	130.06	Nickel-cadmium accumulators
Elecon Engineering Co. Ltd.	73.31	13.58	2.22	25.35	27.14	29.30	396.77	111.21	Material handling equipment
Precision Wires India Ltd.	73.16	37.97	3.48	28.75	29.17	10.50	109.72	40.91	Copper winding wires
Elgi Equipments Ltd.	71.47	15.23	4.81	29.21	29.62	26.33	22.61	102.34	Compressors
Kennametal Widia India Ltd.	71.11	7.49	11.32	12.30	35.77	18.61	57.77	206.32	Machine tools

Company Name	Revenue (Million $)	5-yr CAGR Revenues (%)	Net Income (Million $)	5-yr CAGR Net Income (%)	RoCE (%)	P/E Ratio	1-yr Stock Return (%)	Market Cap (Million $)	Economic Activity
Nicco Corpn. Ltd.	68.87	-10.71	-3.32	NA	4.41	-8.25	55.00	17.08	Jelly filled cables
Timken India Ltd.	68.23	15.71	7.50	35.29	42.99	23.32	113.94	220.08	Tapered roller bearing
Nippo Batteries Co. Ltd.	67.44	2.50	2.39	-7.49	17.04	15.42	8.38	35.37	Dry cells
Kirloskar Pneumatic Co. Ltd.	67.30	33.92	0.32	-7.30	13.75	175.62	225.58	75.04	Compressors
Mcnally Bharat Engg. Co. Ltd.	66.80	16.86	0.60	5.42	31.41	67.05	158.90	51.51	Turnkey projects
Automotive Stampings & Assemblies Ltd.	66.32	NA	0.91	NA	11.75	28.61	33.36	29.39	Stampings & laminations
IFB Industries Ltd.	63.89	3.25	-7.82	NA	-5.24	-3.72	172.44	9.28	Washing machines
Manugraph India Ltd.	63.65	18.13	6.77	72.70	59.69	13.49	565.48	166.35	Printing machinery
Bharat Bijlee Ltd.	63.20	13.29	6.31	NA	50.54	11.48	199.93	86.41	Transformers
Amara Raja Batteries Ltd.	61.54	15.44	1.98	-14.95	5.67	18.57	45.70	40.93	Storage batteries
Wartsila India Ltd.	61.50	-3.28	5.90	12.39	18.03	17.99	143.24	125.78	Diesel engine generator sets
Hitachi Home & Life Solutions (India) Ltd.	61.25	8.30	1.29	8.47	16.43	17.02	97.14	43.21	Window/split airconditioners
Emco Ltd.	59.53	23.24	2.18	43.13	29.05	25.31	116.24	84.78	Transformers
Ion Exchange (India) Ltd.	58.83	7.66	1.09	NA	6.22	30.40	115.92	33.38	Water treatment plants
NRB Bearings Ltd.	57.05	12.08	6.20	17.53	36.36	11.49	77.48	83.28	Ball or roller bearings
Lloyd Electric & Engineering Ltd.	56.23	24.12	2.52	33.35	19.82	17.18	298.87	86.81	Air conditioners & refrigerator accessories
Ador Welding Ltd.	55.96	6.05	6.17	40.47	18.53	13.69	427.49	130.65	Welding electrodes / sticks / wires / fluxes
HMT Ltd.	54.84	-20.45	1.36	NA	7.06	359.42	102.81	1,016.19	Tractors
Petron Engineering Construction Ltd.	54.71	10.84	1.72	42.21	47.84	13.42	85.21	37.49	Turnkey projects
Praj Industries Ltd.	54.15	37.11	4.95	56.88	84.75	36.86	290.90	201.40	Brewery machinery

Company Name	Revenue (Million $)	5-yr CAGR Revenues (%)	Net Income (Million $)	5-yr CAGR Net Income (%)	RoCE (%)	P/E Ratio	1-yr Stock Return (%)	Market Cap (Million $)	Economic Activity
Kei Industries Ltd.	52.74	40.68	1.91	118.10	51.45	14.44	201.86	55.39	Cables & other conductors
Hindustan Powerplus Ltd.	52.50	4.89	1.31	-1.49	9.84	57.96	219.39	76.13	Diesel engines
Subhash Projects & Mktg. Ltd.	52.26	3.08	0.85	11.26	18.65	65.72	549.26	87.52	Turnkey projects
Universal Cables Ltd.	51.45	10.28	0.89	NA	9.96	17.89	233.23	59.32	Cables & other conductors
Honda Siel Power Products Ltd.	50.45	4.50	1.81	-16.90	9.49	19.07	19.29	34.67	Portable generating sets
Walchandnagar Industries Ltd.	49.19	0.60	0.91	-11.57	12.47	18.42	52.47	32.33	Industrial machinery
Esab India Ltd.	48.97	5.59	4.63	18.50	68.92	17.83	245.43	156.01	Welding electrodes / sticks / wires / fluxes
TRF Ltd.	47.47	9.93	0.90	-4.33	28.54	31.44	79.47	29.08	Material handling equipment
Fedders Lloyd Corpn. Ltd.	47.45	6.70	0.78	0.00	11.88	16.03	238.14	32.64	Air conditioning machines / systems
Electrotherm (India) Ltd.	46.68	60.38	3.07	NA	36.21	5.14	326.19	22.47	High frequency melting furnaces
Bhagyanagar Metals Ltd.	39.76	2.15	6.13	29.90	28.80	4.09	45.29	23.13	Jelly filled cables
Bharati Shipyard Ltd.	39.08	21.74	6.22	81.22	63.23	24.30	131.10	151.59	Trawlers
Torrent Cables Ltd.	35.25	24.98	3.38	NA	74.02	11.70	225.51	45.05	Cross linked polyethylene cables (XLPE)
ABC Bearings Ltd.	34.19	7.29	2.62	39.77	50.38	10.68	121.12	33.64	Ball or roller bearings
Swaraj Engines Ltd.	32.52	-2.34	3.51	-4.01	44.85	12.45	43.59	46.07	Diesel engines
Khaitan Electricals Ltd.	27.60	3.42	0.56	-10.30	14.30	8.62	123.28	8.79	Fans
WS Industries (India) Ltd.	27.27	-2.37	0.48	NA	17.24	29.12	173.42	24.82	Electrical insulators, nec
Surana Telecom Ltd.	26.57	11.23	2.83	19.91	24.74	5.09	-15.32	14.90	Jelly filled cables
Paramount Communications Ltd.	25.62	-2.77	0.29	-21.10	10.33	19.73	762.80	33.63	Jelly filled cables

Company Name	Revenue (Million $)	5-yr CAGR Revenues (%)	Net Income (Million $)	5-yr CAGR Net Income (%)	RoCE (%)	P/E Ratio	1-yr Stock Return (%)	Market Cap (Million $)	Economic Activity
VST Tillers Tractors Ltd.	25.51	7.24	1.33	0.03	19.13	7.99	44.85	14.16	Power tillers
Birla Power Solutions Ltd.	25.38	10.04	0.40	-24.89	12.91	9.62	84.30	10.96	Portable generating sets
Fairfield Atlas Ltd.	25.08	36.02	0.81	NA	12.29	28.46	84.16	49.80	Gears
Igarashi Motors India Ltd.	24.15	12.81	0.72	-9.16	3.37	34.59	109.97	63.75	AC motors, others
Vindhya Telelinks Ltd.	23.75	-17.69	0.10	-57.22	-0.77	123.90	98.04	40.83	Jelly filled cables
FAL Industries Ltd.	22.95	1.48	0.23	-17.41	10.76	48.84	155.90	7.55	Vacuum cleaners
RPG Cables Ltd.	22.54	-25.45	-9.65	NA	-27.16	-2.15	161.67	17.86	Cables & other conductors
Eimco Elecon (India) Ltd.	22.14	8.94	1.99	0.99	18.61	25.52	81.15	51.15	Mining machinery
Jyoti Ltd.	21.37	-9.06	-0.67	NA	17.59	23.81	232.38	17.86	Motors & generators
GMM Pfaudler Ltd.	20.58	17.53	1.73	32.80	23.20	15.87	112.19	39.21	Chemical machinery
ECE Industries Ltd.	19.81	-1.35	0.29	-0.77	-6.85	66.83	94.11	17.77	Electrical machinery
Hindustan Dorr-Oliver Ltd.	19.61	17.17	0.25	NA	6.46	72.19	393.39	36.43	Turnkey projects
Diamond Cables Ltd.	18.98	22.52	-1.03	NA	12.82	8.84	493.47	20.10	Cables & other conductors
Tudor India Ltd.	17.39	13.93	-0.38	NA	4.37	NA	18.22	16.70	Storage batteries
Kabra Extrusiontechnik Ltd.	17.33	15.88	1.10	9.91	16.55	11.61	72.12	17.52	Extrusion presses
Avery India Ltd.	16.85	-3.95	0.58	20.21	8.09	13.55	39.61	14.57	Weighing machinery
GEI Hamon Inds. Ltd.	16.11	30.32	0.50	NA	22.75	18.62	90.52	13.45	Heat exchangers
Birla Ericsson Optical Ltd.	16.09	-14.53	0.16	-41.75	-3.58	27.09	37.98	21.92	Cables & other conductors
Revathi Equipment Ltd.	16.01	4.91	5.99	15.46	21.05	14.87	93.23	65.65	Drilling machines
Veejay Lakshmi Engg. Works Ltd.	15.84	-2.45	1.62	NA	20.05	11.02	-15.31	13.18	Textile machinery
Sulzer India Ltd.	15.59	9.99	1.31	21.90	38.63	4.76	79.61	24.77	Textile machinery
UT Ltd.	15.52	-3.73	0.42	NA	18.66	17.16	160.98	15.44	Gears
Gujarat Apollo Equipments Ltd.	15.49	1.29	1.20	11.07	17.91	12.18	98.50	21.57	Other construction machinery

Company Name	Revenue (Million $)	5-yr CAGR Revenues (%)	Net Income (Million $)	5-yr CAGR Net Income (%)	RoCE (%)	P/E Ratio	1-yr Stock Return (%)	Market Cap (Million $)	Economic Activity
Elpro International Ltd.	13.51	6.58	0.58	16.36	-8.76	14.49	133.73	12.55	Lightning arresters, voltage limiters, etc.
Flex Engineering Ltd.	13.45	9.82	1.40	NA	7.18	11.49	42.92	12.80	Packaging machinery
Bilpower Limited	13.41	30.96	0.94	27.12	28.54	5.89	156.74	11.15	Stampings & laminations
Hercules Hoists Ltd.	12.42	22.71	1.52	56.57	41.62	12.40	161.32	23.36	Other cranes
Pitti Laminations Ltd.	12.22	19.02	1.14	NA	54.97	13.57	134.43	17.74	Stampings & laminations
International Combustion (India) Ltd.	12.04	19.43	0.50	NA	18.96	18.39	333.02	16.51	Mining, construction machinery
Shakti Pumps (India) Ltd.	10.68	6.26	0.27	4.13	24.66	39.44	298.75	13.98	Pumps
Premier Ltd.	10.60	-2.94	2.50	NA	0.28	3.42	64.97	19.67	Machine tools
Stone India Ltd.	10.60	3.99	0.25	NA	2.08	21.12	1,145.54	23.96	Railway & tramway equipment
Modison Metals Ltd.	9.63	19.41	1.01	39.45	33.56	10.52	160.25	13.04	Contactors
Wendt (India) Ltd.	9.62	18.69	1.76	20.21	43.72	16.63	62.35	30.88	Machine tools
Panasonic Carbon India Co. Ltd.	9.58	-0.63	1.39	-1.91	21.86	12.60	38.00	15.83	Welding machinery
Aksh Optifibre Ltd.	8.70	-17.51	-0.74	NA	-1.33	11.60	97.98	36.84	Wires & cables, insulated
Disa India Ltd.	7.71	21.41	1.03	34.42	25.14	12.78	187.92	27.05	Metallurgical machinery
High Energy Batteries (India) Ltd.	7.25	9.45	0.43	18.89	42.82	24.97	139.58	8.45	Storage batteries
Nesco Ltd.	6.26	16.96	1.42	NA	454.17	17.68	470.09	60.68	Textile machinery
Kilburn Engineering Ltd.	6.21	-16.25	9.30	NA	-4.47	7.74	360.12	9.20	Dryers
Karuna Cables Ltd.	3.89	5.89	0.08	NA	13.06	22.26	97.35	8.65	Cables & other conductors
GR Cables Ltd.	3.72	-7.78	0.76	NA	1.20	50.12	56.39	6.27	Jelly filled cables
Best & Crompton Engg. Ltd.	3.54	-24.04	-0.59	NA	-45.22	NA	11.67	14.43	Electrical machinery, nec

Company Name	Revenue (Million $)	5-yr CAGR Revenues (%)	Net Income (Million $)	5-yr CAGR Net Income (%)	RoCE (%)	P/E Ratio	1-yr Stock Return (%)	Market Cap (Million $)	Economic Activity
Integra Hindustan Control Ltd.	3.34	12.77	0.19	23.41	34.46	26.12	144.9	6.17	Switching apparatus
Birla Kennametal Ltd.	3.24	23.09	0.40	91.01	34.85	22.24	96.13	9.80	Machine tools
Taneja Aerospace & Aviation Ltd.	3.01	4.29	0.71	NA	18.13	65.47	700.06	74.40	Aircrafts
GG Dandekar Machine Works Ltd.	2.77	-1.33	0.67	-1.92	32.55	11.34	2.46	7.96	Rice mill machinery

Source: Prowess (Center for Monitoring the Indian Economy)

Food & Beverage

Company Name	Revenue (Million $)	5-yr CAGR Revenues (%)	Net Income (Million $)	5-yr CAGR Net Income (%)	RoCE (%)	P/E Ratio	1-yr Stock Return (%)	Market Cap (Million $)	Economic Activity
ITC Ltd.	2,954.67	NA	498.05	NA	37.94	22.34	68.93	12,029.24	Cigarettes
Nestle India Ltd.	539.36	NA	57.25	NA	127.39	29.09	64.36	2,061.98	Dairy products
Mcdowell & Co. Ltd.	406.49	NA	6.08	NA	12.56	57.39	221.68	513.26	Ethyl alcohol
Britannia Industries Ltd.	368.08	NA	34.06	NA	43.59	25.19	60.01	705.95	Biscuits
Godfrey Phillips India Ltd.	295.81	NA	14.45	NA	27.10	19.43	202.97	339.75	Cigarettes
Triveni Engineering & Inds. Ltd.	232.52	NA	22.62	NA	57.21	10.96	4,518.71	303.32	Sugar
Glaxosmithkline Consumer Healthcare Ltd.	229.02	NA	16.63	NA	22.80	25.19	71.75	562.25	Malted milk foods
Balrampur Chini Mills Ltd.	211.43	NA	28.45	NA	33.05	14.21	122.69	558.70	Sugar
Cadbury India Ltd.	201.20	NA	10.50	NA	16.63	24.84	31.74	399.24	Chocolate confectionery
Radico Khaitan Ltd.	174.46	NA	6.72	NA	27.38	39.36	189.71	304.12	Rectified spirit
EID-Parry (India) Ltd.	174.19	NA	23.70	NA	23.83	21.19	204.64	452.94	Sugar
VST Industries Ltd.	155.04	NA	12.28	NA	56.48	14.83	115.85	171.97	Cigarettes
Sakthi Sugars Ltd.	145.69	NA	6.14	NA	9.39	8.07	155.78	78.97	Sugar
United Breweries Ltd.	143.71	NA	3.19	NA	12.84	52.59	44.66	338.73	Beer
Mawana Sugars Ltd.	133.44	NA	11.44	NA	37.72	9.55	88.20	109.18	Sugar
Bajaj Hindusthan Ltd.	119.38	NA	4.50	NA	29.21	23.09	169.60	736.79	Sugar
Simbhaoli Sugar Mills Ltd.	116.10	NA	2.69	NA	49.85	6.73	201.42	45.03	Sugar
Bannari Amman Sugars Ltd.	114.54	NA	9.92	NA	20.17	16.96	139.09	214.22	Sugar
Dhampur Sugar Mills Ltd.	114.13	NA	2.20	NA	21.32	18.64	179.02	146.67	Sugar

Company Name	Revenue (Million $)	5-yr CAGR Revenues (%)	Net Income (Million $)	5-yr CAGR Net Income (%)	RoCE (%)	P/E Ratio	1-yr Stock Return (%)	Market Cap (Million $)	Economic Activity
Hatsun Agro Products Ltd.	103.14	NA	0.17	NA	7.76	28.75	211.9	30.13	Milk
Jagatjit Industries Ltd.	90.79	NA	-0.19	NA	-2.60	47.40	53.50	76.38	Liquors
Oudh Sugar Mills Ltd.	85.69	NA	2.54	NA	28.94	11.10	39.38	44.88	Sugar
Mohan Meakin Ltd.	83.23	NA	0.77	NA	11.24	50.78	358.40	27.70	Indian made foreign liquors
GTC Industries Ltd.	80.20	NA	4.48	NA	-3527.49	8.32	257.14	38.66	Cigarettes
Kesar Enterprises Ltd.	67.97	NA	0.02	NA	37.22	12.34	279.68	24.70	Sugar
Upper Ganges Sugar & Inds. Ltd.	65.59	NA	3.85	NA	33.87	7.48	81.33	41.53	Sugar
Heritage Foods (India) Ltd.	60.48	NA	2.30	NA	29.05	11.12	103.39	33.42	Milk
Kothari Products Ltd.	48.08	NA	8.75	NA	9.41	6.23	64.84	69.22	Tobacco products
Khoday India Ltd.	46.98	NA	0.89	NA	15.65	NA	42.48	44.13	Indian made foreign liquors
Riddhi Siddhi Gluco Biols Ltd.	45.16	NA	0.90	NA	14.57	12.14	514.06	17.85	Starches
GM Breweries Ltd.	44.28	NA	0.17	NA	10.49	8.84	262.48	10.61	Rectified spirit
Shaw Wallace & Co. Ltd.	43.65	NA	-5.65	NA	-2.28	34.51	-12.00	152.80	Liquors
IFB Agro Inds. Ltd.	43.59	NA	0.42	NA	7.00	NA	172.01	10.55	Rectified spirit
Rajshree Sugars & Chemicals Ltd.	43.19	NA	3.81	NA	24.81	10.26	73.40	40.59	Sugar
Dharani Sugars & Chemicals Ltd.	38.47	NA	0.23	NA	12.92	9.34	92.73	22.48	Sugar
Dwarikesh Sugar Inds. Ltd.	37.37	NA	6.05	NA	33.91	9.52	55.65	57.54	Sugar
Shree Renuka Sugars Ltd.	34.62	NA	0.54	NA	NA	34.17	81.94	259.85	Sugar
Rana Sugars Ltd.	32.05	NA	4.05	NA	27.31	7.29	41.79	31.22	Sugar
Thiru Arooran Sugars Ltd.	31.32	NA	0.57	NA	10.27	NA	28.23	38.90	Sugar
Lotte India Corpn. Ltd.	27.30	NA	0.27	NA	5.99	216.90	29.42	19.72	Chocolate & sugar confectionery

Company Name	Revenue (Million $)	5-yr CAGR Revenues (%)	Net Income (Million $)	5-yr CAGR Net Income (%)	RoCE (%)	P/E Ratio	1-yr Stock Return (%)	Market Cap (Million $)	Economic Activity
Vadilal Industries Ltd.	26.88	NA	0.32	NA	12.79	20.57	79.83	4.72	Icecreams & kulfi
Tilaknagar Industries Ltd.	24.98	NA	0.32	NA	42.22	16.25	48.74	6.65	Indian made foreign liquors
JK Sugar Ltd.	22.74	NA	2.08	NA	27.04	4.61	54.84	14.13	Sugar
Sukhjit Starch & Chemicals Ltd.	22.36	NA	0.61	NA	11.10	13.52	64.65	11.64	Starches
Gayatri Sugars Ltd.	17.26	NA	1.18	NA	18.26	6.56	52.90	14.94	Sugar
Ravalgaon Sugar Farm Ltd.	15.96	NA	1.03	NA	36.67	10.81	40.36	8.87	Chocolate & sugar confectionery
Indian Sucrose Ltd.	15.40	NA	1.34	NA	51.53	3.21	278.42	12.63	Sugar
SKM Egg Products Export (India) Ltd.	15.01	NA	1.28	NA	22.07	10.04	8.06	11.52	Egg powder
Empee Sugars & Chemicals Ltd.	14.65	NA	0.02	NA	9.59	14.31	251.54	21.80	Sugar
Riga Sugar Co. Ltd.	14.52	NA	0.46	NA	15.04	8.32	115.84	7.43	Sugar
Champagne Indage Ltd.	8.55	NA	1.25	NA	15.58	58.92	662.15	95.61	Wines
Carnation Nutra-Analogue Foods Ltd.	6.48	NA	0.57	NA	52.06	39.15	254.28	12.72	Protein concentrates
Mount Everest Mineral Water Ltd.	2.46	NA	-0.26	NA	-6.71	413.41	293.64	38.52	Mineral waters

Source: Prowess (Center for Monitoring the Indian Economy)

Media Entertainment

Company Name	Revenue (Million $)	5-yr CAGR Revenues (%)	Net Income (Million $)	5-yr CAGR Net Income (%)	RoCE (%)	P/E Ratio	1-yr Stock Return (%)	Market Cap (Million $)	Economic Activity
Zee Telefilms Ltd.	147.10	17.65	36.88	-9.50	11.35	51.99	-5.13	1,518.77	Broadcasting media
Sahara India Mass Communication Ltd.	47.94	92.11	1.48	31.23	12.80	73.85	30.20	124.70	Broadcasting media
Balaji Telefilms Ltd.	44.72	57.81	9.43	57.52	34.36	17.52	46.70	193.19	Entertainment content provider
New Delhi Television Ltd.	41.28	22.11	6.63	6.65	24.01	83.32	79.42	291.44	Broadcasting media
UTV Software Communications Ltd.	34.89	11.36	3.54	24.70	25.29	25.42	2.08	76.20	Entertainment content provider
Pentamedia Graphics Ltd.	32.58	-22.89	1.56	-43.48	2.63	61.83	-14.75	34.71	Animation content provider
TV Today Network Ltd.	31.61	NA	3.73	NA	15.67	28.07	1.65	124.83	Broadcasting media
Sri Adhikari Brothers Television Network Ltd.	19.68	16.69	0.02	-60.93	9.11	143.97	-0.67	20.29	Entertainment content provider
Television Eighteen India Ltd.	18.51	35.99	4.43	37.40	17.13	42.83	119.77	201.31	Entertainment content provider
ETC Networks Ltd.	10.60	NA	1.64	NA	18.87	8.30	-20.01	13.55	Broadcasting media
Cinevistaas Ltd.	9.45	-1.09	0.31	-31.13	4.73	67.51	-6.25	8.59	Entertainment content provider
BAG Films Ltd.	8.29	NA	0.65	NA	22.48	16.44	9.72	14.83	Entertainment content provider
Pritish Nandy Communications Ltd.	7.93	23.35	0.91	11.09	11.81	10.42	-21.77	12.48	Entertainment content provider
Crest Animation Studios Ltd.	6.49	13.01	-0.09	NA	2.78	67.63	67.43	62.25	Animation content provider
Media Matrix Worldwide Ltd.	5.01	161.59	-0.04	NA	3.15	128.04	-69.42	26.19	Animation content provider
Jain Studios Ltd.	2.30	-2.13	0.02	-49.11	-2.27	159.34	15.03	9.42	Broadcasting media
Aastha Broadcasting Network Ltd.	1.73	202.67	0.03	22.42	-5.07	NA	201.96	8.75	Broadcasting media
GV Films Ltd.	0.66	-2.44	0.08	-16.06	0.26	43.58	87.33	19.41	Entertainment content provider

Source: Prowess (Center for Monitoring the Indian Economy)

Metals

Company Name	Revenue (Million $)	5-yr CAGR Revenues (%)	Net Income (Million $)	5-yr CAGR Net Income (%)	RoCE (%)	P/E Ratio	1-yr Stock Return (%)	Market Cap (Million $)	Economic Activity
Steel Authority Of India Ltd.	7,542.14	13.97	1,549.31	NA	74.91	3.56	3.25	5,214.63	Finished steel
Tata Steel Ltd.	3,801.61	17.40	789.58	52.40	63.25	5.40	15.57	4,627.16	Finished steel
Hindalco Industries Ltd.	2,376.87	35.27	302.13	16.77	18.88	9.37	17.13	2,976.17	Aluminium, unwrought
Ispat Industries Ltd.	2,048.94	37.66	158.20	185.49	13.84	2.96	-39.48	290.89	HRC & flat rolled products
JSW Steel Ltd.	1,975.03	56.37	197.75	NA	33.75	3.60	-16.15	766.24	HRC & flat rolled products
Essar Steel Ltd.	1,484.91	21.60	134.13	NA	28.51	1.63	12.35	289.51	HRC & flat rolled products
National Aluminium Co. Ltd.	1,051.23	15.32	280.65	19.27	42.98	11.17	25.22	3,277.19	Aluminium, unwrought
Sterlite Industries (India) Ltd.	972.51	16.03	24.19	-8.03	6.70	66.14	81.26	2,509.40	Copper
Jindal Stainless Ltd.	789.68	NA	55.88	NA	24.73	4.63	19.68	283.12	Flat rolled products
Bhushan Steel & Strips Ltd.	651.80	24.56	34.85	28.02	17.55	4.34	-7.27	137.56	CRC & flat rolled products
Jindal Steel & Power Ltd.	630.75	52.51	117.20	50.76	35.81	8.27	85.47	1,064.05	Iron & steel
Hindustan Zinc Ltd.	620.59	12.18	148.94	48.60	38.30	13.95	98.97	2,305.68	Zinc
Jindal Iron & Steel Co. Ltd.	514.99	14.38	55.16	86.35	38.48	6.63	62.29	427.39	HRC & flat rolled products
Uttam Galva Steels Ltd.	490.87	29.85	21.44	NA	31.54	3.58	2.62	71.23	Flat rolled products
Mukand Ltd.	384.88	14.67	42.00	72.24	8.33	3.44	116.32	145.45	Flat rolled products
Usha Martin Ltd.	356.80	17.15	9.29	4.31	10.80	14.36	105.20	170.29	Articles of iron & steel
Tube Investments Of India Ltd.	355.67	9.71	22.40	24.58	24.52	15.45	118.26	443.18	ERW precision tubes
PSL Ltd.	327.39	57.67	7.28	16.89	37.26	18.96	65.65	170.50	Tubes & pipes
Shah Alloys Ltd.	279.05	23.69	10.05	34.13	30.83	4.76	159.15	60.74	Stainless steel

Company Name	Revenue (Million $)	5-yr CAGR Revenues (%)	Net Income (Million $)	5-yr CAGR Net Income (%)	RoCE (%)	P/E Ratio	1-yr Stock Return (%)	Market Cap (Million $)	Economic Activity
Jindal Saw Ltd.	257.15	24.47	12.78	14.85	19.49	18.26	68.52	418.08	Tubes & pipes
Welspun-Gujarat Stahl Rohren Ltd.	252.98	80.84	7.69	160.87	43.17	21.52	113.64	227.91	Tubes & pipes
Electrosteel Castings Ltd.	223.50	11.77	20.15	-0.01	15.31	12.85	21.54	188.25	Tubes & pipes
Kalyani Steels Ltd.	210.31	56.46	9.77	NA	20.67	12.13	187.72	270.72	Alloy steel, nec
Maharashtra Seamless Ltd.	197.10	35.12	19.35	37.11	31.99	14.02	87.10	321.50	Seamless tubes & pipes
KEC International Ltd.	187.97	-5.04	5.75	-0.51	23.44	18.68	86.49	213.20	Towers & lattice masts
Shree Precoated Steels Ltd.	180.07	NA	6.73	NA	21.45	19.09	199.53	123.02	Clad, plated/coated flats
Sujana Metal Products Ltd.	159.55	16.75	6.87	21.69	13.76	8.52	752.22	57.94	Flat rolled products
Monnet Ispat Ltd.	134.11	41.14	27.76	87.79	22.44	4.53	10.15	125.26	Sponge iron
Hindustan Copper Ltd.	133.92	4.08	12.72	NA	82.19	53.50	63.95	997.16	Copper
Mahindra Ugine Steel Co. Ltd.	133.40	17.46	10.95	NA	63.87	7.81	77.12	85.70	Alloy steel, nec
Kalpataru Power Transmission Ltd.	128.72	27.83	6.51	12.58	41.63	21.14	227.23	190.20	Towers & lattice masts
Man Industries (India) Ltd.	115.99	41.31	4.16	75.19	21.95	20.55	193.71	112.60	Tubes & pipes
Gillette India Ltd.	101.79	12.11	13.91	25.81	33.20	38.11	13.59	524.84	Razors & razor blades
Jyoti Structures Ltd.	100.01	13.75	2.62	11.47	41.16	21.60	90.22	86.63	Towers & lattice masts
Madras Aluminium Co. Ltd.	97.30	12.80	9.59	6.79	29.01	12.03	18.92	118.58	Aluminium, unwrought
LG Balakrishnan & Bros. Ltd.	92.83	18.85	3.75	35.13	29.03	17.43	26.97	66.64	Tools, implements, etc.
Southern Iron & Steel Co. Ltd.	81.79	34.27	8.88	NA	NA	5.70	78.31	111.05	Pig iron
Indian Charge Chrome Ltd.	72.14	27.96	6.16	NA	36.77	4.54	-8.44	13.76	Charge chrome
Lanco Industries Ltd.	71.79	25.44	4.76	204.49	28.52	12.02	-8.94	43.78	Pig iron
Tata Metaliks Ltd.	71.00	27.21	14.55	84.42	117.96	5.90	-11.88	73.62	Pig iron
GMR Industries Ltd.	70.45	20.53	4.25	5.29	14.75	16.65	224.14	110.78	Ferro chromium
Tata Sponge Iron Ltd.	60.71	16.33	13.84	45.40	88.06	4.30	-3.81	48.97	Sponge iron

Company Name	Revenue (Million $)	5-yr CAGR Revenues (%)	Net Income (Million $)	5-yr CAGR Net Income (%)	RoCE (%)	P/E Ratio	1-yr Stock Return (%)	Market Cap (Million $)	Economic Activity
Tinplate Co. Of India Ltd.	60.31	18.71	6.93	NA	22.66	6.89	97.31	62.89	Tin plates, sheets & strips
Maharashtra Elektrosmelt Ltd.	59.78	9.11	11.87	NA	225.25	6.45	709.09	48.55	Ferro manganese
Raipur Alloys & Steel Ltd.	55.06	39.34	4.12	NA	36.12	7.72	18.88	22.03	Sponge iron
Remi Metals Gujarat Ltd.	47.51	144.76	-13.76	NA	-16.61	0.84	16.45	20.08	Seamless tubes & pipes
Ratnamani Metals & Tubes Ltd.	47.00	30.12	3.01	44.41	36.43	12.25	477.28	53.75	Tubes & pipes
TTK Prestige Ltd.	43.49	6.71	0.87	0.92	11.61	24.36	277.57	33.94	Cookers
Ahmednagar Forgings Ltd.	37.40	13.70	2.84	NA	26.56	14.52	157.68	78.38	Forgings
Bihar Sponge Iron Ltd.	37.18	10.60	65.09	NA	-15.37	23.99	-12.77	18.37	Sponge iron
MM Forgings Ltd.	36.96	18.18	2.19	8.09	23.50	12.87	46.08	38.43	Forgings
Ferro Alloys Corpn. Ltd.	35.15	-5.94	1.37	NA	32.70	20.50	70.12	62.49	Ferro alloys
Tayo Rolls Ltd.	31.68	9.81	1.38	5.41	19.03	13.39	14.25	18.20	Flat rolled products
Lakshmi Precision Screws Ltd.	31.40	11.09	0.92	4.59	18.11	15.69	29.86	14.65	Screws, bolts, nuts etc.
RPG Transmission Ltd.	30.21	-5.96	1.06	NA	-6.78	9.01	389.22	41.14	Towers & lattice masts
Sterling Tools Ltd.	28.60	24.59	1.66	16.58	28.46	14.67	45.95	25.43	Screws, bolts, nuts etc.
Oil Country Tubular Ltd.	28.16	9.25	0.32	-3.60	30.37	-78.38	-8.43	15.85	Seamless tubes & pipes
Everest Kanto Cylinder Ltd.	17.30	NA	0.49	NA	9.67	20.34	20.00	66.03	LPG cylinders/ containers
Indian Aluminium Co. Ltd.	17.24	-42.12	-0.35	NA	-0.24	9.51	37.81	259.12	Aluminium foils
Enkei Castalloy Ltd.	17.19	31.86	1.35	42.48	32.71	15.91	115.20	30.56	Aluminium castings
Parekh Aluminex Ltd.	17.05	28.81	1.18	51.17	35.57	13.52	55.70	21.48	Other aluminium products
Shree Ganesh Forgings Ltd.	13.00	20.36	0.64	50.83	62.20	16.60	21.17	14.94	Forgings
Steelcast Ltd.	12.94	26.58	0.71	NA	52.78	12.21	213.39	13.54	Steel castings
Gandhi Special Tubes Ltd.	12.28	11.13	2.24	17.57	43.74	8.02	97.61	20.86	Tubes & pipes
Hoganas India Ltd.	11.64	13.09	0.96	8.35	17.50	14.92	25.97	11.90	Granules/pig iron powders

Company Name	Revenue (Million $)	5-yr CAGR Revenues (%)	Net Income (Million $)	5-yr CAGR Net Income (%)	RoCE (%)	P/E Ratio	1-yr Stock Return (%)	Market Cap (Million $)	Economic Activity
Investment & Precision Castings Ltd.	10.72	25.15	1.48	27.98	49.89	11.12	135.80	17.57	Castings
Om Metals Ltd.	10.57	8.95	0.74	39.28	23.53	13.11	458.96	34.35	Articles of iron & steel
Titanor Components Ltd.	5.77	11.19	1.57	NA	58.54	18.06	72.68	25.00	Misc. base metals

Source: Prowess (Center for Monitoring the Indian Economy)

Pharmaceutical & biotech

Company Name	Revenue (Million $)	5-yr CAGR Revenues (%)	Net Income (Million $)	5-yr CAGR Net Income (%)	RoCE (%)	P/E Ratio	1-yr stock Return (%)	Market Cap (Million $)	Economic Activity
Ranbaxy Laboratories Ltd.	971.66	17.77	119.89	22.20	26.32	70.66	-37.12	3,303.31	Drugs & medicines
Cipla Ltd.	545.66	25.47	93.09	25.22	33.00	27.42	46.01	2,899.54	Drug formulations
Dr. Reddy's Laboratories Ltd.	393.03	28.53	14.88	1.65	3.60	42.96	11.84	1,625.25	Drugs & medicines
Glaxosmithkline Pharmaceuticals Ltd.	341.18	10.88	75.70	34.01	52.14	19.86	54.24	2,181.28	Drug formulations
Nicholas Piramal India Ltd.	317.08	23.28	38.54	29.27	20.83	33.93	8.37	1,353.15	Drug formulations
Lupin Ltd.	276.95	79.03	18.70	54.03	18.12	23.12	8.49	707.17	Rifampicin
Cadila Healthcare Ltd.	268.70	19.87	29.86	28.37	19.19	20.61	-3.87	726.49	Drug formulations
Aurobindo Pharma Ltd.	263.61	9.23	7.97	-14.01	7.23	122.04	20.72	558.60	Drugs & medicines
Sun Pharmaceutical Inds. Ltd.	237.65	16.90	69.48	29.59	16.36	31.25	31.99	2,952.02	Drug formulations
Wockhardt Ltd.	200.35	0.25	47.22	14.72	23.97	19.05	20.98	1,100.80	Drug formulations
Aventis Pharma Ltd.	185.70	8.89	33.75	48.69	58.02	24.72	39.09	832.14	Drug formulations
Ipca Laboratories Ltd.	166.88	14.77	17.67	30.08	27.32	12.94	0.20	235.03	Drug formulations
Pfizer Ltd.	156.93	15.89	10.34	8.03	25.19	41.54	48.67	608.63	Drug formulations
Biocon Ltd.	156.66	NA	39.63	NA	29.07	34.24	-1.30	1,161.11	Bio-tech base drugs
Orchid Chemicals & Pharmaceuticals Ltd.	156.66	13.90	7.05	-4.28	11.05	29.28	34.73	378.75	Drugs & medicines
Matrix Laboratories Ltd.	152.82	71.60	29.61	NA	35.73	32.66	14.44	781.11	Drugs & medicines
Torrent Pharmaceuticals Ltd.	122.81	4.61	12.03	3.03	15.51	28.23	61.18	413.84	Drug formulations
Glenmark Pharmaceuticals Ltd.	122.35	29.93	14.43	23.97	20.88	74.32	68.05	839.51	Drug formulations
Novartis India Ltd.	111.08	-10.08	14.80	-8.84	35.45	20.24	-17.33	400.75	Drug formulations
Abbott India Ltd.	107.73	9.64	23.24	30.48	56.82	18.44	12.38	252.73	Drug formulations
Unichem Laboratories Ltd.	96.63	15.50	10.25	23.85	33.23	13.52	30.61	202.32	Drug formulations

Company Name	Revenue (Million $)	5-yr CAGR Revenues (%)	Net Income (Million $)	5-yr CAGR Net Income (%)	RoCE (%)	P/E Ratio	1-yr stock Return (%)	Market Cap (Million $)	Economic Activity
Merck Ltd.	94.92	8.34	16.13	31.39	47.75	12.00	5.81	202.89	Drug formulations
JB Chemicals & Pharmaceuticals Ltd.	85.82	16.32	13.44	21.85	24.79	11.31	15.43	162.60	Drug formulations
Divi'S Laboratories Ltd.	83.39	18.07	15.01	32.53	40.92	27.98	13.65	425.38	Drugs & medicines
FDC Ltd.	80.63	19.16	12.40	18.26	26.12	13.58	-18.71	214.96	Drug formulations
Panacea Biotec Ltd.	77.88	12.01	6.83	3.01	21.12	28.61	83.88	354.26	Drug formulations
Shasun Chemicals & Drugs Ltd.	75.59	12.37	7.05	8.70	27.71	13.11	16.86	94.98	Drugs & medicines
Strides Arcolab Ltd.	69.53	23.38	6.63	26.09	18.98	32.64	61.70	249.84	Drug formulations
Elder Pharmaceuticals Ltd.	69.29	12.31	4.58	31.82	19.79	17.84	49.56	99.57	Drug formulations
Wyeth Ltd.	65.89	2.06	8.86	8.05	24.16	40.48	34.02	348.62	Drug formulations
Aarti Drugs Ltd.	60.29	13.97	3.20	12.54	19.20	9.40	-34.76	29.06	Anti dysentery medicaments
Ind-Swift Ltd.	56.70	26.33	5.82	37.23	32.98	6.83	-25.79	46.22	Drug formulations
Ind-Swift Laboratories Ltd.	54.42	28.36	6.02	55.10	26.56	9.11	-43.25	72.25	Drugs & medicines
Dabur Pharma Ltd.	53.58	NA	5.13	NA	10.36	37.54	1.51	204.49	Drug formulations
Nectar Lifesciences Ltd.	50.16	14.57	2.86	22.54	28.42	15.87	-17.18	72.73	Drugs & medicines
Indoco Remedies Ltd.	49.38	12.00	5.71	11.35	27.62	16.14	-8.73	95.69	Drug formulations
Astrazeneca Pharma India Ltd.	48.08	15.50	5.85	19.88	48.44	31.29	63.03	250.19	Drug formulations
Surya Pharmaceutical Ltd.	41.19	21.07	1.91	14.90	30.71	7.99	145.38	36.08	Antibiotics
Ajanta Pharma Ltd.	40.64	2.29	1.69	-15.45	8.88	11.50	15.79	21.08	Ayurvedic medicaments
Natco Pharma Ltd.	39.00	16.66	0.35	NA	9.94	96.89	2.19	86.32	Drug formulations
Dishman Pharmaceuticals & Chemicals Ltd.	36.34	NA	6.48	NA	26.02	34.20	58.29	290.82	Drug formulations
TTK Healthcare Ltd.	34.62	5.89	0.09	-27.66	9.85	NA	32.02	9.54	Drug formulations
Ambalal Sarabhai Enterprises Ltd.	34.32	-8.16	-2.60	NA	-8.39	NA	12.05	15.51	Drug formulations
Marksans Pharma Ltd.	32.70	31.48	3.20	52.65	38.76	11.30	30.45	63.95	Drugs & medicines

Company Name	Revenue (Million $)	5-yr CAGR Revenues (%)	Net Income (Million $)	5-yr CAGR Net Income (%)	RoCE (%)	P/E Ratio	1-yr stock Return (%)	Market Cap (Million $)	Economic Activity
RPG Life Sciences Ltd.	31.55	-7.97	-1.06	NA	8.38	33.25	51.29	40.88	Drug formulations
Granules India Ltd.	31.30	28.00	1.51	26.21	18.81	18.38	0.77	29.87	Paracetamol
Fulford (India) Ltd.	29.95	1.44	2.67	NA	88.58	14.21	22.46	46.59	Drug formulations
Morepen Laboratories Ltd.	29.69	-16.74	-10.79	NA	-7.51	NA	-10.54	26.55	Drugs & medicines
Solvay Pharma India Ltd.	29.03	NA	5.31	NA	54.62	14.79	60.83	64.07	Drugs & medicines
Zandu Pharmaceutical Works Ltd.	25.87	0.75	2.07	27.60	24.52	20.79	45.56	44.55	Ayurvedic medicaments
Kopran Ltd.	25.01	-7.43	-8.27	NA	-5.60	NA	-28.65	30.95	Drugs & medicines
Themis Medicare Ltd.	23.10	16.61	6.38	65.52	18.53	5.63	-21.93	37.58	Drug formulations
Ankur Drugs & Pharma Ltd.	19.26	116.79	1.13	162.34	28.63	26.37	171.59	32.01	Drug formulations
Krebs Biochemicals & Inds. Ltd.	18.01	13.92	1.69	-10.60	12.24	NA	-51.26	14.97	Drug formulations
Wanbury Ltd.	17.56	48.47	1.59	NA	32.66	14.11	80.75	29.98	Drugs & medicines
Jupiter Bioscience Ltd.	16.13	29.85	3.22	29.49	19.17	6.40	5.26	27.68	Trimethoprin
Hiran Orgochem Ltd.	13.93	16.55	0.31	9.26	20.40	13.19	297.85	29.76	Drugs & medicines
Suven Life Sciences Ltd.	13.52	10.92	0.86	-1.75	8.32	46.18	-8.19	47.02	Drugs & medicines
Gufic Biosciences Ltd.	12.73	NA	0.77	NA	33.01	33.28	-48.69	32.52	Drugs & medicines
Anuh Pharma Ltd.	12.26	22.50	1.07	13.78	25.26	17.89	-5.57	21.51	Antibiotics
Vivimed Labs Ltd.	11.84	NA	1.09	NA	45.75	16.31	-31.05	24.83	Drugs & medicines
Lyka Labs Ltd.	11.63	-14.80	-0.61	NA	1.84	13.16	-5.70	18.01	Drug formulations
Syncom Formulations (India) Ltd.	10.29	0.41	0.68	2.35	22.87	6.05	1.32	11.83	Drug formulations
Shilpa Medicare Ltd.	8.71	16.99	0.75	61.34	39.64	16.77	141.92	14.75	Drugs & medicines
Venus Remedies Ltd.	7.75	18.30	0.92	54.58	45.82	23.51	308.13	45.20	Drugs & medicines
Sharon Bio-Medicine Ltd.	5.38	NA	0.09	NA	8.77	20.32	142.06	15.29	Drugs & medicines
Zenotech Laboratories Ltd.	1.28	50.41	-0.93	NA	-16.86	NA	-14.17	33.09	Drug formulations

Source: Prowess (Center for Monitoring the Indian Economy)

Power

Company Name	Revenue (Million $)	5-yr CAGR Revenues (%)	Net Income (Million $)	5-yr CAGR Net Income (%)	ROCE (%)	P/E Ratio	1-year Stock Return (%)	Market Cap (Million $)	Economic Activity
NTPC Ltd.	5,226.39	7.34	1,319.77	11.14	12.05	14.27	29.75	19,882.81	Thermal power generation
Reliance Energy Ltd.	945.62	13.28	88.06	5.05	8.00	21.36	24.57	2,904.21	Generation/Distribution
Tata Power Co. Ltd.	899.22	23.01	125.31	18.23	7.92	16.06	25.71	2,014.51	Generation/Distribution
Neyveli Lignite Corpn. Ltd.	686.70	4.70	275.78	25.34	19.03	9.61	21.61	2,993.19	Thermal power generation
CESC Ltd.	545.35	6.48	34.24	NA	14.99	10.81	59.87	415.05	Generation/Distribution
Torrent Power AEC Ltd.	302.66	7.87	24.25	25.56	18.40	11.55	95.48	338.45	Generation/Distribution
Torrent Power SEC Ltd.	217.06	10.81	9.08	22.77	20.05	9.45	92.63	100.18	Generation/Distribution
Gujarat Industries Power Co. Ltd.	169.29	9.31	23.56	12.56	17.82	9.76	-8.76	230.14	Power generation—gas
Jaiprakash Hydro Power Ltd.	69.32	NA	11.61	NA	11.54	33.85	10.99	377.18	Hydro electricity
Webel SL Energy Systems Ltd.	12.87	32.90	0.50	50.11	61.63	21.21	431.63	26.13	Solar photovoltaics
Energy Development Co. Ltd.	1.93	20.04	0.75	85.33	13.41	39.94	207.53	26.68	Generation/istribution

Source: Prowess (Center for Monitoring the Indian Economy)

Retail

Company Name	Revenue (Million $)	5-yr CAGR Revenues (%)	Net Income (Million $)	5-yr CAGR Net Income (%)	RoCE (%)	P/E Ratio	1-year Stock Return (%)	Market Cap (Million $)	Economic Activity
Pantaloon Retail (India) Ltd.	246.45	51.53	8.76	50.94	25.00	102.15	243.05	1,047.78	Retail trade
Shoppers' Stop Ltd.	116.06	26.96	4.33	NA	73.49	71.45	21.26	353.02	Retailing
Trent Ltd.	52.61	47.11	4.33	8.84	9.49	54.93	59.67	288.15	Retail trade
Piramyd Retail Ltd.	NA	NA	NA	NA	NA	NA	-9.57	54.11	Retail trade

Source: Prowess (Center for Monitoring the Indian Economy)

Specialty Chemical

Company Name	Revenue (Million $)	5-yr CAGR Revenues (%)	Net Income (Million $)	5-yr CAGR Net Income (%)	RoCE (%)	P/E Ratio	1-yr Stock Return (%)	Market Cap (Million $)	Economic Activity
Micro Inks Ltd.	215.92	30.00	24.45	34.62	18.28	16.43	1.04	367.70	Printing inks
Pidilite Industries Ltd.	202.39	13.99	17.40	9.99	31.26	22.73	137.51	470.67	Specialty chemicals, adhesives
Bayer Cropscience Ltd.	193.36	7.37	5.99	39.22	13.82	47.32	-3.97	233.04	Pesticides
BASF India Ltd.	168.36	14.27	8.63	13.70	24.30	16.11	50.52	159.82	Organic chemicals
Ciba Specialty Chemicals (India) Ltd.	131.57	4.82	6.16	8.46	19.37	20.62	101.12	171.49	Specialty chemicals
Clariant (India) Ltd.	82.98	7.15	4.21	3.65	29.51	18.96	31.40	92.07	Dyes & pigments

Source: Prowess (Center for Monitoring the Indian Economy)

INDUSTRY AVERAGES

Cumulative figures for industry groups

Industry	RoCE (%)	Revenues (Million $)	Net Income (Million $)	Market Cap (Million $)	PE Ratio
Air transport	26.70	993.73	82.76	2,675.55	28.97
Automobile	26.96	16,404.51	1,032.84	23,267.17	19.22
Automobile ancillaries	31.18	4,924.47	389.71	8,801.82	21.39
Banking services	41.94	35,335.53	4,029.81	54,837.41	13.48
Beverages & tobacco	31.57	4,757.84	539.39	14,189.49	22.28
Cement	12.74	4,798.29	351.79	8,927.62	21.58
Cement	12.03	5,548.13	298.16	9,095.29	24.17
Chemicals	19.96	133,678.55	6,197.11	113,830.85	18.95
Coal & lignite	17.37	185.87	46.53	590.33	13.09
Computer software	23.54	9,017.99	1,746.81	73,909.90	35.49
Construction	20.62	6,686.11	398.60	12,863.00	25.63
Crude oil & natural gas	39.97	11,199.83	2,961.55	40,428.29	11.93
Dairy products	50.34	1,075.26	77.36	2,710.30	27.40
Drugs & pharmaceuticals	20.32	7,738.64	852.65	28,226.16	29.75
Electrical machinery	16.24	5,400.24	177.88	9,144.96	30.16
Electricity	12.14	9,148.58	1,893.65	29,812.52	14.65
Financial institutions	5.81	509.79	-28.45	1,982.40	-1,813.43
Food & beverages	26.46	12,775.48	943.40	24,110.72	21.54
Information technology	23.57	9,034.48	1,750.35	73,998.96	35.45
ITES	46.82	16.49	3.54	89.06	17.51
Media-print	13.44	371.05	17.17	944.19	46.58
Metals & metal products	33.93	33,947.23	4,244.53	31,132.94	7.10
Mining	39.88	11,900.97	3,117.57	42,144.05	11.87
Non Electrical machinery	23.25	7,281.44	564.80	23,146.11	31.15
Other Food products	18.17	1,385.27	56.92	1,357.85	26.43
Petroleum products	21.86	97,655.19	4,019.43	50,846.33	14.57
Sugar	24.78	1,907.41	158.25	3,054.08	16.15
Tea & coffee	12.87	585.15	64.07	1,869.92	23.32
Trading	24.55	15,452.12	534.78	9,310.90	15.60
Vegetable oils & products	20.89	3,064.55	47.41	929.08	14.79

Source: Prowess (Center for Monitoring the Indian Economy)

MARKET CAPITALIZATION

This data has been ranked based on the respective market capitalizations. The minimum market capitalization for inclusion in this table is $100 million.

Company Name	Market Cap (Million $)	Revenue (Million $)	5-yr Revenue CAGR (%)	Net Income (Million $)	5-yr Net Income CAGR (%)	RoCE %	P/E (x)
Oil & Natural Gas Corpn. Ltd.	37,207.15	10,932.11	18.90	2,950.69	29.03	45.35	11.10
Reliance Industries Ltd.	26,885.20	16,632.15	29.23	1,720.84	25.80	18.83	12.89
NTPC Ltd.	19,882.81	5,226.39	7.34	1,319.77	11.14	12.05	14.27
Tata Consultancy Services Ltd.	18,752.30	1,829.80	NA	416.23	NA	NA	36.35
Infosys Technologies Ltd.	18,518.23	1,560.93	50.68	432.81	45.35	52.26	37.52
Bharti Tele-Ventures Ltd.	15,051.76	1,844.61	388.42	275.15	332.50	25.98	67.97
Wipro Ltd.	14,232.60	1,653.68	25.26	339.73	43.81	41.39	37.82
Indian Oil Corpn. Ltd.	14,071.89	36,360.08	10.47	1,111.51	14.89	20.82	20.13
ITC Ltd.	12,029.24	2,954.67	10.28	498.05	22.56	37.94	22.34
ICICI Bank Ltd.	11,630.16	2,807.96	63.79	455.73	80.28	18.12	22.82
State Bank Of India	11,036.73	8,827.49	8.65	978.30	15.98	59.90	10.55
Hindustan Lever Ltd.	9,407.82	2,502.21	0.06	272.12	2.20	44.91	34.74
Bharat Heavy Electricals Ltd.	7,925.22	2,454.73	9.09	216.68	9.73	21.70	28.82
Housing Development Finance Corpn. Ltd.	7,182.37	758.56	10.65	235.59	20.87	9.28	27.96
Suzlon Energy Ltd.	6,037.50	435.80	65.79	82.15	66.36	56.50	99.55
Tata Motors Ltd.	5,293.92	4,608.31	18.36	281.13	77.00	32.83	17.71
Satyam Computer Services Ltd.	5,293.14	787.32	38.61	170.51	41.99	31.59	27.57
GAIL (India) Ltd.	5,245.92	3,206.86	10.86	444.07	17.80	29.93	9.58
Steel Authority Of India Ltd.	5,214.63	7,542.14	13.97	1,549.31	NA	74.91	3.56
Larsen & Toubro Ltd.	5,158.28	3,049.63	12.52	223.60	23.56	29.65	30.18
HDFC Bank Ltd.	4,967.70	865.92	36.46	151.26	40.85	43.18	28.89
Bajaj Auto Ltd.	4,872.10	1,516.63	12.10	165.72	2.81	18.78	24.25

Company Name	Market Cap (Million $)	Revenue (Million $)	5-yr Revenue CAGR (%)	Net Income (Million $)	5-yr Net Income CAGR (%)	RoCE %	P/E (x)
Tata Steel Ltd.	4,627.16	3,801.61	17.40	789.58	52.40	63.25	5.40
Maruti Udyog Ltd.	4,318.88	3,063.36	7.36	194.00	20.93	30.49	19.23
HCL Technologies Ltd.	3,942.14	328.87	29.33	74.83	10.50	11.65	52.90
Hero Honda Motors Ltd.	3,844.21	1,956.05	30.73	184.20	33.37	75.64	19.48
Punjab National Bank	3,310.68	2,301.38	11.45	320.48	28.14	61.99	10.01
Ranbaxy Laboratories Ltd.	3,303.31	971.66	17.77	119.89	22.20	26.32	70.66
National Aluminium Co. Ltd.	3,277.19	1,051.23	15.32	280.65	19.27	42.98	11.17
National Mineral Devp. Corpn. Ltd.	3,108.70	506.82	23.05	171.69	36.40	56.26	11.10
Neyveli Lignite Corpn. Ltd.	2,993.19	686.70	4.70	275.78	25.34	19.03	9.61
Hindalco Industries Ltd.	2,976.17	2,376.87	35.27	302.13	16.77	18.88	9.37
Sun Pharmaceutical Inds. Ltd.	2,952.02	237.65	16.90	69.48	29.59	16.36	31.25
Reliance Energy Ltd.	2,904.21	945.62	13.28	88.06	5.05	8.00	21.36
Cipla Ltd.	2,899.54	545.66	25.47	93.09	25.22	33.00	27.42
Grasim Industries Ltd.	2,868.34	1,635.22	7.56	201.30	30.60	24.98	14.26
Bharat Petroleum Corpn. Ltd.	2,854.77	14,902.10	12.74	219.50	6.60	19.08	-91.49
Videsh Sanchar Nigam Ltd.	2,749.60	751.10	-13.94	171.90	-2.08	13.30	15.93
Mahindra & Mahindra Ltd.	2,686.52	1,738.53	12.11	115.02	13.95	27.27	20.09
Siemens Ltd.	2,659.13	438.68	11.92	34.40	33.94	41.35	45.93
Sterlite Industries (India) Ltd.	2,509.40	972.51	16.03	24.19	-8.03	6.70	66.14
Gujarat Ambuja Cements Ltd.	2,460.33	688.57	18.38	106.43	1.82	18.49	23.89
Hindustan Petroleum Corpn. Ltd.	2,438.93	15,438.23	14.34	290.30	3.85	20.98	52.17
Jet Airways (India) Ltd.	2,369.28	991.93	17.11	89.09	107.58	27.70	24.44
Hindustan Zinc Ltd.	2,305.68	620.59	12.18	148.94	48.60	38.30	13.95
Associated Cement Cos. Ltd.	2,249.80	1,033.85	10.91	86.00	NA	17.58	17.63
Container Corpn. of India Ltd.	2,192.65	453.82	19.15	97.41	19.27	39.30	21.01

Company Name	Market Cap (Million $)	Revenue (Million $)	5-yr Revenue CAGR (%)	Net Income (Million $)	5-yr Net Income CAGR (%)	RoCE %	P/E (x)
Glaxosmithkline Pharmaceuticals Ltd.	2,181.28	341.18	10.88	75.70	34.01	52.14	19.86
Reliance Capital Ltd.	2,146.95	67.60	-8.53	24.05	3.15	8.81	38.29
Videocon Industries Ltd.	2,084.04	3.17	-2.73	-0.40	NA	8.35	46.83
Mahanagar Telephone Nigam Ltd.	2,082.58	1,280.13	0.09	213.40	-2.90	8.58	11.00
Canara Bank	2,073.76	1,990.33	9.89	252.16	36.28	69.64	10.49
Nestle India Ltd.	2,061.98	539.36	8.94	57.25	20.67	127.39	29.09
Tata Power Co. Ltd.	2,014.51	899.22	23.01	125.31	18.23	7.92	16.06
Mangalore Refinery & Petrochemicals Ltd.	1,932.18	4,873.36	46.31	199.95	NA	36.07	8.67
Motor Industries Co. Ltd.	1,894.35	597.18	11.64	85.18	28.79	45.57	24.46
Bharat Forge Ltd.	1,877.65	299.21	18.04	36.71	28.66	46.55	43.37
ABB Ltd.	1,853.62	555.86	25.82	35.07	32.92	38.72	41.85
UTI Bank Ltd.	1,812.61	524.29	32.15	76.04	45.64	47.90	19.02
Infrastructure Development Finance Co. Ltd.	1,809.96	164.40	20.22	69.10	15.29	9.75	20.36
I-Flex Solutions Ltd.	1,799.56	205.20	35.52	44.92	23.33	25.00	43.07
Kotak Mahindra Bank Ltd.	1,703.46	127.45	14.95	19.29	6.44	35.57	80.57
Industrial Development Bank of India Ltd.	1,657.24	2,059.93	3.87	105.68	-18.06	15.72	15.17
Bharat Electronics Ltd.	1,653.45	733.65	16.49	100.70	32.64	48.57	15.69
Dr. Reddy's Laboratories Ltd.	1,625.25	393.03	28.53	14.88	1.65	3.60	42.96
Bank of Baroda	1,608.63	1,709.41	5.62	153.83	6.13	54.58	12.07
Zee Telefilms Ltd.	1,518.77	147.10	17.65	36.88	-9.50	11.35	51.99
Patni Computer Systems Ltd.	1,504.43	159.56	NA	52.40	NA	25.34	30.02
Oriental Bank of Commerce	1,434.63	922.50	8.78	165.02	21.11	74.22	10.99
Bank of India	1,361.95	1,568.36	5.38	77.28	14.50	39.56	13.88
Nicholas Piramal India Ltd.	1,353.15	317.08	23.28	38.54	29.27	20.83	33.93
Jaiprakash Associates Ltd.	1,348.75	686.15	NA	47.19	NA	17.97	10.36

Company Name	Market Cap (Million $)	Revenue (Million $)	5-yr Revenue CAGR (%)	Net Income (Million $)	5-yr Net Income CAGR (%)	RoCE %	P/E (x)
Financial Technologies (India) Ltd.	1,294.22	7.26	145.26	2.12	NA	15.16	184.05
Ultratech Cement Ltd.	1,283.00	712.88	NA	0.65	NA	7.54	104.50
Union Bank of India	1,260.62	1,266.73	9.35	163.42	48.01	58.55	9.25
Indian Petrochemicals Corpn. Ltd.	1,240.28	2,152.36	13.69	179.58	33.18	30.71	5.18
Dabur India Ltd.	1,231.95	289.45	4.01	33.63	13.76	51.85	32.80
Indian Hotels Co. Ltd.	1,222.56	201.84	7.50	24.06	-1.34	6.60	44.63
Corporation Bank	1,220.71	605.65	7.74	91.40	11.49	41.29	10.78
Tata Tea Ltd.	1,210.26	202.96	-0.45	29.30	0.69	15.24	33.60
Asian Paints Ltd.	1,188.53	537.76	11.33	39.43	12.23	44.70	26.58
Biocon Ltd.	1,161.11	156.66	NA	39.63	NA	29.07	34.24
Indian Overseas Bank	1,160.80	1,062.76	11.24	148.04	74.43	86.81	7.30
Wockhardt Ltd.	1,100.80	200.35	0.25	47.22	14.72	23.97	19.05
Tata Chemicals Ltd.	1,098.98	704.07	15.31	77.40	23.76	16.08	12.13
DSP Merrill Lynch Ltd.	1,082.63	83.68	31.99	30.08	43.79	40.47	30.35
Petronet LNG Ltd.	1,078.13	445.22	NA	-6.47	NA	4.41	54.94
Jindal Steel & Power Ltd.	1,064.05	630.75	52.51	117.20	50.76	35.81	8.27
Shipping Corpn. of India Ltd.	1,049.01	771.87	5.96	322.71	54.44	23.08	3.51
Pantaloon Retail (India) Ltd.	1,047.78	246.45	51.53	8.76	50.94	25.00	102.15
Syndicate Bank	1,027.92	952.77	9.44	91.57	13.32	97.88	8.37
HMT Ltd.	1,016.19	54.84	-20.45	1.36	NA	7.06	359.42
Tata Teleservices (Maharashtra) Ltd.	999.84	183.52	66.12	-119.97	NA	-23.92	-7.54
Hindustan Copper Ltd.	997.16	133.92	4.08	12.72	NA	82.19	53.50
HCL Infosystems Ltd.	996.79	450.41	11.99	30.18	12.69	32.21	31.87
Sesa Goa Ltd.	954.84	352.18	42.73	105.09	129.71	126.79	7.51
Great Eastern Shipping Co. Ltd.	950.62	465.73	17.82	183.82	48.66	26.04	3.91

Company Name	Market Cap (Million $)	Revenue (Million $)	5-yr Revenue CAGR (%)	Net Income (Million $)	5-yr Net Income CAGR (%)	RoCE %	P/E (x)
Aditya Birla Nuvo Ltd.	945.84	451.78	10.86	25.85	NA	11.60	30.26
United Phosphorus Ltd.	899.25	254.29	NA	12.34	NA	15.12	63.23
Ashok Leyland Ltd.	898.73	1,115.57	12.74	61.68	28.16	19.62	11.78
Crompton Greaves Ltd.	886.66	512.76	6.26	26.09	NA	26.74	28.67
Essar Oil Ltd.	875.48	241.67	35.53	2.24	-17.01	-0.62	-56.63
Engineers India Ltd.	871.12	206.85	15.62	25.60	-2.25	20.89	27.03
Andhra Bank	854.55	644.64	11.77	118.20	33.95	63.14	7.86
Allahabad Bank	845.18	864.24	12.59	123.13	50.86	106.91	6.53
Nirma Ltd.	844.97	496.64	4.92	64.69	3.99	16.61	10.47
Glenmark Pharmaceuticals Ltd.	839.51	122.35	29.93	14.43	23.97	20.88	74.32
Aventis Pharma Ltd.	832.14	185.70	8.89	33.75	48.69	58.02	24.72
Bharat Earth Movers Ltd.	831.43	424.89	7.03	39.84	64.41	40.27	19.31
Colgate-Palmolive (India) Ltd.	825.85	243.76	-0.31	25.75	16.95	77.51	30.35
Chennai Petroleum Corpn. Ltd.	808.19	3,918.72	24.05	135.68	33.06	29.80	4.83
Matrix Laboratories Ltd.	781.11	152.82	71.60	29.61	NA	35.73	32.66
JSW Steel Ltd.	766.24	1,975.03	56.37	197.75	NA	33.75	3.60
Titan Industries Ltd.	758.14	258.49	12.46	5.67	5.28	20.23	72.47
Cummins India Ltd.	739.80	299.26	9.47	31.19	6.09	27.55	21.36
Bajaj Hindusthan Ltd.	736.79	119.38	11.98	4.50	1.18	29.21	23.09
Cadila Healthcare Ltd.	726.49	268.70	19.87	29.86	28.37	19.19	20.61
Indiabulls Financial Services Ltd.	721.63	11.81	NA	5.37	NA	16.67	58.42
Lupin Ltd.	707.17	276.95	79.03	18.70	54.03	18.12	23.12
Britannia Industries Ltd.	705.95	368.08	6.72	34.06	24.05	43.59	25.19
Castrol India Ltd.	701.52	355.72	5.36	28.94	-9.03	52.83	22.45
Godrej Consumer Products Ltd.	681.83	137.15	NA	20.36	NA	173.67	27.33

Company Name	Market Cap (Million $)	Revenue (Million $)	5-yr Revenue CAGR (%)	Net Income (Million $)	5-yr Net Income CAGR (%)	RoCE %	P/E (x)
Gammon India Ltd.	677.78	198.18	21.57	8.67	30.67	27.20	40.09
Century Textiles & Inds. Ltd.	665.91	670.70	4.09	24.92	31.08	14.44	22.72
Jubilant Organosys Ltd.	660.44	339.47	19.72	25.75	61.47	25.43	26.02
Amtek Auto Ltd.	649.87	115.61	50.60	11.83	51.15	20.03	29.60
Kirloskar Brothers Ltd.	641.44	172.41	15.35	11.53	32.36	33.59	23.58
EIH Ltd.	639.80	129.26	6.10	7.53	-14.50	10.44	41.50
Hindustan Construction Co. Ltd.	638.90	344.36	24.12	16.82	52.08	22.77	24.16
Procter & Gamble Hygiene & Health Care Ltd.	614.98	172.93	9.07	28.32	10.68	57.47	22.40
Pfizer Ltd.	608.63	156.93	15.89	10.34	8.03	25.19	41.54
Flextronics Software Systems Ltd.	577.05	108.27	34.69	24.58	23.46	33.82	22.39
Sterling Biotech Ltd.	574.13	88.62	33.38	17.99	27.02	22.14	23.35
Gateway Distriparks Ltd.	574.07	21.29	46.86	7.90	141.85	27.92	40.85
Raymond Ltd.	566.52	267.43	-6.94	18.89	21.26	8.68	24.06
Vijaya Bank	563.08	532.14	12.81	86.49	48.42	60.06	7.89
Glaxosmithkline Consumer Healthcare Ltd.	562.25	229.02	6.27	16.63	-5.60	22.80	25.19
Rashtriya Chemicals & Fertilizers Ltd.	559.84	653.38	4.03	32.04	32.07	18.89	18.88
Kochi Refineries Ltd.	559.54	3,634.89	21.11	191.39	29.06	45.68	3.11
Balrampur Chini Mills Ltd.	558.70	211.43	18.78	28.45	39.92	33.05	14.21
Aurobindo Pharma Ltd.	558.60	263.61	9.23	7.97	-14.01	7.23	122.04
Nagarjuna Construction Co. Ltd.	558.04	270.11	40.56	12.96	21.58	26.03	32.40
Jammu & Kashmir Bank Ltd.	539.56	365.92	10.76	26.15	-0.86	58.90	10.73
TVS Motor Co. Ltd.	538.79	754.83	16.59	31.59	10.15	23.00	17.82
Mphasis BFL Ltd.	533.60	56.31	15.41	11.40	157.88	11.46	42.43
Gillette India Ltd.	524.84	101.79	12.11	13.91	25.81	33.20	38.11
Moser Baer India Ltd.	520.94	307.47	54.28	13.80	6.60	3.19	-150.11
Apollo Hospitals Enterprise Ltd.	517.48	135.62	15.95	11.13	13.44	23.22	41.85

Company Name	Market Cap (Million $)	Revenue (Million $)	5-yr Revenue CAGR (%)	Net Income (Million $)	5-yr Net Income CAGR (%)	RoCE %	P/E (x)
Arvind Mills Ltd.	515.83	386.92	6.97	28.94	NA	11.52	13.25
Lakshmi Machine Works Ltd.	514.59	260.24	20.95	3.30	-6.82	34.16	26.29
Mcdowell & Co. Ltd.	513.26	406.49	NA	6.08	NA	12.56	57.39
Centurion Bank Of Punjab Ltd.	509.15	92.91	-4.73	5.71	-6.06	29.86	40.59
HT Media Ltd.	508.97	143.00	NA	6.21	NA	12.58	71.07
Thermax Ltd.	506.28	220.85	18.70	12.57	11.32	21.75	28.76
MMTC Ltd.	502.95	2,077.68	16.29	11.50	22.88	6.42	20.05
National Fertilizers Ltd.	497.27	797.81	7.06	36.57	35.76	20.54	11.79
ITI Ltd.	482.40	316.70	-8.08	-172.18	NA	-70.84	-10.17
BF Utilities Ltd.	479.83	4.06	NA	-1.09	NA	2.14	-468.13
Uco Bank	475.98	896.53	12.97	78.56	56.65	92.80	10.19
Max India Ltd.	475.26	32.43	12.14	0.12	-57.27	2.15	69,704.82
Pidilite Industries Ltd.	470.67	202.39	13.99	17.40	9.99	31.26	22.73
Motherson Sumi Systems Ltd.	464.71	144.95	28.82	14.11	31.87	43.84	30.42
Voltas Ltd.	453.09	329.48	12.90	11.46	55.75	26.76	30.28
EID-Parry (India) Ltd.	452.94	174.19	-7.27	23.70	14.11	23.83	21.19
Gujarat Fluorochemicals Ltd.	445.62	40.33	6.74	10.14	2.08	10.00	41.08
Tube Investments of India Ltd.	443.18	355.67	9.71	22.40	24.58	24.52	15.45
Balkrishna Industries Ltd.	443.14	114.19	30.38	14.35	54.34	44.51	26.65
Hotel Leelaventure Ltd.	434.92	58.34	16.03	10.46	39.74	9.16	26.85
Marico Ltd.	433.48	216.77	8.00	16.77	15.61	39.93	21.68
Phoenix Mills Ltd.	431.31	6.56	6.69	2.44	NA	20.91	129.63
Yes Bank Ltd.	428.32	10.93	NA	-0.85	NA	NA	36.95
Jindal Iron & Steel Co. Ltd.	427.39	514.99	14.38	55.16	86.35	38.48	6.63
Indraprastha Gas Ltd.	426.84	120.05	136.76	21.07	203.49	43.85	18.94

Company Name	Market Cap (Million $)	Revenue (Million $)	5-yr Revenue CAGR (%)	Net Income (Million $)	5-yr Net Income CAGR (%)	RoCE %	P/E (x)
Goodlass Nerolac Paints Ltd.	426.09	242.96	11.18	20.90	25.13	34.08	18.86
Divi'S Laboratories Ltd.	425.38	83.39	18.07	15.01	32.53	40.92	27.98
Jindal Saw Ltd.	418.08	257.15	24.47	12.78	14.85	19.49	18.26
CESC Ltd.	415.05	545.35	6.48	34.24	NA	14.99	10.81
Torrent Pharmaceuticals Ltd.	413.84	122.81	4.61	12.03	3.03	15.51	28.23
Ballarpur Industries Ltd.	413.64	456.60	6.67	38.20	23.03	13.68	10.57
India Cements Ltd.	411.54	315.23	-0.28	1.04	-25.67	3.88	35.18
Aban Loyd Chiles Offshore Ltd.	411.24	65.94	31.93	11.75	58.08	16.32	24.65
Madras Cements Ltd.	408.44	202.23	11.43	12.71	8.12	10.70	28.72
Birla Corporation Ltd.	407.12	327.33	6.96	19.74	NA	23.08	20.95
Alfa Laval (India) Ltd.	401.60	119.75	21.96	17.84	29.76	53.17	24.64
Novartis India Ltd.	400.75	111.08	-10.08	14.80	-8.84	35.45	20.24
LIC Housing Finance Ltd.	397.74	259.14	11.65	32.67	5.77	8.84	10.62
Gujarat Gas Co. Ltd.	397.55	127.15	24.62	15.55	19.02	36.97	17.57
SRF Ltd.	395.81	264.21	7.66	11.52	13.59	13.95	23.81
Kirloskar Oil Engines Ltd.	395.52	293.52	8.72	39.52	16.23	20.64	6.08
Shree Cement Ltd.	395.13	164.33	10.29	6.61	37.90	9.26	35.12
Mahavir Spinning Mills Ltd.	394.48	437.60	20.21	27.45	15.94	20.61	11.79
Dredging Corpn. of India Ltd.	392.22	119.37	12.30	25.75	9.29	17.23	11.96
Godrej Industries Ltd.	391.46	187.96	2.98	17.22	4.13	13.57	25.98
Exide Industries Ltd.	389.06	339.81	9.58	17.56	9.59	23.60	18.52
Indusind Bank Ltd.	382.87	286.54	10.54	46.71	50.22	44.31	9.48
Orchid Chemicals & Pharmaceuticals Ltd.	378.75	156.66	13.90	7.05	-4.28	11.05	29.28
Jaiprakash Hydro Power Ltd.	377.18	69.32	NA	11.61	NA	11.54	33.85
Hinduja TMT Ltd.	374.62	31.34	79.89	15.92	34.08	13.45	31.29

Company Name	Market Cap (Million $)	Revenue (Million $)	5-yr Revenue CAGR (%)	Net Income (Million $)	5-yr Net Income CAGR (%)	RoCE %	P/E (x)
Monsanto India Ltd.	372.43	90.92	28.63	17.45	44.87	25.48	18.03
Sintex Industries Ltd.	369.01	162.75	24.16	12.25	32.58	14.61	22.75
Micro Inks Ltd.	367.70	215.92	30.00	24.45	34.62	18.28	16.43
Sundram Fasteners Ltd.	365.10	235.72	19.15	15.77	10.23	30.40	21.68
Chambal Fertilisers & Chemicals Ltd.	363.71	611.48	14.57	50.14	12.26	17.12	7.48
Sundaram-Clayton Ltd.	359.50	145.49	21.72	12.14	18.69	33.44	26.99
Panacea Biotec Ltd.	354.26	77.88	12.01	6.83	3.01	21.12	28.61
Hexaware Technologies Ltd.	353.35	58.36	-6.87	9.85	-3.24	17.28	22.60
Shoppers' Stop Ltd.	353.02	116.06	26.96	4.33	NA	73.49	71.45
IL & FS Investsmart Ltd.	351.79	25.80	NA	7.51	NA	56.28	28.29
Wyeth Ltd.	348.62	65.89	2.06	8.86	8.05	24.16	40.48
DCM Shriram Consolidated Ltd.	345.38	433.03	16.80	23.73	25.15	20.54	11.13
IVRCL Infrastructures & Projects Ltd.	344.29	239.43	37.77	12.89	45.06	35.11	23.12
Tata Infotech Ltd.	344.08	176.74	13.01	18.24	45.75	34.98	15.26
Gujarat Narmada Valley Fertilizers Co. Ltd.	339.89	442.71	9.71	50.91	27.65	31.20	5.28
Godfrey Phillips India Ltd.	339.75	295.81	3.75	14.45	8.60	27.10	19.43
United Breweries Ltd.	338.73	143.71	NA	3.19	NA	12.84	52.59
Torrent Power A E C Ltd.	338.45	302.66	7.87	24.25	25.56	18.40	11.55
ING Vysya Bank Ltd.	337.69	258.12	2.44	-8.68	NA	36.67	37.23
Bombay Dyeing & Mfg. Co. Ltd.	337.11	260.92	3.60	6.04	-9.25	7.24	29.71
State Bank Of Travancore	336.82	540.73	12.06	56.17	30.05	116.59	6.36
Asahi India Glass Ltd.	336.21	157.17	25.60	17.77	52.99	22.28	23.77
Bongaigaon Refinery & Petrochemicals Ltd.	331.52	1,210.42	29.96	108.70	71.50	100.26	4.81
State Bank Of Bikaner & Jaipur	330.97	498.71	10.43	46.74	11.30	55.07	9.36
SKF India Ltd.	330.78	158.76	15.82	12.87	41.96	34.69	20.94

Company Name	Market Cap (Million $)	Revenue (Million $)	5-yr Revenue CAGR (%)	Net Income (Million $)	5-yr Net Income CAGR (%)	RoCE %	P/E (x)
Alstom Projects India Ltd.	329.48	194.17	54.74	10.89	NA	12.28	34.11
Berger Paints India Ltd.	328.38	215.58	13.42	11.85	17.07	35.59	21.36
State Bank of Mysore	328.17	343.04	9.70	46.65	33.59	69.52	6.92
Areva T & D India Ltd.	321.64	198.84	15.99	4.82	65.07	29.40	42.95
Maharashtra Seamless Ltd.	321.50	197.10	35.12	19.35	37.11	31.99	14.02
Asian Star Co. Ltd.	321.35	240.30	14.70	5.01	-6.44	26.98	50.95
Patel Engineering Ltd.	320.96	106.22	18.31	8.85	21.69	17.56	30.82
Adani Exports Ltd.	320.39	3,072.02	36.87	24.61	-0.49	33.06	13.03
Bank of Maharashtra	318.98	629.93	11.12	40.25	14.46	74.12	11.10
Greaves Cotton Ltd.	317.71	165.96	1.52	14.11	NA	50.38	21.49
Tata Investment Corpn. Ltd.	315.63	26.69	18.82	25.54	24.74	24.03	8.99
Geodesic Information Systems Ltd.	315.34	9.15	NA	4.34	198.91	42.08	48.08
ABG Shipyard Ltd.	315.14	85.60	34.36	10.17	99.67	121.05	30.99
Syngenta India Ltd.	311.70	141.88	NA	16.43	NA	30.37	19.15
Karnataka Bank Ltd.	311.09	239.44	10.22	33.44	29.30	72.62	8.52
Polaris Software Lab Ltd.	306.62	152.04	35.61	12.14	7.50	10.37	38.06
Himatsingka Seide Ltd.	306.47	31.65	4.09	10.55	2.66	16.78	27.35
ICI India Ltd.	306.25	220.73	0.42	10.72	-5.96	11.78	31.43
Atlas Copco (India) Ltd.	305.44	99.85	27.72	5.25	27.60	33.53	27.88
Gujarat Mineral Devp. Corpn. Ltd.	304.20	83.92	11.56	23.50	22.45	10.66	23.04
Radico Khaitan Ltd.	304.12	174.46	NA	6.72	NA	27.38	39.36
Triveni Engineering & Inds. Ltd.	303.32	232.52	0.98	22.62	NA	57.21	10.96
Rolta India Ltd.	301.31	78.63	14.28	23.49	11.41	18.74	12.06
Spicejet Ltd.	300.95	0.45	NA	-6.52	NA	-50.93	-64.66
Blue Dart Express Ltd.	299.83	104.17	17.46	8.87	25.97	37.61	27.08

Company Name	Market Cap (Million $)	Revenue (Million $)	5-yr Revenue CAGR (%)	Net Income (Million $)	5-yr Net Income CAGR (%)	RoCE %	P/E (x)
Adlabs Films Ltd.	297.95	18.66	18.27	4.70	31.89	26.12	56.31
Deccan Chronicle Holdings Ltd.	297.71	37.65	NA	7.28	NA	17.90	31.14
Punjab Tractors Ltd.	295.29	214.20	-4.68	14.30	-13.94	19.48	10.03
IBP Co. Ltd.	291.92	3,098.41	14.82	13.38	7.13	12.96	-4.34
New Delhi Television Ltd.	291.44	41.28	22.11	6.63	6.65	24.01	83.32
Ispat Industries Ltd.	290.89	2,048.94	37.66	158.20	185.49	13.84	2.96
Dishman Pharmaceuticals & Chemicals Ltd.	290.82	36.34	NA	6.48	NA	26.02	34.20
Essar Steel Ltd.	289.51	1,484.91	21.60	134.13	NA	28.51	1.63
Trent Ltd.	288.15	52.61	47.11	4.33	8.84	9.49	54.93
Rico Auto Inds. Ltd.	285.71	161.88	22.99	8.01	21.68	38.78	31.76
Carborundum Universal Ltd.	285.47	81.90	5.84	8.73	8.16	25.84	27.86
Jindal Stainless Ltd.	283.12	789.68	NA	55.88	NA	24.73	4.63
Mahindra Gesco Developers Ltd.	282.25	20.78	40.71	1.78	8.84	8.88	123.33
Gujarat State Fertilizers & Chemicals Ltd.	280.65	627.51	5.48	31.38	46.65	22.33	5.49
Essar Shipping Ltd.	275.50	192.59	15.37	65.60	42.90	18.19	3.46
Cranes Software Intl. Ltd.	272.68	29.97	65.35	10.20	275.65	39.69	22.04
Kalyani Steels Ltd.	270.72	210.31	56.46	9.77	NA	20.67	12.13
Bata India Ltd.	270.70	164.59	-1.31	-14.26	NA	-34.12	-79.73
MRF Ltd.	270.63	689.59	5.62	6.55	-21.83	10.96	109.65
Federal Bank Ltd.	266.15	307.29	6.26	20.48	14.20	71.73	8.09
Apollo Tyres Ltd.	264.93	605.12	14.51	15.37	-2.32	14.37	16.08
KSL & Inds. Ltd.	263.77	34.91	-18.50	2.43	-28.49	5.15	46.46
Astra Microwave Products Ltd.	262.06	17.28	53.03	3.88	64.88	65.28	30.81
Essel Propack Ltd.	261.17	58.39	6.68	9.29	10.66	11.37	25.77
Shree Renuka Sugars Ltd.	259.85	34.62	NA	0.54	NA	NA	34.17

Company Name	Market Cap (Million $)	Revenue (Million $)	5-yr Revenue CAGR (%)	Net Income (Million $)	5-yr Net Income CAGR (%)	RoCE %	P/E (x)
Taj GVK Hotels & Resorts Ltd.	259.57	26.24	28.44	5.02	NA	27.63	37.08
United Breweries (Holdings) Ltd.	258.62	33.41	-16.21	0.16	-42.03	-5.77	-43.50
Shrenuj & Co. Ltd.	256.54	111.24	21.62	2.54	7.45	26.56	91.10
Jain Irrigation Systems Ltd.	255.43	164.33	38.09	6.11	NA	17.35	26.38
Ambuja Cement Eastern Ltd.	254.78	107.33	14.41	10.24	102.31	22.69	23.17
Sasken Communication Technologies Ltd.	253.95	50.97	24.19	4.93	7.87	23.14	49.18
Mercator Lines Ltd.	253.93	127.43	78.01	39.64	122.9	69.45	5.71
Asian Hotels Ltd.	252.89	58.69	17.38	5.79	-6.75	12.74	30.99
Abbott India Ltd.	252.73	107.73	9.64	23.24	30.48	56.82	18.44
GHCL Ltd.	251.34	135.20	9.15	9.22	12.72	19.93	15.16
HFCL Infotel Ltd.	250.82	57.57	48.29	-21.27	NA	-3.50	-10.54
Astrazeneca Pharma India Ltd.	250.19	48.08	15.50	5.85	19.88	48.44	31.29
Strides Arcolab Ltd.	249.84	69.53	23.38	6.63	26.09	18.98	32.64
Fertilisers & Chemicals, Travancore Ltd.	246.73	230.47	-4.95	-38.00	NA	-19.97	-21.20
Alok Industries Ltd.	245.79	302.12	30.11	20.35	33.16	16.14	10.61
Ingersoll-Rand (India) Ltd.	243.43	113.76	3.14	25.41	15.94	8.95	33.03
Unitech Ltd.	241.24	115.76	18.92	6.80	20.35	16.50	30.63
Gokaldas Exports Ltd.	238.76	164.59	NA	9.00	NA	38.10	23.34
Hindustan Oil Exploration Co. Ltd.	235.98	20.35	12.30	8.75	29.15	31.81	29.73
Ipca Laboratories Ltd.	235.03	166.88	14.77	17.67	30.08	27.32	12.94
South India Corpn. (Agencies) Ltd.	234.88	278.54	-8.71	7.08	5.69	20.40	19.32
Bayer Cropscience Ltd.	233.04	193.36	7.37	5.99	39.22	13.82	47.32
Indo Gulf Fertilisers Ltd.	231.87	154.17	NA	12.94	NA	13.05	15.78
Gujarat NRE Coke Ltd.	230.87	64.74	56.80	20.63	184.16	113.39	7.96
Gujarat Industries Power Co. Ltd.	230.14	169.29	9.31	23.56	12.56	17.82	9.76

Company Name	Market Cap (Million $)	Revenue (Million $)	5-yr Revenue CAGR (%)	Net Income (Million $)	5-yr Net Income CAGR (%)	RoCE %	P/E (x)
Crisil Ltd.	229.84	20.40	21.06	5.04	11.39	30.38	38.84
Aftek Infosys Ltd.	228.30	31.58	56.88	10.76	50.56	18.59	15.58
Welspun-Gujarat Stahl Rohren Ltd.	227.91	252.98	80.84	7.69	160.87	43.17	21.52
Indo Rama Synthetics (India) Ltd.	227.40	509.08	4.88	15.96	NA	12.29	12.32
Finolex Industries Ltd.	224.64	223.12	8.97	21.80	14.85	19.22	18.83
Karur Vysya Bank Ltd.	222.48	156.24	7.99	23.94	8.17	55.13	8.44
3M India Ltd.	221.46	61.65	18.51	5.80	100.91	35.98	31.48
Timken India Ltd.	220.08	68.23	15.71	7.50	35.29	42.99	23.32
Blue Star Ltd.	218.73	209.67	14.20	8.90	11.00	36.56	22.16
Gujarat Alkalies & Chemicals Ltd.	217.75	291.00	10.50	32.79	NA	34.59	4.39
FDC Ltd.	214.96	80.63	19.16	12.40	18.26	26.12	13.58
Graphite India Ltd.	214.27	124.55	29.85	10.91	23.04	13.85	19.63
Bannari Amman Sugars Ltd.	214.22	114.54	18.15	9.92	21.85	20.17	16.96
KEC International Ltd.	213.20	187.97	-5.04	5.75	-0.51	23.44	18.68
Dena Bank	210.23	444.32	1.87	13.86	-11.50	58.60	-5.89
Balmer Lawrie & Co. Ltd.	206.39	240.13	8.64	6.78	15.81	18.72	21.06
Kennametal Widia India Ltd.	206.32	71.11	7.49	11.32	12.30	35.77	18.61
Alembic Ltd.	205.23	130.12	7.88	11.83	12.81	18.57	14.76
Finolex Cables Ltd.	204.70	148.50	3.82	6.99	-15.32	7.58	24.55
Dabur Pharma Ltd.	204.49	53.58	NA	5.13	NA	10.36	37.54
Havell's India Ltd.	203.79	151.55	44.54	6.94	55.85	43.26	19.29
Merck Ltd.	202.89	94.92	8.34	16.13	31.39	47.75	12.00
Bilcare Ltd.	202.78	36.95	34.98	5.54	54.05	28.95	28.64
Unichem Laboratories Ltd.	202.32	96.63	15.50	10.25	23.85	33.23	13.52
Gulf Oil Corpn. Ltd.	201.80	108.06	22.21	4.55	31.57	7.30	41.41

Company Name	Market Cap (Million $)	Revenue (Million $)	5-yr Revenue CAGR (%)	Net Income (Million $)	5-yr Net Income CAGR (%)	RoCE %	P/E (x)
Simplex Infrastructures Ltd.	201.77	227.06	25.35	5.72	38.84	16.60	20.67
Praj Industries Ltd.	201.40	54.15	37.11	4.95	56.88	84.75	36.86
Television Eighteen India Ltd.	201.31	18.51	35.99	4.43	37.40	17.13	42.83
GTL Ltd.	201.11	123.75	-2.72	24.04	-14.31	8.55	16.19
Hikal Ltd.	200.81	44.31	14.02	7.75	14.58	21.00	22.71
PTC India Ltd.	199.43	452.93	200.08	5.46	NA	17.48	28.00
Automotive Axles Ltd.	199.29	69.53	21.81	5.14	31.51	46.05	23.79
Subex Systems Ltd.	197.19	26.49	30.15	5.75	38.14	24.21	24.54
Thomas Cook (India) Ltd.	196.98	28.36	11.54	6.24	9.75	34.25	32.27
BOC India Ltd.	194.22	96.45	1.30	6.36	NA	16.41	11.62
Balaji Telefilms Ltd.	193.19	44.72	57.81	9.43	57.52	34.36	17.52
Deepak Fertilisers & Petrochemicals Corpn. Ltd.	192.15	120.32	-2.00	18.13	6.46	19.36	9.65
Kalpataru Power Transmissíon Ltd.	190.20	128.72	27.83	6.51	12.58	41.63	21.14
JK Cement Ltd.	189.16	96.24	NA	1.43	NA	11.68	49.54
3I Infotech Ltd.	189.04	50.85	39.79	4.00	10.86	9.51	25.55
Electrosteel Castings Ltd.	188.25	223.50	11.77	20.15	-0.01	15.31	12.85
Coromandel Fertilisers Ltd.	188.23	359.60	21.15	15.73	7.56	16.23	10.57
Kalyani Brakes Ltd.	187.48	95.60	22.41	7.37	31.30	39.43	23.77
Welspun India Ltd.	185.46	109.73	8.24	8.77	NA	14.55	18.34
Honeywell Automation India Ltd.	184.28	65.58	4.67	1.93	-5.24	9.91	41.37
Varun Shipping Co. Ltd.	182.81	88.40	16.16	18.57	55.69	15.94	6.52
Macmillan India Ltd.	181.58	29.10	18.21	9.86	15.29	32.44	18.20
ISMT Ltd.	177.77	119.76	15.05	0.37	NA	8.00	9.02
Shriram Transport Finance Co. Ltd.	177.18	78.72	29.97	11.21	67.78	18.50	10.53
S Kumars Nationwide Ltd.	174.88	78.69	-7.55	-45.98	NA	0.60	9.98

Company Name	Market Cap (Million $)	Revenue (Million $)	5-yr Revenue CAGR (%)	Net Income (Million $)	5-yr Net Income CAGR (%)	RoCE %	P/E (x)
Aztec Software & Technology Services Ltd.	173.54	18.71	43.17	3.34	29.09	12.21	37.89
Somplast Leather Inds. Ltd.	172.02	NA	NA	NA	NA	NA	NA
VST Industries Ltd.	171.97	155.04	-1.78	12.28	28.04	56.48	14.83
Ciba Specialty Chemicals (India) Ltd.	171.49	131.57	4.82	6.16	8.46	19.37	20.62
PSL Ltd.	170.50	327.39	57.67	7.28	16.89	37.26	18.96
Jindal Poly Films Ltd.	170.40	262.31	13.96	17.45	52.02	16.75	9.60
Usha Martin Ltd.	170.29	356.80	17.15	9.29	4.31	10.80	14.36
Eveready Industries (India) Ltd.	169.26	169.48	-2.20	10.53	40.33	8.62	9.96
JM Financial Ltd.	169.13	3.13	33.46	2.15	46.60	32.79	85.34
Igate Global Solutions Ltd.	168.51	98.10	43.26	6.08	111.61	4.55	22.81
Bajaj Auto Finance Ltd.	167.41	37.07	14.63	12.72	21.36	28.66	12.72
Emami Ltd.	166.77	51.28	8.82	6.70	11.59	36.34	21.57
Manugraph India Ltd.	166.35	63.65	18.13	6.77	72.70	59.69	13.49
Mastek Ltd.	164.95	58.05	22.38	10.77	9.99	36.53	14.71
CMC Ltd.	162.86	176.42	10.85	5.16	12.93	22.04	41.33
JB Chemicals & Pharmaceuticals Ltd.	162.60	85.82	16.32	13.44	21.85	24.79	11.31
Kesoram Industries Ltd.	162.23	392.95	19.02	7.62	16.34	10.24	24.53
BASF India Ltd.	159.82	168.36	14.27	8.63	13.70	24.30	16.11
Avaya Globalconnect Ltd.	158.30	75.61	12.32	5.66	NA	24.46	11.65
Infotech Enterprises Ltd.	157.56	34.95	35.59	5.07	16.67	17.35	32.49
Eicher Motors Ltd.	157.29	505.65	44.48	13.38	29.98	22.50	3.18
Esab India Ltd.	156.01	48.97	5.59	4.63	18.50	68.92	17.83
KSB Pumps Ltd.	155.88	75.94	10.15	6.97	17.17	35.98	19.00
Himachal Futuristic Communications Ltd.	155.18	96.07	-6.09	-38.39	NA	-8.71	-4.20
Dalmia Cement (Bharat) Ltd.	155.08	118.41	6.89	7.33	8.82	9.14	18.14

Company Name	Market Cap (Million $)	Revenue (Million $)	5-yr Revenue CAGR (%)	Net Income (Million $)	5-yr Net Income CAGR (%)	RoCE %	P/E (x)
Amtek India Ltd.	154.99	78.93	56.39	9.28	50.37	26.11	11.77
Cholamandalam Investment & Finance Co. Ltd.	154.89	48.86	8.33	7.74	13.37	15.09	17.07
Tata Elxsi Ltd.	154.35	44.54	9.63	5.98	31.41	70.06	21.96
Anant Raj Inds. Ltd.	154.18	5.39	8.86	0.07	NA	5.68	249.41
Shaw Wallace & Co. Ltd.	152.80	43.65	-25.62	-5.65	NA	-2.28	34.51
HEG Ltd.	152.13	124.12	3.22	9.35	6.25	11.30	18.00
Forbes Gokak Ltd.	151.63	106.83	5.62	5.67	-4.32	12.33	18.82
Bharati Shipyard Ltd.	151.59	39.08	21.74	6.22	81.22	63.23	24.30
Shriram Investments Ltd.	150.39	77.77	31.71	10.65	46.64	19.11	13.27
Ansal Properties & Infrastructure Ltd.	149.53	44.02	6.00	3.10	11.97	16.73	23.91
FAG Bearings India Ltd.	147.93	84.54	14.94	7.02	33.84	33.65	15.22
Dhampur Sugar Mills Ltd.	146.67	114.13	8.86	2.20	NA	21.32	18.64
IFCI Ltd.	146.17	327.01	-12.60	-100.77	NA	3.56	-1.57
Mukand Ltd.	145.45	384.88	14.67	42.00	72.24	8.33	3.44
NIIT Technologies Ltd.	144.63	42.76	NA	9.15	NA	18.67	15.21
Opto Circuits (India) Ltd.	144.61	17.99	33.87	4.33	40.89	40.42	25.11
Geometric Software Solutions Co. Ltd.	143.20	21.69	24.33	4.70	0.44	28.83	32.94
Nucleus Software Exports Ltd.	143.18	15.23	54.36	3.60	86.58	26.81	23.76
Rei Agro Ltd.	141.95	192.05	45.58	8.60	69.69	29.73	12.80
Madhucon Projects Ltd.	141.30	69.65	25.50	3.70	32.05	24.84	37.73
Nagarjuna Fertilizers & Chemicals Ltd.	141.20	289.05	-2.72	6.71	-23.61	7.88	9.83
Chettinad Cement Corpn. Ltd.	138.31	114.08	16.71	6.35	34.13	16.30	17.41
Prism Cement Ltd.	138.28	120.68	8.74	5.87	NA	17.74	24.06
Scandent Solutions Corpn. Ltd.	138.25	29.10	NA	2.43	NA	14.72	30.78
Prithvi Information Solutions Ltd.	138.25	43.80	NA	4.72	NA	50.46	14.84

Company Name	Market Cap (Million $)	Revenue (Million $)	5-yr Revenue CAGR (%)	Net Income (Million $)	5-yr Net Income CAGR (%)	RoCE %	P/E (x)
India Infoline Ltd.	137.65	4.98	NA	3.97	NA	46.52	28.14
Bhushan Steel & Strips Ltd.	137.56	651.80	24.56	34.85	28.02	17.55	4.34
Tamil Nadu Newsprint & Papers Ltd.	136.98	166.23	8.03	8.63	18.50	8.68	10.29
Century Enka Ltd.	136.97	255.35	3.68	11.95	0.21	9.64	11.84
Videocon International Ltd.	135.79	909.80	10.57	-3.07	NA	8.75	2.51
Abhishek Industries Ltd.	134.17	188.30	35.35	9.15	NA	16.15	11.79
CCL Products (India) Ltd.	133.23	25.21	17.21	6.89	42.34	37.08	15.74
Ador Welding Ltd.	130.65	55.96	6.05	6.17	40.47	18.53	13.69
HBL Nife Power Systems Ltd.	130.06	74.04	17.14	4.19	6.81	23.98	28.44
Birla Global Finance Ltd.	129.69	16.00	-13.62	7.04	-2.31	11.10	29.29
NIIT Ltd.	129.32	64.50	-13.26	3.63	-35.50	14.65	33.83
Escorts Ltd.	127.64	286.01	0.60	-71.26	NA	-6.83	-4.45
Grindwell Norton Ltd.	127.19	68.93	10.64	6.63	22.52	29.26	18.53
Goetze (India) Ltd.	126.81	116.68	20.42	5.01	16.97	18.84	23.75
India Glycols Ltd.	126.20	144.45	30.17	17.95	32.76	28.08	7.05
Navneet Publications (India) Ltd.	126.10	62.40	13.76	7.12	5.68	29.23	14.60
Wartsila India Ltd.	125.78	61.50	-3.28	5.90	12.39	18.03	17.99
Monnet Ispat Ltd.	125.26	134.11	41.14	27.76	87.79	22.44	4.53
Ramco Industries Ltd.	125.07	57.72	7.01	6.55	12.75	22.66	16.75
TV Today Network Ltd.	124.83	31.61	NA	3.73	NA	15.67	28.07
Sahara India Mass Communication Ltd.	124.70	47.94	92.11	1.48	31.23	12.80	73.85
Aptech Ltd.	123.46	23.10	NA	-13.93	NA	-13.04	-9.95
Ruchi Soya Inds. Ltd.	123.44	881.06	15.07	9.91	17.03	18.63	12.10
Rain Calcining Ltd.	123.31	82.78	16.44	2.73	NA	6.86	14.11
Shree Precoated Steels Ltd.	123.02	180.07	NA	6.73	NA	21.45	19.09

Company Name	Market Cap (Million $)	Revenue (Million $)	5-yr Revenue CAGR (%)	Net Income (Million $)	5-yr Net Income CAGR (%)	RoCE %	P/E (x)
SREI Infrastructure Finance Ltd.	122.55	29.45	-2.65	6.43	24.53	14.68	14.01
Gati Ltd.	121.22	80.83	11.74	3.29	9.87	25.01	30.60
Ashapura Minechem Ltd.	120.62	113.88	52.82	3.12	33.22	25.80	22.76
Morarjee Realties Ltd.	119.94	14.14	-26.84	-2.16	NA	-1.01	9.17
Bank of Rajasthan Ltd.	118.93	128.20	5.29	7.96	23.72	54.18	96.91
Madras Aluminium Co. Ltd.	118.58	97.30	12.80	9.59	6.79	29.01	12.03
Vesuvius India Ltd.	117.99	44.93	31.41	5.51	21.74	39.48	18.28
Aarti Industries Ltd.	117.94	155.44	22.98	10.58	35.66	24.21	10.23
Oriental Hotels Ltd.	117.71	30.36	10.39	3.49	-2.66	11.88	27.59
KPIT Cummins Infosystems Ltd.	114.89	44.29	50.77	5.15	46.49	25.10	21.26
Sterlite Optical Technologies Ltd.	114.47	84.24	NA	2.32	NA	6.11	39.94

Source: Prowess (Center for Monitoring the Indian Economy)

INDEX